The European Culture Area

The European Culture Area

A Systematic Geography
Fourth Edition

Terry G. Jordan-Bychkov
AND
Bella Bychkova Jordan

ROWMAN & LITTLEFIELD PUBLISHERS, INC.
Lanham • Boulder • New York • Oxford

ROWMAN & LITTLEFIELD PUBLISHERS, INC.

Published in the United States of America
by Rowman & Littlefield Publishers, Inc.
4501 Forbes Blvd, Suite 200, Lanham, Maryland 20706
http://www.rowmanlittlefield.com

12 Hid's Copse Road, Cumnor Hill, Oxford OX2 9JJ, England

British Library Cataloging in Publication Information Available

Library of Congress Cataloging-in-Publication Data

Jordan-Bychkov, Terry G., 1938–
    The European culture area : a systematic geography / Terry G. Jordan-Bychkov and
Bella Bychkova Jordan.—4th ed.
        p.   cm.
    Includes bibliographical references and index.
    ISBN 0-7425-1628-8 (alk. paper)
    1. Europe—Geography.   2. Europe—Description and travel.   I. Bychkova Jordan,
Bella.   II. Title.

D907 .J67   2002
914—dc21   2001019736

Printed in the United States of America

♾ ™ The paper used in this publication meets the minimum requirements of American
National Standard for Information Sciences—Permanence of Paper for Printed Library
Materials, ANSI/NISO Z39.48-1992.

Contents

Preface

The fourth edition of *The European Culture Area* reflects our geographical interpretation of a fascinating, influential, and ever-changing part of the world. Firmly based in our experiences gained during 30 seasons of European travel and field research, it reflects journeys from Gibraltar to North Cape, from the westernmost promontories of Ireland to the Russian steppes and taiga, from Cyprus to Iceland and the Faeroes. It also reflects a decade of living in European Russia.

Extensively revised from its 1996 predecessor, the present edition reveals Europe at the threshold of a new century. The book derives from the rich humanistic tradition of geography and represents our attempt to interpret Europe as a cultural entity. We treat Europe both as one and many, as a people adhering to an overarching culture while at the same time exhibiting a bewildering internal regional variety.

Throughout the book, preference will be given to the indigenous form of place names, as for example *Napoli* instead of *Naples* and *Bayern* instead of *Bavaria*. We believe the English forms of these toponyms serve no useful purpose and often lead to confusion. One American tourist bound for the wonders of Florence reportedly refused to get off the train at the station bearing the placard "Firenze," convinced that the conductor intended to cheat him! Why bother to learn names that the local citizenry do not use? Some exceptions have been made. The names of independent countries appear in English form, even though this leads us to the absurdity of calling Hrvatska "Croatia" and Deutschland "Germany." Also, if a river, city, mountain range, or other geographic feature extends across linguistic borders and is as a result known by more than one native name, then the English version receives preference. Thus, we use *Danube* instead of *Donau/ Duna/Dunarea*. The index directs the reader from English to native toponym forms.

Similarly, we give preference to the metric system and centigrade thermometer, which enjoy almost universal usage in Europe. A conversion table is included (see Metric and Centigrade Conversion Table). Also, since metric measures often appear in abbreviated form, such as *km* instead of *kilometer*, we offer a key to these in the same table.

Use is also made of the internationally approved letter code abbreviations for European and neighboring countries. In Europe, they are used in postal zip codes for international mail and also appear on oval-shaped placards affixed to the rear end of cars and trucks. We employ them in bibliographies, on many maps, and in some captions. For example, the code for Germany is D (see Official Letter Codes and Native Names for Countries). Also in that same table we list the native forms of the names for countries.

Statistical subdivisions of most countries appear on maps throughout the text, in order to present a more detailed geographical pattern of data. While based upon administrative and censal units, our subdivisions almost always represent some lumping of units, in order that the maps not become overly complicated.

We include only part of Russia in Europe. For statistical purposes, our "Eurorussia" includes the following administrative regions, or *raions:* North, Northwest, Central, Volga–Vyatsk, Central Chernozem, Povolzhsky (Volga), North Caucasus, and Urals, in addition to the Kaliningrad exclave on the Baltic.

Numerous persons have contributed to the writing of the fourth edition by providing ideas, suggestions, data, assistance, and criticism. Our research assistant, Damon Scott, deserves our special thanks, as do the professors who read earlier drafts and offered suggestions for improvement, including Grigory Ioffe of Radford University, Charles F. Gritzner of South Dakota State University, Mary Lee Nolan of Oregon State, Ary J. Lamme III of the University of Florida, Brad Baltensperger of Michigan Tech, and John U. Marshall of York University. Other valuable contributions came from professors Andreas Grotewold, Bruce S. Young, Kirk H. Stone (†), Kazimierz J. Zaniewski, John Sallnow, Wilbur Zelinsky, Michael Kukral, Robert A. Sirk, Dale J. Stevens, Robin Elisabeth Datel, Ramesh Dhussa, H. Gardiner Barnum, and Joseph Brownell. Most of all, we are indebted to Susan McEachern of Rowman & Littlefield, who believed in this book and made possible its fourth edition.

Dr. John Cotter of Austin created all of the attractive, functional cartographic work for this book. His maps reveal the human touch that can only be achieved the old-fashioned way, by rejecting computer graphics and employing instead a skilled hand and sensitive eye. We are fortunate to have had his services. Long may his eyes remain keen and his hand steady.

Word-processing for the fourth edition was most ably done by Joanne Sanders of the University of Texas at Austin geography staff. She not only typed with skill and speed, but also caught diverse errors in the manuscript. She is a consummate professional.

The modest success of three previous editions of *The European Culture*

Area reflects in part the resurgence of interest in regional geography and in the humanistic method of study. Renewed and growing attention to the geography of Europe was also revealed in the 1992 establishment and subsequent growth of a "European Specialty Group" within the Association of American Geographers. Earlier editions of *The European Culture Area* have been translated into Italian and Japanese, suggesting an international appeal, and the book has often been cited in European scholarly journals, both within and outside the discipline of geography. The fourth edition now renews the availability of *The European Culture Area* to the English-speaking countries, presenting the geography of a dynamic and influential region at the dawn of a new century.

Metric and Centigrade Conversions and Abbreviations

Length

1 meter (m) = 3.281 sq. ft.   1 ft. = 0.348 m.
1 kilometer (km) = 0.621 mi.   1 mi. = 1.609 km.
1 centimeter (cm) = 0.3937 in.   1 in. = 2.54 cm.

Area

1 sq. m. = 10.764 sq. ft.   1 sq. ft. = 0.092 sq. m.
1 sq. km. = 0.386 sq. mi.   1 sq. mi. = 2.59 sq. km.
1 hectare (ha) = 2.471 acres   1 acre = 0.405 ha.
100 ha. = 1 sq. km.

Volume/Capacity

1 cu. m. = 35.3 cu. ft.   1 cu. ft. = 0.028 cu. m.
1 cu. cm. = 0.061 cu. in.   1 cu. in. = 16.39 cu. cm.
1 liter (l) = 0.264 gal.   1 gal. = 3.785 l.
1 hectoliter (hl) = 2.84 bushels   1 bushel = 0.35 hl.

Weight

1 kilogram (kg) = 2.2 pounds (lbs)   1 lb. = 0.45 kg.
1,000 kg. (1 metric ton) = 2,205 lbs.   1 ton = 0.91 metric ton
100 kg. = 1 centner (ct) = 220.5 lbs.

Temperatures

To convert from centigrade to Fahrenheit: multiply by 9, divide by 5, add 32

Official Letter Codes and Native Names for Countries

European Countries

A	Austria (Österreich)
AL	Albania (Shqiperi)
AND	Andorra
AR	Armenia (Hayastan)
B	Belgium (Belgie/Belgique)
BG	Bulgaria (Balgarija)
BIH	Bosnia-Herzegovina (Bosna-Hercegovina)
BY	Belarus
CH	Switzerland (Helvetia)
CY	Cyprus (Kipros)
CZ	Czechia (Čechy)
D	Germany (Deutschland)
DK	Denmark (Danmark)
E	Spain (España)
EST	Estonia (Eesti)
F	France
FL	Liechtenstein
FR	Faeroe Islands (Føroyar) (part of DK)*
GB	United Kingdom (in some venues, UK is used)
GBZ	Gibraltar (possession of the United Kingdom)*
GE	Georgia (Sakartvelo)
GR	Greece (Hellas or Hellada)
H	Hungary (Magyarorszag)
HR	Croatia (Hrvatska)

* dependent territory

I	Italy (Italia)
IRL	Ireland (Eire)
IS	Iceland (Island)
L	Luxembourg
LT	Lithuania (Lietuva)
LV	Latvia (Latvija)
M	Malta
MC	Monaco
MD	Moldova
MK	Macedonia (Makedonija)
N	Norway (Norge)
NL	Netherlands (Nederland)
P	Portugal
PL	Poland (Polska)
RO	Romania
RSM	San Marino
RUS	Russia (Rossiya)
S	Sweden (Sverige)
SF or FIN	Finland (Suomi)
SK	Slovakia (Slovensko)
SLO	Slovenia (Slovenija)
UA	Ukraine (Ukraina)
V	Vatican City (Citta del Vaticano)
YU	Yugoslavia (Jugoslavija)

Neighboring Non-European Countries

ASE	Azerbaijan
DZ	Algeria
—	Chechnya (Ichkhería)**
ET	Egypt
HKJ	Jordan
IL	Israel
IR	Iran
IRQ	Iraq
KWT	Kuwait
KZ	Kazakhstan
LAR	Libya
MA	Morocco
RL	Lebanon

** independence not internationally recognized

SYR	Syria
TCY	Turkish Cyprus**
TM	Turkmenistan
TN	Tunisia
TR	Turkey

** independence not internationally recognized

CHAPTER 1

Europe Defined

What is Europe? The answer is not as simple as you might imagine, for Europe represents, in the words of Norwegian geographer Leif Ahnström, "an elusive notion." *The Economist,* a well-known British news magazine, devoted its February 12, 2000, issue to "What Is Europe?"

The Continental Myth

Most people would define Europe as a *continent.* You may recall from elementary school days reciting the names of the family of continents, in which Europe held a place of full membership. Support for the continental status of Europe appears in various dictionaries and in the writings of numerous geographers. For example, *Webster's New World Dictionary* defines Europe as a "continent between Asia and the Atlantic Ocean," while the British geographer Lionel Lyde entitled his textbook *The Continent of Europe.* In this view, then, we are led to believe that Europe constitutes a distinct *physical* entity, because a continent is a sizable landmass standing more or less separate from other landmasses. North and South America, connected by the narrow Isthmus of Panama, form continents, as do Africa, linked to Asia only by the severed land bridge at Suez, and Australia, fully separated from other landmasses by surrounding seas.

Europe, however, cannot meet the definition of a continent since it does not form a separate landmass. To be sure, the Mediterranean Sea provides a clear separation from Africa in the south, while the Atlantic and Arctic Oceans well define Europe's western and northern limits, but in the east, the notion of continentality founders. Only the beginning of a water separation appears in the southeastern fringe, where an arm of the sea reaches northward from the Mediterranean, through the Aegean, Dardanelles, and Bosporos to the Black Sea, and still beyond to the Sea of Azov. There the division ends, for to the north stretches the vast East European Plain. Instead of a narrow isthmus similar to Panama or Suez, the map reveals a wedge of land broadening steadily to the east, welding Europe and Asia into one large continent called **Eurasia**. Europe lacks a clear-cut oceanic border in the east and as a result is not a continent. In fact, a glance at a map of the Eastern Hemisphere reveals Europe as simply one rather small appendage of Eurasia, merely a westward-reaching peninsula. At most, Europe forms only about one-fifth of the area of Eurasia.

The erroneous belief that Europe possesses the characteristics of a continent came down to the modern day from the civilizations of the ancient Mediterranean, in particular from the Greeks and Romans (fig. 1.1). The Greco-Roman worldview in turn owed much to other, older cultures. One theory concerning the origin of the words *Europe* and *Asia* relates them to the Semitic Assyrian-Phoenician *ereb* ("sunset") and *acu* ("sunrise"). The

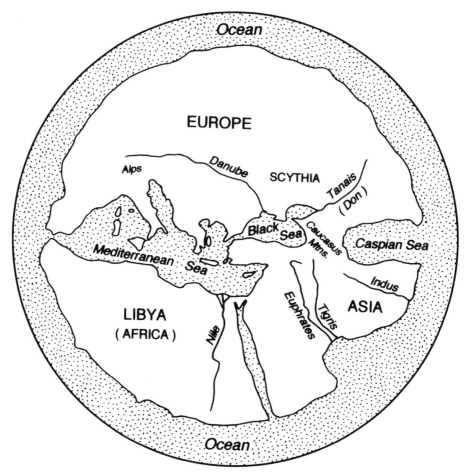

Figure 1.1.   World map drawn by the ancient Greek geographer Hecataeus ca. 500 b.c. He erroneously linked the Caspian Sea to the open ocean so that Europe and Asia joined only at the Caucasus isthmus. (*Source:* Adapted from Parker 1960.)

"land of the sunset," Europe, may have first appeared as an entity among the peoples of the Fertile Crescent, meaning simply "the western land." Also, an ancient, mythological ruler of Sidon in Phoenicia reputedly had daughters named *Europa* and *Asia*. The legendary Europa married the Greek king of gods, Zeus, and accompanied him back to the Aegean, while her sister remained in the east.

From their vantage point on the Aegean, the ancient Greeks perceived a world divided into three parts—Europe, Africa (then called Libya), and Asia—and the Romans accepted the Greek outlook. Greece was always a nation of seafarers, and its sailors from the time of Ulysses and earlier had charted the marine separation between Europe and Africa. In addition, the classical Greeks knew of the division of Africa and Asia, for the Phoenicians before them had circumnavigated the African continent. The Argonauts and other Greek explorers had probed into the Black Sea, founding trading colonies as far away as present-day Ukraine. Intrepid Greek merchants probed beyond the Black Sea to the shores of the landlocked, saltwater Caspian Sea. Certain Greek scholars evaluating the information brought back by traders assumed that the saline Caspian was part of the ocean. To them, the Caucasian isthmus between the Black and Caspian Seas was the only land bridge connecting Europe and Asia (fig. 1.1). Little did they know that the Caspian was an inland sea, with no opening to the ocean, and that north of the Caspian stretched a huge expanse of land. Certain other classical scholars, including Strabo, Pomponius Mela, and Ptolemy, mistakenly believed that only a narrow isthmus lay north of the Black Sea and the Sea of Azov, separating them from the Arctic Ocean, and they placed the Europe–Asia border along the course of the Don River (the ancient Tanais) (fig. 1.2). Their lack of accurate information led them to whittle down the expansive Russian plains to a narrow land bridge. The classical Greeks and Romans, then, believed in a threefold division of the landmasses, and Europe was to them a separate physical entity, a mere geographic term.

From the Greeks and Romans, the concept of the three continents passed intact to monastic scholars of the medieval period. Perpetuation of the classical view became guaranteed when a Christian religious significance was attached to it in the Christian church. Religious-inspired cartography produced the famous "T in O" map. The church simplified the map of the known world in such a way that the pattern of land and seas formed the letters T, for *terrarum* ("earth") and O, for *orbis* ("circle"), suggesting that God had shaped the world in a sort of Latin shorthand. The Mediterranean Sea represented the lower bar of the T, and the top of the map was east rather than north. The Nile River (or Red Sea)–Aegean Sea–Black Sea–Don River line formed the horizontal bar of the T. Some medieval Christian scholars created water separations of Europe, Asia, and Africa by severing Suez and widening the Don to marine proportions. The letter O lay between the outer perimeter of the three continents and the presumed edge of the world (fig. 1.3). On many such ethnocentric Christian maps, the cen-

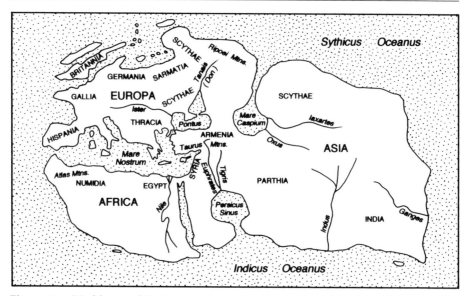

Figure 1.2.   World map of the Roman geographer Pomponius Mela, drawn in A.D. **43.** The Caspian Sea is still depicted as an arm of the ocean, but Russia has also been narrowed to form an isthmus. (*Source:* Adapted from Parker 1960.)

ter of the world was the holy city of Jerusalem, while the lost Garden of Eden lay far out in the inaccessible reaches of hinter Asia. We should not judge "T in O" maps by modern standards because their purpose, as interpretative art, was to depict religious mysteries and offer a stylized stage for the Christian drama, rather than to picture the world accurately. In any case, medieval scholars perpetuated the pre-Christian notion of Europe as a continent.

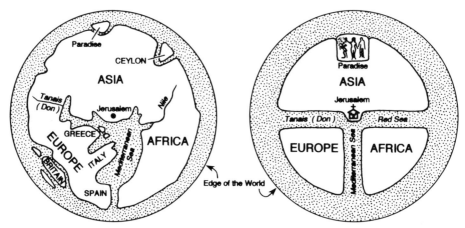

Figure 1.3.   Two versions of the medieval European "T in O" map. Europe remained, as in classical times, a separate continent. (*Source:* Adapted from Woodward 1985.)

Even after the Age of Discovery added new continents to the world map, some erroneous views persisted. As late as 1532, cartographers such as Grynaeus continued to show Russia as a narrow isthmus (fig. 1.4). Later in that century, a fairly accurate world map first appeared. It revealed that no isthmus existed north of the Black Sea and that the Don was a rather insignificant river whose headwaters did not even approach the great frozen ocean to the north. Instead of a relatively narrow land bridge, the mapmakers of Europe encountered a 2,000-kilometer-wide wedge of land between the White Sea in the north of Russia and the Sea of Azov in the south.

Europe was not, after all, a continent, but a 2,000-year-old belief is not easily discarded. Even to the present day, as we have seen, some continue to speak of the "continent of Europe." In the absence of an isthmus, geographers began looking for other environmental features to use as Europe's eastern border. The Swedish geographer Philip J. von Strahlenberg lamented in 1738 that "every one who is conversant in Geography knows that there has, for a considerable time, been a disagreement among geographers about the certainty . . . of the boundaries between . . . Europe and Asia." He and others felt that even if it was not a continent, perhaps it could still be bounded physically. Maybe Europe was a **subcontinent** like India, walled off from the rest of Eurasia by the Himalaya Mountains. Attention soon fell upon the Urals, a low mountain range running in a north–south

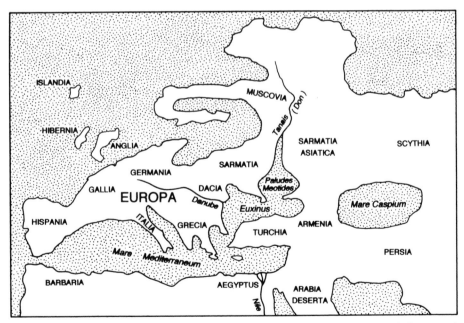

Figure 1.4.   A portion of the world map by Grynaeus, 1532. Russia remains an isthmus and the headwaters of the Tanais (Don) River incorrectly lie near the Arctic shore. Europe is still a continent. (*Source:* Adapted from Parker 1960.)

direction across the heart of Eurasia, as the best border, and many adopted this view (fig. 1.5). The Uralian border today enjoys greater acceptance than any other, even though it severs Russia in half (fig. 1.6). Another range, the impressive snow-capped Caucasus Mountains, provided another link in the border of Europe, stretching between the Black and Caspian Seas. Certain other geographers, more sensitive to the nuances of terrain, suggested that Europe did not extend beyond those regions where the land lay partitioned into small, discrete landform units, banishing to the Asian world the great expanses of unbroken plains that dominate the Eurasian interior, including most of Russia (fig. 1.6) (see chapter 2).

Some other geographers, continuing the ancient classical tradition, award certain rivers the status of European border. The Don formed one part of Strahlenberg's proposed border, and the Dnipro and Ural Rivers found similar honor among certain scholars. The suggestion has also been made that Europe should exclude all areas of interior, Arctic and Indian Ocean drainage, leaving as European only those lands whose rivers drain to the Atlantic Ocean, Baltic, Mediterranean, and Black Seas (fig. 1.6).

Still others prefer a climatic border, defining Europe as a temperate, well-watered land flanked by deserts, steppes, and frigid subarctic wastes. To the south lies the great arid belt consisting of the Sahara, Arabian, and

Figure 1.5.   The Ural Mountains, long regarded by many as the eastern border of Europe. The view here is in the far north, near the Arctic Ocean, on the eastern boundary of Russia's Komi Republic. The month is June, but snow still caps the northern Urals. (Photo by T.G.J.-B. 1997.)

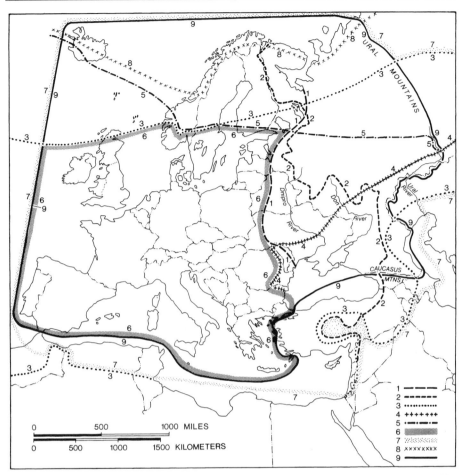

Figure 1.6. The European ecumene: diverse proposals for defining Europe physically. Mountain ranges, rivers, drainage basins, terrain patterning, and climatic traits have all been suggested. Borders: 1. eastern border of small discrete terrain regions, beyond which lie boundless plains; 2. western border of interior Arctic–Indian Ocean drainage; 3. Herbert Louis's borders, based on warmth and rainfall; 4. northern limit of the steppe grasslands; 5. northern limit of temperate climates; 6. the European ecumene narrowly defined, including lands accepted by all who seek to bound Europe on a physical environmental basis; 7. the European ecumene most broadly defined, including lands accepted by at least one scholar seeking a physical boundary; 8. southern border of Arctic tundra; and 9. the most widely accepted border of Europe today. Europe, environmentally, thus becomes a temperate, well-watered land of variegated terrain. Louis oddly extended it far into southern Siberia, off our map. (*Sources:* Hahn 1881, plate 3; Louis 1954, map following 80; Wolf 1982, 31; Parker 1953, 1960.)

Central Asian Deserts (fig. 1.7). The geographer Herbert Louis adopted this southern border, placing it at the limits of nonirrigated farming. He further proposed that Europe reached only as far north and east as those lands having at least two months averaging +15° Celsius or warmer and a total of four months above +10°C, a limit judged critical for grain cultivation (fig. 1.6). Some scholars would also exclude from Europe the steppe grasslands that intrude from Asia north of the Black Sea, regarding them as alien in appearance and utilization. The northern tundras, beyond the tree line in an Arctic environment, merit similar disapproval from a few. From all these attempts at bounding the European ecumene emerges an image of a temperate, humid land of highly variegated terrain.

But of what value are these diverse suggestions for an environmentally determined Europe? Why, in fact, does the concept of "Europe" survive so long after continentality has been disproven? Why do we teach courses in the geography of Europe, instead of Eurasia? Why is there a "European Specialty Group" within the Association of American Geographers? In-

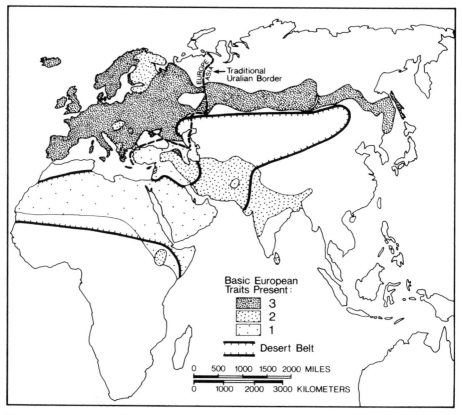

Figure 1.7.   Europe defined geographically on the basis of Christian religion, Indo-European language, and Caucasian race. Note how Europe, so defined, nestles against but does not intrude into the great desert belt to the south.

deed, why do the Europeans themselves continue to believe that a separate and distinct Europe exists? Why do they speak of their "common European home"? Clearly, the answers do not lie in the contrived and discordant physical boundaries previously discussed. Instead, we must agree with the Russian geographer, E. M. Murzayev, who concluded that "any attempt to divide Europe from Asia on a systematic physical-geographical basis is doomed to fail."

Europe as a Human Entity

Let us instead seek a definition of Europe based in human, rather than environmental, characteristics. Europe is a *culture* that occupies a *culture area*. A culture may be defined as a community of people who hold numerous features of belief, behavior, and overall way of life in common, including ideology, technology, social institutions, and material possessions. A culture area is any region inhabited by people of a particular culture, a land upon which the visible imprint of that culture has been placed. Geographer W. H. Parker perhaps put it best when he said that Europe represented "a cultural concept" and that "its eastern limits have been cultural and never long stable." Europeans belong to a cultural community rooted in a Judeo–Christian–Hellenic heritage—in short, *Western Civilization*.

During the long period of belief in continental status, Europe evolved and expanded as a culture area. Only gradually, and amid confusion that lingers still today, did Europe make the transition from physical to human entity. As late as the 1200s, *Europe* continued to mean simply a continent, though by then some had adopted the view that Europeans were distinctive as the descendants of Japheth, one of the sons of the biblical Noah. Slowly, in the period 1300 to 1600, *Europe* came to mean "Christendom," says Denys Hay, "and the emotional content of the word Europe significantly increased." A European self-consciousness, centered in the church, emerged. By 1571, the pope revealingly referred to "Europeans, or those who are called Christians." *Europe* acquired a positive, cultural meaning, and Europeans now had a distinctive worldview based in a vivid and flattering self-image. Four centuries later, in 1991, another Roman pope exhorted Europe to return "to its Christian roots." In that same year, the president of Turkey, frustrated at the failure of his dominantly Muslim country to be accepted as a member of the European Union (EU), lamented that "some people maintain that the EU should be a Christian club." When Turkey, in 1997, was denied even the right to *apply* for EU membership, the country's prime minister angrily attributed this action to "religious discrimination." About that same time, a British periodical described "a Muslim crescent curling threateningly around the southern and eastern edges of Europe" (*Economist*, 6 August 1994). Finally, in 1999, Turkey's candidacy for EU membership was accepted, but considerable doubt exists concerning whether this application will ever be approved.

Christianity, for at least the last eight centuries, has allowed Europeans to remain a self-conscious, distinct culture (table 1.1). The church helped create a we-versus-they mentality that separated Christian/European from barbarian/heathen/infidel/fiend. All along the outer margins of Europe, religion still today engenders a virulent sense of separation and demonization, causing Spaniards to despise Arabs; Greeks, Bulgars, and Armenians to hate Turks; Russians to revile Chechens; Serbs to murder Bosnians and Albanians; and Georgians to battle Ossetians and Abkhazis (see fig. 3.17). Even in the very heart of Europe and in the present century, the religious issue has remained sufficiently potent to deny European residence, and even life itself, to Jews.

The second basic cultural trait that helps define Europe as a human entity is *language.* The great majority of Europeans speak one or another of the **Indo-European** tongues, an extended family of related languages that all derive from a common ancestral speech. Flanking the Indo-Europeans

Table 1.1. European Self Identity: A Checklist

Category	Europe/Self	Non-Europe/Alien
Physical Habitat	Marine	Continental
	Occident	Orient
	Temperate	Extreme
	Rimland	Heartland
	Northern	Southern
Religion	Christian	Non-Christian
	Roman	Orthodox
	Secular	Believer
Race	Fair complexion	Dark complexion
Ideology/politics	Democratic	Authoritarian
	Uniting	Dividing
	Postnational	Nationalist
	Social democracy	Communism
	Peace/stability	War/turmoil
Culture	Civilization	Nature/barbarism
	Reason	Emotion
	Teacher	Pupil
	Progress	Stasis
	Cosmopolitan	Parochial
	Tolerance	Intolerance
	Wisdom	Immaturity
	Postmodern	Traditional/modern
Economy	Postindustrial	Industrial/agrarian
	Tertiary	Primary/secondary
	Core	Periphery
	Developed	Colonial

Source: Adapted, with modification and addenda, from Painter 2000.

are speakers of other language families, such as Uralic, Altaic, Caucasic, Afro-Asiatic, or Euskera (fig. 1.8). The language pattern will be considered in greater detail in chapter 4.

Race provides the third basic human trait that helps distinguish Europeans from their neighbors. Europe is the homeland of the **Europoid** (*or Caucasian*) race. Beyond the Sahara Desert to the south, in Africa, live the **Negroid** peoples, while most Asians belong to the **Mongoloid** race. In other words, Europeans, as Caucasians, differ in physical appearance from neighboring peoples, and these differences have become enmeshed in their self-identity. Racism remains common among Europeans, as in virtually all cultures. The question of race will be addressed in chapter 5.

In a narrow sense, then, Europe can be defined as those parts of the Eastern Hemisphere where the people are Christians, speak an Indo-European language, and exhibit Europoid physical traits (fig. 1.7). For the sake of simplicity, we might sever the awkward "tail" of European culture extending eastward along the line of the Trans-Siberian Railroad, perhaps

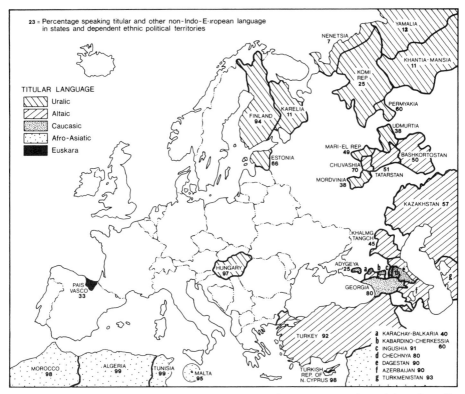

Figure 1.8. The non-Indo-European borderlands of Europe, as indicated by ethnically based independent states and dependent territories of five different language families. While these nominal, non-Indo-European groups do not always form a majority in these territories, their ethnicity remains strong enough to dilute the "European-ness" of the areas. Only the Hungarians do not occupy a peripheral position. Can we bound Europe accordingly?

cutting it off at the point where Altaic and Uralic speakers cause a constriction and forking, very near the widely accepted Uralian border (figs. 1.7 and 1.8).

By the sixteenth century, when continentality was proven invalid, the human Europe was already well developed. This evolution of a culture area explains not only the numerous efforts to find a satisfactory eastern boundary for Europe since the 1500s, but also the remarkable survival of the myth of continentality in the face of contradictory evidence. Cartographers, aware that Europe differed from Asia, were simply trying to express this idea on their maps. Continentality had become merely a surrogate for culture.

Still, if Europe is to be defined in terms of human characteristics, then the three basic criteria of religion, language, and race hardly suffice, for European culture is complex and has changed remarkably through time. In order to define *modern* Europe, we must add many more defining traits to the basic ones. Any such list must necessarily be subjective, and the resultant definition can only be a personal one, but that should not deter the search. The following are suggested as additional ways in which Europeans differ from their neighbors:

1. **A well-educated population.** The European culture, more than most others, places a high value on the written word as opposed to oral tradition. As a result, more than 90% of all Europeans in most countries are literate, and in some nations it is illegal not to be. In Germany, for example, 99% of the population can read and write, and in Spain the proportion is 97% (see chapter 6). By contrast, as near as the southern shore of the Mediterranean, in Morocco, only about half of the people are literate as is also true in India to the east.

2. **A healthy population.** Europeans enjoy a far-above-average life expectancy—well in excess of 70 years in some countries. Perhaps an even better measure of health is provided by the *infant mortality rate*—the number of children per thousand who do not survive to the age of 1 year. For much of Europe, the rate stands below 10, while across the Mediterranean and Aegean one encounters rates such as Turkey's 43 (see chapter 6). Most Europeans benefit from modern medical facilities and an abundant, nutritious diet.

3. **Stabilized population size.** The European population is scarcely growing at present; *zero population growth* has essentially been achieved. In fact, some European countries, such as Germany and Ukraine, have declining populations (see chapter 6). In startling contrast, all countries in neighboring North Africa and Asia Minor, as well as in Africa and Asia at large, experience more than 1.5% annual natural increase in the population and suffer an ongoing "population explosion."

4. **A wealthy population.** The typical European receives enough not only for the necessities of life, but also for many luxuries. The net result is

a very high standard of living, as judged by the precepts of Western Civilization (see chapter 6). In areas adjacent to Europe, the large majority of Africans and Asians, often less materialistic in their outlook, achieve a bare subsistence and live in what Europeans call poverty. Per capita incomes drop drastically as one crosses into Africa or Asia.

5. **An urbanized population.** The great majority of Europeans live in cities and towns of 10,000 or more population, and in some countries the proportion exceeds 80% (see chapter 8). By way of comparison, only 28% of the people in India, 30% in China, 44% in Egypt, and 27% in Sudan are urbanites.

6. **An industrialized economy.** All sectors of industry, especially the services, are well developed in Europe and collectively employ the far greater part of the labor force. Some even speak of Europe as an "industrial civilization" (see chapters 9 and 10). By contrast, agriculture remains the dominant form of economy in most of Africa and Asia.

7. **A dense transportation network.** Europe is crisscrossed by an unparalleled system of highways, railroads, canals, pipelines, and airline routes (see chapter 10). Few areas can be called remote, and the "friction of distance" has been minimized. By contrast, in much of Asia and Africa a network scarcely exists, few people own automobiles, and movement of people over any considerable distance remains rare.

8. **Freely elected governments.** Europeans invented democracy and took the first major steps toward limiting the power of leaders, producing political freedom and pluralism (see chapter 7). Competing ideologies are tolerated, and *individualism*, the cardinal European virtue, flourishes in such political conditions. In most of Africa and Asia, by contrast, authoritarianism and collectivism remain the rule.

9. **Part of the European zone of continuous settlement**—that thickly populated western section of Eurasia separated from Asia and Africa by deserts and Arctic wastelands (see chapter 6).

By this necessarily personal definition, then, Europe includes that part of the Eastern Hemisphere where people are not merely Christian, Caucasian, and Indo-European, but also educated, free, healthy, individualistic, wealthy, materialistic, mobile, urbanized, employed preponderantly in industry, and demographically stable. As a result of sharing these and other diverse, important traits, Europeans are, in the barely exaggerated words of the Italian Luigi Barzini, "all basically the same kind of people, comfortable in each other's countries and in each other's homes." David Gress refers to this European culture complex as "a synthesis of democracy, capitalism, science, human rights, . . . individual autonomy, and the power of unfettered human reason." It rests firmly on the glory of ancient Greece, layered over by the Renaissance, Enlightenment, and modern science. Europeans developed a *geo-ideology*, if you will, which links this common cultural heritage—**Western Civilization**—to a particular piece of the earth's surface.

European Great Ideas

If a single word can epitomize the human Europe, it is *dynamism*. Europe provided nearly all **great ideas**—those that have, for better or worse, substantially changed human existence and destiny—in the past millennium. To see the distinctiveness of Europe, to appreciate the degree to which this culture area has been a center of innovation, one need but plot on a map the place of origin of the great ideas that have revolutionized life since about A.D. 1000 (fig. 1.9).

Among the great ideas of Europeans is *democracy*, the child of classical Greece. It reappeared in medieval Iceland, in the infant Switzerland, in the Magna Carta of England, and in the Teutonic city-states of the Middle Ages, before bursting forth over much of Europe in the late 1700s and 1800s. Nowhere in Asia or Africa did this noble idea arise of its own accord, for tyranny and servitude have been the rule there. The *Age of Discovery*, primarily the accomplishment of Italian and Iberian Europeans, allowed Europe to discover the remainder of the world, rather than the converse. The peoples of the great Asian civilizations did not choose to follow the stepping-stone islands to discover and colonize America or Australia. It was not the Chinese who sent traders and explorers to Europe but rather the Italian Marco Polo who journeyed to China. In the process, as they encountered strange and to them barbarous foreign cultures, Europeans developed a heightened self-awareness that helped shape their geo-ideology.

The *printing press* employing *moveable type*, a gift from the artisans of the German Rhine Valley, had a tremendous impact in most parts of the world, revolutionizing people's means of communication. The concept of *the earth's sphericity*, developed by the classical Greeks, was revived by Italians and Iberians in the Age of Discovery, and the Polish astronomer Nicolaus Copernicus was the first to proclaim the heliocentric concept that the *earth revolves about the sun*. If Copernicus dealt a first great blow to human ego by removing the earth from the center of the universe, his fellow European Charles Darwin struck another in his *theory of evolution* by proposing that humans were animals of humble biological ancestry rather than divine creatures made in the image of God. Gregor Mendel provided the basis for *genetic science*, and Sigmund Freud, born a short distance from Mendel in Czechia, founded modern psychology, the scientific study of the mind. The Englishman Isaac Newton, in his *laws of motion and gravity*, established modern physics, while the German-born Swiss resident Albert Einstein, through his *theory of relativity*, greatly enhanced our understanding of the universe. Discovery of bacterial and viral *causes of disease*, the beginning of modern medicine, was the work of the German country doctor Robert Koch and the Frenchman Louis Pasteur. Marie Sklodowska Curie, a native of Poland and citizen of France, pioneered the study of *radioactivity*, with her husband Pierre (the word *curie* became the unit of measurement for this property), ushering in the atomic and nuclear age. The Russian Dmitry Mendeleyev developed the periodic table of the

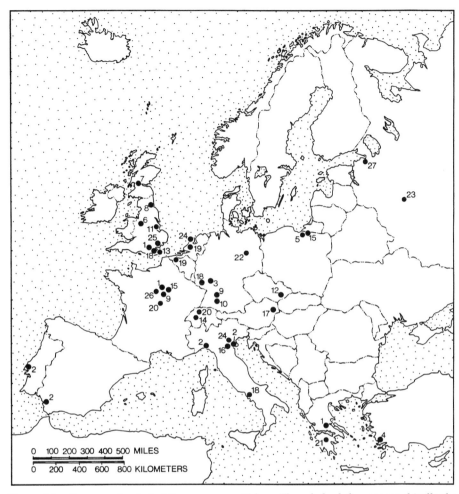

Figure 1.9.   Sources of selected European great ideas. These help define geographically the European culture area. Key: 1. democracy (ancient Greece, French Revolution, Magna Carta); 2. Age of Discovery (Genova, Venèzia, Cádiz, and Lisboa); 3. printing press (Johannes Gutenberg, at Mainz); 4. concept of the spherical earth (classical Greeks at Miletus, now in Turkey); 5. concept of heliocentric solar system (Nicolaus Copernicus in Frombork); 6. Industrial Revolution (English Midlands); 7. steam engine (James Watt in Glasgow); 8. railroad (northeast England); 9. internal combustion engine (Étienne Lenoir in Paris, and Nikolaus Otto and Gottlieb Daimler in Germany); 10. automobile (Daimler and Carl Benz in Germany); 11. laws of motion and gravity, providing the basis of modern physics (Isaac Newton in England); 12. science of modern genetics (Gregor Mendel in Morava); 13. theory of evolution (Charles Darwin in England); 14. theory of relativity (Albert Einstein in Bern); 15. discovery of bacterial and viral causes of diseases (Robert Koch in Ostpreussen and Louis Pasteur in Paris); 16. radio (Guglielmo Marconi in Bologna); 17. modern study of the mind (Sigmund Freud in Wien); 18. socialism (Karl Marx in Trier and London, and Tommaso Campanella in Italy); 19. productive capitalism (Holland and Vlaanderen); 20. nationalism (Switzerland and France); 21. nation-state (Greece); 22. expressways (Germany); 23. orbital satellites and manned space flight (Russia); 24. microscope and telescope (Hans Lippershey and Zacharias Janssen in Holland, and Galileo in Padova); 25. digital computer (Charles Babbage in England); 26. early research on radioactivity (Pierre Curie and Marie Sklodowska Curie in France); and 27. periodic table of chemicals (Dmitry Mendeleyev in St. Petersburg).

chemical elements, working in St. Petersburg in the 1890s. Dutch and Italian inventors perfected the first *microscope* and *telescope,* allowing humans for the first time to inspect objects too small or too distant to be studied with the naked eye.

The most far-reaching impact resulted from the *Industrial Revolution* (see chapter 9), the invention of diverse machines and harnessing of inanimate power that began in Great Britain in the 1700s. Its technology became a hallmark of European civilization and involved countless crucially important inventions, including the steam engine, railroad, internal combustion engine, automobile, expressway, radio, orbital satellites, manned space flight, and digital computer, to mention but a few. All of these came from Europe (fig. 1.9). Prometheus was unbound, and it was Europeans who loosened his bonds. *Modernity* and the concept of *progress,* quintessentially European, sprang into being.

Other cornerstones of modernity were also laid in Europe, including capitalism, socialism, nationalism, and the nation-state. *Productive capitalism,* distinguished by the application of capital to innovation in order to elevate levels of production, spread from an early nucleus in the 1500s in the Low Countries, and soon "overtly commercial values" permeated European civilization, leading to an economic miracle that spread prosperity through a larger segment of the population than ever before in world history. When linked to the Industrial Revolution, productive capitalism reshaped the world. *Socialism* arose in Europe as a movement to spread prosperity still more widely and to prevent the migration of great wealth back into the hands of the few. Rooted in Italian Tommaso Campanella's 1602 *City of the Sun,* socialism appeared as a fully developed ideology in the nineteenth-century works of Karl Marx, a German. Practiced in moderation, socialism led to the enviable quality of life achieved in the Scandinavian welfare states, but applied in despotic, perhaps Asian extremes, it led to the economic and political catastrophe of Russian Communism.

Nationalism, in which citizens transferred allegiance from the monarch to the state, with potentially dangerous results, began perhaps in medieval Switzerland and later appeared more forcefully in revolutionary France. Still later came, as another gift from Europe, the most virulent form of nationalism, the *nation-state,* in which nationality became linked to a common language and/or religion. The nation-state concept, perhaps born in the early nineteenth-century Greek struggle for independence from the Turks, subsequently infected most of Europe and much of the world at large.

Collectively, the impact of these diverse European great ideas has been prodigious. Try to imagine a world never touched by them. The Eurocentric notion that European culture is, as a result, a *superior* one follows easily. Certainly most Europeans believe this to be true. Listen, for example, to the words of the great German writer Thomas Mann. In his 1924 novel *The Magic Mountain,* Mann described two opposed principles in conflict for

possession of the world—"force and justice, tyranny and freedom, superstition and knowledge, permanence and change. One may call the first Asiatic, the second European because Europe was a center of rebellion, the
domain of intellectual . . . activity leading to change, while the Orient was
characterized by quiescence and lack of change." Similar, even stronger
views found expression in the works of the famous Greek author Nikos
Kazantzakis, who grew to manhood on the very outermost periphery of
Europe, confronting a hostile, alien culture. Kazantzakis, in his book *Report
to Greco,* compared his own culture to that of Asia Minor. Greece, he wrote,
"is the filter which . . . refines brute into man, eastern servitude into liberty,
barbaric intoxication into sober rationality." Cultural impulses received
from the East, from Asia, were refined and transubstantiated by the Greeks
into more civilized forms. Greece's "fated location" on the borders of Asia
produced, said Kazantzakis, "a mystic sense of mission and responsibil-
ity," a buffer against the "barbaric" and "bestial" East (i.e., Turkey).

When confronted by Eurocentricism and cultural arrogance, we should
remind the Europeans that many of their gifts to the world proved malevo-
lent and destructive, in some cases threatening the very existence of the
human race. Europe gave us ethnic cleansing, genocide, fascism, religious
inquisitions, imperialism, colonialism, mechanized total warfare, and eco-
cide. In the words of geographer Yi-fu Tuan, Europeans, by discarding "the
ageless fear of the greater power and potency of nature," assumed "an
arrogance based on the presumed availability of almost unlimited power."
Europe means progress, but where that progression ultimately will lead, to
good or evil, remains unclear. Europeans developed a high culture, but it
could not, in the final analysis, prevent them from committing unspeakable
atrocities, even in the German heart of Europe, nor does it allow them to
control the powerful technology they unleashed.

Geographer James Blaut suggests that the rise of Europe was not due
to the superiority of its culture, but instead to the wealth Europeans seized
through conquest and colonialism. No, European culture is not superior.
In fact, the world might be a better place had it never existed. As such,
we should regard Europe merely as a *distinctive* culture, one devoted to
individualism, innovation, acquisition, and change. Nor should we forget
that other parts of the world also contributed "great ideas."

Europe Bounded

Earlier, we rejected the diverse attempts to find physical borders for Europe
(fig. 1.6), while at the same time presenting a map based on the three basic
European traits (fig. 1.7). Now, we must seek more refined, culturally based
limits.

Perhaps the best place to begin our search is with the subjective perceptions of Europeans themselves. Listen when they speak, and you will hear revealing, if often bigoted, remarks such as:

"Africa begins at the Pyrenees." (Alexandre Dumas, Frenchman)

"We were once, and will be again, Europeans." (Latvia's prime minister, 1991)

"The principles of Europe can't exactly be implanted in Bulgaria." (Vladimir Andreev, Bulgarian filmmaker, 1995)

"Scratch a Russian and you will wound a Tatar." (Napoléon Bonaparte)

"Russians: a European people or some mongrel Asian one?" (Steven Erlanger, 1995)

"Can we become a part of Europe?" (anonymous Albanian, 1992)

"When the rest of [medieval] Iberia was under Arab domination, Catalonia was part of Europe, an important difference." (Catalunya's director of linguistic policy, 1991)

"We are not part of the civilized world now." (Yasar Kemal, Turkish novelist, 1999)

"Turkey—the Europe you don't know; the Asia you will discover." (Turkish National Tourist Bureau, 1995)

"Of course we are part of Europe." (Ismail Cem, Turkey's foreign minister, 1998)

"Napoli must stop being a Middle Eastern city." (Sergio Baronci, Italian bureaucrat)

"Ukraine: a shell concealing an Eurasian core." (Michael Wines, 1999)

"Poland—a suburb of Europe." (Jerzy Jedlicki, 1999)

"Certain of our Polish characteristics do not conform with Western mentality." (Edmund Lewandowski, Lodz professor, 1995)

"We dress in Western clothes and drink espresso, but our minds are Oriental." (Aleksandr Tijanic, Serbian information minister, 1999)

"With our mother country Croatia behind us, we will unite not with the barbaric hordes, but with Europe." (Kresimir Zubac, Bosnian Croat politician, 1996)

"After 5 decades of Soviet occupation, we are now anew becoming a part of Europe." (Lennart Meri, president of Estonia, 1994, on the withdrawal of the last Russian troops from his country)

"By their spiritual makeup, Russians are Oriental people." (N. A. Berdiaev, 1990)

"The liquid manure of Western Civilization is seeping through our borders." (Aleksandr Solzhenitsyn, Russian author, 1994)

Implicit in many such remarks is the notion that Russia and some other eastern European states do not belong in Europe. One member of the Ukrainian parliament recently distinguished the "Europeanized Slavs" in the western part of his country from the "Russo-Slavs" of the eastern region. Witold Orlowski, a Pole, noting that his country would soon create a barrier–border along its eastern frontier, at the instigation of the European Union, declared that "Europeans are drawing the borderline of Europe for the next 50 years and don't care about Ukraine, Belarus, and Russia."

Still, we should not forget that Mikhail Gorbachev, the former Russian leader, coined the term "our common European home," and, as Milan Hauner notes, many Russians today ask "what is Asia to us?" Most geographers seek to compromise, drawing the border of Europe *through* Russia, thereby claiming the western part of it—*Eurorussia*—for the European culture area (fig. 1.10). We will do precisely that in this text, whenever a statistical boundary of Europe is required.

Europeans even tease each other about the Asian issue. A 1996 advertisement by a Danish-owned ferry boat line that takes cars and passengers to the Swedish port of Malmö advised prospective customers that "Asia begins in Malmö," then suggested that the common Swedish road sign warning of a wildlife crossing—a picture of a moose inside a red triangle—actually meant everything from "restaurant" to "opera"!

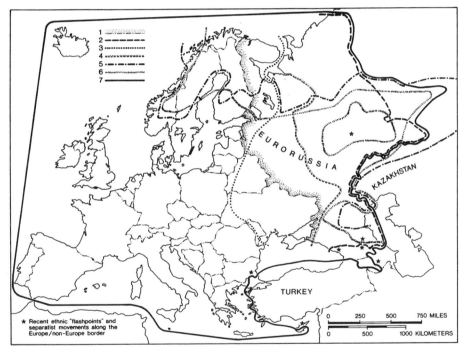

Figure 1.10. Proposed culture-based borders of Europe. 1. western border of Russia; 2. eastern border of Europe proposed by the Russian geographer E. M. Murzayev, based upon internal administrative units; 3. border proposed by the German geographer Banse, 1912; 4. border proposed by the French geographer Thevet, 1575; 5. border of the "European space economy," according to geographer Andrew Dawson, 1993; and 6. borders of "sedentary agricultural Europe," proposed by the Frenchman Francis Delaisi, 1929. The seventh border is the one used when defining Europe for statistical purposes throughout this book. (*Sources:* Parker 1960; Delaisi 1929, 24–25; Hahn 1881, plate 3; Murzayev 1964; Dawson 1993.)

In some places, a sharp cultural border for Europe seems simple to draw, as is true in the Mediterranean and the Aegean Seas, where different shores belong to sharply contrasted cultures. The same holds true along the partition line on the island of Cyprus, where, in the words of one UN official, crossing from the Greek to the Turkish sector "is like suddenly stepping into Asia." Greek Nicosia's "skyline is an enormous wall of high-rises," while Turkish Lefkosa's consists of "low, red-tiled roofs, homes to craftsmen and shopkeepers." We deal in these places with Christian–Islamic confrontation and dichotomy.

In recent times, some segments along this well-defined border of Europe have become flash points of conflict, separatism, and ethnic cleansing, as happened in Cyprus in 1974; in Bulgaria, where expulsions of ethnic Turks flared anew in the late 1980s; in Azerbaijan, where the Armenian Christian minority in Nagorno–Karabakh Province rebelled; in Georgia, where Abkhazi Muslims seceded amid civil war in 1993; in the Russian Caucasus, where Islamic Chechnya continues a struggle for independence; and even along the Volga, where Muslim Tatarstan has achieved autonomy (figs. 1.8, 1.10, and 1.11). In some of these conflicts, "Asian-ness" was flaunted, as in Cyprus, where Turkey code-named its 1974 invasion "Attila," after the Hunnic warrior from Asia who attacked Europe long ago. In the aftermath, Turkish Cypriots quickly expunged Greek place names from the map in their new republic. The border of Europe tends to grow sharper as a result of such conflicts.

Still, seeking a sharp cultural border for Europe proves futile in some places, especially in the East. There, the attempt to draw a precise line separating Europe from Asia becomes a fool's errand, with no two geographers agreeing (fig. 1.10). There, at least, Europe has no sharp borders. As long ago as the 1920s, geographers had "largely emancipated themselves from the hypnotic effect of terms like Europe and Asia," wrote the geographer Marion I. Newbigin, stressing instead the gradual transition from European to non-European. The Russian geographer Murzayev agreed, concluding that "there is no clear boundary" (fig. 1.10). The absence of a sharp border for Europe becomes even more evident when the various defining criteria are mapped. Even if the definition includes only the three basic traits—religion, language, and race—transitional zones appear in both south and east (fig. 1.8).

The Caucasus region reveals a chaotic cartography when we limit consideration to just two traits, religion and language (fig. 1.11). Indeed, the Caucasus—which gave us the very name "Caucasian"—is "a limboland between Asia and Europe" (*Economist*, 16 November 1996). The United Nations lists both Armenia (a Christian, Indo-European–speaking country) and Georgia (also a Christian land), as part of Asia. Both countries lie beyond the main ridge of the Caucasus Mountains, a range Michael Specter called "one of the great fault lines of the world, where Christian Orthodoxy and Islam, East and West, make their edgy meeting." Georgian geographer

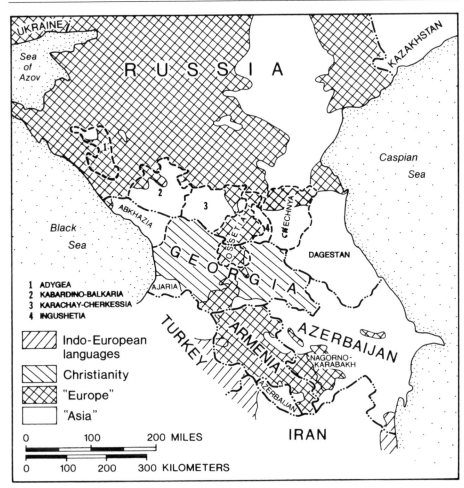

Figure 1.11. Europe and Asia in the Caucasus, based on the distribution of Christianity and the Indo-European languages. Notice how complicated the border of Europe becomes even when only these two criteria are employed.

Revaz Gachechiladze claims that his country "persists in being a European nation." But are Georgians and Armenians Europeans? Yes and no. A "fault line" does not exist in the Caucasus, but a fault zone does.

The absence of sharp boundaries for the European culture area becomes even more apparent when we map all eleven of the earlier-mentioned human-defining characteristics of Europe. A broad transitional zone emerges. From a core in central and northwestern Europe, where all the defining traits appear, "European-ness" declines gradually to the peripheries, especially in the east and south. Europe, culturally, yields slowly to Asia and Africa (fig. 1.12). "But," you might protest, "how could Greece—the very mother of Europe—display fewer than half of the European traits?" Well, you need only know that, as recently as the 1950s,

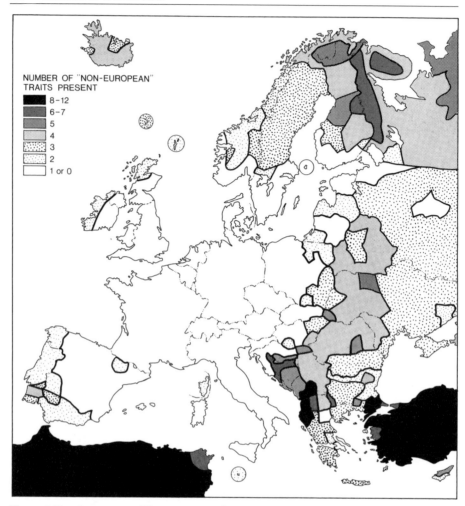

Figure 1.12.   A measure of European-ness, by province, based upon twelve European traits. A pronounced core–periphery pattern is revealed—a pattern that we will encounter repeatedly in subsequent chapters. Key: 1. over 80% Christian; 2. over 80% Indo-European; 3. over 90% Caucasian; 4. infant mortality rate below 12; 5. per capita gross domestic product is at least 40% of the EU average; 6. over 90% of people literate; 7. 300 or more kilometers of highway per 100 square kilometers of territory; 8. less than 25% of workforce employed in agriculture; 9. over 50% of people live in towns and cities; 10. less than 0.5% annual natural population increase; 11. lies inside the European zone of continuous settlement (see fig. 6.1); and 12. no substantial restrictions of democracy today.

Greeks spoke of "going to Europe" when they traveled to Paris, London, or Frankfurt. Things have changed since the time of Pericles and Plato.

Advance and Retreat

Once we adopt the notion that Europe should be defined in human terms, then we must also realize that its geographic extent can change. People and ideas are mobile, and so is Europe. To bound Europe today means drawing different lines than would have been used 1,000 or 2,000 years ago (fig. 1.13). Both expansion and retreat have marked Europe's past. One thousand years before Christ, a small European nucleus had formed around the shores of the eastern Mediterranean, a Greek embryo of Western Civilization. The Greeks had to fight off the Asiatic Persians among others to preserve their infant European culture. By the beginning of the Christian Era, Europe coincided with the territorial extent of the Roman Empire, a considerable expansion from the nucleus of 1000 B.C., though the core still lay in the Mediterranean basin.

The passage of still another millennium, to about A.D. 1000, brought

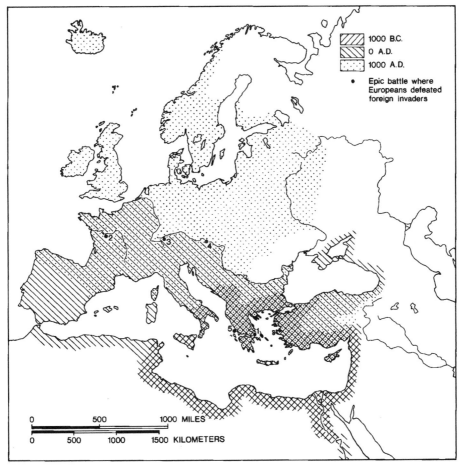

Figure 1.13.   Territorial extent of Europe, 1000 B.C. to A.D. 1000. Europe shifted north and west. The battles include: 1. Marathon and Salamis (Greeks defeated Persians, 490 and 480 B.C.); 2. Tours (Franks turn back Arabs, A.D. 732); 3. Lechfeld (Germans rout the Asiatic nomads at their deepest penetration into Europe in A.D. 955); 4. Wien (European alliance three times repelled the Turks in 1529, 1532, and 1683); and 5. Lepanto (Spaniards and Venetians crush Turks, 1571). (*Source:* In part after Whittlesey 1949.)

dramatic areal changes. The Arabs, driven by the evangelical spirit of a new religion, Islam, wrested away all of North Africa, most of Iberia, and the larger islands in the Mediterranean Sea. The deepest intrusion of the Arabs reached into central western France, where they were finally turned back on the battlefield of Tours. Asiatic horsemen from the East, the Magyars, penetrated as far as southern Germany, where a major battle was fought on the Lechfeld in A.D. 955. After long years of raiding, these mounted warriors eventually abandoned all but a foothold in the grassland of Hungary, where their linguistic descendants still remain today. The first thousand years after Christ were not, however, entirely years of retreat. The loss of North Africa was paralleled by an expansion into heathen Germanic and Slavic realms, which Christian missionaries brought into the European community.

The territorial ebb and flow of Europe continued into the present millennium. Spaniards and Portuguese, gripped by a religious fervor reminiscent of the earlier Muslim expansion, drove the Arabic Moors from Iberia, a reconquest that was completed in 1492. But in the East two serious setbacks occurred. The Tatars, or Golden Horde, followed the path of their earlier Asiatic kinsmen, sweeping across southern Russia to fall on Europe in the 1200s. Scarcely had they fallen back into Russia when a new peril appeared in Asia Minor, where the Muslim Turks overwhelmed the Greeks and pressed on beyond the Dardanelles–Bosporos to seize permanently the center of eastern Christendom, Constantinople, which they renamed Istanbul. From there the Turks spread northward to occupy most of the Balkan Peninsula. Repeatedly, Europe's warriors gathered to turn the Turks back from the gates of Wien and also at the naval battle of Lepanto off the Greek coast, preserving European culture. The Turkish tide gradually receded, leaving only Muslim relics in the Balkans and a small Turkish bridgehead on the north shore of the Dardanelles and Bosporos around Istanbul. Even the most persistent efforts by Europeans failed to destroy this bridgehead, and it, along with Asia Minor, remains lost to Europe.

Another area of contest within the last thousand years has been Palestine. The Europeans seized a temporary foothold in the Holy Land during the Crusades, only to suffer eventual defeat. Renewed efforts to claim the area began with the Zionist movement, the British takeover after World War I, the flood of Jewish migration after the Nazi disaster, and the creation of Israel. To be sure, the Israelis are not Christian, and they abandoned the Indo-European Yiddish language in favor of Semitic Hebrew, but in standard of living and economic development, their nation represents a transplanting of Europe to the eastern Mediterranean shores. Indeed, Zionist leader Max Nordau declared in 1929 that "we Jews intend to go to Palestine as the emissaries of civilization and to extend the boundaries of Europe to the banks of the Euphrates" (quoted in Hasson).

The truly spectacular European expansion, however, has been accomplished over the past 400 to 500 years by Germanic peoples, Slavs, and

Iberian Latins. The French scholar Pierre Chaunu views this global expansion as primarily the work of "Latin Christendom," including the adherents to both its Roman Catholic and Protestant components. Germanic-speaking peoples, in particular the English, created overseas Europes in Anglo-America, Australia, New Zealand, and South Africa, while Spaniards and Portuguese transplanted much that is European in large parts of Latin America. The overseas activities of the Iberians and Germans coincided with a major Slavic expansion overland, accomplished by the Russians, who busily pushed Europe deep into the previously alien heartland of Eurasia and on beyond to the Pacific shore.

In addition to the middle-and upper-latitude areas to which large European populations were transplanted bodily, and by destroying or subjugating the native peoples, great tropical colonial empires were established by the Spaniards, Portuguese, British, French, Dutch, Belgians, and Germans. In the entire world, only China, Japan, Thailand, Iran, Arabia, and Turkey avoided falling under European imperial rule at some time between 1500 and 1950. Colonialism brought the imprint of Europe. Consequently, India has a railroad system founded by the British, Haitians speak a form of French, and Filipinos adhere to the Roman Catholic faith. Europeans carried their mode of life throughout the world, transplanting it to thinly occupied lands or grafting it onto societies too firmly rooted to be dislodged (fig. 1.14). The world has been Europeanized in numerous, fundamental ways. Even those few areas never ruled from Europe have felt its cultural impress. Japan accepted the Industrial Revolution, China adopted Marxist socialism, and Turkey replaced Arabic script with the Latin alphabet.

At the same time, other parts of the world also helped shape Europe. Influence flowed both ways, and the European way of life has been profoundly altered in the process. Indeed, prior to about A.D. 1500, Europe could best be regarded as peripheral to the great culture centers of the Old World, receiving far more than it gave. Even Christianity, the traditional basis for much of Europe's distinctiveness, originated in the Middle East and attained its first major foothold in Asia Minor (see chapter 3). African Arabs taught Iberians some of the navigational secrets that permitted the Age of Discovery, and Muslims preserved much ancient Greco-Roman knowledge during Europe's lengthy Dark Age. Asiatic philosophical influences reached some European intellectuals, such as the twentieth-century German writer Hermann Hesse. Agriculture originally reached Europe from a western Asian hearth (see chapter 11), and the later introduction of American Indian crops, such as the potato, tomato, tobacco, and maize, greatly altered the European agrarian system.

Nor has European influence always found acceptance overseas. Recent events suggest a substantial, rising resistance to Europeanization, as is seen in the demise of colonialism and the Islamic cultural revival. In Africa, Islam rather than Christianity is the fastest-growing religious faith, and generations of Christian missionaries failed to make significant inroads in

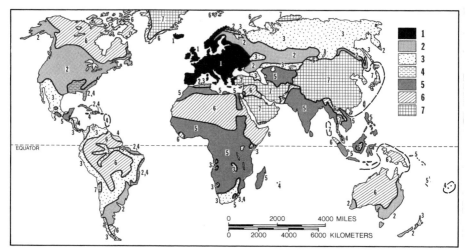

Figure 1.14.   The Europeanization of the world. Key: 1. European hearth area, A.D. 1500; 2. neo-European areas; population and culture almost wholly of European derivation; 3. mixed European and aboriginal areas, but culture strongly influenced or dominated by European practices; 4. plantation culture; small European-derived minority traditionally dominated a large non-European labor force; 5. exploitative or custodial occupation by Europeans in colonial era; minute numbers of Europeans implanted some durable customs and artifacts; 6. loose, ineffective, or brief European control and impact; and 7. areas never directly occupied or controlled by Europeans, but indirect penetration of European influence often significant. (*Source:* Modified from Zelinsky 1966, 74–75.)

India, China, or Japan. Finally, demographic stagnation means that Europeans form an ever-smaller part of the world population, a trend that will presumably further undermine their influence.

Still, the importance of Europe remains profound. Let us turn our attention now to a geographical analysis of this small but remarkable corner of the world.

Sources and Suggested Readings

Ahnström, Leif. 1993. "Europe: Culture Area, Geo-ideological Construct, or Illusion?" *Norsk Geografisk Tiddskrift* 47:57–67.

Barzini, Luigi. 1983. *The Europeans.* New York, USA: Simon & Schuster.

Beeley, Brian W. 1978. "The Greek–Turkish Boundary: Conflict at the Interface." *Transactions of the Institute of British Geographers* 3:351–366.

Berdiaev, N. A. 1990. *Istoki i Smysl Russkogo Kommunizma.* Moskva, RUS: Nauka.

Blaut, James M. 1993. *The Colonizer's Model of the World: Geographical Diffusionism and Eurocentric History.* New York, USA: Guilford.

Chaunu, Pierre. 1979. *European Expansion in the Later Middle Ages.* Trans. Katharine Bertram. Amsterdam, NL: North-Holland.

Cuisenier, Jean, ed. 1979. *Europe as a Cultural Area.* 's Gravenhage, NL: Mouton.

Dawson, Andrew H. 1993. *A Geography of European Integration.* London, GB: Belhaven.

Delaisi, Francis. 1929. *Les deux Europes.* Paris, F: Payot.

Dodgshon, Robert A. 1992. "The Role of Europe in the Early Modern World-system: Parasitic or Generative?" *Political Geography* 11:396–400.

Fells, John, and Józef Niznik. 1992. "What Is Europe?" *International Journal of Sociology* 22:201–207.

Fischer, Eric. 1943. *The Passing of the European Age: A Study of the Transfer of Western Civilization and Its Renewal in Other Continents.* Cambridge, Mass., USA: Harvard University Press.

Gachechiladze, Revaz, with R. A. French. 1995. *The New Georgia: Space, Society, Politics.* College Station, USA: Texas A&M University Press.

Graham, Brian, ed. 1998. *Modern Europe: Place, Culture, and Identity.* London, GB: Arnold.

Gress, David. 1999. *From Plato to NATO: The Idea of the West and Its Opponents.* New York, USA: Free Press.

Hahn, F. G. 1881. "Zur Geschichte der Grenze zwischen Europa und Asien." *Mitteilungen des Vereins für Erdkunde zu Leipzig*, 83–104.

Hasson, Shlomo. 1996. "Frontier and Periphery as Symbolic Landscapes." *Ecumene* 3:146–166.

Hauner, Milan. 1990. *What Is Asia to Us? Russia's Asian Heartland Yesterday and Today.* Boston, USA: Unwin Hyman.

Hay, Denys. 1968. *Europe: The Emergence of an Idea.* 2nd ed. Edinburgh, GB: University Press.

Hebbert, Michael J., and Jens C. Hansen, eds. 1990. *Unfamiliar Territory: The Reshaping of European Geography.* Aldershot, GB: Avebury.

Jedlicki, Jerzy. 1999. *A Suburb of Europe.* Budapest, H: Central European University Press.

Kazantzakis, Nikos. 1966. *Report to Greco.* New York, USA: Bantam.

Lewis, Martin W., and Kären E. Wigen. 1997. *The Myth of the Continents: A Critique of Metageography.* Berkeley, USA: University of California Press.

Louis, Herbert. 1954. "Über den geographischen Europabegriff." *Mitteilungen der Geographischen Gesellschaft in München* 39:73–93.

Lyde, Lionel. 1926. *The Continent of Europe.* London, GB: Macmillan.

Meinig, D. W. 1969. "A Macrogeography of Western Imperialism." In *Settlement and Encounter*, ed. Fay Gale and Graham H. Lawton. Melbourne, AUS: Oxford University Press, 213–240.

Murzayev, E. M. 1964. "Where Should One Draw the Geographical Boundary between Europe and Asia?" *Soviet Geography: Review and Translation* 5:15–25.

Newbigin, Marion I. 1924. *The Mediterranean Lands: An Introductory Study in Human and Historical Geography.* London, GB: Christophers.

Painter, Joe. 2000. "Transnational Citizenship and Identity in Europe." Paper read at the Twenty-ninth International Geographic Congress, Seoul, Korea.

Parker, W. H. 1953. "Europe and the New Civilization." *Canadian Geographer* 3:53–60.

———. 1960. "Europe: How Far?" *Geographical Journal* 126:278–297.

Pred, Alan. 1995. *Recognising European Modernities.* London, GB: Routledge.

Strahlenberg, Philip J. von. 1738. *An Historico-geographical Description of the North and Eastern Parts of Europe and Asia.* London, GB: J. Brotherton et al.

Tuan, Yi-fu. 1989. "Cultural Pluralism and Technology." *Geographical Review* 79:269–279.

Whittlesey, Derwent. 1949. *Environmental Foundations of European History*. New York, USA: Appleton.

Wintle, Michael, ed. 1996. *Culture and Identity in Europe*. Avebury, GB: Aldershot.

Wolf, Eric R. 1982. *Europe and the People without History*. Berkeley, USA: University of California Press.

Woodward, David. 1985. "Reality, Symbolism, Time, and Space in Medieval World Maps." *Annals of the Association of American Geographers* 75:510–521.

Zelinsky, Wilbur. 1966. *A Prologue to Population Geography*. Englewood Cliffs, N.J., USA: Prentice Hall.

CHAPTER 2

Habitat

While Europe constitutes a human and largely cultural entity, its natural setting should not be slighted in a geographical analysis. The story of the human Europe has been acted out in a habitat on a segment of the physical earth—a peninsula composed of many constituent peninsulas attached to the western extremity of Eurasia. In this chapter we will consider Europe's terrain, climate, vegetation, soils, and waters.

The physical environment of Europe has influenced the inhabitants' way of life in diverse ways, and we cannot understand Europe thoroughly without knowing the nature of the habitat. At the same time, Europeans have massively altered their environment, for both better and worse, to the extent that a "natural" habitat no longer exists. To the geographer, environment, people, and place remain abstractions unless considered together. This intertwining of way-of-life and habitat, this *cultural ecology*, provides another focus of the present chapter.

The European Mountains

The European land is highly varied, ranging from high, rugged mountains to featureless flat plains. We employ a threefold classification of terrain types: mountains, hills, and plains (fig. 2.1).

Mountains lie largely in the southern half of Europe, except for one major chain in Scandinavia, and most ranges are oriented in an east–west direction. The southern concentration of mountains is largely a result of *plate tectonics*, as the African and Eurasian plates slowly collide, a process begun some 50 million years ago—recent by geologic standards. The collision has caused folding, fracturing, and uplifting of the earth's surface, thus building the mountains.

The *Bética Mountains* parallel the south coast of Spain and consist of several ridges, including the *Sierra Nevada*, with several valleys in between.

Figure 2.1.   Terrain regions. (*Sources:* Raisz 2000; Embleton 1984.)

The Bética stretch from the Rock of Gibraltar to the vicinity of Valencia, where they disappear beneath the sea, only to emerge again to the east as the Baleares Islands. The Bética area, which includes peaks of more than 3,350 meters, served as the final stronghold of the Moors, or Arabs, and their influence is seen in the architecture of the city of Granada, which lies in one of the longitudinal valleys at the foot of the Sierra Nevada. Many Arabic place names also survive as a Moorish relic, including Gibraltar, derived from *gebel-al-Tariq* ("rock of Tariq"), a Moorish ruler. The last Arab revolt against Spanish rule, in the late 1500s, occurred in the Bética range, and villages founded by the Berbers—an African tribal group that accompanied the Moorish invasion—still today retain a special cultural character. Truly, Europe meets Africa in these mountains. The southernmost ridge of the Bética range fronts on the Mediterranean Sea, creating a rocky and picturesque coast, but in places the mountains draw back from the shore, allowing small pockets of coastal plain, called *huertas* (literally "gardens"). These permit intensive irrigation agriculture, as in the Huerta of Valencia, famous for its orange groves. The *Ibérica Mountains* form a fragmented arc trending inland north and northwest from the general area of Valencia, where they join the Bética range. They do not exceed elevations of 2,300 meters and offer little hindrance to transportation.

The *Pyrenees* form a true barrier range along the border of Spain and France. Rivers cutting back into the main, northern ridge of the Pyrenees from the Spanish and French sides are not longitudinally aligned, and as a consequence no low passes have been carved out by adjacent headwaters. The resultant isolation aided the survival of Andorra, a mountain nation whose people long relied on smuggling as a livelihood. The lesser, southern ridges of the Pyrenees are also difficult to pass, since the rivers that sever them have cut deep gorges. The barrier effect of the Pyrenees was overcome by tunnel construction, connecting the Val d'Aran, a small part of Spanish territory lying north of the main Pyrenean ridge, to Spain. A lower, westward mountain projection from the Pyrenees is the *Cordillera Cantabrica*, reaching 2,600 to 2,750 meters at the highest and paralleling the north coast of Spain. The steepest face of this fault-block range faces north, to the Atlantic, producing a rocky coast with numerous small protected bays called *rías*, and long used as fishing harbors.

Farther south in Iberia lie the *Central Sierras*, an east–west mountain complex about the same height as the Cantabrica and bearing several local names, in particular the sierras of *Gredos*, *Guadarrama*, and *Gata* in Spain and the *Serra de Estrêla* in Portugal. Still farther south one finds other parallel, lower mountain areas, most notably the *Sierra Morena*. Collectively, the Iberian ranges partition the peninsula, fostering sectionalism and even political separatism.

The *Alps*, the highest and most famous European mountains, stretch from the French Riviera in an arc eastward through Switzerland to Wien on the bank of the Danube (fig. 2.2). The inhabitants use almost countless local names to designate different parts of the range, such as the *Cottienne*, *Maritime*, *Berner*, *Dolomitic*, and *Julian Alps*. The range is divided into 3 parts—the southern, western, and eastern Alps. Bordering the Mediterranean, the southern Alps form the narrowest segment of the range and consist of one main ridge along the French–Italian border. About the latitude of Grenoble and Torino, the southern section gives way to the western Alps, in the process acquiring a second main ridge to parallel the first and changing direction to arc eastward. Extending as far east as the border of Austria, the western Alps form the highest and most spectacular part of the range, with deeply incised valleys and impressive remnant glaciers. Mont Blanc, towering 4,813 meters above sea level, is the highest in Europe. Deep, sheersided, U-shaped valleys, hollowed out by glaciers during the Ice Age, sometimes have floors 2,750 meters lower than the adjacent peaks.

Figure 2.2.   Spur ridges of the eastern Alps, bearing a winter's snow cover. While the Alps appear formidable, low passes and water gaps make them relatively easy to traverse. (Photo by T.G.J.-B. 1974.)

While impressive in appearance, the southern and western Alps never served as a true barrier. So many low passes exist through which invaders can move that the Italians, who live south of the mountains and look to them as a natural border, refer to the range as the "magnificent traitor." The Carthaginian general Hannibal successfully moved a cavalry of elephants and 30,000 men through the southern Alps to attack Italy. Centuries later came various German tribes from the north, who slipped through to deal a deathblow to the Roman Empire. The ease of access through the western Alps is attributable to streams. The valley lying between the two ridges is drained by a succession of rivers, including the Isère, Arc, Rhône, Reuss, and Rhine. All of these sever the northern ridge, providing access into the heart of the range as they flow into the plains and hills beyond the Alps. Headwater tributaries of these rivers have cut into the southern ridge directly opposite streams flowing to the Po River of Italy, producing a series of remarkably low passes. The most famous of these are the Mont Cenis (2,083 meters), Great Saint Bernard (2,470 meters), and Simplon (2,010 meters) Passes, lying on ancient routes from Italy to France, as well as the St. Gotthard and Splügen Passes (both 2,100 meters), linking the German-speaking lands with Italy. This combination of river gaps and low passes produces the "magnificent traitor."

The eastern Alps, much broader than the other 2 sections, reach a width of 240 kilometers along a line from Verona to München. Instead of one longitudinal valley, 2, 3, or even 4 exist, guiding the courses of rivers such as the Inn, Adige, Mur, and Drau. The peaks of the eastern Alps rarely exceed 3,000 meters. In spite of their greater width, the eastern Alps are also relatively easy to cross. The great north–south route is the Brenner Pass (1,375 meters), carved by tributaries of the Inn and Adige Rivers through the middle of three ridges found in this part of the Alps. Water gaps created by these and other rivers sever the northern and southern ridges.

The *Appennini Mountains,* the backbone of the Italian Peninsula, branch out from the southern Alps in the Riviera region, arc gently to approach Italy's Adriatic shore, and then return to the western coast to form the toe of the Italian boot. Structurally, they reappear in the island of Sicilia. The Appennini, narrow and low, offer many easy passes and have never presented much of a barrier.

The *Dinaric Range* begins at the Alps near the point where Italy, Slovenia, and Austria meet and stretches southeastward along the Adriatic coast through the western Balkan Peninsula, continuing as the *Pindhos Mountains* and others through to the tip of the Pelopónnisos in Greece. While not unusually high, the Dinaric Range is in many sections rugged and difficult to traverse, especially in areas of *karst* topography, where water filtering down from the surface dissolved permeable limestone, forming numerous large sinks or troughs called *dolines* and *polje* that are used for farming. One of the few easy passages through the Dinaric Range occurs in the extreme north, near the juncture with the Alps, where Pear Tree Pass allows access from the plains of Hungary into the *Po–Veneto Plain* of Italy, another "betrayal" by the magnificent, traitorous mountains that rim the northern edge of the Italian Peninsula. Both Hunnic and Gothic warriors poured through Pear Tree Pass to attack the Roman Empire. To the south, about midway through Albania, the Dinaric Range becomes more open and accessible, a condition that persists through Greece.

Just east of Wien, across the Danube River in Slovakia, the *Carpathian Mountains* begin, almost as a continuation of the Alps. Their directional course inscribes a huge mirror-image of the letter C through southern Poland, a corner of Ukraine, and Romania, ending as they began on the shores of the Danube, at the Iron Gate. The southern part of the Carpathians in Romania bears the name Transylvanian Alps. High elevations rarely occur in the Carpathians—few peaks are over 2,500 meters—and they form a narrow range with numerous low passes. South of the Iron Gate on the Danube, the same mountain structure turns back eastward in two prongs as the *Stara Planina* and *Rodopi Mountains,* mainly in Bulgaria. To the east, the *Crimean Mountains* occupy the southern side of a large peninsula jutting into the Black Sea in Ukraine and shelter the famous resort of Yalta from the east European winter. Still farther east and in the popular mind serving as boundaries for Europe lie the *Caucasus Mountains,* a towering, rugged range that has provided refuge for numerous small ethnic groups between the Black and Caspian Seas, and the *Urals,* a low, easily penetrated mountain ridge reaching from the Arctic Ocean shore southward into central Eurasia (figs. 1.5 and 1.6). In the Caucasus, 6,431-meter-high Mount Elbrus is the tallest peak. Arabs refer to the Caucasus as "the mountains of languages," reflecting the ethnic variety.

The final major mountain area of Europe is the *Kjølen Range,* the spine of the Scandinavian Peninsula in Norway and Sweden. Heavily glaciated in the Ice Age, it retains remnant glaciers today. As a result, the soil cover is extremely thin or absent altogether, and the coastline is deeply indented by ice-carved fjords—U-shaped glacial valleys later flooded by the ocean. One of the most spectacular is the long, narrow Hardanger Fjord ("Hairstring Fjord"). The Kjølen Range has very few inhabitants, but at the upper end of most fjords, a small patch of flat, unflooded land known as a *vik* occurs, backed by a steep headwall and flanked by nearly perpendicular valley sides (fig. 2.3). Long ago the inhabitants derived their very name, Vikings ("people of the inlet"), from these small plains. Virtually forced by the local Kjølen terrain to look outward, down the fjord to the sea, the Vikings became famous as traders and sea raiders.

Earthquakes and Vulcanism

Closely linked to the mountain ranges of Europe, particularly in the southeast and on the island of Iceland, are the related phenomena of *earthquakes,*

Figure 2.3.   A branch of the Sognefjord and an inhabited vik at its head. In the Norwegian Kjølen Range, only small agricultural areas occur. The fjords provide an excellent transportation facility. (Photo by T.G.J.-B. 1981.)

vulcanism, and *tsunamis* (tidal waves) (fig. 2.4). The mountain areas most repeatedly and catastrophically affected include the Appennini, Caucasus, Rodopi, and Dinaric/Pindhos, as well as many islands of the eastern Mediterranean and Iceland. Huge losses of life sometimes accompany European earthquakes, as was the case when 60,000 Sicilians died in an early twentieth-century disaster and 25,000 Armenians in 1988. The fatalities are often caused by the collapse of stone houses and tiled roofs, both common in southern Europe.

Volcanoes can also bring grief. The eruption of Vesùvio near Napoli in A.D. 79 destroyed the Roman city of Pompeii, while on Sicilia over 500 recorded eruptions of Etna, the largest continental volcano in the world, claimed an estimated 1 million lives over the past 2,500 years. The perpetually active volcano called Stromboli lies in the Aeolian Isles, north of Sicilia.

The most violent and powerful volcanic eruption ever known in Europe occurred on the small Greek Aegean Island of Thíra, today merely a shattered, sea-flooded caldera. Thíra erupted and collapsed with incredible force about 1625 B.C. The noise was likely heard as far away as Scandinavia and central Africa; a huge tsunami, perhaps 200 meters tall, crashed against the shore of nearby islands; and the sky was soon blackened with falling volcanic debris. Parts of the large nearby island of Kriti may have become temporarily uninhabitable as volcanic ash killed vegetation. Altogether, some 54 cubic kilometers of material was removed in the explosion of Thíra, in the process probably giving rise to the legend of the lost continent

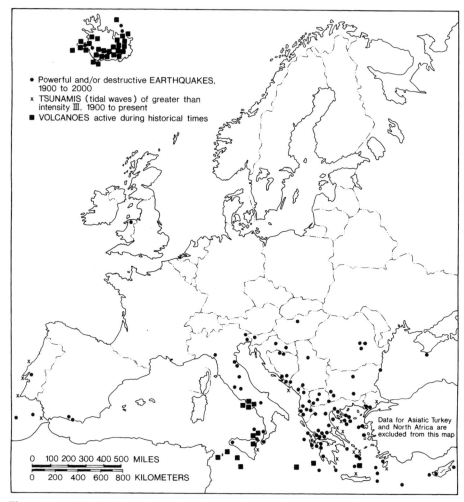

Figure 2.4.   1971, Earthquakes, vulcanism, and tsunamis in Europe. (*Sources:* Kárník 1971, 2:203; Simkin et al. 1989; data supplied by U.S. Geological Survey, National Earthquake Information Center website, <wwwneic.cr.usgs.gov/neis/epic/epicglobal.html> [last accessed: 2000]. Check this website for updates.)

of Atlantis. Archaeologists found the remains of dwellings beneath 30 meters of ash cover on the remnant of Thíra.

On the mountainous island of Iceland, astride a tectonic plate divide at the opposite territorial extremity of Europe from Thíra, vulcanism and earthquake activity occur frequently. Iceland, with 30 volcanic systems, has experienced over 250 eruptions in the past 1,100 years. Recently, a new island—Surtsey—appeared as a volcanic peak off Iceland's southern shore, and a massive eruption occurred on a nearby, older island, creating a natural harbor. Small wonder that this northern island is called "the land of fire and ice."

The Plains of Europe

Plains are concentrated in the north and east, in contrast to the southern dominance of mountains (fig. 2.1). A large, compartmentalized lowland, collectively called the *Great European Plain*, extends from the foot of the Pyrenees in southwestern France, bending northward and eastward along the coast through Germany and Poland as far as the Baltic states. Many different sections of the Great European Plain can be distinguished, each bearing its own name and special character.

European landscapes tend to be small, and to know Europe well, we should think in terms of diminutive regions, each with its own identity, both physically and culturally. All facets of European culture, from languages to the pattern of independent states, reflect this compartmentalization. Europeans, then, do not think geographically at the scale of the Great European Plain but instead distinguish its constituent parts.

Beginning in the southwest, the first segment encountered is the *Basin of Aquitaine*, largely fertile and producing France's famous Bordeaux wines. Only the sandy section bordering the coast, the *Landes*, is infertile. The basin connects to neighboring lowlands through two famous and important natural corridors: the Gap of Carcassonne, leading eastward to the Mediterranean Sea and guarded by the walled town of the same name, and the Gate of Poitou, a plains pathway some 65 kilometers wide, leading into the north of France toward Paris. Moorish invaders coming up from Spain entered the Basin of Aquitaine by way of Carcassonne and turned northward to the Gate of Poitou, where they were met and defeated by Frankish forces near Tours in A.D. 732. Later, the basin provided a natural core area for the development of the medieval feudal states of Aquitaine and Gascogne. The orientation of the basin, facing outward toward the Atlantic, contributed to its long dominance by English rulers.

Beyond the Gate of Poitou lies a second major part of the Great European Plain, the *Paris Basin*, occupying the larger part of northern France. In surface configuration this basin resembles a series of concentric, progressively larger saucers, with the city of Paris and the surrounding district, known as the Île de France, occupying the smallest, central saucer. In every direction from Paris, the land rises gently until a sharp drop-off is reached, formed by outward-facing *cuestas*, or escarpments. From the foot of each cuesta, the countryside again gradually increases in elevation until another cuesta is reached. To the east, seven such cuestas are present in at least fragmentary form (fig. 2.5). These escarpments proved valuable as natural defense walls for France in wars with Germany. Invaders had to fight their way up the steep cuesta slopes in the face of French fortifications in order to reach Paris. The city of Verdun, which lies at the foot of one of the east-facing cuestas, was the scene of bitter fighting in World War I, and 600,000 Germans and French died fighting for command of the slope during a 6-

Figure 2.5.   An outward-facing cuesta near the Paris Basin city of Troyes, looking toward the city of Paris. Such cuestas protect the capital of France. As recently as World War I, they played a strategic role. The fertility of the Paris Basin is suggested by the expanse of grain fields. (Photo by T.G.J.-B. 1978.)

month period in 1916. This series of natural defense lines made the Île de France an ideal birthplace for the French state (see chapter 7).

Across the English Channel in the southeastern part of the island of Great Britain lies a third segment of the Great European Plain, the *English Scarplands*. It is in many respects simply a continuation of the Paris Basin, including a series of west-facing cuestas. The Cotswolds and Chilterns are eroded hilly areas along the cuesta lines. At the eastern foot of the hilly escarpments are long valleys, oriented roughly southwest to northeast, including the Vale of Oxford and the once-marshy Fens. Just as the Paris Basin served as the nucleus of the French state, so the English Scarplands witnessed the initial nation building by the Saxon invaders of Britain.

North from the Paris Basin, the Great European Plain again narrows to form a gateway, Vlaanderen, centered in western Belgium. As is true of Carcassonne and Poitou, Vlaanderen possesses strategic value. In World War I, "Flanders Fields" connoted bitter fighting and high casualties, and its name lives on in the English poetry and literature of that era. Beyond the Vlaanderen constriction, the Great European Plain once again broadens to the north and east to form the *Low Country*, distinguished by almost total flatness. It consists of the communal delta of the Rhine, Maas, Schelde, Ems, and several lesser rivers. The greater part of the Low Country lies in the Netherlands, whose very name describes the terrain. Some of the area lies below the level of the sea. Much of the land that the Dutch struggle to keep is quite fertile, but the Low Country also contains sizable sandy districts, including the Kempenland on the Belgium–Netherlands border, as well as areas of peat bog.

On the east, the Low Country borders the much larger *North European Plain,* which broadens as it extends through Germany, Denmark, southernmost Sweden, and Poland, increasing from 160 kilometers in width at the German–Dutch border to nearly 500 kilometers in the Polish lowlands to the east. The North European Plain, the western half of which has traditionally been called the North German Plain, differs markedly from the Low Country. It displays considerably more surface irregularity, a great part of which can be attributed to the effects of the Ice Age, in particular the last southward advance of the glaciers from their Scandinavian source. Parallel chains of *moraine* hills, glacial deposits formed wherever the ice mass paused in its retreat to leave behind a greater thickness of debris, extend east–west across the North European Plain, from the Jylland Peninsula of Denmark on into northern Poland, parallel to the Baltic shore. Between the hill chains are extensive zones covered with a layer of *ground moraine,* or *till,* where the continental glaciers deposited less material. The till surface is quite irregular or hummock with many enclosed depressions of widely varied sizes that contain lakes or bogs. These are so numerous that the coastal part of the North European Plain is called the Baltic Lake Plain. The glaciers did not entirely cover the plain, but even the areas south of the ice mass were altered by its proximity. Beyond the terminal moraine, the southernmost line of glacially deposited hills, meltwater streams from the ice mass washed down finer sand and gravel, forming what are known as *outwash plains.* These remain today as infertile heath areas. The Lüneburger Heath south of Hamburg provides an example.

If the Ice Age produced much inferior land, it also helped form some of the most fertile districts of the plain. Winds sweeping down from the ice mass picked up fine particles of earth and carried them to the southern edge of the plain, where the lowlands give way to a zone of hilly terrain. The forced ascent blunted the velocity of the winds, causing them to drop at the foot of the hills much of their load of dust. These wind-deposited, fine-textured parent materials, known as *loess,* weathered into fertile and easy-to-work soils. The greatest depths of loess accumulated in numerous "embayments" of the North European Plain, called *Börde,* which reach south into the hills.

To the east, beyond a parted veil of hill areas, large lakes, and the inhospitable Pripyat Marsh, lies the greatest of all the lowlands, the expansive *East European Plain* (fig. 2.1), spanning the entire breadth of the European peninsula from the Arctic Ocean in the north to the Black Sea in the south. This plain is not drawn on the "European" scale. Its vastness lends an alien aspect, and invading European armies, such as those led by Napoléon Bonaparte and Adolf Hitler, felt overwhelmed here. A huge independent state, Russia, arose to match this great plain, and its size, too, is atypical for Europe. Small wonder that most Europeans look upon huge Russia, seated in this massive lowland, as marginally European.

That is not to say that internal variety is entirely lacking in the East European Plain. In the southern, unglaciated part, three major east-facing cuestas parallel the Dnipro, Don, and Volga Rivers, vaguely reminiscent of the Paris Basin but on a far grander scale. The northern half of the plain abounds in the same glacial features that dominate the North European Plain. Four advances of the ice sheets from Scandinavia left terminal and recessional moraines, with large, flat, poorly drained lowlands called *polesiye* in the till plains between the moraine walls. The recessional moraine that follows the line from Warszawa to Minsk in Belarus, Smolensk, and Moskva has served as an east–west route of both transport and invasion.

To the north lies another fairly extensive plains region, the *Fenno-Scandian Shield*. Massively glaciated and underlain by ancient rocks, some of which lie exposed at the surface, the shield is centered in Finland and Russian Karelia. Two great moraine walls, called the Salpausselkä, parallel the south coast of Finland and serve to dam up much of the interior, producing an intricate system of connecting lakes. The Finns and Karelians long used these waterways as their dominant mode of transportation, but in the age of highways, roads follow sinuous *eskers*—high ground laid down as the beds of ancient rivers flowing in hollows beneath the glaciers. The eskers run at right angles to the Salpausselkä and provide some of the main north–south highway links. Parts of Sweden also belong to the Fenno-Scandian Shield, including the lake-rich *Central Swedish Lowland*.

All of the other plains areas lie in the south, wreathed by the mountain ranges that dominate that part of Europe. Most are small, with the bordering ridges always visible. An exception is the large *Hungarian Basin*, also known as the Pannonian Plain, surrounded by the Alps, Carpathians, and Dinaric Range and including the nation of Hungary, as well as parts of every neighboring country. The fringing mountains provide no isolation for the Hungarian Basin. The Italian lands are easily reached through the Pear Tree Pass, while the Black Sea lies beyond the Iron Gate on the Danube, where the river severs the Carpathians from the Stara Planina. In the northwestern corner of the basin, the Moravian Gate provides egress north to the Great European Plain, and the valley of the upper Danube leads on beyond Wien into southern Germany. Greece and the Aegean are accessible southward through the long, narrow Vardar–Morava Depression, a rift valley wedged between the Dinaric Range and Stara Planina. Numerous low passes in the Carpathian Mountains lead toward Russia. Through one or another of these numerous leaks and seams in the mountain wall representatives of just about every major linguistic group in Europe and adjacent parts of Asia have passed as conquerors or refugees, and the recorded history of the basin is one of continued turbulence. It has witnessed conflict between Roman and barbarian, Turk and Christian, Hun and German, Magyar and Slav. Warpaths have also been trade routes from the time of the amber trade through the Moravian Gate several thousand years ago. The diverse ethnic makeup of the basin today, including German, Hungarian, Slav, and Romanian, is the heritage of a long history of warfare, trade, and migration.

The *Valachian Plain* and *Maritsa Valley* form two small, fingerlike lowlands reaching eastward into the Balkan Peninsula from the Black Sea, flanking the Stara Planina on both sides. The Valachian Plain measures only about 300 by 125 kilometers in size, a typical European dimension. Valachia has witnessed the comings and goings of a great variety of invaders and migrating peoples, including the Huns, Slavs, Magyars, and Mongols. Today, the Valachian Plain is the heartland of the Romanians, who have somehow managed to preserve a language derived from the Roman armies, perpetuating an isolated eastern bastion of Romance speech.

The Po–Veneto Plain of northern Italy, rimmed by the Alps and Appennini, is the only sizable plains area in that country. It represents a continuation of the structural depression containing the Adriatic Sea, filled to above the level of the sea with materials brought down from the surrounding mountains by streams and ice. Glaciers moving down into the fringe of the Po–Veneto Plain from the north deposited moraines, which dammed up the mouths of tributary Alpine valleys, creating a chain of beautiful natural lakes, including Como, Maggiore, Lugano, Iseo, and Garda. South of the moraine dams is an infertile outwash plain, beyond which lies the greater part of the Po–Veneto Plain, an area of fertile, river-deposited soils. At the juncture of alluvium and outwash, the groundwater table reaches the surface, resulting in an east–west line of springs called *fontanili*. From ancient times, the fontanili attracted human settlement, and today a row of cities, including Torino and Milano, traces the course of the spring sites. Still another line of cities, including Parma, Modena, and Bologna, lies along the southern edge of the plain, at the foot of the Appennini. The western, uppermost part of the plain served as the political nucleus of Italian unification in the nineteenth century, and today the same area contains the industrial heart of the nation.

France's gateway to the Mediterranean is the *Languedoc Plain*, a narrow coastal lowland reaching from the Pyrenees to the Riviera. Two strategic routes connect the plain to the heart of France: To the west one finds access through the previously mentioned Gap of Carcassonne to the Basin of Aquitaine, and the Rhône–Saône Corridor leads north into the Paris Basin.

The mountain ranges of Iberia divide that peninsula into a series of separate plains, each of which is home to people of a distinct subculture. The *Lowland of Andalucía*, wedged in between the Bética Mountains and the Sierra Morena in far southern Spain, is a land of olive groves dotted with place names that recall the Moorish occupation. The main river draining the lowland is the Río Guadalquivir, a name derived from *Wadi-al-Kabir*,

Arabic for "the great river." The narrow *Portuguese Lowland*, which fronts the Atlantic coast of Iberia, and the *Ebro Valley* in northeastern Spain are the other major peripheral Iberian lowlands. The interior plains of Iberia, collectively known as the *Meseta*, differ from all the others in Europe previously discussed because they are elevated plateaus rather than lowlands, standing about 800 meters above sea level. The Central Sierras divide the plateau into two parts, *Old* and *New Castilla,* the homeland of the people who have traditionally dominated and ruled Spain. The New Castilla Meseta contains the capital city of Madrid and also includes both Extremadura in the southwest and the plains of La Mancha near the center.

The European Hills

The third and final terrain category includes the major **hill** areas of Europe. Hills dominate the European midsection, just as mountains occur mainly in the south and plains in the north (fig. 2.1). From the coast of France, a broad, compartmentalized belt of hills extends eastward through central Germany.

Among the more important constituent hilly districts are *Bretagne* (also known as the *Armorican Massif*) in western France, the *Massif Central* to the southeast, and the *Hercynian Hills,* which reach across Germany and into Czechia. The Hercynian region is itself subdivided into a myriad of small, separate hill complexes—mostly fault-block uplifts—such as the Ardennes of Belgium and Luxembourg, Vosges of eastern France, Schwarzwald, Jura, Harz, Bohemian Forest, and Sudety. Scattered among these hill units are equally numerous small plains, such as the Bohemian Basin, Upper Rhine Plain, and Alpine Foreland, the latter a small plateau just north of the Alps. These many small plains have long served as clusters of dense population, and the weblike gateways linking them have been routes of trade and invasion. The intervening hill areas, more sparsely settled, retain remnant forests and sometimes provided refuge for retreating ethnic minorities, such as the Celts of Bretagne and the Protestants of the Massif Central.

Some major hill lands lie outside the main belt in central Europe, including the highlands of the British Isles. In Great Britain, hills dominate the west and north, confining the English Scarplands to the southeastern part of the island. *Cornwall* is the hilly peninsula reaching southwest to Land's End, and the *Cambrian Mountains* occupy the larger part of the province of Wales. Geographer Estyn Evans aptly called the jagged coastlines where these and other western hills meet the sea "the tattered ends of Europe." The *Pennine Chain* and hilly *Lake District* of northern England blend into the *Scottish Highlands.* On the island of Ireland, a hill rim parallels the coast except in the east, including among others the mountains of Mourne, Antrim, Wicklow, and Knockmealdown. In northern Ireland, where the effects of glaciation appear abundantly, numerous elongated, streamlined hills called *drumlins* occur. Glaciers planed off the drumlins, and the long axis of such hills parallels the direction of ice flow. The hills of the British Isles have been the primary refuges of the Celtic people, where they were, for a time at least, able to resist the Anglo-Saxon invaders and preserve their customs and language. Gaelic, Erse, and Welsh are still spoken today as mother tongues in parts of the hills. In contrast, the lowlands and plains were invariably the scene of early Celtic defeat and assimilation. In Roman times the pattern was identical, for while the legions of Rome were able to secure the English Scarplands, they rarely ventured out against fierce hill tribes such as the Picts. Hadrian's Wall, built across the waist of Great Britain to restrain the Picts, still stands as a monument to Roman failure in the hilly north.

If a recurrent trait can be detected in the terrain makeup of Europe, it is, as suggested earlier, *compartmentalization*. The segmentation into numerous peninsulas and islands helps create this image, but it is heightened by the fact that individual terrain units are small and possess individuality. The Basin of Aquitaine differs from its neighbor, the Paris Basin, and the western Alps differ from the eastern Alps. Rarely does homogeneity of terrain dominate a sizable area, and each small landform district possesses its own special character.

Human Modification of Terrain

If terrain influences Europeans in certain ways, then they have most assuredly responded in kind. The "everlasting hills" have not been as drastically altered as some other facets of the European physical environment, but the work of the ever-active human hand is definitely visible. One example is *terracing*. This ancient technology, probably derived from the mountain fringe of the Fertile Crescent in the Middle East, has enabled people to "level" mountains for agricultural use. In the Mediterranean lands, where level terrain is in short supply, terraced hillsides are common, especially in Greece.

People even build hills. On the North European Plain near Berlin, for example, stands the Teufelsberg, or "Devil's Mountain." Building material for the Teufelsberg came from the rubble of the war-destroyed German capital, and the peak reaches sufficient height to provide a ski slope in winter. In eastern Ireland, there are numerous small hills called *motes*, erected as fortifications by invading Normans in the Middle Ages. Similar artificial hills or mounds dot the delta plains on the approach to the ruins of Pella, the capital of the Macedonian empire in northern Greece at the time of Alexander the Great (fig. 2.6). If people build, they also excavate, forming open-pit mines that scar the landscape in many regions.

Tunneling represents another device by which Europeans have modified terrain, in this case to reduce the barrier effect of mountain ridges.

Figure 2.6. A huge artificial mound at the ancient Danish capital of Jelling, on the Jylland Peninsula. Europe abounds in such anthropogeomorphic features, helping produce the image of a thoroughly humanized landscape of great antiquity. (Photo by T.G.J.-B. 1981.)

Norway has begun to impose an effective highway network upon the Kjølen Range in this way, and the Pyrenees have lost much of their barrier effect. Even the gentle Appennini are now pierced. Nowhere has tunneling been so frequently employed as in the western Alps because that range lies in the core of Europe, where the need for effective, rapid ground transportation is greatest. Italy is now linked to both France and Germany by tunneled routes.

Major Climate Types

Tucked safely north and west of the Eastern Hemisphere's great desert belt, Europe enjoys climates that are generally humid and exceptionally mild, considering the rather high latitudes involved. These temperate, moist conditions favored Europe and helped it become one of the major homelands of humanity.

Three major climate types exist (fig. 2.7). One is the **marine west coast,** bearing a name that describes both its location and predominant *air mass.* An air mass is just that—a large volume of air relatively uniform in temperature and moisture content. Marine air masses, which in Europe originate over the Atlantic Ocean, are moisture-laden, cool in summer, and mild in

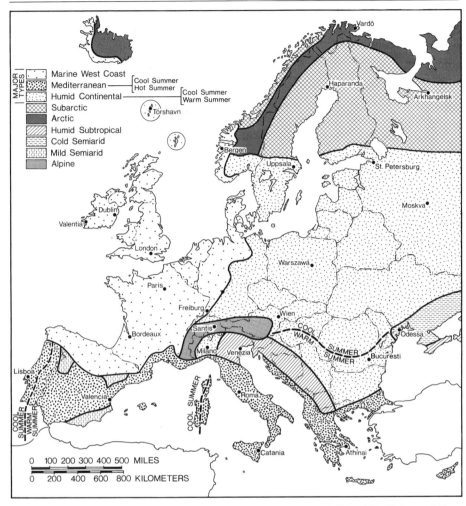

Figure 2.7.   Climate types. (*Sources:* Köppen et al. 1930–1936; Wallén 1970; Flohn and Fantechi 1984.)

winter. Coming ashore from the west, since Europe lies in the wind belt of the *westerlies*, this marine air meets little topographic resistance, due to the east–west alignment of most mountain ranges. It regularly penetrates deeply into Europe, producing the marine west coast climate zone. This includes the British Isles, northern Iberia, most of France, western Germany, the Low Country, and part of the fjord coast of Norway (fig. 2.7). Temperatures remain mild all year, with cool summers and relatively pleasant winters. The coldest month averages above freezing and generally below 7°C. Temperatures do not differ greatly between winter and summer. Dublin, Ireland, averages only 10°C warmer in July than in January, and the difference at Tórshavn in the Faeroe Islands is only 7°C. The majority of January nights in London do not have frost. Even in the Shetland Islands, far to the north, snow is relatively rare, occurring only 3 days in the winter of 1991–1992, for example, and temperatures rarely fall below −10°C.

Occasional bitter cold waves do occur in the marine west coast climate, but many winters pass without one. London has recorded −16°C, and in one severe cold spell in February 1929, the temperature remained constantly below freezing for 226 hours in the British capital. A bitter cold spell struck western Europe again in December 1996 and January 1997, causing more than 200 deaths and freezing over the River Thames above London. Still, the appearance of a few palm trees at places on the southwest Irish coast suggests the overall mildness of the winters. It was not always so. During the colder climatic phase known as the Little Ice Age, from about A.D. 1200 to 1800, the marine west coast winters were more severe. The canals of Holland more often froze over, permitting the ice skating shown in the paintings of some of the Dutch masters.

Marine west coast summers are cool, with July averages generally below 21°C, and sweaters or coats feel comfortable on many days. Heat waves, with temperatures above 32°C, do occur rarely in parts of the marine west coast area. The record high temperature at Paris is 38°C. Severe heat waves occurred in the marine west coast region in 1976 and again in 1995 and 1997, with temperatures soaring to 31°C to 33°C. A severe drought accompanied the 1995–1997 episode, especially in England.

Because the marine air masses contain great amounts of moisture, the west coast climate is quite humid, with adequate precipitation all year round. Normally between 50 and 100 centimeters fall each year, though some stations record more. In plains areas, amounts are rather modest, as for example Paris, which receives only 58 centimeters annually, and London 62 centimeters. The cool temperatures retard evaporation as does prevalent cloudiness, and precipitation is adequate to produce humid conditions. Stations situated at the western edge of hills and mountains receive considerably more precipitation. Freiburg, Germany, at the western foot of the Schwarzwald, averages 86 centimeters annually, and the slopes above Bergen, Norway, on the west flank of the Kjølen Range, receive 213 centimeters in an average year. This increased amount of precipitation is the product of the so-called *orographic* factor. Humid air masses moving from the west must rise over hill and mountain barriers, which block the path. In rising, the air mass cools, lowering its ability to hold moisture in an evaporated state, and the excess is precipitated on west-facing slopes.

Very little precipitation typically falls on any given day in the marine west coast areas. Gentle showers or drizzles are the rule. Paris, for example, has its modest annual precipitation spread over 188 days, or about 0.3 of a centimeter per rainy day, involving over half of all days in the year. A pervasive wetness, then, results from persistent light rain and feeble evaporation, rather than from large amounts of rainfall. On one occasion, London had 72 consecutive days in which precipitation fell. Clouds obscure the sun most of the time, and the marine west coast climate seems unpleasant to most people. Seventy percent or even more of the daylight hours each year are marred by cloudiness, and the British Isles average less than 1,500 hours of sunshine annually, about 4 hours per day or less. Fog and mist also commonly occur, and one town in Denmark reports an average of 54 foggy days each year. This cheerless climate drives numerous inhabitants to seek vacations in the sunny southern part of Europe. Jean Rouaud summed it up nicely: "in the lower Loire," in the west of France, "rain is a life companion."

The precipitation and cloudiness reach the marine west coast climate region borne by an endless succession of *cyclonic storms,* centers of low pressure embedded in the wind belt of the westerlies. European weather reports assign personal names to these low-pressure centers, much as we do for tropical hurricanes, in alphabetical sequence, and they are so numerous that names such as "Xiste" occur by midsummer.

In most cases, these storms are gentle, as the modest precipitation amounts suggest, but on occasion they reach violent proportions. For example, a cyclonic storm struck England and northwestern France on October 15–16, 1987, the most severe recorded in 250 years, bringing sustained winds of 70 to 115 and gusts of 175 kilometers per hour (kph). Millions of trees were felled, 13 people died, and extensive property damage occurred. Then, in late December 1999, 2 different unusually violent storms struck the French coast within 3 days of each other, bearing hurricane-force winds of 175 and 200 kph, respectively. Spires on the Notre Dame Cathedral in Paris toppled, hundreds of thousands of trees fell, and at least 120 persons died, over half of them in France. About 80% of the French forested area experienced damage, and the historic woodland of Fontainebleau near Paris lost over half of all its trees.

Generally, winds are gentler, and often they come so regularly and from such predictable directions as to have names. One of the best known is the *Föhn* of southern Germany, a warm, dry wind from the south that results when a cyclonic storm moves just north of the Alps. The low pressure draws winds over the mountains from the Mediterranean lands, dropping orographic precipitation and growing cooler in ascent, and then descending into Germany, warming as they progress downslope. A föhn blowing in midwinter can produce a sudden false springtime, with fair skies and pleasant temperatures, a delightful though short-lived respite from the dreary, damp winter conditions.

Southern Europe, in particular the 3 southward-reaching peninsulas of Iberia, Italy, and Greece, is dominated by the **Mediterranean** type of climate. Also included are the various European islands of the Mediterranean, southern coastal France, and the Adriatic coast of Croatia (fig. 2.7). The most distinguishing trait of the Mediterranean climate is the concentration of precipitation in the winter season, with exceptionally dry summers. Generally, less than one-tenth of the annual precipitation falls in the quarter-year comprising the summer months of June, July, and August, and the month of July is almost totally rainless. Lisboa, Portugal, averages only 0.5 of a centimeter in July; Roma, Italy, 1.8; and Athínai, Greece, 0.8. This seasonality of precipitation reflects the transitional position of the Mediterranean basin between the humid marine west coast to the north and the parched Sahara in the south. In winter, the Mediterranean lands lie in the belt of the westerlies and receive the impact of precipitation-producing marine air masses and migrating storm centers, while in summer the region comes more under the influence of a great subtropical high-pressure center, which causes fair weather in North Africa and the Mediterranean peninsulas alike. Winter precipitation usually occurs as rainfall in the small lowland plains, but snow is common in the numerous mountain ranges concentrated in the Mediterranean climate region. Accumulated snow in the highlands is of crucial importance to farmers because the meltwater runoff in spring and summer provides a source of irrigation water for the drought season.

Occasionally, the summer drought expands to include the entire year, causing serious water shortages. Southern and central Spain suffered such a prolonged drought in the 1990s. Even the olives—hearty trees able to endure dry conditions—began to die. At the pilgrimage village of El Rocío in Andalucía, priests held a high mass in December 1995 to pray for the advent of the normal winter rains. After 2 wet years, the drought in Andalucía resumed in 1998.

Temperatures in the Mediterranean climate are warmer than those of the marine west coast area because of a more southerly location and a lower incidence of cloudiness. Summers are hot in the greater part of the Mediterranean climate zone, with July averages usually in the 24°C to 28°C range. The record high temperature at Athínai is 40.5°C, at Valencia, Spain, 42.8°C, and at Catania, Sicilia, 40°C, the highest ever recorded in Italy. Because the relative humidity in summer tends to be low, fairly rapid nighttime cooling occurs. A cool summer subtype of the Mediterranean climate also appears in places, confined to the Atlantic littoral of Portugal and certain other windward coastlines (fig. 2.7). In the cool summer subtype, averages for the warmest months do not exceed 22°C. Throughout the Mediterranean climate area, except in the mountain ranges, winters remain mild and extended periods of frost are unknown. Groves of citrus dot the lowlands of the Mediterranean, a good indicator of the absence of severe cold. The record low of −7°C for Athínai is typical of the region. Cloudiness is at a minimum, particularly in the summer, a striking contrast to the marine west coast. Parts of Italy receive more than 2,500 hours of sunshine per year, almost twice as much as the British Isles.

The local winds of the Mediterranean reflect its location between the marine west coast and the desert. Winter storm centers moving through the basin draw cold, damp winds down from the north, including the *mistral* and the *bora*. The mistral blows with fury down the Rhône–Saône Corridor into the Mediterranean coastal fringe of France and on beyond to the islands of Corsica and Sardegna, while the bora strikes the eastern coast of Italy from across the Adriatic Sea. From the opposite direction, dry, hot *sirocco* winds are drawn up from the Saharan region by cyclonic storms to afflict southern Italy and Greece. A similar wind, the *leveche*, brings hot, dusty conditions on occasion into the south of France, while in Andalucía the same phenomenon is called the *solano*. All serve to introduce parched, warm continental tropical air from the Sahara Desert to the south. In Italy, the sirocco blows from 30 to 50 times annually, lasting 80 to 120 days per year and occurring most often from March through May and again in November. The Saharan winds are least common in summer, but when they do happen in that season, the searingly hot effects are most unpleasant and damaging to crops and orchards.

The third of the major climate types found in Europe, the **humid continental,** dominates the eastern part of the culture area, from southern Scandinavia to the eastern Balkans and deep into Russia (fig. 2.7). Here, as the climate's name implies, *continental* air masses, born over the vast Eurasian interior and frozen Arctic Ocean, prevail over those of marine origin. These air masses display a great annual range of temperature, becoming very cold in the winters and surprisingly warm in the summers, producing a climate given to seasonal extremes. In particular, the winters are colder and become progressively more bitter toward the east. The disasters that befell the armies of Adolf Hitler and Napoléon Bonaparte in Russia were in no small part the work of numbing cold. January averages in the humid continental area range from about $-12°C$ up to freezing, and low readings below $-20°C$ are common. In the bitter winter of 1986–1987, Moskva recorded $-26°C$ and St. Petersburg $-29°C$. A blizzard in February 1999 produced heavy snowfall that cut off more than 200 villages and towns in Hungary for several days. The difference between January and July averages runs double or more the annual range of many marine west coast stations. Winter temperatures are low enough to cause a durable snow cover to develop, with usually at least one month in which the ground remains blanketed. In more eastern areas, the continuous snow cover can last for three or four months. Rivers, lakes, and shallow ocean inlets freeze over, including the Baltic Sea. Occasionally, during winter in the East European Plain, the heart of the humid continental climate zone, cloudy and mild spells of weather occur. Russians, who prefer clear, cold conditions, contemptuously refer to these marine-influenced spells as "European" weather.

Summer temperatures are remarkably similar to those in the marine west coast area. The July average at Moskva and Warszawa is identical to that at Paris, and most stations fall in the 16°C to 21°C range for the warmest month average. Only in the southern extremity of the humid continental area, in the Balkans, and in an outlier in the upper Po–Veneto Plain does a warm summer subtype of the humid continental climate occur (fig. 2.7). In this zone, July averages exceed 22°C, and some summer days are unpleasantly hot. Throughout the humid continental climate region, precipitation is adequate if not abundant at all seasons, owing in part to the low evaporation rate associated with cool and cold weather. Between 48 and 65 centimeters of precipitation can be expected each year at typical humid continental stations, only slightly less than is the rule in marine west coast areas.

Minor Climate Types

The greater part of Sweden and Finland lies in the zone of the **subarctic** climate, more severe than the humid continental (fig. 2.7). Only one to three months average over 10°C, and the proximity to the pole in a continental location means bitter, dark winters. Summers are very cool and short, and winter is clearly the dominant season. In January 1987, a temperature of − 45°C was recorded in Norway's Kjølen Range. The precipitation total is modest and comes mainly as snow, but the resultant climate is humid, due to very low evaporation. At these high latitudes, darkness prevails in the winter months and daylight is fleeting. One of every ten Finns suffers from Seasonal Affective Disorder, a depression caused by the prevailing darkness; to offset the problem, an extravagant use of public lighting is employed. Few Europeans choose to live in this cold zone, and most of those who do have come to exploit the fisheries or mineral wealth, such as northern Sweden's iron ore.

Still more severe is the **arctic** climate, a region largely devoid of trees (fig. 2.7). It lacks a summer altogether, and the warmest month averages below 10°C. Surprisingly, the adjacent Barents Sea, part of the Arctic Ocean, does not freeze in winter, and the entire Norwegian coast and the Russian Arctic port of Murmansk remain open to shipping, thanks to the influence of the easternmost branch of a warm ocean current known as the North Atlantic Drift.

The Dinaric Range and coastal portion of the Po–Veneto Plain are characterized by the **humid subtropical** climate, similar to the Mediterranean area in temperature but lacking the pronounced summer drought. Here, the summers are hot with high humidity, and the July visitor to Venèzia may well be reminded of New Orleans or Brisbane.

Nearly all of Europe receives adequate precipitation, even if it is seasonal as in the Mediterranean. The only exceptions are some peripheral semiarid regions. In these places, the great desert belts of Africa and Eurasia gently touch Europe. Two minor types result: (1) the **cold semiarid** climate, typical of the lands north of the Black and Caspian Seas that share the bitter continental winter, made all the more fierce here by the absence of trees to block the wind; and (2) the **mild semiarid** climate, sharing the temperatures of the Mediterranean winter but lacking its precipitation (fig. 2.7). The mild semiarid districts lie in Iberian *rain shadow* areas east of the Bética, Ibérica, and Cantabrica Mountains, where the moisture-bearing westerlies are orographically drained of their moisture. Included are the

Ebro Valley, the coastal huertas flanking the Bética Mountains, and the western reaches of the Meseta in Old Castilla.

The final type, the **Alpine** climate, occurs to some extent in all the mountain ranges of Europe, even though it is shown in figure 2.7 only in the Alps. The key causal factor is elevation above sea level. Mountain heights cause the climate to be colder, so that Säntis in Switzerland, for example, actually has an arctic climate, differing only in the enormous amount of orographic precipitation, a total of almost 250 centimeters annually. The Alpine climate varies greatly from valley to valley and slope to slope, creating a pattern too chaotic to map on a small scale.

All of the minor climate types occur in peripheral parts of Europe and are, as a consequence, only marginally "European." Recognizing their alien character, relatively few Europeans choose to live in such regions. We can regard the marine west coast, Mediterranean, and humid continental climates as "core" European, while the minor types represent a transition toward non-European conditions.

Human Influence on Climate

Europeans, usually unintentionally, alter the climate, both on a local scale and more broadly. They live preponderantly in cities, each of which, in some measure, suffers from air pollution and experiences temperature alteration (fig. 2.8).

London's *anthropoclimate* has been studied for centuries, and we know a lot about the human-induced changes there. As early as 1661, John Evelyn wrote in reference to London that "the weary traveler, at many miles distance, sooner smells, than sees the city." When the coal smoke poured through a myriad of chimneys, "London resembles the face rather of Mount Etna, the Court of Vulcan, Stromboli, or the suburbs of hell than an assembly of rational creatures." In more recent times, geographers came to speak of London's "heat island," a reference to the fact that temperatures are consistently higher over the built-up portion of the city than over the surrounding rural greenbelt. Minimum nighttime temperatures are at times 7°C higher over the central portion of London than in the greenbelt, and daytime maxima are also higher. This results from the inability of heat radiation from surfaces to penetrate the pollution haze that hangs over the city; the retention of heat by paved streets and buildings; and the heat produced locally by fuel combustion in vehicles, factories, and homes. At times, isotherms—lines connecting points with the same temperature—take on the same shape as the London urban area.

Human activity also influences rainfall and humidity characteristics of the London area. More thunderstorms occur over the city, more precipitation, and a distinctly higher absolute humidity than in adjacent rural areas. The cause lies both in the greater amount of thermal convection resulting

Figure 2.8.   Air quality sign in Wien. The people of the city can learn the latest readings of various air pollutants. Two levels of "smog alarm" are posted, based on levels of ozone, carbon monoxide, dust, sulfur dioxide, and nitric dioxide. (Photo by T.G.J.-B. 1995.)

from more surface heating and in the superabundance of microscopic particulate matter associated with air pollution. Drops of condensation are built around such nuclei. A decrease in coal burning has lessened the degree of air pollution in London since about 1960, but the heat island persists. This same effect can be detected in many other areas of Europe. In fact, every city has a heat island, and severe air pollution remains a problem in many countries.

Ozone buildups, caused when emissions from automobiles and factories interact chemically with sunlight, have reached crisis levels in the center of Europe. Germans, who delight in driving fast, "a basic right" in their view, now face mandatory speed limits as low as 90 kph during air pollution alert episodes. The corridor of worst air pollution, including not only ozone but also particulate matter, lies in the humid continental climate, along the southern margins of the North European Plain and in the Bohemian Basin, from eastern Germany and Czechia into Poland. This corridor, not coincidentally, also appears as the worst concentration of *acid rain,* a phenomenon best revealed by damage to forests (fig. 2.9). Various chemicals released into the air as a consequence of burning fossil fuels are cleansed from the atmosphere by precipitation. The resultant rainfall has a much higher than normal acidity, diminishing soil fertility, poisoning bod-

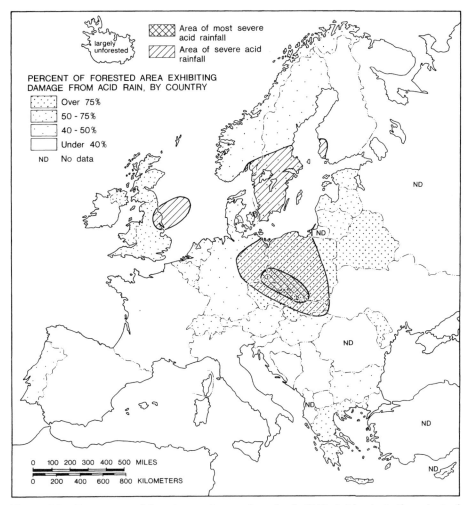

Figure 2.9.   Percentage of forest area damaged or dead, 1998. Acid rain is the principal cause of forest damage and death. Subnational data are shown only for Germany. (*Source: Statistical Yearbook 1999 for Foreign Countries,* Stuttgart, D.: Metzler-Poeschel; various national statistical yearbooks.)

ies of water, and damaging vegetation. Air pollution extends to the outer-most peripheries of Europe, as in the far north, where the phenomenon called "Arctic haze" recently appeared.

Also found on a wide scale and likely the result of human activity is a pan-European warming of climate. In effect, the entire core of the culture area seems to have become a huge heat island. Recent decades have been unusually warm, Atlantic cyclones have taken more northerly tracks, and sirocco-type winds off the Sahara have increased in both frequency and duration. Reflecting the increased warmth, Alpine glaciers lost a third to a half or their ice mass in the twentieth century. For example, the Aletsch

Glacier in Switzerland retreated almost 2 kilometers and lost about 100 meters of thickness in the 1900s. By contrast, the Icelandic and Kjølen Glaciers have grown since 1950, but this is not inconsistent with climatic warming, since a hotter world is also a wetter world, providing the northern glaciers more snow while still not increasing temperatures to the melting point. At the lower latitudes, where the Alpine glaciers are found, snowfall has decreased markedly since the 1970s, not just in the Alps but throughout the temperate zone in Europe. The glaciers of the Caucasus have also retreated.

Vegetation Regions

The distribution of natural vegetation in Europe can best be revealed in a map of *floristic provinces* (fig. 2.10). To a considerable degree, these provinces coincide with the climate types discussed earlier, not surprising given the fact that climate has a major shaping influence upon plant life. So do people. In fact, Europeans have so massively altered the vegetative cover that we cannot know precisely what these biotic provinces were like in a natural state. For this reason, biogeographers often speak of *potential* vegetation.

The **Atlantic** floristic province was once largely covered by a broadleaf deciduous forest, consisting of trees that drop their leaves during the dormant season in winter. *Oaks* served as the dominant species, and other common trees included the ash, linden, beech, and birch. Elms, maples, willows, and hornbeams were also well represented among the canopy trees. In the vegetative understory grew yews, hollies, and hazel shrubs, beneath which lay a ground cover of ivy, heather, anemone, ferns, bracken, primrose, and wild strawberry.

No fully intact Atlantic biotic system survives today, so pervasive has been the human influence. Clearing the forest for agricultural use led to widespread destruction of the deciduous broadleaf forest, a process begun in earnest about A.D. 500 by the Germanic peoples. Charcoal burners also exacted a toll on the Atlantic woodlands, as in the Belgian province of Brabant, where in the place of the once great Forest of Carbonnière ("charcoal makers"), an unwooded plain meets the eye today. This devastation by farmers and burners continued unabated into the 1300s, when pestilence and warfare greatly reduced the population. The Hundred Years' War between France and England proved so destructive of human life in the Basin of Aquitaine as to give rise to the local folk saying that "the forests returned to France with the English."

Following this respite, the Atlantic forests were subjected to a renewed attack by ax wielders. Population decline proved to be temporary, and a final phase in the clearing occurred in the 1500s and 1600s. To the renewed

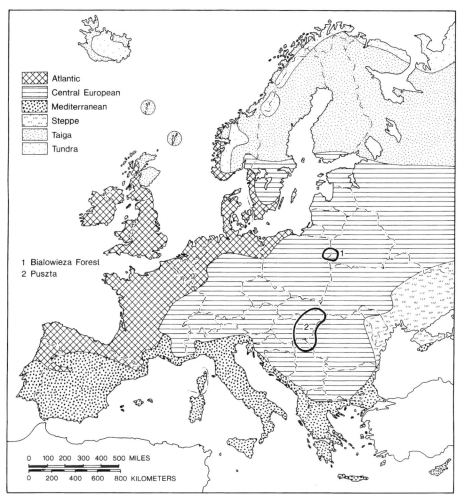

Figure 2.10.   Floristic provinces. (*Sources:* Jalas and Suominen 1972–1976; Polunin and Walters 1985.)

demands of an expanding farm population were added the needs of English, French, and Dutch shipbuilders, as well as other artisans. By 1550, England suffered from acute timber shortages, and France reached the same predicament a century later. Both came to rely on their American colonies to supply much-needed lumber. Considerable forests remained in Ireland during the late 1500s, for contemporary documents mention the difficulty of conducting military campaigns against Irish rebels in their woodland refuges. It seems likely that the English felled many Irish woods to destroy these hideouts. Profit-hungry landlords completed the process of deforestation in Ireland in the 1600s, selling the timber abroad. By the year 1700, woodlands had vanished from the Irish scene, and oak virtually disappeared from the pollen record after that time. In England, similarly deforested, the word *wold* (as in Cotswold), which originally meant "forest," came to mean instead "an upland area of open country."

So catastrophic was the assault on the woodland that in several countries lying within the Atlantic floristic province, less than 10% of the land bears a forest cover today, and much of this meager woodland results from twentieth-century *afforestation,* the replanting of forests (fig. 2.11). Hill districts of the British Isles have been the scene of some of the most impressive afforestation projects, especially the Scottish Highlands and islands. However, trees planted in these projects tend to be commercially valuable exotics such as Douglas fir and Sitka spruce. The soil must be regularly limed, often by helicopter drop, to counteract natural acidity so that the desired exotic trees will survive.

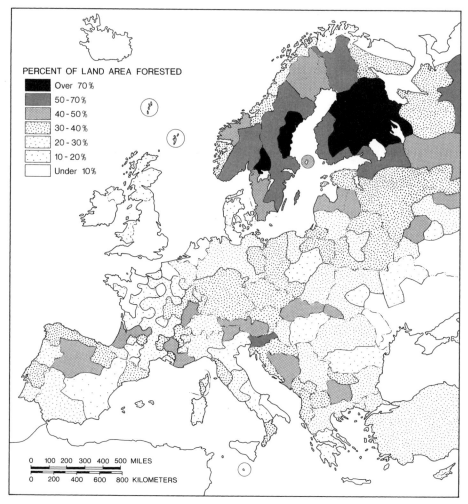

Figure 2.11.   Percentage of land forested. Deforestation is greatest in the west and south.

Only scattered patches of forest containing native Atlantic trees remain. Some owe their existence to royal protection, as for example England's Sherwood Forest. In places, rough terrain, unattractive to farmers, sheltered a remnant of woods (fig. 2.12). The tiny vestiges of Atlantic woodland are today carefully tended, with heavy penalties for unauthorized cutting. Often, these tidy groves resemble parks more than natural woodlands, particularly to the American eye. Western Europeans value remnant forests as recreational areas and have laid out a splendid network of hiking trails, and one rarely finds a forest area not open to the public.

Representative of the destruction of the Atlantic forests of Europe are wide expanses of treeless *moors* and *heaths,* especially in the British Isles and Denmark. As a general rule, *heath* is the term used for hilly areas or undulating plains, while *moor* describes level surfaces. Both are covered with a variety of low shrubs, including heather, juniper, and gorse (reed-like, with abundant yellow flowers). Peat bogs abound. Experts now believe that nearly all such areas are human induced, except in small exposed heights and coastal locations. Fire, used to create pastureland, was appar-

Figure 2.12. **"The forest's in trouble on Wenlock Edge,"** according to an old English saying. Reference is to a ridge in the Scarplands of western England near the border of Wales. Only the steep slopes of Wenlock Edge, unattractive to farmers, retain a forest cover. In contrast, the fertile vales below lie stripped of trees and is well cultivated. The remnant forests resemble dark caps on the steep leading edges of a succession of great earthen "waves." (Copyright Aerofilms Limited, London.)

ently the most important device employed to establish these open land-scapes.

Ironically, these heaths and moors are themselves now under human attack and rapidly declining in area. Afforestation projects are partly responsible, and one can still see the rock fences that once enclosed Scottish sheep pastures zigzagging through new forests of spruce and fir. In other cases, especially in Denmark, heaths have been converted to agricultural use, especially improved pastures for dairy cattle (fig. 2.13). In other words, people first removed the forests in ancient times to produce rough pasture of heath, and then much later they destroyed the heath to obtain a better grassland. Clearly, the concept of *natural* vegetation is largely alien to Europe.

The **central European** floristic province lies east of the Atlantic woodlands, covering the core of the culture area. Here, the *beech* dominates the natural climax forest, with many oak, larch, and hornbeam. Unlike the Atlantic forest, the central European province has abundant coniferous needleleaf evergreen trees such as fir, spruce, and the Scottish pine, espe-

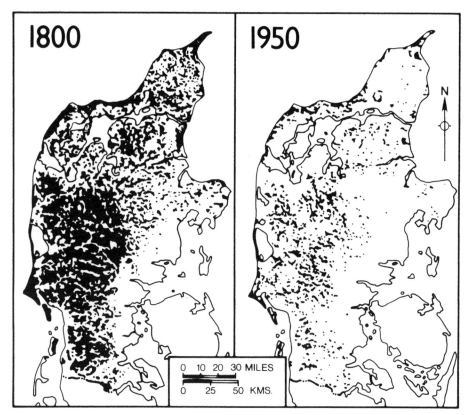

Figure 2.13.   Reduction of heaths in the Jylland Peninsula of Denmark, 1800–1950. This land was reclaimed for agricultural use. (*Source:* Thorpe 1957, 88.)

cially in hilly, mountainous, and sandy regions. The understories are similar to those in the Atlantic forest, and orchids and sedges also abound.

While less catastrophically influenced by human activity, the mixed deciduous/coniferous forest of central Europe has also been greatly altered. As in areas farther west, Germanic farmers engaged in a great era of forest clearance during the Middle Ages to create new farming colonies (fig. 2.14). Often, evidence of the initial clearing survives in the present-day village and town names. In Germany, the common suffixes -rod, -rot, -reuth, and the like, as in Wernigerode, Heiligenroth, and Bayreuth, are all related to the modern German verb roden ("to root out" or "to clear"). The German suffix or prefix brand indicates that the original clearing was accomplished by burning, for it derives from a Germanic root word meaning "fire."

Germanic forest removal typically began with small, roughly round clearings. As population grew, the settlers worked communally to push the perimeter of farmland outward at the expense of the forest, until finally the clearings of adjacent villages joined, sometimes leaving small isolated groves of trees at points farthest from the settlements (fig. 2.15). Less common and confined mainly to valleys in central Germany and southern Poland, a second linear pattern of clearing began with a long, narrow cut along the valley to serve as a road. The colonists each received a ribbon-shaped farm stretching in a narrow strip back away from the road. Each colonist family cleared their own property. In the absence of communalism, the more ambitious settlers rapidly cleared the forest toward the hinter portions of their land, while their neighbors lagged behind, producing an uneven linear swath of farmland advancing from the valley toward the adjacent ridge crest.

Figure 2.14. The retreat of woodland in central Europe, A.D. 900–1900. (Source: Otto Schlüter, as reproduced in Darby 1956a.)

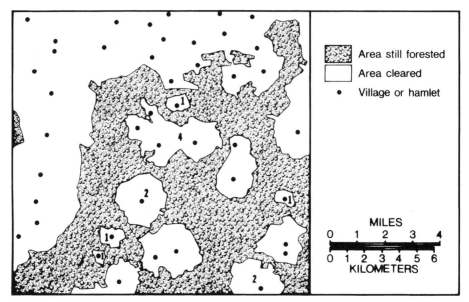

Figure 2.15. Stages of forest clearance in the southeastern outskirts of München, Germany, showing typical Teutonic clearance at almost every stage curiously preserved to the modern day. The smaller clearings (#1) are suggestive of the early stage, while those marked #2, almost perfectly circular, reflect a somewhat later stage. Symbol #3 indicates the earliest phase of coalescence of adjacent clearings, while #4 illustrates more mature coalescence. To the north and west, more complete clearing occurred. (*Source:* Brunhes 1920, 81.)

From the Germans, extensive clearance of the central European forests spread east to the Slavs, who had already made modest inroads before A.D. 500. Slavic forest removal is indicated by place names containing the word elements *kop, lazy,* and *paseky,* all of which specifically indicate "clearing."

A conservation movement arose in time to rescue substantial wooded areas in the central European floristic province. As in the west, the nobility, anxious to preserve recreational hunting grounds, took the lead. An example, rare because it stands in the middle of a great city, is Berlin's *Tiergarten* (literally "animal garden"), long the royal hunting preserve of the Hohenzollern family. It survived until the winter of 1945–1946, when desperate inhabitants of the destroyed capital cut the trees for firewood. The Tiergarten has since been replanted. Terrain also protected some of the forest, for woodland cover on steep slopes was generally spared by the farmers. So close became the identification between forest and hilly or mountainous areas in Germany that the word *wald* ("forest") appears as the name for areas of rough terrain, as in Schwarzwald ("Black Forest").

Much of the woodland standing in central Europe today (fig. 2.11) consists of artificially planted tree farms. The science of forestry arose in eastern Germany in the late 1700s, but the result was single-species commercial forests, with trees growing in orderly Germanic rows, like soldiers standing in rank. These monocultural woodlands lack biodiversity and represent ecological disasters.

The most impressive remnant of the original central European woodland is the Bialowieza Forest on the eastern margin of the North European Plain, straddling the border between Poland and Belarus (fig. 2.10). It encompasses some 127,000 hectares and about 4% is preserved as a national park in Poland. Earlier, it enjoyed royal protection. The Bialowieza Forest houses at least 4,000 plant species, including immense specimens of hornbeam, spruce, and oak. Here, and only here, one can glimpse the great forest of the European heartland in something resembling its pristine condition, but access is strictly regulated.

No native open grasslands existed within the original central European woodland, and the prairies of the central Hungarian Basin, called the *Puszta* or *Alföld* (fig. 2.10), are apparently human induced, maintained by fire and grazing. A fair amount of woodland survives in the Puszta, causing it to be described as a "wooded steppe." Traditionally, the Hungarians raised large herds of open-range cattle there.

To the south, generally corresponding to the climate region of the same name, lies the **Mediterranean** floristic province. The natural vegetation consisted of relatively open forests of broadleaf evergreen live oaks and olives, as well as Aleppo and stone pines, chestnuts, myrtles, walnuts, cypresses, and, in the mountains, firs. The dominant tree was the holm oak. Beneath and between the trees grew an evergreen shrub layer of juniper, honeysuckle, heather, and spiny broom. The ground cover included various grasses, especially esparto, as well as spurge and spleenwort.

This vegetative cover must withstand the pronounced summer drought of the Mediterranean region. Most trees and shrubs exhibit *sclerophyllous* features—an exceptional development of protective external tissue, as in the thickening of leaves and bark, in order to retard evaporation. This is well illustrated by the thick, deeply fissured bark of the cork oak and the stiff, leathery leaf of the olive. Also, leaves are small, and the upper side is shiny, further retarding evaporation.

The destruction of the Mediterranean evergreen forest has been virtually complete. Alteration began in prehistoric times, and the initial effect was probably to produce a parkland in which live oaks were scattered in a grassland. Stretches of this sort of vegetation can still be seen in Extremadura, on the Meseta of southwestern Spain. In most cases, though, a far more complete alteration was achieved.

The process was well under way by Homer's time, some 3,000 years ago. He wrote of ongoing forest removal, both accidental and purposeful. In the rainless summers, "fierce fire rages through the glens on some parched mountainside, and the deep forest burns. The wind driving it whirls the flames in every direction." Shipbuilding also took a heavy toll, including the "thousand" ships launched for the sake of fair Helen of Troy. Homer, in describing battlefield carnage, compared the deaths of warriors to the felling of trees, and a soldier speared in the throat "fell as an oak, or a poplar, or tall pine tree which craftsmen have felled in the hills with freshly whetted axes to be a ship's timber," while another warrior, speared just below the ear, "fell as an ash, on the crest of a distant hill, which is smitten by the bronze ax and falls to the ground." Timber also provided charcoal for smelting, particularly after the use of iron replaced bronze. The construction of buildings, including temples and palaces, demanded still more lumber, until finally a shortage of wood forced acceptance of stone as the primary Mediterranean building material. Considerable damage had already occurred by the 400s B.C., prompting the classical Greek writer Plato to compare deforested, eroded Attiki to "the skeleton of a sick man, all the fat and soft earth have been wasted away, leaving only the bare framework of the land" (fig. 2.16).

People, then, using both fire and ax, assaulted the Mediterranean woodlands in ancient times and continued the destruction for many centuries. Unfortunately, the forest proved unable to reestablish itself after having been cleared for two major reasons. First, most of the Mediterranean open forest occupied steep slopes, for mountainous terrain dominates southern Europe. With the trees removed from the slopes, the soil washed away with

Figure 2.16.   Deforested, rocky landscape on the Aegean island of Patmos. Thousands of years of grazing, accidental fires, and the need for lumber have left this Greek hillside denuded of forest, with much exposed rock. Tall stone fences have been built to separate adjacent herds of goats and sheep. Most of the Greek islands were once much more forested than they are today. (Photo by T.G.J.-B. 1971.)

the winter rains, stripping the mountains to bare rocky skeletons unfit for reforestation. The second retarding factor in woodland regeneration was the lowly goat, a domestic animal of great importance to most Mediterranean rural people. Quite at home in the rugged terrain, the goat devours the tender young shoots of trees newly broken through the soil. Still, much timber survived in the classical period, as is indicated by the writings of numerous scholars of the time. Destruction continued in postclassical times. Venetian and Genovese merchant fleets and Byzantine, Spanish, and Portuguese imperial navies made the same demands on the forests as had their Greek and Roman predecessors. The craftsmen of Firenze, Toledo, and Byzantium (modern Istanbul) needed charcoal as had their classical forerunners, and the ever-present herdsmen and farmers continued to regard the woodland as an enemy to be conquered.

Expanses of bare rock devoid of vegetation today represent the most extreme result of human activity in the Mediterranean (fig. 2.16). More common, however, are regions covered with thickets of evergreen shrub growth a meter or more in height, known in French as *maquis*, in Italian as *macchia* or *maki*, and in Spanish as *matorral*. Such thickets served as hiding places by the French underground in World War II, with the result that the resistance movement became known as the Maquis. Areas of *garrigue* vegetation, a thin cover of scattered dwarf evergreen scrub less than a meter high and rooted in very shallow soil or in fissures in bare rock, also abound. In either case, maquis or garrigue, the habitat is badly damaged and of little further use. Some limited afforestation has been accomplished in the Mediterranean floristic province in recent times, but often with exotics such as Australian eucalyptus, now especially widespread in Portugal.

The **steppe** floristic province, dominated by tallgrass prairies, lies in far southeastern Europe, in Ukraine, and southern parts of Eurorussia. It represents an extension of the expansive grasslands that dominate the heart of Asia, reaching eastward to Mongolia and beyond. As such, the steppes appear alien to the European eye and are, at best, only peripherally a part of Europe. Pointed like an extended finger toward Europe, this *steppe corridor* served repeatedly as a natural route of invasion by mounted Asiatic nomad–warriors, who found the treeless country suited to their mode of warfare and the abundant grasses excellent for their flocks and herds. For a thousand years and more, wave after wave of Asian intruders passed this way—Hun, Bulgar, Magyar, Avar, and Tartar. Most remained to become more or less Europeanized.

The great prairie that led the Asian nomadic tribes into Europe has largely vanished. The steppe proved too fertile to escape the plow, and today domesticated grasses, mainly wheat, grow in place of the natural grassland.

The **taiga** floristic province, sometimes called the *boreal* forest, is also peripheral to Europe. These are the great coniferous evergreen woodlands of the north, and they, too, represent a projection westward from an Asian core. Dominant species include the Norway spruce, Scottish pine, and various firs. The downy birch, a broadleaf deciduous tree, also abounds, as do the gray alder and larch. In poorly drained places, abundant due to the heavy hand of glaciation, peat bogs and mires support a growth of mosses, grasses, and shrubs, while some hilly areas have heaths. Europeans have also found the taiga province inhospitable. It remains thinly populated and a refuge for non-Indo-European Finnic peoples. Most of the land retains a forest cover, as in Finland, 76% wooded (fig. 2.11). The taiga represents the last substantial forest in Europe and is the focus of a large lumbering and paper-pulp industry (fig. 2.17). As a result, most of the taiga is no longer a natural forest but instead is planted and regularly harvested. Nor does this represent a new industry. For centuries the northern lands have supplied lumber for the European core countries, and the coat-of-arms of Taivalkoski County in Finland's northern Kainuu region shows forest trees and a two-man saw.

The final floristic province, the **tundra,** occupies lands north of the tree line along the Arctic coast of Scandinavia and Russia, Iceland, in the higher elevations of the Kjølen Range (where it bears the name *fjell*), and above the limit of forest growth in certain mountain ranges such as the Alps. Tundra vegetation consists largely of lichens, mosses, sedges, rushes, dwarf beech and birch, stunted or creeping evergreen shrublets, and some grasses. Rarely do these plants exceed 30 centimeters in height, though in the transition zone between the tundra and taiga, scrub birch forests grow

Figure 2.17.   Logs floating to Joensuu, Finland, in the taiga region of the Fenno-Scandian Shield. The great needleleaf evergreen forests of the European north provide the basis for a large-scale wood-processing industry, dealing in lumber and pulp. (*Source:* Photo by T.G.J.-B. 1985.)

somewhat taller. The brief Arctic summer brings an outburst of flowery plants of unique coloring and beauty. *Permafrost,* or permanently frozen subsoil, occurs in some places, causing waterlogging of the upper layers and a variety of surface soil hummocks. As a result, walking across the tundra in summer can be very difficult. Few Europeans live here, leaving it as a refuge for the Sami people and other Finnic minorities. The tundra, too, serves more to bound Europe than as a part of it.

Forest Death

Of crucial significance to the fate of the remnant woodlands of Europe, whether natural or artificial, is the recently detected phenomenon of "forest death." Around 1975, forestry experts began to notice tree damage, especially in needleleaf species. Then, as if some critical threshold had been crossed, the percentage of trees exhibiting damage increased rapidly. In western Germany, only 8% of the forest showed visible damage in 1982, in the form of leaf or needle loss or discoloration, but a year later the proportion had increased dramatically to 34%, and by 1984 to 50%. Switzerland's forest damage rose from 17% in 1984 to 40% by 1988 and 65% by 1998 (fig. 2.9). In Czechia, well over two-thirds of the woodland exhibited damage by 1988, a proportion that rose to 96% a decade later, and forest death was widespread in the hill lands along the border with eastern Germany. The Schwarzwald of southwestern Germany became another center of the phenomenon. Even peripheral lands such as Greece, Norway, the Kola Peninsula of northern Russia, and Estonia have damage in half of their forests, and annual reports by the European Union reveal that in the 1990s "there is an overall tendency toward a worsening of the forest condition in Europe." The culprit, almost certainly, is acid rain (fig. 2.9). Unless drastic corrective action is taken, by-products of the industrial age will complete the deforestation of Europe begun millennia ago by ax-wielding agriculturists.

Soil Regions

Climate, vegetation, and parent materials combine to yield a variety of soil types in Europe, varying greatly in texture, depth, and fertility. Scientists recognize eleven or more major soil groups in Europe, displaying a highly complex spatial pattern. For our purposes, we use instead a simplified four-fold classification, keyed to fertility (fig. 2.18).

Highly fertile soils encompass those derived from several different parent materials, including loess—human wind-borne, fine-grained periglacial deposits; alluvium—riverine deposits; and volcanic ash. Loess-derived soils occur in a fragmented belt from northern France to Ukraine

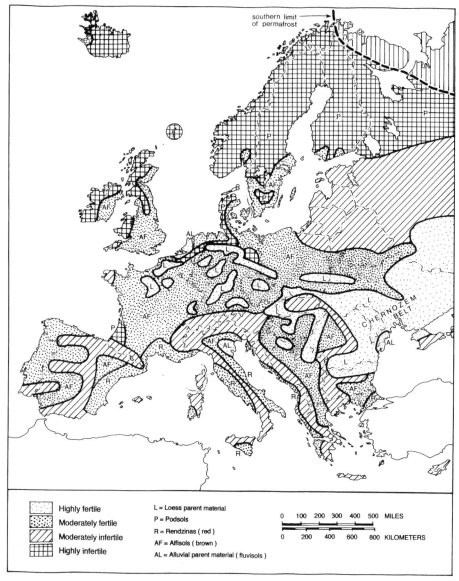

Figure 2.18.   Soil regions. This simple classification conceals an incredibly complex pattern. Note the core/periphery pattern of fertility and infertility. (*Sources:* Food and Agriculture Organization and the UN Educational, Scientific, and Cultural Organization [FAO–UNESCO] 1981; FAO–UNESCO 1988; Garnett 1945.)

in plains and valleys beyond the southern margins of the glaciated lands (fig. 2.1). Loess weathered into a dark-colored, fertile, fine-textured, deep, and easily filled soil. In Ukraine and Russia, this soil is called *chernozem* ("black earth"), and the organic matter of decaying prairie grasses added to the fertility. Loessial soils elsewhere, mainly on the Great European

Plain, had a light forest cover, lacking the thick sod of the prairies, and attracted farmers from ancient times to the present day. Alluvial soils—or fluvisols—dominate the Low Country and also occur in smaller pockets elsewhere, as in broad river valleys and certain Mediterranean lowlands. Dark volcanic soils, called *andosols*, occur too locally to be revealed on the map of Europe, but are highly fertile and attract dense agricultural populations to the environs of volcanoes in Italy and Greece.

A second category consists of **moderately fertile** soils. Of these the most widespread are the so-called brown forest soils, classified as *alfisols* because of a high content of iron and aluminum. Most occur on the Great European Plain. Limestone also weathered into fertile soils, called *rendzinas*. These appear widely in the three Mediterranean peninsulas, where they are called *terra rossa* ("red earth") (fig. 2.18).

Moderately infertile soils, still usable for farming if fertilized, can be found in the central part of the East European Plain and in montane areas further to the west. These have a lighter color, often gray or light brown, and have excessive acidity or deficient humus. Most mountain ranges can best be classified as moderately infertile, with cultivable valleys interspersed with ridges where soils are thin and stony.

The **highly infertile** soils lie mainly in northern Europe. These *podsols* ("white earth" or "ash-colored soils") are highly acidic and humus-starved. Leaching—the downward movement of plant nutrients to lower soil layers—is the cause of the humus deficiency. Before these sterile soils can yield harvests, the farmer must add lime and compost to counteract the acidity and infertility. Sandy areas such as outwash plains are also highly infertile.

Anthrosols

Farmers and herders greatly modified all of these soil types. In the process, they sometimes created artificial soils called anthrosols. The topsoil is often produced by composting. Celts living on the coasts of Scotland and Ireland formerly created soil for rocky fields by composting seaweed.

The human impact on soils can be seen in other ways, too. Deep plowing mixes soil layers—called horizons—and irrigation can cause surface deposits of salt or other sediments to accumulate. Soil erosion has also occurred widely, especially in the limestone-derived rendzinas of the Mediterranean. In Spain, about half of all farmland in some provinces is severely eroded, prompting land abandonment in places. Some Spanish fields lost up to a meter of soil through erosion. Terra rossa, in fact, is actually a subsoil, from which the upper horizons have been eroded (fig. 2.19).

Spain was also the scene, in 1998, of one of Europe's worst episodes of soil pollution, when 420,000 cubic meters of toxic mud burst from the waste reservoir of a zinc mine in the Andalucía Lowland and spread 30 kilometers

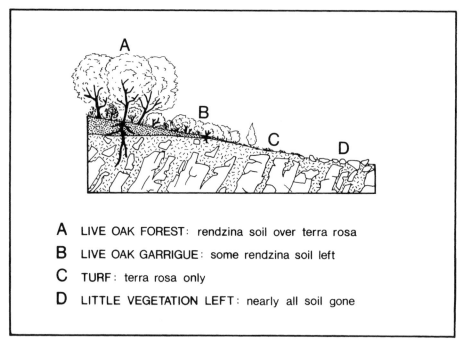

A LIVE OAK FOREST: rendzina soil over terra rosa

B LIVE OAK GARRIGUE: some rendzina soil left

C TURF: terra rosa only

D LITTLE VEGETATION LEFT: nearly all soil gone

Figure 2.19. Diagram of Mediterranean floral and edaphic destruction. The alterations involve forest removal and subsequent erosion and overgrazing. Large areas of southern Europe have been degraded in this way. (*Sources:* Delano Smith 1979, 283; Braun-Blanquet 1936.)

downstream. Belarus lost a huge area of farmland to radioactive contamination from the Chernobyl disaster in 1986.

Hydrogeography

The waters of Europe, including flanking seas, connecting straits, rivers, and marshes, intertwine intimately with occupation. Europe's highly indented coastline causes most parts of the culture area to be no more than 650 kilometers from the sea. Only 8 sizable independent countries in Europe lack a coastline, as contrasted to 29 major states that enjoy access to the sea. Winter ice troubles only the Baltic and White Seas.

These **flanking seas,** named on the accompanying map (fig. 2.20), are in turn linked by numerous strategic **straits,** facilitating a movement of people and goods around the perimeter of Europe. Control over the connecting straits has long been the goal of many competing European powers, and many of these waterways have often been militarily contested. The Bosporos and the Dardanelles, two narrows that join the Black and Aegean Seas, have alternately been controlled by the seagoing Greeks, most notably in the period of the Byzantine empire, and by the land-based Turks, who

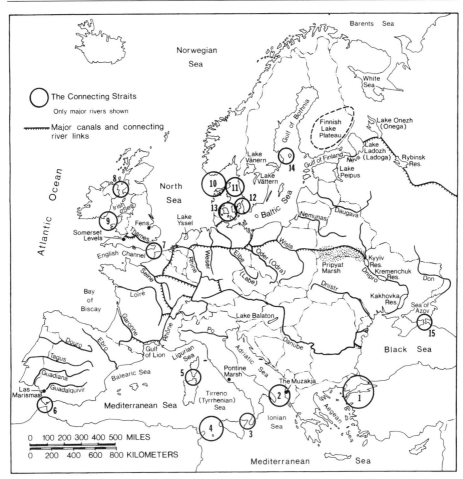

Figure 2.20. Hydrogeographic features. Europe is characterized by a highly indented coast-line of surrounding seas and connecting straits. Key to connecting straits: 1. Dardanelles–Bosporos; 2. Otranto; 3. Messina; 4. "waist" of the Mediterranean; 5. Bonifacio; 6. Gibraltar; 7. Dover; 8. North Channel; 9. Saint George's Channel; 10. Skagerrak; 11. Kattegat; 12. Øre-sund; 13. the Belts; 14. Åland; and 15. Kerch.

presently control these strategic straits. Similarly, Arabs and Spaniards contested Gibraltar before it fell to the British, who hold it as a vestige of a sea-based empire. Wider, but still of great strategic importance, the so-called waist of the Mediterranean divides the sea into two halves. Control of the axis from Sicilia to Tunisia, spanning the waist and including the islands of Pantelleria, Lampedusa, and Malta, was contested first by the Roman and Carthaginian Empires, and the victors assembled a circum-Mediterranean state of great durability. Arabs later ruled the waist. The Axis Powers in World War II, which controlled Sicilia and Tunisia, never broke the British hold on Malta, allowing west–east Allied access from Gibraltar to Suez to continue.

On the Atlantic front of Europe, the most crucial strait is at Dover. Briefly, this white-cliffed passage and the adjacent English Channel served as the core of a Norman French state, but ultimately it became a natural moat and trade route for the British. Instead of joining the mainland to Britain, Dover came to separate them. Denmark and Sweden have long commanded the several entries to the Baltic Sea.

The great, navigable **rivers** of Europe lie disproportionately on the Great European Plain. Flowing in a southeast-to-northwest direction, each has a major port city at its juncture with the sea. Canals interconnect these streams, providing a splendid waterway system. Most of eastern and southeastern Europe drains to the Black Sea, in particular through the great Danube, which, rising in southern Germany, passes through or borders nine independent states and is known by five different names along its course. The rivers of southern Europe, not being navigable, generally lack port cities at their mouth. Iberia drains largely to the Atlantic in the west, and the important European Mediterranean rivers include only the Ebro, Rhône, and Po.

Many European rivers have been greatly modified by human action, both deliberate and accidental. Some seas and streams, in particular the Wisla River, are severely polluted—laced with heavy metals such as lead and mercury, coal-mine salts, and organic carcinogens. Others, such as the Dnipro River, have had their character greatly altered by reservoir construction. The Drin, a minor river of northern Albania, has been completely transformed from a gorge-cutting mountain stream to a stair step of three lakes, now open to boat traffic. Many rivers of the Great European Plain have been *channelized* and *canalized* with locks and small dams to enhance transport, and the great rapids at the Iron Gate of the Danube, where the river cuts through at the Carpathian–Stara Planina juncture, have been dynamited away. River banks are often manicured and lined with facing stones, giving them an artificial appearance.

Marshes were once common in many parts of Europe, but the majority of wetlands have been drained and converted to agriculture. The *Fens* in the English Scarplands disappeared in this way, as did the nearby Somerset Levels, the Pontine Marshes near Rome, much of Las Marismas (a huge salt marsh at the mouth of the Guadalquivir in Spain), the Muzakja in Albania, and many others. Some marshes were, instead, created by human action, as in the Val di Chiana in Toscana, Italy. There, Etruscan forest removal in ancient times began siltation, which in time clogged the valley's drainage system, forming a large malarial marsh and allowing the Tevere River to eventually capture the area from the Arno. Later, farmers drained the Val di Chiana marshes and made them productive. The greatest surviving European wetland, the Pripyat Marsh, lies along the border of Belarus and Ukraine.

Dutch Coastline Alteration

The coastlines of Europe have also been altered by human action. Nowhere is this change more evident than in the Low Country, where the Dutch live on the "wrong" end of a huge geomorphological seesaw. Their deltaic homeland in the Low Country is gradually sinking, at the rate of about 20 centimeters per century, coincident with an increase in elevation along the Swedish shore of the Baltic Sea. Since the end of the period of Pleistocene glaciation about 10,000 B.C., the coastal fringe of the Netherlands has sunk some 20 meters. Silt brought in and deposited by the Rhine, Maas, and Schelde Rivers has partially offset the sinking of the land, but without active human efforts, the coastline would have drastically deteriorated.

Before the encroachment by the sea began, the ancient Dutch coast was apparently quite straight and paralleled by a protective wall of sand dunes. The only breaks in the dunes occurred where the many distributaries of the Rhine, Maas, and Schelde cut through to reach the North Sea. As thousands of years passed and the level of some lands on the inland side of the dunes fell below sea level, parts of the Low Country flooded. Driven by storms, the North Sea broke through the sand dune barrier in the northern and southwestern Netherlands and permanently inundated large areas. This deterioration can still be seen today, especially in the north. The Friesche Islands, which lie in an east–west string along the northern coast, represent all that remains of the sand dune wall in that sector, and the shallow saltwater Waddenzee, which separates the islands from the coast, was once dry land. Besides the Waddenzee, the other major marine incursion helped create a huge flooded river mouth, or estuary, where the Rhine, Maas, and Schelde Rivers came to the sea on the southwestern coast.

Still, deterioration continued. Parts of the coastal margin of the Low Country fragmented into marshy tidal islands, and numerous lakes formed in depressions. From time to time storm tides broke through to join some of these lakes to the sea. When the Romans came to this region, they found a large freshwater lake just south of the Waddenzee, fed and drained by a distributary of the Rhine, and called it the Flevo Lacus. The Roman lake became a saltwater embayment of the North Sea, when a series of storms about A.D. 1200 cut through the ribbon of dry land separating it from the Waddenzee. This created the shallow, saline Zuider Zee ("southern sea") to replace Flevo Lacus. Other freshwater lakes in the coastal fringe awaited their turn to be joined to the sea.

Another type of deterioration involved the slow eastward migration of what remained of the sand dune barrier. The prevailing westerly winds gradually moved the dunes inland, and the sea followed close behind. A fortress built during the Roman occupation on the landward side of the dunes was covered by drifting sands, disappeared, and was soon forgotten after the legions left, only to reappear during the Christmas season in the year 1520 on the *seaward* side of the dune wall. Soon thereafter the ruins were flooded by the advancing North Sea. This involved an eastward migration of about 3 kilometers in 1500 years, and it is estimated that in the vicinity of the city of 's Gravenhage the dunes have moved at least 5 to 8 kilometers.

Human action to resist the environmental deterioration gained momentum over the last 1,500 to 2,000 years. At first, the early Dutch inhabitants did nothing more than pile up mounds of earth upon which to build their homes. These mounds, variously called *terp* (Dutch), *warft* (Frisian), and *wurt* (Low German), can be seen today in parts of the Low Country and are generally still inhabited (fig. 2.21). During periods of high water, the *terpen* temporarily became little islands protecting the people in clustered dwellings on top. These mounds, 4 to 12 meters high, varied in area from 1.5 to 16 hectares. The terpen were built mainly from the third to the tenth centuries A.D., and some 1,500 of them still survive at least in rudiment. Somewhat later, in the A.D. 900s, the Dutch began placing obstructions along the coast to catch and hold accretions of sand and silt and built walls to trap silt being washed down the rivers. In these ways they induced island building in the delta (fig. 2.22).

Dike building began about A.D. 900 in the extensive tidal marsh areas

Figure 2.21.   An ancient terp in the Dutch coastal province of Friesland. This artificial mound dates from the earliest period of the Dutch battle against the sea and today contains the church and cemetery of the village of Jelsum. Before the era of dike building, the countryside all around the terp was subject to periodic inundation by the waters of the sea. (Copyright Marianne Dommisse, from Netherlands Information Service, used with permission.)

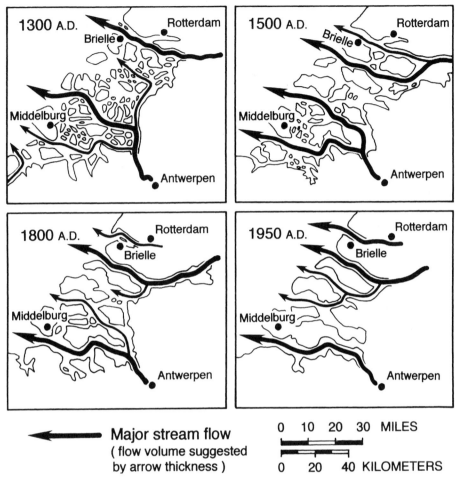

Figure 2.22. Humans at work modifying the Dutch coastline, 1200–1950. Both the advance of the North Sea and the subsequent work of humans to push back the waters are evident in these maps of the Rhine–Maas–Schelde estuary in the Zeeland Province of the Netherlands. The Delta Project is not shown. (*Source: Westermanns Atlas zur Weltgeschichte* 1963, 2:97.)

of Vlaanderen and Zeeland, provinces of what are today the southern Netherlands and adjacent Belgium. The dikes protected lands above the low-tide level that were subject to periodic flooding, and sluice gates were opened at low tide to allow gravity discharge of the water that had accumulated through seepage. Such protected areas became known as *polders*, a term first used in 1138 in Flanders Plain. Dike building and poldering spread northward into the province of Holland, where Count William "the Diker" directed poldering in an area of peat bogs, lakes, and marshes south of Amsterdam in the early 1200s. A peak of dike construction occurred in the 1300s to protect cropland from the unpredictable seas, lakes, and rivers.

The development of polders in areas too low to be drained by gravity at low tide awaited the invention of a mechanical water lifter. The windmill, known in the Low Country at least since the late 1100s, initially served only as a grinder of grain, but in the year 1408 the windmill was first employed as a water lifter and by the 1600s had achieved general use for this purpose. The same westerlies that pushed the waters against the Dutch shores and caused the retreat of the protective sand dunes were harnessed to reclaim the land. Within several centuries nearly all of the marshes and bogs had been converted into polders, with a resultant increase in population and food production.

Drainage of the numerous freshwater lakes dotting the coastal fringe of the Low Country represented the next advance in Dutch reclamation technology. Two centuries of experimentation with the windmill convinced engineers that sizable water bodies could be converted to agricultural use, and between 1609 and 1612 the combined work of 49 windmills laid dry a 7,300-hectare freshwater lake. Other small lakes were drained in quick succession. More-powerful water lifters were needed to allow reclamation of large lakes and oceanic inlets, and for these the Dutch had to wait until the nineteenth and twentieth centuries, when steam- and, later, electric-engine pumps became available. Between 1840 and 1846, a dike was built around the 60-kilometer circumference of the freshwater Haarlemmer Lake, covering 17,800 hectares west of Amsterdam. Then three British-built steam-engine pumps worked continually for five years, from 1847 to 1852, to drain the lake. Haarlemmer was the largest water body yet to surrender to the Dutch at that time, but the greatest projects still lay in the future.

The treacherous Zuider Zee had been a menace to the Low Country ever since its formation. Its waters needed only a strong north wind to send them raging against the vulnerable sea dikes protecting the polderland to the south, and over the years the Zee had claimed many victims. A severe flood in 1916 finally prompted the Netherland government to take action on the Zuider Zee Project and actual work began seven years later. The key to the project, a huge sea dike called the *Afsluitdijk,* was completed 7 years later, cutting off the mouth of the Zuider Zee from the ocean and greatly reducing the amount of protective dike exposed to the open sea by shortening the coastline (fig. 2.23). The streams flowing into the Zee soon flushed it clean of salt water, creating the freshwater Lake Yssel. The dike included sluices to allow for outflow of water and locks to accommodate shipping. The hated name Zuider Zee disappeared from the map, and perhaps the only group of people who mourned its demise were the saltwater fishermen, mainly Frisians, whose livelihood was destroyed. The highway and railroad built on the new dike provided greatly shortened transport links between western and eastern parts of the Netherlands.

The second part of the project has involved the diking and draining of 4 large polders from the floor of the old Zuider Zee. The *Wieringer* Polder in the far northern part was actually drained before all of the sea dike was finished, becoming dry in 1931. Experimentation established the best

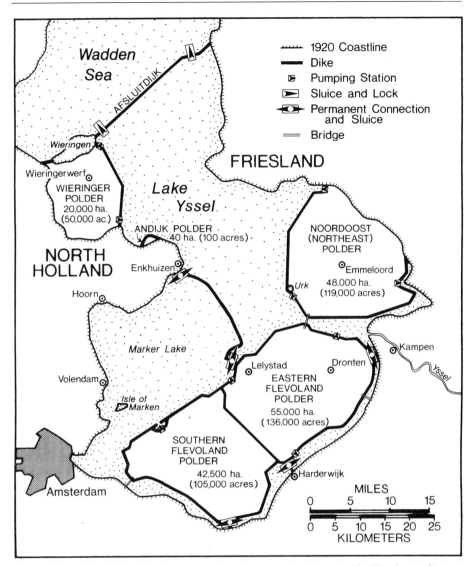

Figure 2.23.   The Zuider Zee Project produced a dramatic change in the Dutch coastline, as well as converting what remains of the old saltwater Zee into the freshwater Lake Yssel.

sequence of crops to remove salinity from the soils, and soon the Wieringer Polder was colonized by Dutch farmers. Settlement was completed in 1941, and the area is a fully integrated part of the Netherlands, largely indistinguishable from surrounding districts. The other major polders include the *Noordoost,* drained by electric pumps in 1936–1942 and colonized by the early 1960s; *Eastern Flevoland,* named for the ancient Roman lake and laid dry in 1957; and *Southern Flevoland,* pumped free of water in 1968 and today absorbing suburban spillover from the adjacent cities of Holland, as well as providing parkland. The remainder of Lake Yssel remains undrained, serving as a freshwater supply and recreational area.

With the Zuider Zee Project, the Dutch turned back the major marine encroachment on their northern coast. The other principal danger area lies in the southwestern province known as Zeeland, where the Rhine–Maas–Schelde estuary passes through six large gaps in the old sand dune barrier. This delta country was no stranger to storm floods from the sea, but the attention of the Dutch government was finally attracted by an especially severe disaster in 1953. Between January 31 and February 2, 160-kph winds from the northwest pushed river water back up into the estuary, breaking down dikes and spilling into the farmlands and towns of the islands in the estuary. More than 80 breaches were made in the dikes, and some 150,000 hectares were flooded with seawater. About 1,800 persons drowned, 100,000 were evacuated, and damage reached enormous proportions. The storm could easily have been catastrophic. A strategic dike along the north bank of the Rhine–Maas channel called the Nieuwe Waterweg, protecting the densely settled heartland of Holland to the north, held—barely. Had it collapsed, the homeland of 3 million people would have been inundated and many more persons drowned.

To prevent such an occurrence in the future, the government approved the *Delta Project* (fig. 2.24). Four large new sea dikes closed off most of the

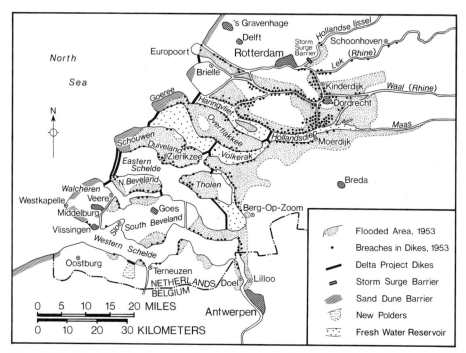

Figure 2.24.   The Delta Project was designed to protect the southern Dutch coast and prevent another catastrophic flood like the one in 1953. (*Sources:* Wagret 1968; van Veen 1962.)

mouths of the Rhine–Maas–Schelde estuary, with a freshwater lake on the landward side. The Nieuwe Waterweg remained open so as not to disrupt Rhine River shipping, but elaborate new water-diversion systems and storm-surge barriers directed the flow of the Rhine and Maas into the adjacent lake in case a storm tide backs up the river as in 1953. The lake can absorb the river flow for several days without spilling over its dikes, and the excess water can then escape through sluices to the sea when the storm subsides. The western Schelde estuary also remains open since it serves the major Belgian port of Antwerpen, but dikes along the estuary shore were raised and strengthened. Little land reclamation occurred in the Delta Project, only about 16,200 hectares, for the goal was preservation rather than expansion.

The Low Country, then, was human-made. Without the effort of the inhabitants, the seacoast would lie far to the interior, and Europe would be deprived of some of its richest farmland and largest cities (fig. 2.25).

Coastal Silting

More commonly, Europeans have modified the coastline unintentionally, especially on the three Mediterranean peninsulas. Bays have been silted up to become dry land, rivers rendered unnavigable, ports made landlocked,

Figure 2.25.   Cattle grazing at low tide on the seaward side of the huge dike protecting the lowlands bordering the North Sea in Schleswig–Holstein Province, Germany, at the far eastern tip of the Low Country. (Photo by T.G.J.-B. 1981.)

and islands near the coast joined to the mainland (fig. 2.26). Most of these changes occurred in historic times, some very recently.

Mediterranean people wrought these changes by destroying forests and allowing massive amounts of soil to erode. The results have been spectacular. The Greek geographer Strabo, writing about 2,000 years ago, noted that the Adriatic tides reached to Ravenna in northern Italy, a city 10 kilometers inland today. Palos de la Frontera on the Odiel River, from which Columbus departed on his voyage of discovery in 1492, is now silted up for 1.5 kilometers below the former docks. Even more impressive is the silting that occurred in the area of Monte Circeo, a mountain on the western coast of Italy. According to the Homeric epic *Odyssey*, Monte Circeo formed an island in preclassical times, and it retained that status even as late as 300 B.C. Several centuries later, siltation joined it to the Italian mainland. Where Ulysses once sailed, farmers labor today in fertile fields. Today, the Ionian Greek isle of Levkás is also in the process of being joined to the mainland.

Europeans, then, inherited and greatly altered a temperate, well-watered, forested, fertile enclave, compartmentalized by terrain and

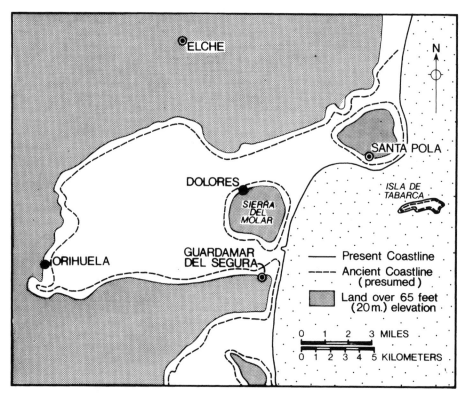

Figure 2.26. Coastline alteration by siltation since ancient times, Alicante District, Mediterranean coastal Spain. Materials eroded from the adjacent Bética Mountains have filled a sizable bay and joined several islands to the mainland. Similar siltation occurred in other Mediterranean areas. (*Source:* Smith 1979, 332.)

flanked on all sides by the sea and less hospitable lands where cold, aridity, and barrenness prevail. In this comfortable niche, European civilization arose and flowered. It is tempting to attribute the human Europe to the gentle land and the isolation offered by the less-favored periphery, but that interpretation would be simplistic. Similar favored lands elsewhere in the world produced cultures fundamentally different from that of Europe. The explanation for the European culture area must be sought mainly elsewhere, for Europe is largely a self-written drama. The remainder, and appropriately larger part, of the book is devoted to the interworkings of culture that contain the key to understanding Europe geographically.

Sources and Suggested Readings

Alexander, David. 1984. "The Reclamation of Val-di-Chiana (Tuscany)." *Annals of the Association of American Geographers* 74:527–550.

Ashwell, Ian Y., and Edgar Jackson. 1970. "The Sagas as Evidence of Early Deforestation in Iceland." *Canadian Geographer* 14:158–166.

Barr, Brenton M., and Kathleen Braden. 1988. *The Disappearing Russian Forest*. Totowa, N.J., USA: Rowman & Littlefield.

Bennett, Charles F., Jr. 1975. "Human Influences on the Ecosystems of Europe and the Mediterranean." In *Man and Earth's Ecosystems: An Introduction to the Geography of Human Modification of the Earth,* ed. Charles F. Bennett Jr. New York, USA: Wiley, 121–144.

Bennett, Hugh H. 1960. "Soil Erosion in Spain." *Geographical Review* 50:59–72.

Bischoff, Uwe. 1992. "Der Scirocco: Untersuchungen zur Häufigkeit und Dauer über Mittel- und Süditalien." *Erdkunde* 46:52–57.

Bishop, Kevin H. 1997. "Liming of Acid Surface Waters in Northern Sweden." *Transactions of the Institute of British Geographers* 22:49–60.

Braun-Blanquet, J. 1936. "La forêt d'yeuse Languedocienne." *Mémoires de la Société des Sciences Naturelles de Nîme* 5.

Brunhes, Jean. 1920. *Human Geography*. Chicago, USA: Rand McNally.

Carter, Francis W., and David Turnock, eds. 1993. *Environmental Problems in Eastern Europe*. London, GB: Routledge, Chapman & Hall.

Chandler, T. J. 1965. *The Climate of London*. London, GB: Hutchinson.

Conrad, Victor. 1943. "The Climate of the Mediterranean Region." *Bulletin of the American Meteorological Society* 24:127–145.

Darby, H. Clifford. 1956a. "The Clearing of the Woodland in Europe." In *Man's Role in Changing the Face of the Earth,* ed. William L. Thomas Jr. Chicago, USA: University of Chicago Press, 183–216.

———. 1956b. *The Draining of the Fens*. 2nd ed. Cambridge, GB: Cambridge University Press.

Dunbar, Gary S. 1983. "The Forests of Cyprus under British Stewardship." *Scottish Geographical Magazine* 99:111–120.

Duncan, A. M., D. K. Chester, and J. E. Guest. 1981. "Mount Etna Volcano: Environmental Impact and Problems of Volcanic Prediction." *Geographical Journal* 147:164–178.

Embleton, Clifford, ed. 1984. *Geomorphology of Europe*. New York, USA: Wiley.

Europe's Environment: The Second Assessment. 1999. Amsterdam, NL: Elsevier.

Fleure, H. J. 1960. "The Loess in European Life." *Geography* 45:200–204.

Flohn, Hermann, and Roberto Fantechi, eds. 1984. *The Climate of Europe: Past, Present, and Future*. Hingham, Mass., USA: D. Reidel.

Food and Agriculture Organization and the UN Educational, Scientific, and Cultural Organization. 1981. *Soil Map of the World*. Vol. 5, *Europe*. Paris, F: United Nations.

————. 1988. *Soil Map of the World: Revised Legend*. Roma, I: United Nations.

Garnett, Alice. 1945. "The Loess Regions of Central Europe in Prehistoric Times." *Geographical Journal* 106:132–143.

Gentilcore, R. Louis. 1970. "Reclamation in the Agro Pontino, Italy." *Geographical Review* 60:301–327.

Goudie, Andrew. 1990. *The Landforms of England and Wales*. Oxford, GB: Basil Blackwell.

Graham, Edward. 1993. "The Urban Heat Island of Dublin City during the Summer Months." *Irish Geography* 26:45–57.

Grenon, Michel, and Michel Batisse, eds. 1989. *Futures for the Mediterranean Basin: The Blue Plan*. Oxford, GB: Oxford University Press.

Hulme, Mike, and Elaine Barrow. 1997. *Climates of the British Isles: Past and Future*. London, GB: Routledge.

van Hulten, M.H.M. 1969. "Plan and Reality in the IJsselmeerpolders." *Tijdschrift voor Economische en Sociale Geografie* 60:67–76.

Jackson, E. L. 1982. "The Laki Eruption of 1783: Impacts on Population and Settlement in Iceland." *Geography* 67:42–50.

Jalas, Jaako, and Juha Suominen. 1972–1976. *Atlas Florae Europaeae*. Helsinki, SF: Suomalaisen Kirjallisuuden Kirjapaino Oy.

Jeftic, Ljubomir, John D. Milliman, and Giuliano Sestini, eds. 1993. *Climatic Change and the Mediterranean*. Sevenoaks, Kent, GB: Edward Arnold.

Kárník, Vít. 1971. *Seismicity of the European Area*. Vol. 2. Dordrecht, NL: D. Reidel.

King, Russell, Lindsay Proudfoot, and Bernard Smith. 1997. *The Mediterranean: Environment and Society*. London, GB: Arnold.

Köppen, Wladimir, et al. 1930–1936. *Handbuch der Klimatologie*. Berlin, D: Borntraeger.

Lambert, Audrey M. 1985. *The Making of the Dutch Landscape: An Historical Geography of the Netherlands*. 2nd ed. London, GB: Seminar Press.

Malmström, Vincent H. 1960. "Influence of the Arctic Front on the Climate and Crops of Iceland." *Annals of the Association of American Geographers* 50:117–122.

Peterson, D. J. 1993. *Troubled Lands: The Legacy of Soviet Environmental Destruction*. Boulder, Colo., USA: Westview.

Polunin, Oleg, and Martin Walters. 1985. *A Guide to the Vegetation of Britain and Europe*. Oxford, GB: Oxford University Press.

Pryde, Philip R., ed. 1995. *Environmental Resources and Constraints in the Former Soviet Republics*. Boulder, Colo., USA: Westview.

Raisz, Erwin. 2000. "Physiography of Europe." In *Goode's World Atlas*. 20th ed. Ed. John C. Hudson and Edward B. Espenshade Jr. Chicago, USA: Rand McNally.

Ryan, William, and Walter Pitman. 1998. *Noah's Flood*. New York, USA: Simon & Schuster.

Scarth, A. 1983. "Nisyros Volcano." *Geography* 68:133–139.

Sigurdson, Haraldur, et al. 1985. "The Eruption of Vesuvius in A.D. 79." *National Geographic Research* 1:332–387.

Simkin, Tom, et al. 1989. *This Dynamic Planet: World Map of Volcanoes, Earthquakes, and Plate Tectonics*. Washington, D.C., USA: Smithsonian Institution.

Smith, C. Delano. 1979. *Western Mediterranean Europe*. London, GB: Academic.

Statistical Yearbook 1999 for Foreign Countries. Stuttgart, D.: Metzler-Poeschel.

Steigenga-Kouwe, S. E. 1960. "The Delta Plan." *Tijdschrift voor Economische en Sociale Geografie* 51:167–175.

Tansley, Arthur G. 1939. *The British Isles and Their Vegetation*. London, GB: Cambridge University Press.

Thirgood, J. V. 1981. *Man and the Mediterranean Forest*. London, GB: Academic.

Thorarinsson, Sigurdur. 1966. *Surtsey: The New Island in the North Atlantic*. New York, USA: Viking.

Thorpe, Harry. 1957. "A Special Case of Heath Reclamation in the Alheden District of Jutland, 1700–1955." *Publication of the Institute of British Geographers* 23:87–121.

Tooley, Michael J., and Saskia Jelgersma, eds. 1992. *Impacts of Sea-level Rise on European Coastal Lowlands*. Oxford, GB: Basil Blackwell, Institute of British Geographers, Publication No. 27.

U.S. Geological Survey, National Earthquake Information Center. <http://www-neic.cr.usgs.gov/neis/epic/epic_global.html> [last accessed: 2000].

van Veen, Johan. 1962. *Dredge, Drain, Reclaim: The Art of a Nation*. 5th ed. 's Gravenhage, NL: Nyhoff.

Wagret, Paul. 1968. *Polderlands*. Trans. Margaret Sparks. London, GB: Methuen.

Wallén, Carl C. 1970. *Climates of Northern and Western Europe*. Amsterdam, NL: Elsevier.

Westermanns Atlas zur Weltgeschichte. 1963. Pt. 2. Braunschweig, D: Georg Westermann.

Williams, Michael. 1970. *The Draining of the Somerset Levels*. London, GB: Cambridge University Press.

CHAPTER 3

Religion

Of all the human traits mentioned in chapter 1 that define "Europe," the single most important is Christianity. As recently as A.D. 1500, the faith and culture remained very nearly synonymous, with Christianity confined almost exclusively to Europe. Christian Europeans had been in combat with Muslims in the Mediterranean for seven centuries, strengthening their sense of cultural identity. Pope John Paul II, in 1982, claimed that European identity "is incomprehensible without Christianity," that the faith "ripened the civilization of the continent, its culture, its dynamism, its activeness, its capacity for constructive expansion on other continents." The pope admonished a highly secularized Europe to "revive those authentic values that gave glory to your history."

The Christian heritage, more than any other single trait, still today provides the basis for the European image of "we versus they." Christianity underlies and inspires both the good and bad aspects of Europe: its great art, literature, music, and philosophy as well as its religious wars, genocides, and inquisitions. One cannot imagine European culture devoid of the magnificent cathedrals, altarpieces, crucifixes, and religious statuary. Christianity inspired the *Commentaries* of Saint Thomas Aquinas, Leonardo da Vinci's *Last Supper*, Michelangelo's *David* and Sistine Chapel, the Kremlin in Moskva, and the cathedral at Chartres, Dante's *Inferno* and John Milton's *Paradise Lost*. For many centuries, the church was Europe and Europe was the church. Europeans bear the indelible stamp of Christianity, and even today to depart the Christian lands and enter the bordering Muslim districts is to leave Europe (fig. 3.1).

Pagan Europe

Christianity was not native to Europe. The culture area, to a remarkable extent, is the result of a juxtaposition of different intrusive traits. In pre-

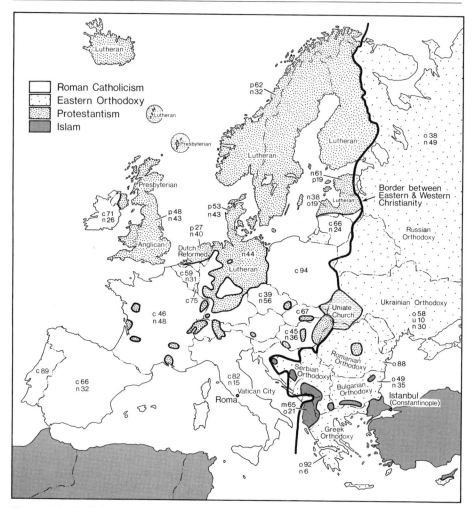

Figure 3.1. Religious groups in Europe. The numbers refer to percentages of the largest group(s) within each country, and the key to abbreviations is: c = Catholic; o = Orthodox; p = Protestant; u = Uniate; m = Muslim; and n = declaring no religious faith. Persons declaring a denomination but listing themselves as nonpracticing or nonreligious are included as members. The figures for RUS are for Eurorussia, as defined in the preface. (*Sources:* Catholic News Service 1993; Gallup Social Surveys Ltd. 1991; *Eurobarometer* 1991, 1995.)

Christian times, Europeans had a *polytheistic* culture, worshipping multiple divinities. Most groups practiced *animism,* nature religions that imbued objects such as rocks, heavenly bodies, mountains, forests, and rivers with souls.

A bewildering array of spirits, gods, and goddesses ruled over war, fertility, woodlands, high places, caves, harvests, death, lightning, navigation, earthquakes, volcanoes, moon, sun, winds, and a hundred other domains. The Germanic Thor hurled thunderbolts, the Greek Aphrodite governed love and fertility, and the Roman Mars assisted in warfare. Thousands of shrines and altars dedicated to these divinities dotted the ancient landscape of Europe, many of which survive in ruins (fig. 3.2). Some pre-Christian deities achieved more importance than others, often gaining acceptance over fairly large areas. A mother/fertility/love goddess, referred to by the Romans as *Magna Mater*—the great mother—was widely venerated throughout the Mediterranean lands, and *Mithras,* a male god derived from Persia, achieved widespread worship among the Roman military class. Especially strong in Greece, the *Mystery Cults* had a main center at Eleusis near Athínai. Their rites are little known since they occurred in secret (giving us the word *elusive*), but we do know they offered eternal life to the faithful. In the western and northern fringes of Europe, astronomy-based religions of early Indo-European origin held sway, leaving us mega-

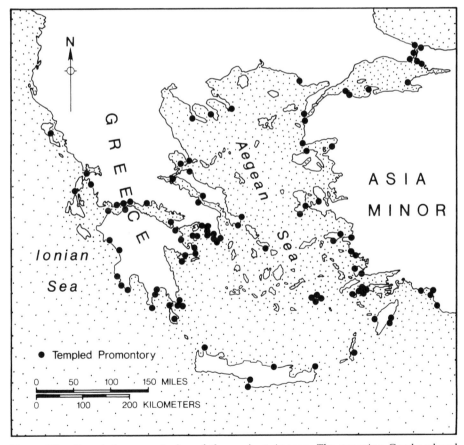

Figure 3.2. Templed promontories of the ancient Aegean. The seagoing Greeks placed great importance upon promontories, both as hazards to sailing and as landmarks. Temples both heightened the visibility of the promontories and allowed placation of the relevant gods. (*Source:* Semple 1927.)

lithic ruins such as Stonehenge, which is believed to have been a rather sophisticated observatory.

In other words, pre-Christian Europe was religiously divided and chaotic. That the culture area should have been converted to a radically different, *monotheistic* faith, Christianity, seems amazing. Originally, the worship of a single male divinity had been confined to Afro-Asiatic-speaking nomadic herders of the Near Eastern deserts. This tribal Semitic shepherd-god seemed ill suited to the agricultural, polytheistic Indo-Europeans.

Diffusion of Christianity

The key figure in the remarkable diffusion of Christianity to Europe, the Apostle Paul, bridged the Semitic and Greek cultures; he presented monotheism in terms understandable and appealing to Europeans. Christianity also proved, throughout the centuries of conversion, adept at absorbing elements of the native religions of Europe. *Sun*day, devoted to a Roman god of the sun, became the Christian sabbath; the old multiple divinities survived as saints; the Virgin Mary annexed the devotion afforded to the Mediterranean Magna Mater; Jehovah replaced the old king of the gods, Zeus/Jupiter/Thor; and the Mystery Cults' promise of eternal life was honored by Christianity. Marian veneration remains strongest in the Mediterranean lands even today (fig. 3.3).

Pagan places of worship typically became Christian shrines and churches. For example, a rural church in Scotland stands atop a prehistoric artificial mound venerated since ancient times, the Alvestra Monastery in south-central Sweden abuts standing stones dating from pre-Christian antiquity, and Canterbury Cathedral, seat of the Church of England, rests on the foundations of a solar-oriented pagan temple (fig. 3.4). Sacred groves from pagan times still stand protected alongside Greek monasteries, and springs holy to the pre-Christian Irish remain pilgrimage sites today.

Christianity destroyed the animistic belief that humans were part of Nature, replacing it with the doctrine that God had given his people dominion over the environment. By removing the animistic sacredness of Nature, Christianity perhaps opened the way for the massive environmental modification that endangers European survival today.

Initially, Christianity spread from city to city in the Roman Empire, leaving the intervening rural areas pagan (fig. 3.5). The Latin word *pagus*, meaning "rural district," is the root of both the word *pagan* and *peasant*. Similarly, the isolated, unconverted dwellers of the heaths gave rise to the word *heathen*. Christianity in Europe was at first an urban faith.

Perhaps one key to the concentration of the first European Christians in the cities of the Roman Empire lies in the Jewish Diaspora. Early in the Christian Era, the Romans dispersed most Jews from Israel, in an attempt to quell their rebellions against imperial authority. Jews came as refugees

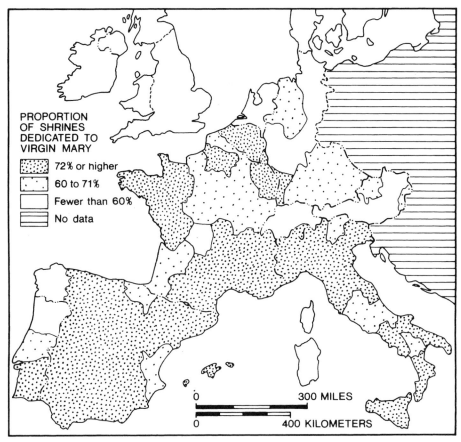

Figure 3.3.   Proportion of pilgrimage shrines dedicated to the Virgin Mary in modern Europe. Marian devotion is greatest in the Mediterranean lands, where the Magna Mater was venerated in pre-Christian times. Spain alone has some 22,000 Marian shrines. Catholic shrines dedicated to Christ and various saints are most common in the northern and Alpine lands. (*Source:* Nolan and Nolan 1989, 121.)

to almost every Roman city throughout the empire, and they clustered in ethnic neighborhoods. Evidence now suggests that those very neighborhoods often housed the first Christian congregations. In other words, Jewish people in their Diaspora, already monotheists whose holy scriptures formed half the Bible, may have become the earliest Christians in Europe, though many or most Jews did not convert.

Whatever the case, the spread of Christianity remained slow until A.D. 313, when the Roman emperor Constantine issued an edict of toleration for Christianity, which led eventually to its status as state religion. In the centuries that followed, 2 major centers directed the diffusion of Christianity from its Mediterranean base—Latin Roma and Greek Byzantium (present-day Istanbul). The Roman church spread rapidly in the western Mediterranean during the fourth and fifth centuries. Before the fall of the empire,

Figure 3.4.   Kildrummy Church positioned atop an ancient artificial mound in the northern Scottish Highlands where pagans worshipped. Such juxtapositions occur frequently in all parts of Europe. (Photo by T.G.J.-B. 1992.)

Italy, France, and Iberia became converted, and the Germanic tribes who subsequently overran these areas quickly accepted the church. From the western Mediterranean core, Roman missionaries spread far to the north. St. Patrick arrived in Ireland in 432, and a major cultural flowering occurred among the Celtic converts there. Peoples of Britain, missionized from both Ireland and the Continent, converted from the 400s through the early 600s (fig. 3.5).

The pagan tribes of Germany received missionaries from Ireland, Britain, and France beginning in the early 600s, and the Germans in turn carried the church to Scandinavians and Slavic Poles, with both missions completed by about 1100. The pivotal event in Poland occurred in 966, when the principal local ruler allowed himself to be baptized, an event duplicated in Hungary in 973. The European work of Roman missionaries ended in the 1380s with the conversion of the Balts in distant Lithuania. In carrying Christianity to the heathen north, missionaries also took the Latin alphabet, and the zone of Roman mission work is fairly well indicated even today by the use of Latin characters.

The impressive gains in the north were partially offset by losses to Islam. North Africa, where the Roman church was well established, became permanently Muslim in the 700s, and much of Iberia remained under the control of the Muslims for many centuries. Islamic invaders respected those

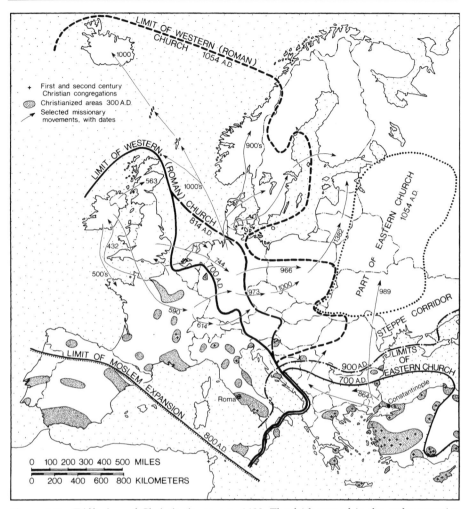

Figure 3.5. Diffusion of Christianity to A.D. 1400. The faith spread in the early centuries by moving from city to city while bypassing rural areas.

religions that possessed a written book of beliefs, and Christianity survived in Moorish Iberia.

Greek Christians, centered in the Byzantine empire, initially converted the Slavic tribes that had spread south of the Danube River into imperial territory. Mission work north of the Danube was hindered by repeated invasions of Asiatic tribes entering Europe through the steppe corridor and Valachian Plain between A.D. 550 and 1050 (fig. 3.5), but finally, in A.D. 989, Ukrainians and Russians became Christians. Missionaries working among the Slavs developed the Cyrillic alphabet, derived from the Greek characters, and the distribution of this script today, with some exceptions, parallels the extent of their church in Europe. Greek Christianity, like its Roman counterpart, lost ground in the south while winning converts in the north.

Soon after 1200 their Byzantine empire collapsed under Turkish pressure, eventually causing the loss of Asia Minor and even the Christian center at Istanbul to Islam.

Christian Fragmentation

Religiously, as in virtually every other facet of culture, Europe displays an overarching unity, a façade partially concealing major internal contrasts. Monolithic Christianity never existed in Europe. From the very first, the more ancient contest between Greek and Roman civilizations dictated fragmentation. The claim of the Latin bishop of Roma to leadership of all Christendom never gained unqualified acceptance by the Greeks and the bishop of Byzantium. The subsequent split of the empire into western and eastern halves, Roman and Greek, presaged a final religious schism. In a separation in A.D. 1054, the western church became Roman Catholicism, the Greek Church Eastern Orthodoxy. The dividing line between Catholicism and Orthodoxy remains the most fundamental religious border in Europe today (fig. 3.1). It has changed little in a thousand years and provides the basis for many of the contrasts between west and east in Europe.

The second great schism occurred in the 1500s, when western Christianity split, the southern lands remaining Catholic and the north becoming Protestant (fig. 3.6). Protestantism arose in different places over several centuries in an attempt to bring about reforms within the Roman church. The pivotal event, the challenge to the church issued by Martin Luther at Wittenberg, Germany, in 1517, evolved into successful secession. The new church quickly spread through northern Germany and the Scandinavian lands, supported by the rulers of individual states. John Calvin furthered the Protestant cause in the mid-1500s from his base in Switzerland, dispersing Puritanism to England, Presbyterianism to Scotland, the Reformed church to the Netherlands and Germany, and the Huguenot faith to France, as well as lesser Calvinist groups to eastern Europe. Also in Switzerland, Ulrich Zwingli led a Protestant movement in the German-speaking cantons. A number of Anabaptist Protestant sects also arose, including the Mennonites in the Netherlands. These people rejected infant baptism and offered the rite only to adult believers. An additional breakaway from Roman Catholicism came in 1534 when King Henry VIII created the Church of England.

The Protestant breakaway reinforced a great north–south cultural divide in Europe. The religious border had pretty much stabilized by 1570, though the dreadful Thirty Years' War between Catholics and Protestants still lay ahead (compare figs. 3.1 and 3.6). As a result of the two Christian schisms, Europe acquired three major religious regions.

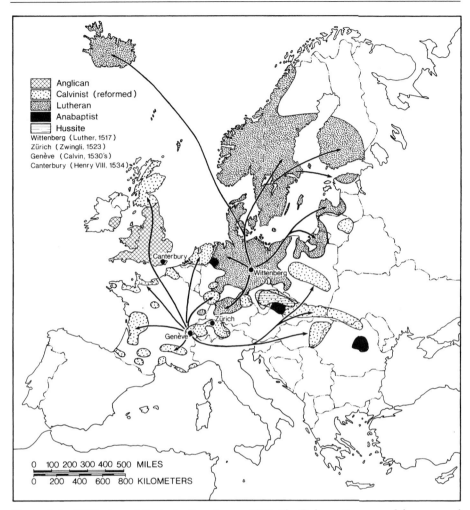

Figure 3.6.   Diffusion of Protestantism to A.D. 1570. The Reformation spread from several different nuclei to influence most of northern and central Europe.

Roman Catholicism

About 250 million Europeans are practicing or nominal **Roman Catholics** today, roughly 35% of the total population. Catholicism possesses a huge region, stretching from Iberia and Italy in the south to Lithuania in the north and from Ireland in the west to Croatia and Hungary in the east. In some countries, such as Spain, where less than 0.5% of the population belongs to other churches, Catholicism is overwhelmingly prevalent, but many regions, particularly along the contact zones with Protestantism and Orthodoxy, exhibit considerable denominational variety.

Roman Catholicism remains a truly united church largely obedient to the papacy, and Vatican City is the seat of a highly centralized administration (fig. 3.7). At the same time, regional differences exist. Irish Catholicism is not the same as Italian or Lithuanian Catholicism, and the church has encouraged national patron saints and other regional qualities to persist. Individual districts and valleys often boast their own patron saints and shrines. For example, in the Bética Mountains south of Granada in Spain lies the highly distinctive region of Las Alpujarras, where the town of Ugijar proudly houses the sanctuary of Our Lady of the Martirio, "patroness of Las Alpujarras." In this manner, Catholicism heightens, and draws strength from, the sense of place.

A vivid Catholic impress has been placed on the countryside in lands loyal to the Roman church. Geographers speak of *cultural landscapes*—the visual, varied trace of human presence—and much of Europe can be said to display a Catholic landscape. Among the most obvious religious contributions to the landscape are *sacred structures,* especially the church building. Europe exhibits many regional contrasts in church size, building material, and architectural style. In Catholic areas, the church structures tend to be large and ornate, in part because the Roman church places great value on visible beauty. Catholic landscapes gain additional distinctiveness from the numerous roadside shrines and chapels that dot the countryside.

Catholicism also influenced the names people placed on the land. In

Figure 3.7.   St. Peter's in the Vatican City, the papal seat and center of European and world Catholicism. The Catholic Church retains a viable central authority, based here in a small independent state. (Photo by T.G.J.-B. 1989.)

Catholic countries, the custom of naming towns for Christian saints remains common. Often, saintly suffixes were added to preexisting settlements, as in Alcazar de San Juan in Spain. The frequency of such sacred names decreases to the north in Europe, and rarely do they occur in Protestant lands. In Germany, about three-quarters of the towns and villages bearing the saintly prefix *Sankt* lie in the Catholic-dominated southern part of the country, including 21% in the province of Bayern alone. Cross the religious divide into Protestant Germany, and saints largely disappear from place names.

Catholicism has also had a distinctive economic imprint on its part of Europe. For example, the Catholic tradition of avoiding meat on Friday and on numerous church holidays greatly stimulated the development of the fishing industry. The church encouraged the use of fish during periods of fasting and penitence, as well as on Friday. Seashore Catholics, such as Basques, Bretons, Galicians, and Portuguese, are among the greatest fishing peoples of Europe. Saint Peter, the original Christian fisherman, holds a place of special veneration in the fishing villages of Catholic Europe. The importance of the Catholic Church to fishing is suggested by the economic crisis in English fishing when Catholic dietary restrictions ended as a result of the Anglican breakaway in the 1500s. Many fishermen were obliged to become sailors, perhaps leading to the great era of English naval exploration, piracy, and overseas colonization.

Pilgrimages

An even more profound economic influence of Catholicism results from the church's enduring practice of religious pilgrimages. Favored holy sites derive considerable financial benefit. In Catholic Europe, tens of millions of pilgrims travel to literally thousands of holy places each year. Pilgrimage sites vary in importance, ranging from small shrines that attract only the faithful from the immediate surroundings to internationally known places sought out by Catholics from all over Europe and America. Pilgrimage sites are unevenly distributed in Europe, even within Catholic areas (fig. 3.8). In France, for example, pilgrimage sites devoted to the Virgin Mary lie mainly in the south and west, with a few isolated clusters elsewhere in the country (fig. 3.3).

Vatican City draws millions of Catholic visitors to Roma each year, adding to the already important tourist trade based on antiquities. As recently as the 1700s, most long-distance travel of people within Europe involved pilgrims going to Roma and a few other religious centers. Many roads developed mainly for pilgrim traffic, complete with hospices at difficult places such as mountain passes. Monks built bridges along these routes.

The major present-day pilgrimage sites, in addition to Roma, include *Lourdes*, a French town at the foot of the Pyrenees in the Basin of Aquitaine

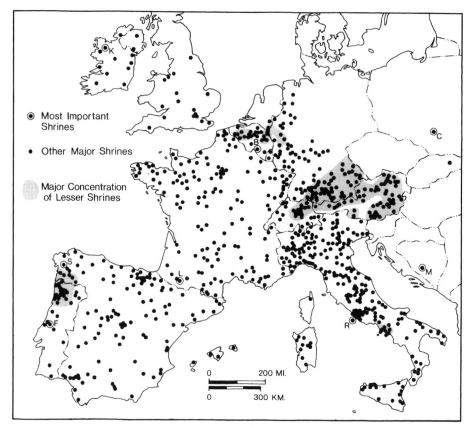

Figure 3.8. Pilgrimage shrines in western Europe. Each dot represents a shrine that is the most important in its diocese and/or draws at least 10,000 pilgrims per year. In the shaded areas, remarkable concentrations of lesser shrines occur. Pilgrimage is largely a Catholic phenomenon, as the distribution suggests. Only a small selection of eastern European shrines is shown. Key to symbols for most famous shrines: B = Beauraing; C = Czestochowa; F = Fátima; K = Knock; L = Lourdes; M = Medjugorje; R = Roma; and S = Santiago de Compostela. (*Source:* In part from Nolan and Nolan 1989, 29, 31, 32.)

where the Virgin Mary supposedly appeared in a vision; *Fátima*, north of Lisboa in Portugal; *Beauraing*, a small place in French-speaking southern Belgium near the border of France; *Knock*, in the hilly west of Ireland; *Czestochowa*, where the greatest icon of Polish Catholicism, the miraculous Black Virgin, is housed; *Medjugorje*, in the Croatian Catholic district of Bosnia–Herzegovina, where the faithful believe the Virgin Mary appeared repeatedly beginning in 1981; and *Santiago de Compostela* in Spanish Galiza, a medieval site associated with St. James (figs. 3.8 and 3.9). Fátima alone attracts over 4 million pilgrims annually, as does Lourdes. In the centennial year of the miracle at Lourdes in 1958, an astounding 8 million visitors came. Small wonder that this small provincial town ranks second in France only to Paris in number of hotels.

Figure 3.9.   Pilgrims at Santiago de Compostela, the greatest of the shrines in Spain and a goal of pilgrims since the Middle Ages. It lies in Galiza. (Photo by T.G.J.-B. 1999.)

Protestantism

Protestantism is the traditional faith of the European north, centered in the lands around the shores of the North and Baltic Seas (fig. 3.1). About 90 million persons presently claim Protestant affiliation, forming roughly 13% of the total population.

In marked contrast to Catholicism, the most profound geographical feature of European Protestantism is its fragmentation into separate denominational regions, a splintering present from the very first, due to the work of multiple Reformation leaders (fig. 3.6). *Lutheranism* has the largest geographical distribution, including the Scandinavian countries, Iceland, Estonia, Finland, Latvia, and half of Germany (figs. 3.1 and 3.10). No central Lutheran authority exists in Europe, and the faith is divided into a series of independent national churches.

The *Anglican* denomination remains the official established church in England, with lesser branches in the other British provinces, as well as in Ireland, and *Presbyterianism,* derived from Calvinism, enjoys the status of official Church of Scotland, with an adult communicant membership of about 800,000. Also in the United Kingdom are an array of so-called free churches that lack official status but are nevertheless traditional denominations of long standing. The largest of these is *Methodism,* with a community

Figure 3.10.   A rural Lutheran church in southwestern Iceland. This modest, Gothic-influenced structure is typical of the Protestant cultural landscape in Iceland, a barren European outpost island in the North Atlantic. (Photo by T.G.J.-B. 1971.)

of about 1.3 million, with lesser numbers of *Baptists* and many others. The *Dutch Reformed* Church, another Calvinist-derived body, is centered in the northern Netherlands and has about 2 million adherents today. In Switzerland, the Protestant majority belongs to a church that combines Calvinist, Lutheran, and Zwinglian influences. About all that remains of the work of Jan Hus, the first Reformation leader, is a community of some 200,000 *Brethren* in Czechia.

All of these traditional Protestant groups in Europe have experienced sharp declines, particularly since about 1900. *Neo-Protestantism* provides an exception. In the past several decades, evangelical-fundamentalist groups, often based in the United States, have begun actively missionizing Europe, both in the Protestant north and the formerly communist east (fig. 3.11). Pentecostals, Jehovah's Witnesses, Seventh-day Adventists, and Baptists have been especially active. Ethnic minorities such as the Sami of the far north and South Asians in the United Kingdom have been particularly attracted to neo-Protestantism. Romania, perhaps typical of eastern Europe, now has about 160,000 converts. In Russia, neo-Protestantism won many new members, especially after 1990.

As a result of the diversity of European Protestantism, no single religious landscape has been produced. As a rule, however, Protestantism possesses far less visibility than Catholicism. Church buildings tend to be

Figure 3.11.   Neo-Protestant church in southern Sweden. The church buildings are humble in appearance. Evangelical Christians have won many converts in Scandinavia and Finland. (Photo by T.G.J.-B. 1989.)

smaller and far less ornate, pilgrimage places are absent, and no wayside shrines line the roadsides (fig. 3.10). Some Protestant groups traditionally rejected all visible ostentation, rendering their presence almost invisible. For example, the modest Methodist chapels of Wales, lacking steeples and stained glass, often prove difficult for the uninitiated even to identify as places of worship (fig. 3.12).

Instead, Protestant influences should be sought in other aspects of European culture. *Individualism,* so central a trait in modern European culture, may have its roots in the Protestant Reformation. The far-reaching *Industrial Revolution* (see chapter 9), which so profoundly reshaped European culture, also likely derives from Protestantism. The inherently dynamic character of Protestantism, the willingness of its adherents to accept change and strive for self-improvement, coupled with the Protestant ethic of hard work and the rejection of Catholic restrictions on lending money for interest, provided necessary social precedents for the Industrial Revolution. Modern industrialism arose in Protestant lands and only belatedly spread into Catholic and Orthodox areas, though nonreligious factors such as the location of coal deposits help explain industrial origin and dispersal. Earlier, Catholic persecution of French Calvinists (or *Huguenots*) and Protestant Flemings, including many skilled artisans, caused an emigration of these craftsmen to England, northern Germany, and Holland. The Protestant

Figure 3.12.   This Methodist chapel in the Lleyn Peninsula of Celtic Wales reflects the architectural simplicity preferred by British "free" churches and helps produce a very subdued religious landscape. (Photo by the T.G.J.-B. 1974.)

countries thereby gained a valuable industrial impetus, while the Catholic lands, particularly France, lagged behind.

Given such attitudinal and cultural contrasts, it is not surprising that the Protestant–Catholic border, helping divide Europe into north and south, witnessed much strife over the centuries. The Thirty Years' War (1618–1648), a Protestant–Catholic contest for possession of the core of Europe, devastated large areas of Germany and Czechia and caused enormous loss of life. Two centuries earlier the Hussite War, a similar contest, also caused much grief. Most of the religious border has since fallen quiet, and the 2 groups learned to live in peace. Only in Northern Ireland, where the population is about evenly divided between Protestants and Catholics, does the feud persist. An intrusive Protestant conquest and colonization occurred in Northern Ireland in the 1600s, followed by centuries of overlordship and attempted conversion by the Protestants. In recent decades, the province suffered from terrorist activity by extremists of both religious groups, with the result that Protestants and Catholics live mainly apart in segregated neighborhoods (fig. 3.13).

Eastern Orthodoxy

As its name implies, **Eastern Orthodox** Christianity prevails in the eastern part of Europe, especially in Greece, most of the Balkans, Ukraine, Belarus,

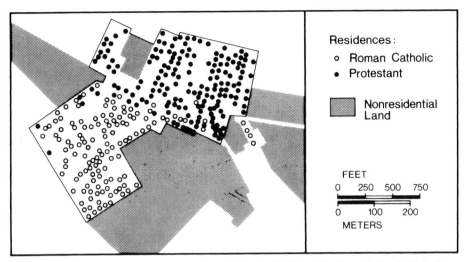

Figure 3.13. On the Protestant–Catholic divide, in Belfast, Northern Ireland. Only here does strife continue on the great north–south religious border in Europe, with the result that people have become residentially segregated along denominational lines. (*Source:* Boal 1969, 37.)

Georgia, and Russia (fig. 3.1). Perhaps 130 million Europeans profess this faith, roughly 18% of the total population of the culture area. The Eastern Church, steeped in mysticism and communalism, retains far more of the Asiatic qualities of the original Christianity, unaltered by the Renaissance, Reformation, and Enlightenment. Though grievously wounded by communism, Orthodoxy enjoys a rejuvenation today.

The patriarch of Constantinople, nominal leader of Orthodoxy, enjoys none of the central authority of the Roman papacy. Orthodoxy long ago began splintering into an array of national churches, including today Greek, Serbian, Bulgarian, Romanian, Russian, Cypriot, Estonian, Georgian, and two Ukrainian Orthodox groups. The leadership at Constantinople, or Istanbul, was permanently weakened when this capital of eastern Christendom fell to the Turks in 1453. Only 4,000 Christians remain in Istanbul today. Most recently, in 1996, the Russian Orthodox Church severed all ties to the patriarch.

Splintering extended still further. In Russia, the ultraconservative *Old Believers* separated from Orthodoxy in the late 1600s, and some 10 million followers lived in different parts of Russia by 1910. Today, only about 70,000 remain, centered in Belarus, Latvia, Lithuania, and Russia, though a revival appears to be underway. Another conservative splinter group, the *Molokans*, dating from the 1700s, once had over a million followers, and today surviving parishes can be found in the Caucasus, south Russia, Ukraine, and Moldova. In 1991, the splintering continued when the *Free Orthodox Church* broke away from established Russian Orthodoxy.

The Orthodox religious landscape shares with that of Catholicism a beauty and vividness, while at the same time being both highly distinctive and regionally varied. Balkan church buildings, borrowing from the colorful and decorative Byzantine architectural style of the Greek south, attract the eye with abundant reds and yellows. Russian churches and monasteries display their own style, often built with wooden onion domes (fig. 3.14).

The Orthodox Church today is experiencing a revival in the Slavic north as churches and monasteries reopen, after seven decades of governmental oppression. In Russia, the Orthodox Church may well become a major element of the rising Russian nationalism.

The East–West Divide

The western border of Orthodoxy remains the most fundamental internal cultural divide in Europe. The importance of this border can hardly be overstated. In the Orthodox realm, east of this line, individualism, personal freedom, and materialism are far more weakly developed, while communalism and the link between religious faith and nationalism possess an ancient strength. Western European democracy and the market economy will find less fertile soil in the east.

The border between eastern and western Christianity is both stable in location and well marked on the cultural landscape. Perhaps the best place to observe this ancient divide is the small Russian town of Pechory, situated directly on the Estonian border, a remarkable outpost of the Greco-Russian religious world. An impressive and beautiful Orthodox monastery, itself a pilgrimage destination, dominates Pechory, announcing visibly this perimeter of the Orthodox realm (fig. 3.15). A scant few kilometers away lies Estonia, belonging to the West, to the domain of the Reformation, Renaissance, and Enlightenment. Pechory, by contrast, is all about eastern mysticism and the mysteries of faith. Russia and the East begin simultaneously here.

A very short distance from Pechory stands the ruined stone fortress of Izborsk, built over a millennium ago to fend off invaders from the west. Just beyond Izborsk, towards the provincial city of Pskov, is the venerated place where the Russian hero-prince, Aleksandr Nevsky, met and crushed a German Catholic military order, the Teutonic Knights, on the ice of frozen Chudskoye Lake in 1242, a victory commemorated by a huge statue and monument. Nevsky's defiant words, "who comes here bearing a sword will die by the sword," are remembered by Russians to the present day.

For a thousand years and more, then, this segment of the great European cultural divide has been marked and defended. All who would understand the multiplicity of Europe should come to this place. Standing there, you might well conclude, instead, that Europe *ends* in this place, that here we find the elusive eastern border of the culture area.

Go stand on this same line much farther south, in the Balkans. Listen,

Figure 3.14.   A venerable wooden Russian Orthodox church, in the town of Suzdal, east of Moskva. Eastern Orthodoxy produces distinctive regional religious landscapes. (Photo by T.G.J.-B. 1999.)

Figure 3.15.   The great monastery at Pechory, in far western Russia, is an Orthodox outpost on Europe's main religious divide. (Photo by T.G.J.-B. 1999.)

with author Michael Ignatieff, to a Serb militiaman—a representative of the Orthodox east—as he explains how the neighboring Catholic Croats (who speak the same language, Serbo-Croatian) differ from Serbs. "Those Croats, they think they're better than us. Think they're fancy Europeans." The guns of war fell silent over a half-century ago at Pechory, but in the Balkans the east–west war has flared anew.

Uniate and Armenian Churches

A fourth, minor division of European Christianity consists of the **Uniate** Church, centered in western Ukraine and adjacent parts of Romania, Slovakia, Hungary, and Poland. Also referred to as "Greek Catholic" or "Ukrainian Catholic," this church claims about 6 million adherents. It is that rarest of hybrids—an attempted merging of eastern and western Christianity, along the religious divide. The Uniate Church derives from the long Catholic Polish and Austrian rule of an Orthodox area. The Catholic monarchs demanded that their Orthodox subjects acknowledge the authority and supremacy of the Roman pope. Beneath that façade of Catholicism, the Uniate Church retained most Orthodox rites and practices, such as a married priesthood. When Polish and Austrian rule ended, Uniate Christians suffered persecution by Russian czarist Orthodoxy and, later, Communists. When freedom of religion was restored in 1990, the church reemerged vigorously in the western part of Ukraine, becoming one statement of national identity. Some 2,000 parishes reopened, and the future of the revitalized Uniate Church seems secure.

The **Armenian** (or *Gregorian*) Church, while a branch of eastern Christianity, is independent of Orthodoxy and never acknowledged the supremacy of the patriarch at Constantinople. This ethnic church, with perhaps 1.5 million adherents, is one of the oldest branches of Christendom and today survives in independent Armenia, the embattled southeasternmost outpost of Europe and Christianity.

Dechristianization

A substantial part of the European population is secularized. Terms such as **dechristianization** and **post-Christian** have been used in describing modern Europe. Some 190 million Europeans profess to be nonreligious, amounting to more than a quarter of the total population. The geographical pattern of dechristianization appears complicated and difficult to generalize (fig. 3.16). In some regions, especially in the north and east, over half of the population is secularized, such as in most of Scandinavia, Eurorussia,

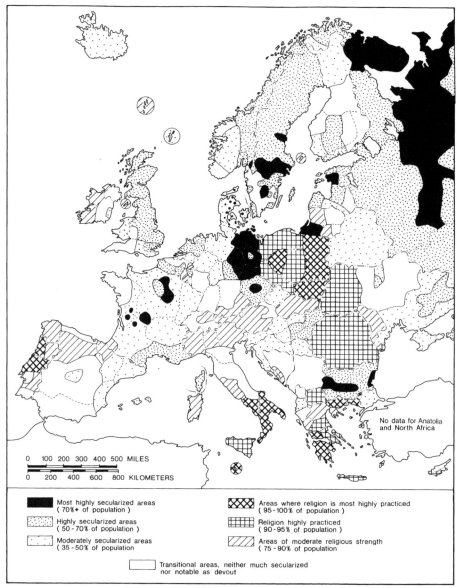

Figure 3.16. Secularization and religious vitality in Europe. *Secular* is defined as some combination of the responses "atheist," "agnostic," "nonreligious," "no religious faith," and "never attend church." (*Sources: Eurobarometer* 1995, 42:B61–B62, and its public-opinion survey in western and eastern Europe by the Gallup Poll Social Survey for the Commission of the European Communities in 1991/1992; Catholic News Service 1993; Media and Opinion Research Department of Radio Free Europe/Radio Liberty Research Institute 1992; Gustafsson 1957, 145; Boulard 1954, 48, 79, folded map at end; Gay 1971, 264–265, 273; Duocastella 1965, 281–282; Knudsen 1986, 7; Lehmann 1998; Krindatch 1996, 44; Nolan and Nolan 1989, 31–32.)

the United Kingdom, the Netherlands, and Czechia. Eastern Germany—the formerly communist area—is thoroughly dechristianized, as are parts of France and Bulgaria. If measured by national units, the most thoroughly secular countries are Estonia, with 61% of its population claiming to be nonreligious, agnostic, and/or atheist; Czechia 56%; Eurorussia 49%; France 48%; Germany and the United Kingdom 44%; Denmark 43%; and the Netherlands 40% (fig. 3.1). In France, fewer than 1 person in 10 goes to religious services even once per year, and the Church of England is regularly attended by a mere 2% of the population. Even in Ireland, once a bastion of Catholic strength, over a quarter of the population today claims no religious faith, and the Irish abandoned the church more rapidly than any other European group in the 1990s.

Within Eurorussia, the northern regions are clearly the most disaffected. In the Republic of Karelia, 62% of the people are indifferent to religion, and in the Komi Republic 55%. The districts along the Volga River, in eastern Eurorussia, are the least dechristianized, ranging between 25% and 35%, though secularization is more pronounced in ethnic minority republics there, such as Chuvashia (47%), Mari El (40%), Mordovia (37%), and Tatarstan (40%) (for locations refer back to fig. 1.8).

By contrast, refuge regions of surviving Christian vitality include a belt from Poland through western Ukraine to Romania, nearly all of Greece, southern Italy, western Iberia, the Irish west, and an area overlapping parts of the Alps and the Po–Veneto Plain. In Greece, 93% of the people claim to be religious and in Portugal 89%. In the German province of Bayern, part of the Alpine zone of religious intensity and a center of Catholicism, the parliament in 1995 passed a law requiring crucifixes to be hung in all school classrooms, defying a supreme court ruling against this practice and citing "the historical and cultural character of Bayern."

The decades-long persecution of the church under communist regimes in the east clearly helps explain the dechristianization pattern, though it does not address the issues of how Polish Catholicism, Romanian Orthodoxy, or the Ukrainian Uniate Church so successfully resisted that oppression or why Scandinavia and Britain are so secular. Arguably, the north never became thoroughly Christianized, lying remote from the centers of church authority. Of the three main divisions of Christianity, Catholicism clearly resisted secularization most successfully, while Protestantism suffered the greatest losses. In formerly Lutheran-dominated Latvia, only 7.5% of the people claim to be practicing Protestants, while in the United Kingdom, almost half the adult population never attends church.

Some apparent dechristianization may, instead, be reaction against the established churches, particularly since these groups often have status as official state churches and are supported by tax revenues. The success of the neo-Protestant movement suggests as much. It works the other way, too. Professed devotion to the church could be the reaction to governmental suppression, as happened in Poland. For these reasons, a better measure of secularization might be the proportion of the population that believes the Christian Easter promise of eternal life. By this measure, Greece at 57% and Poland at 61% appear far less religious, as do Denmark at 26% and Slovenia at 33%.

Though many Europeans hold secular views, the influence of a Christian heritage still permeates the culture of Europe. An entire mindset was shaped by Christianity. That cornerstone of the culture area will persist as long as Europe exists. The two are inseparable. True, some say that secularized Europe lives on "old capital" inherited from Christianity and therefore represents a culture in decline, its basic institutions supported only by inertia, but others counter that agnostic intellectual freedom, unfettered by religious dogma, represents the logical culmination of the European experiment in individualism.

Sects and Cults

Dechristianization has left an emotional and spiritual void in the lives of many Europeans. Some sought to fill this void with political ideologies, such as communism. Indeed, communists took over some of the precepts of Christianity, such as the victorious proletariat ("the meek shall inherit the earth"), spreading the Revolution (missionizing the world), the godly status of Marx and Lenin (presented as new Russian icons, or holy images), and a code of personal moral behavior. For others, nationalism became the new faith, as in Nazi Germany.

Others turn to New Age sects and cults in Europe. In France alone, the government has identified and investigated 172 sects and 800 "groups," with some 260,000 members. Many of these sects engage in mind control and are considered dangerous. Included are the *Holy City of Mandar'om* on a mountaintop in southern France, ruled by a "Cosmic Messiah." More sinister was the *Order of the Solar Temple,* active in both Switzerland and France, which conducted two mass suicides in 1994.

In Britain, the *Druids* have returned to ancient sites such as Stonehenge, and nearby Glastonbury has become the focus of several New Age cults. Concern has also been expressed about the activities of the *Church of Scientology* in Germany and France, and the governments of both countries have brought legal charges against this group, including fraud and tax evasion.

Non-Christian Minorities

The diffusion of Christianity through Europe proved almost complete, leaving little in the way of minority religions. Today, the only substantial non-Christian presence consists of Muslims, or **Islamic** peoples. For the past 1,200 years, the southern and southeastern borders of the European culture area have coincided with the Christian–Muslim religious divide, a boundary that has shifted back and forth amid frequent warfare (fig. 3.1). In modern times, the border has taken on a First World–Third World meaning. Christianity in the Eastern Hemisphere correlates geographically with Europe, prosperity, and high living standards, while Islam connotes non-Europe, the "other," widespread poverty, and increasing resistance to dominance by Europeans. A much higher birth rate in most Islamic areas provides an additional basis for continuing culture conflict. A pronounced "we versus they," "European versus alien" outlook has developed concerning Islam.

As is true of nearly every cultural border, the Christian–Islamic line is in many areas not a sharp one. Only Gibraltar offers a clear-cut division, achieved by systematic ethnic cleansing centuries ago. In fact, nearly 20 million Muslims reside in modern Europe. Most of these live in ancient homelands, including the *Bosnians* (Muslim Slavs of Bosnia–Herzegovina); *Pomaks* (Muslim Slavs of Bulgaria, Serbia, Kosovo, and Macedonia); most *Albanians; Turks* in several countries; and assorted minorities living in the Caucasus, in particular the *Abkhazis* and *Adzhars* of Georgia and, in the Russian Caucasus, about 5 million *Chechens, Ingushis, Dagestanis, Balkaris, Cherkessians,* and others. Another 5 million Muslims—the Turkic Tatars and *Bashkortis*—live in republics on the southeastern margins of Russia's East European Plain and in the Crimean Peninsula of Ukraine (fig. 3.17).

Many other Muslims, at least 8 million in all, are recent immigrants to Europe, particularly from Turkey, North Africa, and Pakistan. France, with 4 million such immigrants, largely *Arabs;* Germany with 2 million, mainly Turks and *Kurds;* and Great Britain, with 1 million, mainly from the Indian subcontinent, house the largest populations. The French port city of Marseille alone has 150,000 Muslims in its population of 800,000, and 43 mosques.

Often, the reaction of Europeans to these Muslim minorities is prejudice, hatred, or worse. A French politician recently spoke of "the smell of Islam" permeating certain neighborhoods in Paris. Even though two-thirds of the North African Muslims of France no longer practice the faith and only 10% are devout, the government in 1999 banned Islamic head scarves for schoolgirls. One French political extremist declared Islam to be "incompatible with our civilization and our laws." Turks and Kurds face similar prejudice in Germany. Many Europeans fear that "calls to Islamic prayer will drown out church bells," as journalist Roger Cohen of the *New York Times* put it. Given these biases, can Muslim immigrants ever be accepted as Europeans?

Hostility is directed not just toward the Islamic immigrants, but also against Muslim peoples living in their ancestral homelands. Catholic Croats and Orthodox Serbs battered Bosnian Muslim enclaves in the 1990s with a ferocity reminiscent of the Crusades. On Europe's southern cultural frontier, Armenians recently warred against Muslim Azeris; Georgians

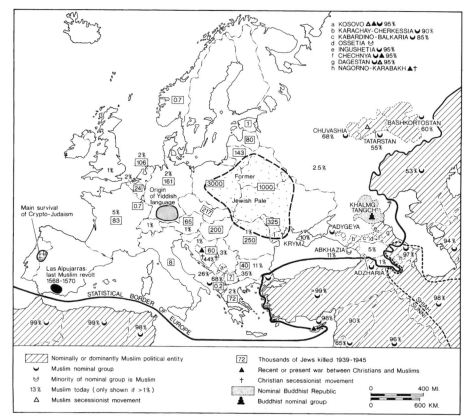

a KOSOVO ▲▲◡ 95%
b KARACHAY-CHERKESSIA ◡ 90%
c KABARDINO-BALKARIA ◡ 85%
d OSSETIA ◡
e INGUSHETIA ◡ 95%
f CHECHNYA ◡▲ 95%
g DAGESTAN ◡▲ 95%
h NAGORNO-KARABAKH ▲†

Figure 3.17.   The non-Christian periphery and former Jewish Diaspora. Islam and Judaism both present Europe with a perceived challenge to the very essence of its culture. Both minorities have been handled harshly. Within YU, separate Muslim data are shown for Kosovo and Crna Gora; the figure shown in YU is for the remainder of Serbia, including Vojvodina. The Jewish dead total shown on the border of UA and BY is the Soviet Union total, less EST, LT, LV, and MD. Of this total, about 625,000 deaths occurred in UA. (*Sources:* Roth 1974, 368–373; King 1992, 419–439.)

against Abkhazis; and Greek Cypriots against Turkish Cypriots (fig. 3.17). Muslim Chechens defy Russian rule today, and their rebel leader declared in 1999 that "we fight to protect our land and the religion of Allah." Other Caucasus Islamic minorities could follow Chechnya's example. Yugoslavia tried to cleanse Kosovo of Albanian Muslims, and Bulgaria, in 1989, expelled hundreds of thousands of Muslim Turks, most of whom later returned. Earlier, in 1877–1878, many Muslims were expelled from Bulgaria, causing it to become a Christian majority country. Tensions between Orthodox Greece and Muslim Turkey never completely relaxed, and the two countries fought a war in the 1920s. Clearly, Islam simultaneously gives focus to European cultural identity and, in the European mind, threatens that very identity. We should not, then, expect an early entry of Turkey into the European Union.

Contrary to some popular perception, Islamic fundamentalism and revival have generally not caught hold among most European Muslims. Indeed, Bosnians and Albanians had become secularized, even before the advent of communism in the 1940s. We often witness, incredibly, dechristianized Europeans battling secularized Muslims. Ethnicity succeeded religiosity and the old struggle continues.

Islam announces its defiant presence in the cultural landscape emphatically. The minarets of mosques pierce the sky as aggressively as the spires of Christendom (fig. 3.18). When Christians overrun and ethnically cleanse Muslim regions, the minarets and mosques are either quickly destroyed, as in Bosnia, or else converted into churches (fig. 3.19). Likewise, the great Orthodox cathedral of Constantinople, St. Sophia's, became a minaret-flanked mosque in Turkish Istanbul.

The other sizable religious minority in Europe consists of adherents to **Judaism,** today numbering only about 1.6 million. Their fate at the hands of Europeans in the twentieth century should cause Muslim minorities to fear for their lives, if they do not already. As recently as 1939, Europe was the world's principal Jewish home and the population stood at 9.7 million, about 60% of all Jews. In 1880, prior to the great Jewish migration to America, about 90% of all Jews resided in Europe. Not only was Europe the principal home of Judaism, but Jews such as Albert Einstein, Felix Mendelssohn, Benjamin Disraeli, Sigmund Freud, and Heinrich Heine had contributed greatly to European history and civilization. It mattered little. Jews, in the final analysis, were not permitted to be Europeans and were murdered by the millions. Only 3.9 million remained in Europe by the end of World War II, over half of whom have since emigrated.

France has more Jews in its population today, 530,000, than any other country, having received 220,000 Jews from Morocco and Algeria when those French colonies became independent in the 1950s and 1960s. French Jews live mainly on the Mediterranean coast and in Paris. Russia and Ukraine each retain only about 300,000 Jews. Reportedly, about 75,000 emigrate annually from Russia and 30,000 from Ukraine. Incredibly, many of these go to Germany, whose Jewish population has risen to 100,000, in spite of the fact that 819 anti-Semitic crimes occurred in that country in 1999 alone. The United Kingdom has 300,000 Jews, most of whom reside in greater London.

The Jewish presence in Europe, now so horribly diminished, had ancient roots. Jews reached Mediterranean Europe in Roman times, after their forced dispersal from Palestine. One major early concentration developed in Muslim Arabic Iberia, where Judaism won toleration, flourished, and eventually claimed perhaps one-fifth of the population. These Iberian Jews, or *Sephardim,* later faced eviction or forcible conversion to Roman Catholicism after the Christian reconquest, leaving behind only *Marranos* ("secret Jews"), and empty *judarias* ("ghettoes"). Their synagogues became churches. To the present day, in certain mountain towns of northern

Figure 3.18.   A Village mosque and minaret amid the ripened wheat fields of Rodos announce the presence of the Muslim minority on this Greek Aegean Island. Rodos is one of the few European areas where Christians and Muslims coexist peacefully. (Photo by T.G.J.-B. 1971.)

Figure 3.19.   The Giralda, a tower on the Roman Catholic cathedral at Sevilla in southern Spain, was originally the minaret of the Great Mosque when the city was Arabic and Muslim. After the reconquest and forced expulsion or conversion of the Muslims, victorious Christians added the bell chamber to the top. In this manner, a Muslim element was retained in the religious landscape. (Photo by T.G.J.-B. 1986.)

Portugal, Marranos still practice Jewish ritual while outwardly adhering to Roman Catholicism (fig. 3.17). Many Sephardic Jews fled Iberia and found new homes, particularly in Protestant countries such as Britain and the Netherlands. Another major Jewish concentration developed in medieval times in western and southern Germany, where the German-derived *Yiddish* language originated. These became the *Ashkenazim*, the second major division of European Jewry. In the late Middle Ages, Ashkenazic Jews, responding to an edict of tolerance and invitation to settle by the Kingdom of Poland, began the migration that created the great concentration in eastern Europe. This *Jewish Pale*, as it came to be called after Russia annexed it and forced the Jews to remain within set borders, became the principal focus of Jewish life and culture in the entire world (fig. 3.17). The Lithuanian city of Vilnius, within the Pale, was at one time the unrivaled center of Jewish culture, the "Jerusalem of the North," with 100 synagogues, libraries, and a population 40% Jewish. The Nazis utterly destroyed the Pale and its inhabitants.

Everywhere the vestigial Jewish identity is perishing. It will play little if any role in twenty-first-century Europe. The pervasive Christian identity and heritage of Europe prevented toleration of this small, creative religious minority. Any self-claim of Europe's cultural superiority, and these are not hard to find, must be measured against the treatment Europeans have afforded religious minorities over the centuries and down to the present day.

Christianity, then, represents the essential feature and underpinning of European culture. Even in an age of secularism, a Christian heritage still identifies Europe and all it represents. But there is more to understanding the distinctiveness of Europe than religious faith. Language provides a second defining trait, and the following chapter is devoted to geolinguistics.

Sources and Suggested Readings

Anderson, James. 1980. "Regions and Religions in Ireland: A Short Critique of the Two Nations Theory." *Antipode* 11:44–53.

Bar-Gal, Yoram. 1985. "The Shtetl—the Jewish Small Town in Eastern Europe." *Journal of Cultural Geography* 5 (2): 17–29.

Bleibrunner, H. 1951. "Der Einfluss der Kirche auf die niederbairische Kulturlandschaft." *Mitteilungen der Geographischen Gesellschaft in München* 36:7–196.

Boal, Frederick W. 1969. "Territoriality on the Shankill–Falls Divide." *Irish Geography* 6:30–50.

Boulard, Fernand. 1954. *Premiers itinéraires en sociologie religieuse.* Paris, F: Éditions Ouvrières Économie et Humanisme.

Boyer, Jean-C. 1996. "La frontière entre protestantisme et catholicisme en Europe." *Annales de Géographie* 105:119–140.

Bronsztejn, Szyja. 1991. "La condition et la répartition de la population juive en Pologne." *Hommes et Terres du Nord*, 42–45.

Catholic News Service. 1993. *Religious Beliefs and Practices in Twelve Countries 1991.* Washington, D.C., USA: Catholic News Service.

Connell, J. 1970. "The Gilded Ghetto: Jewish Suburbanization in Leeds." *Bloomsbury Geographer* 3:50–59.

Doherty, Paul. 1989. "Ethnic Segregation Levels in the Belfast Urban Area." *Area* 21:151–159.

———. 1993. "Religious Denomination in Northern Ireland, 1961 to 1991." *Irish Geography* 26:14–21.

Donkin, R. A. 1978. *The Cistercians: Studies in the Geography of Medieval England and Wales.* Toronto, CDN: Pontifical Institute of Medieval Studies.

Duocastella, Rogelio. 1965. "Géographie de la pratique religieuse en Espagne." *Social Compass* 12:253–302.

Gay, John D. 1971. *The Geography of Religion in England.* London, GB: Duckworth.

Girardin, Paul. 1947. "Les passages alpestres en liaison avec les abbayes, les pèlerinages et les saints de la montagne." *Geographica Helvetica* 2:65–74.

Gustafsson, Berndt. 1957. *Svensk kyrkogeografi, med samfundsbeskrivning.* Lund, S: Gleerup.

Hannemann, Manfred. 1975. *The Diffusion of the Reformation in Southwestern Germany, 1518–1534.* Chicago, USA: University of Chicago, Department of Geography, Research Paper No. 167.

Hard, Gerhard. 1965. "Eine Topographie der Pilgerwege von Deutschland nach Santiago in Spanien aus dem 15. Jahrhundert." *Erdkunde* 19:314–325.

Ignatieff, Michael. 1998. *The Warrior's Honor: Ethnic War and the Modern Conscience.* New York, USA: Henry Holt.

Jouret, Bernard. 1968. "L'influence du protestantisme dans l'économie douroise." *Revue Belge de Géographie* 92:61–74.

Jurkovich, James M., and Wilbert M. Gesler. 1997. "Medjugorje: Finding Peace at the Heart of Conflict." *Geographical Review* 87:447–467.

King, Robert D. 1992. "Migration and Linguistics as Illustrated by Yiddish." In *Reconstructing Languages and Cultures,* ed. Edgar C. Polomé and Werner Winter. Berlin, D: de Gruyter.

Knippenberg, Hans, and Sjoerd de Vos. 1989. "Spatial Structural Effects on Dutch Church Attendance." *Tijdschrift voor Economische en Sociale Geografie* 80:164–170.

Knudsen, Jon P. 1986. "Culture, Power, and Periphery—the Christian Lay Movement in Norway." *Norsk Geografisk Tidsskrift* 40:1–14.

Kress, Hans-Joachim. 1968. *Die islamische Kulturepoche auf der iberischen Halbinsel: Eine historisch-kulturgeographische Studie.* Marburg, D: Geographisches Institut, Universität Marburg.

Krindatch, Alexei D. 1996. *Geography of Religions in Russia.* Decatur, Ga., USA: Glenmary Research Center.

Lambert, E. 1943. "Le livre de Saint Jacques et les routes du pèlerinage de Compostelle." *Revue Géographique des Pyrénées et du Sud-Ouest* 14:5–33.

Lautensach, Hermann. 1960. *Maurische Züge im geographischen Bild der Iberischen Halbinsel.* Bonn, D: F. Dümmler.

Lehmann, Susan G. 1998. "Inter-ethnic Conflict in the Republics of Russia in Light of Religious Revival." *Post-Soviet Geography and Economics* 39:461–493.

Lendl, Egon. 1965. "Zur religionsgeographischen Problematik des europäischen Südostens." *Verhandlungen des Deutschen Geographentages 1963,* 34:129–139.

Martyniuk, Jaroslaw. 1993. "Religious Preferences in Five Urban Areas of Ukraine." *Radio Free Europe/Radio Liberty Research Report* 2 (15): 52–55.

McGrath, Fiona. 1989. "Characteristics of Pilgrims to Lough Derg." *Irish Geography* 22:44–47.

Media and Opinion Research Department of Radio Free Europe/Radio Liberty Research Institute. 1992. "Unpublished Survey in Ukraine." Washington, D.C., USA: Media and Opinion Research Department of Radio Free Europe/Radio Liberty Research Institute.

Mours, Samuel. 1966. *Essai sommaire de géographie du protestantisme réformé français au XVIIe siècle.* Paris, F: Librarie Protestante.

Newman, David. 1985. "Integration and Ethnic Spatial Concentration: Changing Spatial Distribution of Anglo-Jewish Community." *Transactions of the Institute of British Geographers* 10:360–376.

Nolan, Mary Lee. 1983. "Irish Pilgrimage: The Different Tradition." *Annals of the Association of American Geographers* 73:421–438.

Nolan, Mary Lee, and Sidney Nolan. 1989. *Religious Pilgrimage in Modern Western Europe.* Chapel Hill, USA: University of North Carolina Press.

de Planhol, Xavier. 1962. "L'islam dans la physiognomie géographique de la Péninsule Iberique." *Revue Géographique des Pyrénées et du Sud-Ouest* 33:274–281.

Richard, Jann. 1996. "Géographie religieuse et géopolitique en Biélorussie du XVIe siècle a nos jours." *Annales de Géographie* 105:141–163.

Rinschede, Gisbert. 1985. "The Pilgrimage Town of Lourdes." In *Geographia Religionum, 1. Grundfragen der Religions-geographie,* ed. Manfred Buttner et al. Berlin, D: Dietrich Reimer, 1–61.

———. 1992. "Pilgerzentrum Fátima/Portugal." *Geographie Heute* 106:15–22.

Roth, Cecil. 1974. *A History of the Marranos.* 4th ed. New York, USA: Hermon.

Schwartz, Lee. 1991. "A Note on the Jewish Population of the USSR from the 1989 Census Data." *Soviet Geography* 32:433–435.

Semple, Ellen Churchill. 1927. "The Templed Promontories of the Ancient Mediterranean." *Geographical Review* 17:353–386.

Sidorov, Dmitri. 2000. "The Resurrection of the Cathedral of Christ the Savior in Moscow." *Annals of the Association of American Geographers* 90:548–572.

Stanislawski, Dan. 1975. "Dionysus Westward: Early Religion and the Economic Geography of Wine." *Geographical Review* 65:427–444.

Vertovec, Steven, and Cori Peach, eds. 1997. *Islam in Europe.* London, GB: Macmillan and St. Martin's.

Waterman, Stanley, and Barry Kosmin. 1988. "Residential Patterns and Processes: A Study of Jews in Three London Boroughs." *Transactions of the Institute of British Geographers* 13:79–95.

Whelan, Kevin. 1983. "The Catholic Parish, the Catholic Chapel, and Village Development in Ireland." *Irish Geography* 16:1–15.

———. 1988. "The Regional Impact of Irish Catholicism, 1700–1850." In *Common Ground: Essays on the Historical Geography of Ireland,* ed. William J. Smyth and Kevin Whelan. Cork, IRL: Cork University Press, 253–277.

CHAPTER 4

Geolinguistics

Language is the bearer of culture, the principal means by which communication within cultural groups occurs and traditions pass from one generation to another. For these reasons, language identifies cultural groups, and as earlier proposed, the Indo-European tongues provide 1 of the 3 basic distinguishing traits of the culture of Europe. While less crucial than Christianity in distinguishing the culture area, language nevertheless plays a substantial role in creating Europe's human uniqueness. Geolinguistics encompasses the geographical study of languages.

The Indo-European Language Family

Linguistically, Europe presents a crazy-quilt pattern surpassed in complexity by few other parts of the world. A Babel of tongues characterizes the culture area (fig. 4.1). In Europe and Eurorussia, nearly 100 separate and mutually unintelligible languages are spoken, in addition to the almost countless local dialects. Moreover, the complex linguistic geography is ever changing. Over the centuries and millennia, some languages spread and grew, while others retreated to refuge areas, and still others vanished, leaving behind only a few words adopted into surviving tongues or perhaps merely a sprinkling of unintelligible place names.

In the face of this linguistic kaleidoscope, the overarching kinship of the **Indo-European** languages offers some unity and cohesion. The linguistic kinship of the various Indo-European languages can be illustrated by comparing their vocabularies, especially words that describe commonplace things encountered in everyday life. Consider, for example, the word for *three* in various Indo-European tongues: *tre* or *tri* in Erse, Albanian, Italian, Swedish, Russian, Czech, and Serbo-Croatian; *tría* in Greek; *tres* in Spanish; *trei* in Romanian; *thrír* in Icelandic; *trzy* in Polish; and *trys* in Lithuanian.

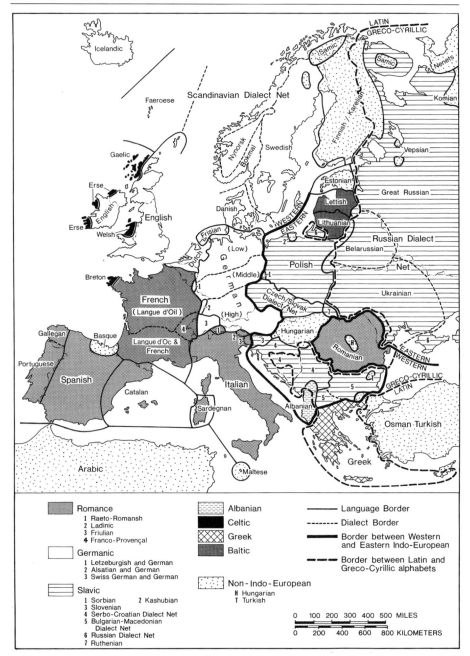

Figure 4.1.   Languages and selected dialects of modern Europe. See also figure 1.8. Many forms of speech normally considered separate languages, such as Swedish or Ukrainian, are perhaps better regarded as dialects enmeshed in nets. (*Sources:* Zaborski 2000; Straka 1979; Alinei et al. 1983; Comrie 1994; Mackenzie 1994.)

Contrast these to the words for "three" in non-Indo-European languages, such as *uç* in Turkish, *kolme* in Finnish, or *három* in Hungarian.

Sometimes kindred words have taken on somewhat different meanings in the various Indo-European languages. For example, the word meaning *stone* in the vanished ancient, ancestral Indo-European speech was *kemen*, from which we derive modern English *cement* (stonelike) and *cemetery* (place of the standing stones); Spanish *camino* ("road"; paved with stones); German *kamin* ("fireplace"; stone hearth); English *chimney* (the part of a house made of stone); Albanian *kaminë* ("heap," "pile," or "mass"; as of stones); and Russian *kamen* ("stone"). In this case, Russian has retained the ancient meaning, but the derivation of all the others can easily be understood. It is these kinships, both the obvious and the obscure, that link languages in the Indo-European family.

The most ancient Indo-European, the parent language, was apparently spoken about 9000 or 10,000 B.C. in the Middle East, in Anatolia and along the borders of modern Turkey, Syria, and Iraq. Its speakers, it seems, were the first farmers—the people who initially domesticated plants and animals. Indo-European apparently spread with agriculture from this ancient hearth area. As they dispersed in different directions, the speakers of the parent language lost contact with each other, causing their speech to diverge. Also, they encountered and absorbed indigenous hunter-gatherers who spoke different languages, and in the process some words and pronunciations were borrowed.

Indo-European Diffusion

In the formative stage of Indo-European speech in Turkish Anatolia, about 8000 B.C., different dialects developed, due to linguistic drift and mixing with alien peoples. A *dialect net* formed, meaning a linguistic continuum in which the speakers of each dialect could understand the neighboring ones but not those spoken farther away in regions with which they had no regular contact. Further fragmentation into separate, mutually unintelligible *languages*, in which adjacent Indo-European peoples could not understand each other, seems to have occurred whenever the dialect net was "torn." That likely happened where the farming frontier, spreading slowly west and north from Anatolia, at the rate of about 1 kilometer every 20 years, encountered physical geographical obstacles. Indo-European pioneer farmers branched around these obstacles, some going one way and some the other. When that occurred, the two groups lost contact with each other for centuries and their speech drifted apart. Generations later, when they coalesced beyond the obstacle, they could not understand each other.

The first such tear, a profound one, apparently occurred about 6000 B.C. when one branch of the Indo-Europeans spread westward from Anatolia into the Aegean isles and beyond, onto the Greek mainland, while the other went north along the Black Sea's western coast (fig. 4.2). The split between western and eastern divisions of Indo-European may instead have been induced by the catastrophic creation of the Black Sea, about 5600 B.C. Scientists recently determined that, prior to then, the Black Sea was a much smaller, interior-drainage lake, lacking a connection to the Aegean and standing 120 meters below sea level (see Ryan and Pitman). The sea suddenly burst through the natural dam at what is today the Bosporos, spilling in and enlarging the Black Sea to its present size. In the process, the large lowland plain adjacent to modern Bulgaria, Romania, and Turkey was inundated—probably the great biblical flood. The Indo-European farmers living in these lowlands fled in different directions, some toward Turkey and Greece, others into the Balkans, likely ripping the dialect net. Whether caused by the Aegean water barrier or the Black Sea flood, this tear produced the divide between **Western** and **Eastern** (formerly called *Centum* and *Satem,* respectively) **Indo-European,** a divide that would later extend all the way to the Baltic Sea, for when the two branches met again to the north, their speech had drifted too far apart to be understood.

Fragmentation continued. The eastern branch perhaps divided at the Stara Planina, with *Thracian* developing to the south among flood refugees in the Maritsa Valley (see fig. 2.1), while in the north, perhaps even beyond the corridor of steppe grasslands, on the margin of the East European Plain, arose the ancestral Balto-Slavs, descendants of others who fled the waters. In their continued northward moving, they apparently divided around the Pripyat Marsh, separating the ancient *Baltic* and *Slavic* languages. The Slavs drove east and north, eventually populating a wedge between the 120-day growing season on the north and the steppes to the south, pushing agriculture as far as the prehistoric technology would allow and providing, in the short run at least, a satisfactory eastern border for "Europe" (fig. 4.2).

Equally profound tears in the dialect net happened at obstacles in the west. From Greece, where *Hellenic* speech developed, some Indo-Europeans migrated across the Strait of Otranto to Italy, apparently giving rise to the *Italic*-speaking group, while others seem to have pressed north about the same time through the Vardar–Morava rift valley, a narrows that restricted contact with the Hellenes to the south. Emerging into the Hungarian Basin, they became the *Danubian* people. The proto-*Celtic* culture evolved later, at the northern foot of the Alps, from the Danubian parent and eventually spread to dominate most of central and northwestern Europe. Other Danubians went north into Scandinavia by way of the Jylland Peninsula of modern Denmark, crossing the infertile outwash plain and following a narrow strip of fertile land along the fjorded east coast of Jylland (fig. 4.2). Those venturing north along this route after about 3500 B.C. apparently became the *Germanic* peoples.

What happened in Iberia remains even less clear. The substantial survival of non-Indo-European languages there into historic times suggests a different linguistic order prevailed. Perhaps farmers speaking Afro-Asiatic

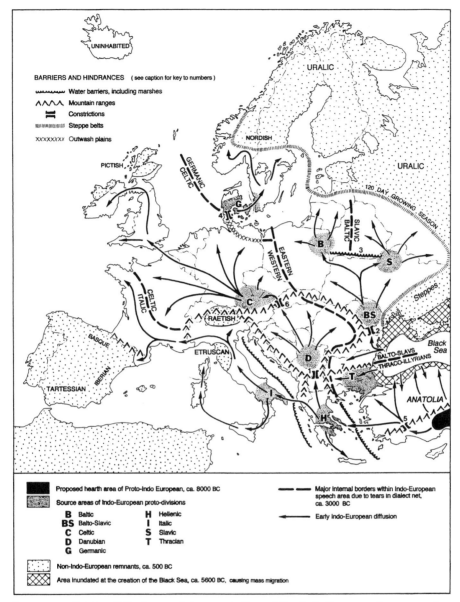

Figure 4.2. Origin, diffusion, and fragmentation of the Indo-European languages from 8000 to 3000 B.C.: a geographical speculation. Residual non-Indo-European speakers survived best in border areas between languages and in harsh environments marginally suited to agriculture. Key to groups: B = proto-Balts; BS = proto-Balto-Slavs; C = proto-Celts; D = Danubic; G = proto-Germanic; H = proto-Hellenes; I = proto-Italic; S = proto-Slavs; and T = proto-Thraco-Illyrians. Key to nonobvious obstacles: 1. Vardar–Morava rift valley; 2. constriction between Carpathians and steppes; 3. Pripyat Marsh; 4. Jylland narrows, a wedge of fertile land between marshes and outwash plains on the west and south and the Schlei Fjord on the east; 5. Cilician Gate, a passage through the Taurus Mountains; 6. Danube water gap; and 7. Stara Planina. (*Sources:* Krantz 1988; Ryan and Pitman 1998; Renfrew 1988, 1989, and personal communication 1999, all with very substantial modifications.)

tongues, belonging to a different language family, spread across North Africa, entered Iberia at Gibraltar, and continued northward until they met their fellow agriculturists, the Indo-Europeans, at the Pyrenees. If so, "Africa begins at the Pyrenees" describes an ancient condition, and the now extinct Tartessian and Iberian tongues were Afro-Asiatic. Basque, apparently an indigenous European language unrelated to either Indo-European or Afro-Asiatic, could have survived along the contact zone of the two immigrant farming peoples (fig. 4.2).

A comparison of the diffusion of the Indo-European languages with that of Christianity reveals similarities as well as differences. Both of these cultural traits, so essential in shaping and defining Europe, arose in very nearly the same place in the Near East, well outside the present limits of the European culture area. Both spread from east to west, reaching Europe by way of the Aegean lands, and both split into eastern, western, and northern divisions. Indeed, the patterning is strikingly similar. Catholicism prevails in the Romance language region, Protestantism in the Germanic areas, and Orthodoxy in the Slavic lands, though exceptions to this generalization abound. Both religiously and linguistically, then, Europe falls into three major, spatially correlated components.

The two diffusions also differed in fundamental ways. The spread of Indo-European occurred much earlier, in prehistoric times. It proceeded wavelike instead of hierarchically from city to city and took far longer to complete—over 5,000 years for Indo-European and just over a millennium for Christianity. Also, the Christian diffusion left essentially no indigenous survivors and no religious equivalents of the Uralic or Basque speakers. Both diffusions demonstrate that in Europe we deal, to a considerable extent, with an *imported* rather than a native culture.

Many geolinguistic changes have occurred in Europe since 3000 B.C., when the Indo-European diffusion had largely run its course, though some features have displayed remarkable durability, such as the western–eastern divide and the tenacious survival of Basque and Uralic minorities. One notable change has been the continued tearing of the several dialect nets to form more and more languages. Over 90% of all Europeans are accounted for by 3 Indo-European divisions—Germanic, Slavic, and Romance, but each of these now contains multiple languages (fig. 4.1).

Romance Languages

The **Romance** languages, Western Indo-European in affiliation and forming 1 of 3 major divisions of the family, today claim about 185 million speakers in Europe, roughly one-fourth of the total population. Romance languages derive from the ancient Italic division of Indo-European (fig. 4.2). One Italic tongue, *Latin*, originally spoken only in the district of Lazio (Latium) around Roma, rose to dominance and achieved a remarkable dispersal.

When a language successfully expands in this manner, its speakers possess some cultural or technological advantage. In the case of Latin speakers, this advantage came in the form of superior political organization, which permitted empire building. Latin was the language of the Roman Empire. It spread with Roman victories, and by about A.D. 100 the Roman Empire, and with it Latin, reached its greatest territorial extent. The Romance tongue was heard on the banks of the Thames, Rhine, and Danube, as well as in North Africa. Few of the cultural groups ruled by the empire resisted linguistic assimilation, though the Greeks did because of their high culture. In fact, many Greek words found their way into Latin. The *Etruscans*, a highly civilized non-Indo-European group living just north of Roma, succumbed linguistically to Latin, but not before giving it the parent words for *people*, *public*, *military*, *autumn*, and other vocabulary that later passed from Romance into English speech. In Iberia, the Romans likely achieved the decisive introduction of Indo-European, wresting it away from the Afro-Asiatic peoples and a scattering of Celts.

When the empire collapsed, the Romance languages retreated but survived remarkably well. Germanic invaders brought their own language to Britain, the west bank of the Rhine, and the Alps, while Slavs and Magyars surged into the Balkans, leaving a lonely linguistic outpost in Romania as a reminder of the former eastern greatness of the Romans (fig. 4.1). In these forfeited areas, only place names survive today as remnants of the Latin tongue. In England, for example, *-caster* and *-chester* suffixes, as in Lancaster or Manchester, derive from *castra* (Latin for "military camp"). Later, when the Moors invaded Iberia beginning in the 700s, the Afro-Asiatic languages, especially Arabic, regained a foothold there, though the Latin-derived *Mozarabic* tongue survived as the language of Christians under Moorish rule. The subsequent defeat of the Moors by the Spaniards and Portuguese reclaimed nearly all of Iberia for the Romance languages and completely extinguished Arabic. Only abundant place names and numerous loanwords survive as reminders of the former Arabic presence (fig. 4.3).

The collapse of the Roman Empire accelerated the fragmentation of Latin into many separate languages. Mozarabic, now extinct like Latin, was only one of these. All of the surviving Romance tongues in modern Europe represent the fragmented legacy of Latin. Today, the Iberian Peninsula is home to three of these languages. Dominating the nation of Spain from the Meseta interior is *Castilian Spanish*, spoken by some 25 million people. Speakers of the *Catalan* language, numbering 9 million, are found in the eastern coastal fringe of Spain, the Baleares Islands, a corner of southern France, Andorra, and a foothold on the Italian isle of Sardegna. Catalan is now the dominant tongue in Barcelona and all of Catalunya, an autonomous region in Spain (fig. 4.4). Even France, which historically extended few rights and privileges to linguistic minorities, permits bilingual French–Catalan highway signs in its southern region, where Catalan is spoken. The Atlantic front of Iberia is home to *Portuguese-Gallegan*, a dialect net with

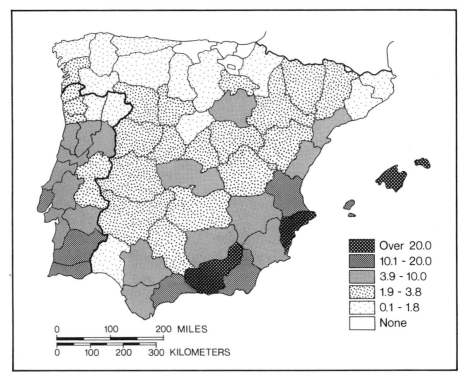

Figure 4.3.   Number of Arabic and Arabized topographic names per thousand square kilometers in Iberia. "Africa begins at the Pyrenees," according to a French saying, and a thousand years ago, that was almost literally true. Arabic and the Islamic faith had pushed European culture northward, almost to the Pyrenees. The subsequent Indo-European, Christian reconquest of Iberia left behind, as a reminder, many place names derived from the Arabic tongue. (*Sources:* After Lautensach 1954; Sopher 1955.)

Figure 4.4.   A sign in the Catalan language welcomes visitors to the independent state of Andorra in the Pyrenees. (Photo by T.G.J.-B. 1986.)

some 12 million speakers. The survival of Portuguese seems guaranteed by political independence, and Gallegan has achieved legal status in the autonomous Spanish province of Galiza, where it is the habitual language of daily use of 68% of the people.

Northward from Iberia, beyond the Pyrenees, is found *French*, the speech of the large majority of France's population as well as of the southern Belgians, or Walloons, the western Swiss, and residents of the Valle d'Aosta in northwest Italy, a total of some 54 million persons. The southern of two principal French tongues, *langue d'oc* gradually retreats before *langue d'oïl*, originally found only in the Parisian north. *Occitan* is the principal dialect in the langue d'oc region and is now being taught in some schools, ending two centuries of government suppression. *Italian*, with more speakers than French, some 58 million, is spoken not only in Italy but also on the island of Corsica, which belongs to France, Canton Ticino in southern Switzerland, and the Nice District on the French Riviera. The Tuscan dialect has become standard Italian speech, a heritage of the cultural greatness of Firenze. Italian has the third largest number of speakers among the languages of Europe.

Along the northern fringe of Romance speech, sheltered in Alpine valleys, are found several minor, dying tongues—*Romansh*, with 30,000 speakers and 2 main dialects in Graubünden (Grischun) Canton, eastern Switzerland; *Ladinic* in Italian South Tirol; and *Friuli* in the easternmost end of the Po–Veneto Plain. Collectively, these three constitute the Raeto-Romanic group. *Sardegnan*, with about 1.6 million speakers, survives on a Mediterranean island and is distinct from Italian.

Romanian, an eastern outlier of the Romance languages, is separated from the larger western area by the interposed South Slavs. This language, spoken by 24 million persons in Romania and adjacent Moldova, has survived in spite of invasions by Slavs, Magyars, and other groups, though the vocabulary is infiltrated with Slavic words. Closely related to Romanian is *Vlakh*, presumably derived from Valachia in southern Romania but today spoken by a few nomadic herding tribes in interior northern Greece and adjacent countries. The Vlakhs apparently descend from Romanians who migrated southward after the collapse of the Roman Empire to find refuge in the Dinaric–Pindhos mountain region. The seasonal shelters of Vlakh nomads may be seen at the foot of Mount Ólimbos in Greece and elsewhere.

The northern border of the Romance languages today, stretching from the English Channel to the head of the Adriatic Sea (fig. 4.1), displays a diverse character that relates to physical geography. Generally, where the border crosses plains, as in Vlaanderen and the upper Rhône Valley of Switzerland, it tends to be unstable and mobile. French advances against Dutch in the former and retreats before German in the latter. But where the language border follows mountain ridges, as in the St. Gotthard Pass region in the western Alps, it has remained unchanged for more than a thousand years. To cross St. Gotthard going north today, as in the Dark Ages, is to leave Romance speech and enter the Germanic lands.

Germanic Languages

The second of the 3 major Indo-European groups, also belonging to the western division of the family, consists of the **Germanic** languages, with about 190 million native speakers in Europe, almost exactly the size of the Romance population. One of every 4 Europeans speaks a Germanic language, and these tongues dominate most of northern and central Europe (fig. 4.1).

Geographical development of the Germanic languages over the past 5,000 years has been volatile. The Germanic branch probably arose, as described earlier, in the isolation of Jylland (fig. 4.2), and from there it spread through the Danish isles and into Scandinavia, absorbing a non-Indo-European race of hunters and fishers, a tall, blond people skilled in long-boat building and sometimes referred to as *Nordish*. From them the early Germanic people apparently adopted a sizable vocabulary, with the result that perhaps a quarter or even a third of all Germanic words today are not Indo-European in origin. The Germanic speakers, in the process, also took on many of the tall, blond racial traits of the indigenous hunter-fishers, as well as their seagoing abilities. In the colder conditions of the north, their grain crops developed into faster-maturing varieties to accommodate the shorter growing season, but the Germanic advance apparently halted at about the northern limits of the humid continental and marine west coast climates (compare figs. 2.7 and 4.2).

There, in the north, the Germanic people remained for millennia on the outer margins of the agricultural, Indo-European world. Then, about 500 B.C., the climate of Scandinavia became colder, in a deterioration that continued to the beginning of the Christian Era. Their response was remarkable. Nearly all Germanic people evacuated the north, boarding longboats and crossing the seas to resettle in the river valleys of northern Germany. These valleys, due to a pattern of springtime flooding that delayed planting and effectively shortened the growing season, had apparently remained largely uncolonized by the resident Celtic Indo-Europeans. The Germanic folk, with their fast-ripening grains, could occupy this riverine environment. Their southward advance continued, eventually displacing the Celts from Germany, leaving behind only a scattering of Celtic place names such as *Alp* ("mountain"), *Halle* ("salt"), and *Rhine* ("river"). With the collapse of the Roman Empire, Germanic tribes such as the Franks, Goths, Burgundians, and Lombards pressed far into Romance territory but usually failed to achieve a permanent implantation of their languages.

Elsewhere, the Germanic longboat invasions continued, bringing Anglo-Saxons to England and, after warmer climatic conditions resumed, accomplishing much agricultural recolonization in Scandinavia. From there, Viking longboats eventually reached the Faeroes, Iceland, and Greenland. For 1,500 years, Germanic longboats assisted the dispersal of these peoples.

In central Europe, about A.D. 700, the Germans developed an innovative, more intensive form of agriculture known as the *three-field system* (see chapter 11) and an effective system of organized government, the *feudal system*. Armed with those new technologies, they began expanding east at the expense of the Slavic peoples about A.D. 800, pushing the German language frontier well into present Poland and also eventually creating the eastern diaspora of Germans that recently returned home. Only a residue of Slavic place names survived in some parts of the North German Plain and Danube Valley as reminders of their former presence (fig. 4.5).

The single most important Germanic language, both in terms of the population of speakers and the number of countries where it serves as mother tongue, is *German.* About 90 million people speak this language, including majorities not just in Germany, but also in Austria, Switzerland, Liechtenstein, and Luxembourg. In addition, German-speaking provinces can be found in Italy (South Tirol, or Alto-Adige), eastern Belgium, and France (Alsace). German is the second language in Europe in number of speakers, surpassed only by Russian. Until very recently, large German minorities remained in many eastern European countries, especially Russia, Hungary, Romania, and Poland, though all of these groups have been greatly depleted by recent *return migration* to Germany after an absence of centuries. During the 6-year span from 1986 through 1992, the peak of the migration, over 1.5 million ethnic Germans departed eastern Europe, including the former Soviet Union, and went to Germany, where automatic

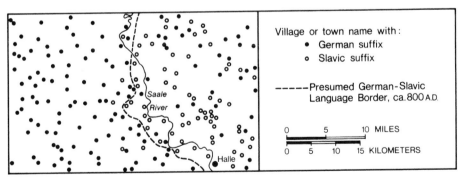

Figure 4.5.   An archaic language border in Germany. About the year A.D. 800, the German–Slavic boundary in central Europe lay roughly along the line of the Elbe and Saale Rivers. German-speaking settlers, in the 800–1300 period, surged eastward across this border, changing the linguistic pattern as they carried their speech far into Slavic territory. But even today, evidence of the old border of A.D. 800 remains in the form of Slavic place names. Villages with name suffixes such as *-itz, -in,* and *-zig* are of Slavic origin. Europe abounds with such archaic linguistic features.

citizenship awaited them. Romania's German minority dwindled from 360,000 in 1977 to only 17,000 by 1998. The German diaspora in eastern Europe has, for all practical purposes, ceased to exist, though many remain in Russia.

A standardized form of German based on Luther's Bible translation is understood and spoken throughout the German language region, but many dialects survive, some of which have become proper languages, unintelligible to speakers of standard German. Most notable are *Letzeburgish*, which is gaining increased usage in Luxembourg; *Alsatian*, the declining German dialect of eastern France; and *Swiss German*, spoken by the majority in Switzerland. Both Letzeburgish and Swiss German support nationalistic sentiment.

Dutch, spoken by 20 million in the Netherlands, northern Belgium, and extreme northern France, also developed as a separate language out of the former German dialect net in the Low German region but with the difference that its speakers never adopted standard German. Also derived from Low German is the *Frisian* language, spoken by about 300,000, mainly in northeastern Netherlands.

English, the closest Germanic relative of Frisian, also derives from Low German and is spoken by some 59 million persons in the United Kingdom, Ireland, and Gibraltar. As a result of the Norman French conquest of England almost a thousand years ago, English absorbed a great many Romance words, totaling perhaps 30% of the present English vocabulary. This mixing of Germanic and Romance, with the resultant richness of vocabulary, provides the distinctiveness of English. Since World War II, English has become the *lingua franca*, or language of international contact, of the western half of Europe and may soon play that role throughout the culture area. In Sweden and the Netherlands, for example, over half of the population now speaks English as a second language (fig. 4.6). Instruction in English has recently increased greatly in eastern Europe and Switzerland.

The northern part of the Germanic language region is dominated by the *Scandinavian* dialect net (fig. 4.1). The independent countries of that part of Europe would have us believe that separate Danish, Norwegian, and Swedish languages exist, but in fact these are mutually intelligible dialects, even in the standard forms promoted by the three governments. For example, some 64% of Norwegians understand "all but a few words" of standard Swedish, and the same is true of 58% of all Danes concerning the *Bokmål* form of Norwegian, 1 of 2 government-recognized dialects in that country (fig. 4.1). In local areas along international borders within Scandinavia, mutual intelligibility is virtually universal. *Isoglosses*, or word boundaries, crisscross Scandinavia without regard to political borders. Politics, it seems, often determines what a "language" is.

Only *Icelandic*, where the Scandinavian dialect net was "torn" by the intervening sea, is properly regarded as a separate language. The Scandinavian dialect net encompasses about 20 million speakers and Icelandic about

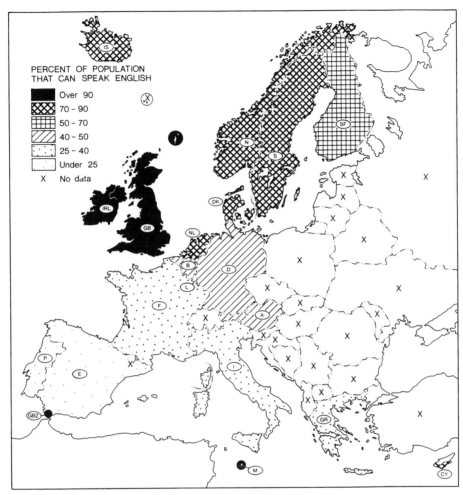

Figure 4.6.   Ability to speak English, as a percentage of total population, by national units and selected dependent territories. (*Sources: Eurobarometer* and selected national statistical yearbooks).

260,000. *Faeroese,* spoken in a small island group between Iceland and Norway, should perhaps also be regarded as a separate Scandinavian language, but long rule by Denmark has altered the local speech to the extent that Faeroese probably fits better in the Scandinavian dialect net.

Slavic Languages

The third of the 3 major Indo-European divisions, and the largest, consists of the **Slavic** languages, which belong to the eastern branch of the family. About 236 million people—one-third of the population of Europe—

including the Eurorussians, speak a Slavic language. Together, the Romance, Germanic, and Slavic divisions account for almost 9 of every 10 Europeans.

The origins of the Slavic languages probably lie somewhere on the margins of the Pripyat Marsh (fig. 4.2) in dim prehistory. The proto-Slavs, who called themselves *Sorby*, achieved the agricultural colonization of the central section of the East European Plain. Slavs might have remained a minor and peripheral linguistic group, had they not, about A.D. 200, invented a new type of curved-blade plow, equipped with a moldboard, that lifted the topsoil and turned it over. Mounted on wheels and pulled by multiple teams of oxen, this plow allowed for the first time the cultivation of heavy clay soils and greatly increased crop production. With this innovation they expanded west and south, entering the chernozem prairie regions. When the Roman Empire collapsed, they pushed deep into the Balkans.

The Slavic region is today separated into a large northern part and a much smaller southern area, divided by a corridor of non-Slavic languages (fig. 4.1). In the north, *Polish* claims about 35 million speakers, the *Czech-Slovakian* dialect net 14 million, and the *Russian* dialect net about 159 million inside Europe. Most sources recognize *Ukrainian* (Little Russian, 42 million speakers), *Belorussian* (White Russian, 10 million), and *Great Russian* (107 million in Europe) as 3 separate languages, and they are now being promoted as such for nationalistic purposes, but we might better regard these as a single multiethnic Russian dialect net that encompasses virtually the entirety of the East European Plain. The Great Russian component, formerly strewn widely through the Soviet Union, in 1996 included about 14.7 million persons living outside Russia in newly independent European countries, three quarters of them in Ukraine. Another 8 million or so Russian speakers still lived in the former Soviet Central Asian republics, plus Azerbaijan, in 1996.

A substantial return migration of Russian speakers to Russia from the former Soviet republics is occurring. Between 1989 and 1996, over 2 million people took part in this mass migration, and the flow continues, though at a lower volume. Many additional ethnic Russians departed Siberia—the Asian part of Russia—to return to Eurorussia in the 1990s. Russian is spoken by more people than any other language in Europe today.

Stretching from the Adriatic to the Black Sea in the Balkan Peninsula, the 3 southern Slavic languages are *Slovenian*, with 2 million speakers, the *Serbo-Croatian* dialect net with 14 million, and the *Bulgarian-Macedonian* dialect net with 11 million. Further complicating the pattern of Slavic languages is an alphabet divide, a fundamental cultural boundary in Europe that separates users of the Latin characters from those employing Greek or Greek-derived Cyrillic letters (fig. 4.1). This literary divide cuts right through the Slavic lands, both northern and southern.

Celtic Languages

All of the other Indo-European groups are small in population and peripheral in location. Most have experienced retreat and some face possible extinction. The **Celtic** division of Western Indo-European clings to refuges on the hilly, cloudy, tattered coasts of northwestern Europe (figs. 4.1 and 4.7). *Welsh,* one of the surviving Celtic tongues, retains about 550,000 speakers in the hills of western Wales, a refuge area called the *Bro gymraeg.* As recently as 1911, Welsh had almost a million speakers, and the subsequent decline caused some to predict "a land where children will not be able to pronounce the names of the places where they live." Indeed, some Celtic languages died in recent times, including *Manx* on the Isle of Man and *Cornish* in Cornwall. In the case of Welsh, the obituary seems to have been premature. The Welsh Language Act of 1993 gave the language legal equality with English, and the Welsh elite began insisting that their children study the ancestral tongue. It is a required language in state schools. A higher percentage of Welsh youth now can speak Welsh than is true of the population at large. The number of speakers stabilized, then began to increase in the 1990s. Welsh newspapers, radio broadcasts, and television channels are now available. The Welsh, it seems, have rejected the arrogant criticism of Englishman John Stuart Mill, who scolded all Celts for choosing "to sulk on their rocks, half-savage relics of past times."

Breton, the Celtic language of western France, has a condition similar to Welsh, retaining a population of about 200,000 and presently enjoying a modest, elite-led revival. Recently, 34 Breton-only schools opened, a radical departure from the not-too-distant past, when French officials banned the language altogether in education, and the number of speakers had declined from perhaps 500,000 in 1970.

By contrast, the situation of *Gaelic* in the *Gaidhealtacht* refuge of the northern highlands and islands of Scotland has become desperate. Bilingual Gaelic-English road markers conceal the fact that only about 80,000 persons, mainly elderly, still speak the language. *Erse,* or Irish Gaelic, has enjoyed governmental protection and support since the independence of Ireland in the 1920s, but it, too, has declined. Its *Gaeltacht* refuge area continues to shrink, and mandatory teaching of Erse in schools ceased in the 1980s. Only about 60,000 persons still use Erse as the language of the household, though anywhere from 500,000 to a million reputedly have at least limited ability in the language. Some Gaeltacht residents protest by defacing the English parts of bilingual signs (fig. 4.8). An Erse revival of sorts is underway in the cities of Ireland, all of which lie outside the Gaeltacht. The first Erse television station began operating in 1996, and 12 all-Erse primary schools opened. Reputedly, 5% of Ireland's population uses Erse frequently in conversation and 2% list it as their mother tongue.

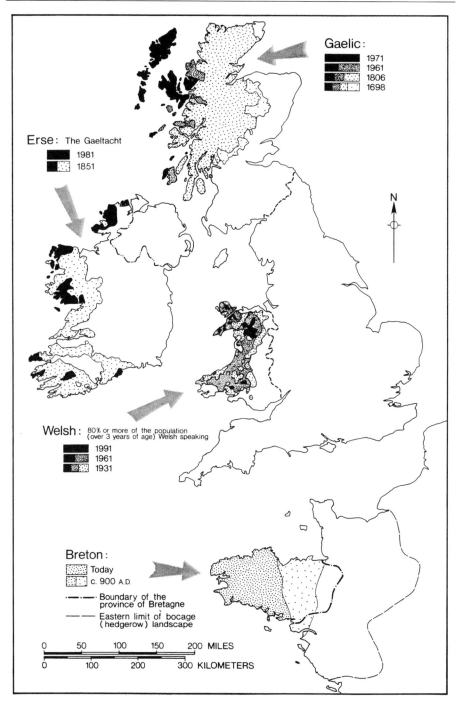

Figure 4.7.   Retreat of the Celtic languages, as represented by Erse, Breton, Scottish Gaelic, and Welsh. The rural refuge areas fragmented as the decline progressed. Today, all but Scottish Gaelic are experiencing a revival, centered in the towns and cities, rather than in the rural refuges. (*Sources:* After Withers 1984, 47, 81, 233, 234; Aitchison and Carter 1999; Hindley 1990).

Figure 4.8.   Defacing of English language on highway signs in the Connemara *Gaeltacht*, Republic of Ireland. The official bilingual policy of the republic is unpopular in both English and Erse areas. (Photo by T.G.J.-B. 1974.)

The present distribution and condition of the Celtic languages in Europe gives no hint of their former greatness. They originated far away, in central Europe. Proto-Celtic likely arose from the ancient Danubian branch of Indo-European, west of the constriction of the Danube water gap, where that great river forces its way between the Alps and Carpathians (figs. 4.2 and 2.1). The hearth area lay along the northern margins of the Alps and in the longitudinal valleys within that range. By the time the Celts, who called themselves the *Gallatae* or *Galls,* can be identified in the archaeological record, about 700 B.C., they exhibited a high culture at places such as Hallstatt in Austria and Lake Neuchâtel in Switzerland, excelling in metalworking and art.

The Celtic decline began when the Germanic peoples surged southward out of Scandinavia about 500 B.C., displacing them from central Europe and creating a Celtic diaspora to the west, south, and east. *Galicia,* a region in southern Poland, derives its name from these prehistoric Celtic refugees, as does *Gala*tia in faraway interior Turkey, another *Galiza* in northwestern Iberia, nearby *Gala*che in western Spain, and *Gaul* (ancient France and Po–Veneto Plain). Most of these refugees soon fell victim to the northward advance of the Romans, which occurred as warmer conditions returned. Pinched between the Romance and Germanic speakers, the Celtic languages retreated west to the rugged refuges where we find them today.

Other Indo-European Groups

The ancient **Hellenic** branch of the Indo-European languages is parent to modern *Greek,* spoken by about 10 million people in Greece and Cyprus. Minorities can be found in surrounding countries such as Albania. While a minor tongue, accounting for less than 1.5% of all Europeans, Greek is not an endangered language. The social morale of its speakers has always been very high, and Greeks still take justifiable pride in the cultural achievements of their ancient ancestors. Greek Orthodox Christianity has also played a major role in the survival and vigor of Greek culture. Self-pride allowed the Greeks to preserve their language even during lengthy periods of rule by the Romans and Turks. Modern Greek is spoken in almost precisely the same region as in the Mycenean Age 13 centuries before Christ and in the area where the dialect net tear apparently produced proto-Hellenic some 8,500 years ago. The language changed—modern Greek is roughly as different from Classical Greek as Italian is from Latin—but remained astoundingly stable geographically.

Neighbors to the Greeks are the speakers of the **Thraco-Illyrian** group, today represented only by *Albanian.* They number over 5 million and reside mainly in Albania, Kosovo Province in Yugoslavia, and western Macedonia. A scattering of Albanian villages can also be found in southern Italy, Crna Gora, and Greece. In the main, contiguous Balkan area of Albanian speech, a dialect net survives, mutually unintelligible in extreme forms. One of the northern, or *Tosk* dialects, has become the standardized form of the language. The ancestral Thraco-Illyrian group, belonging to the Eastern Indo-European division, perhaps originated in the Maritsa Valley of Bulgaria (figs. 2.1 and 4.2), but the ancient geographical development remains poorly understood. Apparently, the Thraco-Illyrian speakers evolved at some point into a mountain people, diffusing through the Stara Planina and Rodopi Range. This may have happened as early as the time of the Black Sea flood. They went as mountain folk over into Illyria, in the Dinaric Range, the present seat of the Albanian language. Eventually, Thraco-Illyrian died out altogether in the eastern Balkans, and modern Albanian occupies a refuge not unlike that of Celtic.

Another minor Eastern Indo-European group consists of the **Baltic** languages, *Lettish* (Latvian) and *Lithuanian,* spoken in two small independent states on the eastern shore of the Baltic Sea (fig. 4.1). Together, these languages have about 4 million speakers. Baltic speech survives close to its presumed area of origin west of the Pripyat Marsh (fig. 4.2). Territory was later lost to both Germanic and Slavic languages, but the Balts have held out in a northern refuge. The recent achievement of political independence by Latvia and Lithuania bodes well for these two endangered languages.

Romany, the Eastern Indo-European speech of many or most of the 7 million or more *Roma,* or "Gypsies" as they are popularly called, is spoken widely, especially in eastern Europe, though not in contiguous or sizable areas. Romania, with 2.4 million, and Bulgaria, with 900,000 Roma, house the largest numbers, representing about 11% of each country's inhabitants. Macedonia has the highest percentage of Roma in the population, 18%. Romany has split into three separate languages and 13 dialects, due to the strewn distribution of the group and the largely nonliterate status of the tongue. The Roma apparently entered Europe in the 1300s as a caste of itinerant Hindu peddlers from the Indus Valley of present Pakistan. In almost every European country they are despised and persecuted.

In the distant, embattled outpost of Europe in the trans-Caucasus region (fig. 1.8) is found another Eastern Indo-European language, *Armenian* with almost 5 million speakers. Only about 73% of Armenians live in their ancient, newly independent homeland. Others live in adjacent parts of Georgia and Azerbaijan, including the disputed territory of Nagorno–Karabakh, held by Armenian armed forces but still legally part of Muslim-dominated Azerbaijan. Still other Armenians form a diaspora, especially in Russia, where over 800,000 reside. Near linguistic kin and neighbors of the Armenians are the *Kurds,* 400,000 of whom have immigrated to Germany, mainly from eastern Turkey, in recent decades.

Non-Indo-European Languages

The Indo-European languages, as suggested earlier, represent one of the defining human traits of the European culture area. Non-Indo-European tongues are both rare, accounting for only 5% of the population, and peripheral in location (figs. 1.8 and 4.1).

On the northeastern margins of Europe live speakers of the **Uralic** language family, an indigenous group whose ancestors retreated to cold, marshy refuges as the Indo-Europeans advanced. Today, they live in a chain of independent countries and autonomous regions from Finland and Estonia eastward through the Karelia and Komi Republics of Russia, among others, as far as Mordvinia (fig. 1.8). These are peoples of the taiga, a land Indo-Europeans never found attractive. Many, particularly the speakers of *Estonian* (1 million) and *Finnish-Karelian* (5 million), adopted agriculture in ancient times from the Indo-Europeans and carried it into the taiga, but certain other Uralic groups, such as the *Sami* (or Lapps, 59,000) and *Nenets*, never became farmers. The Uralic peoples still display a deep veneration for forests, and their graveyards often take on a wooded, wild appearance. These reflect ancient memories from the time they were hunters in the forests, before the Indo-Europeans came. A formidable belt of marshes marks the Uralic–Indo-European border along the present Estonia–Latvia boundary, a line beyond which the Baltic speakers apparently never progressed.

Among the Uralic speakers, only the *Hungarians,* or Magyar, do not live in a peripheral area. Instead, 13 million strong, they occupy the heart of the structural basin that bears their name, almost in the very center of Europe (fig. 4.1). Most live in Hungary, but sizable minorities can also be found in Romania, Slovakia, Slovenia, northern Yugoslavia, and western Ukraine. By their own tradition and historical evidence, the ancient Hungarians, a herding people of the east, entered Europe as invaders in A.D. 895 and found a permanent foothold in areas where a prairie vegetation had been created by earlier human activity in the central European biotic province.

On the southeast, the Indo-Europeans border the **Altaic** language family, mainly Turkic groups. The *Osman Turks* of Anatolia long ago attained footholds in Cyprus and north of the Dardanelles–Bospors. In addition, their long rule of the Balkans left behind minorities in countries such as Bulgaria, where perhaps 1 out of 10 persons speaks Turkish, in spite of 3 attempts in the past century and a half to expel them, most recently in 1989. Another 1.5 million Osman Turks reside as immigrants in Germany. *Tataric,* also a major Turkic language, is centered in Tatarstan, Bashkortostan, and, as a minority, in Krym, the peninsular part of Ukraine (fig. 1.8). Altogether, about 6 million Tatars live in Europe. In small pockets of Moldova, Bulgaria, and southern Ukraine live over 200,000 *Gagauz* speakers, who are Christians and belong to the Oguz branch of Turkic. Europe abounds with such tiny minorities, most of which have not been mentioned here.

The **Caucasic** language family, including most notably *Georgian*, also bounds Indo-European on the southeast (fig. 1.8). To the south, across the Mediterranean Sea, **Afro-Asiatic** languages such as *Arabic* and *Maltese* mark the cultural border of Europe and remind us that the great desert lies not far away in that direction.

The non-Indo-European periphery of Europe is completed by *Basque,* or Euskera, in the southwest, on the Pyrenean borders of Spain and France (fig. 4.1). With perhaps 700,000 speakers, Basque long suffered decline, but a vigorous revival is presently under way. In Spain, establishment of the

Basque Autonomous Province offers abundant hope for the future of this unique language.

Closer inspection, then, reveals that Europe possesses neither Indo-European homogeneity nor linguistic chaos. We discerned a core, where 3 major Indo-European divisions prevail, surrounded by an inner periphery of lesser Indo-European groups and an outer periphery of altogether alien tongues. Moreover, east–west linguistic contrasts are reflected in the major, most ancient division within the Indo-European family and by 2 different alphabets. The Romance–Germanic divide and the split of Slavic into two geographically separate areas provide a significant north–south patterning.

For centuries, many smaller languages declined, and some perished, but recent decades have witnessed the revival of many endangered tongues. We need to look more closely at these opposing trends.

Linguistic Decline and Revival

Why do some languages decline or even die? Why do revivals occur? Geographer Charles Withers, studying Scottish Gaelic, listed four basic processes, each directly or indirectly spatial, for decline. First is a *clearance model*, or decline caused by emigration of speakers to places outside the refuge area, leaving behind a smaller population to perpetuate the language. Second, a *changeover model* describes reduced linguistic viability due to the immigration of an alien population. A third process encouraging linguistic simplification is the *economic development model*. New modes of production, particularly industrialization, accompanied by urbanization, can break up the social structure needed to perpetuate a language. The transition from subsistence farming to working in a factory, even if made within the ethnic area, could be quite destructive in the linguistic sense, particularly if the language of the workplace was not that of the farm. In this context, geographer Keith Buchanan referred to the decline of the Celtic tongues as a "liquidation" carried out by the English in order to produce a loyal and obedient workforce for the mines and factories. Finally, a *social morale model* describes the process by which an ethnic minority, over time, loses pride in its language and voluntarily abandons it. An educational system using solely the majority language produced bilingualism and, indirectly, fostered illiteracy in the minority tongue. Depriving the language of legal and religious status helped convey the same message— the minority tongue is inferior and its use socially degrading. Denying the language access to the printed and broadcast media can hasten the process. All four of these processes were at work until the late twentieth century to diminish or destroy many lesser languages in Europe.

Recent decades have witnessed the opposite process—the revival of endangered languages. Welsh and Breton provide examples, as do numerous languages of the former Soviet Union. Partly these revivals accompanied

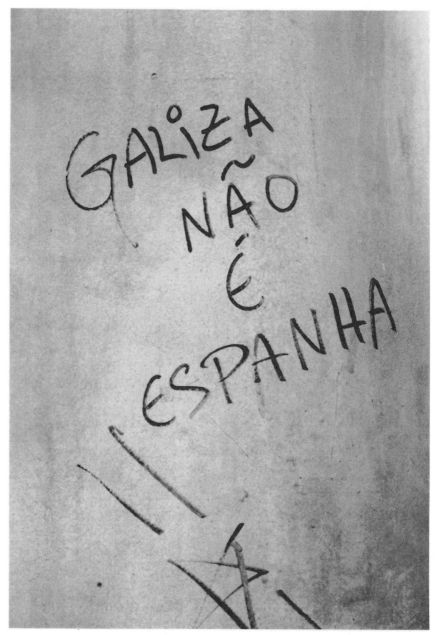

Figure 4.9.   Gallegan-language graffiti greets the visitor to the pilgrimage town of Santiago de Compostela, in the Spanish autonomous province of Galiza. Gallegan is undergoing a modest revival, following repression under the Francisco Franco dictatorship. The message is political—"Galiza is not Spain." (Photo by T.G.J.-B. 1999.)

the collapse of the Soviet empire and have seen migration patterns reverse, counteracting the earlier clearance and changeover models. Russian speakers since 1990 emigrate from Latvia, for example, while Lettish speakers immigrate. The social morale model is reversed, as newly independent governments promote languages like Lettish and stigmatize Russian.

But more is at work in linguistic revival than simply imperial collapse. The rise of a global economy and progress toward a united Europe also contribute. The more globalized and uniform European civilization becomes, the more people want to anchor themselves in a regional or even local culture. An identity with place and region counteracts the trend toward oneness. Ethnolinguistic resurgence occurs.

This movement invariably has political consequences (see chapter 7) and is a *postindustrial* phenomenon (see chapter 9) (fig. 4.9). Indeed, the rapid deindustrialization of Wales after about 1965, which witnessed the widespread closure of mines and factories, coincided with the Welsh revival movement. Buchanan's linguistic liquidation collapsed when the Celtic workforce became unemployed. Whatever the exact causal forces may be, modern Europe is witnessing the widespread rejuvenation of small languages and also regional dialects (fig. 4.10). In the Netherlands, for example, radio broadcasts in the *Limburgs* dialect of the southeast can now be heard.

Figure 4.10.   Bilingual French–Breton sign in Bretagne Province, France. Breton "hid" in isolation behind hedgerows like the one seen here, for a thousand years, gradually retreating before the French language, but today this Celtic language is enjoying a modest revival. (Photo by T.G.J.-B. 1999.)

Next we turn attention to the third of the basic human traits of Europe—the sticky issue of race. As we found true of religion and language, the racial situation is far more complicated than it seems at first glance.

Sources and Suggested Readings

Aitchison, John W., and Harold Carter. 1985. *The Welsh Language 1961–1981: An Interpretive Atlas.* Cardiff, GB: University of Wales Press.
———. 1994. *A Geography of the Welsh Language, 1961–1991.* Cardiff, GB: University of Wales Press.
———. 1999. "Cultural Empowerment and Language Shift in Wales." *Tijdschrift voor Economische en Sociale Geografie* 90:168–183.
Alinei, Mario, et al. 1983. *Atlas Linguarum Europae.* Vol. 1. Assen, NL: van Gorcum.
Becker, Hans. 1971. "Die Volksgruppen der italienischen Ostalpen: Begleitworte zum Versuch einer Kartendarstellung." *Kölner Geographische Arbeiten* D:256–270.
Beynon, Erdmann D. 1941. "The Eastern Outpost of the Magyars." *Geographical Review* 31:63–78.
Blomkvist, Y. E. 1985. "Settlements of the Eastern Slavs." *Soviet Geography* 26:183–198, 268–283.
Buchanan, Keith. 1977. "Economic Growth and Cultural Liquidation: The Case of the Celtic Nations." In *Radical Geography: Alternative Viewpoints on Contemporary Social Issues,* ed. Richard Peet. Chicago, USA: Maaroufa, 125–143.
Chinn, Jeff, and Robert Kaiser. 1996. *Russians as the New Minority.* Boulder, Colo., USA: Westview.
Comrie, Bernard. 1994. "Northern Asia and Eastern Europe." In *Atlas of the World's Languages,* ed. Christopher Moseley and R. E. Asher. London, GB: Routledge, 219–244.
Cornish, Vaughan. 1936. *Borderlands of Language in Europe and their Relations to the Historic Frontiers of Christendom.* London, GB: Sifton.
Cvijic, Jovan. 1918. "The Geographical Distribution of the Balkan Peoples." *Geographical Review* 5:345–361 (includes large color map).
Dami, Aldo. 1960. "Les Rhetoromanches." *Le Globe* 100:25–71.
Dominian, Leon. 1917. *The Frontiers of Language and Nationality in Europe.* New York, USA: American Geographical Society, Special Publication No. 3.
Dugdale, J. S. 1969. *The Linguistic Map of Europe.* London, GB: Hutchinson University Library.
Falc'hun, François. 1963. *Histoire de la langue bretonne d'après la géographie linguistique.* Paris, F: Presses Universitaires de France.
Fernández-Armesto, Felipe, ed. 1994. *The Times Guide to the Peoples of Europe.* London, GB: Times.
Geipel, John. 1969. *The Europeans: An Ethnohistorical Survey.* London, GB: Longman.
Goetschy, Henri, and André-L. Sanguin, eds. 1995. *Langues régionales et relations transfrontalières en Europe.* Paris, F: Harmattan.
Greenberg, Joseph H. 2000. *Indo-European and Its Closest Relatives: The Eurasiatic Language Family.* Stanford, Calif., USA: Stanford University Press.
Grüll, Josef. 1965. "Entwicklung und Bestand der Rätoromanen in den Alpen." *Mitteilungen der Österreichischen Geographischen Gesellschaft* 107:86–103, 117.

Hindley, Reg. 1990. *The Death of the Irish Language: A Qualified Obituary*. London, GB: Routledge.

Jones, Philip, and Michael T. Wild. 1992. "Western Germany's 'Third Wave' of Migrants: The Arrival of the Aussiedler." *Geoforum* 23:1–11.

Kirk, John M., Stewart F. Sanderson, and John D. A. Widdowson, eds. 1985. *Studies in Linguistic Geography: The Dialects of English in Britain and Ireland*. London, GB: Croom Helm.

Krantz, Grover S. 1988. *Geographical Development of European Languages*. New York, USA: Peter Lang.

Lautensach, Hermann. 1954. "Über die topographischen Namen arabischen Ursprungs in Spanien und Portugal." *Die Erde* 6:219–243.

Lundén, Thomas. 1966. "The Finnish-speaking Population of Norrbotten (Sweden)." *Europa Ethnica* 3:98–102.

———. 1988. "Language, Geography, and Social Development: The Case of Norden." In *Language in Geographic Context*, ed. Colin H. Williams. Clevedon, GB: Multilingual Matters, 47–72.

MacGiolla Chríost, Diarmait, and John W. Aitchison. 1998. "Ethnic Identities and Language in Northern Ireland." *Area* 30:301–309.

Mackenzie, J. Lachlan. 1994. "Western Europe." In *Atlas of the World's Languages*, ed. Christopher Moseley and R. E. Asher. London, GB: Routledge, 245–261.

Mallory, J. P. 1989. *In Search of the Indo-Europeans: Language, Archaeology, and Myth*. London, GB: Thames & Hudson.

Marinelli, Olinto. 1919. "The Regions of Mixed Populations in Northern Italy." *Geographical Review* 7:129–148 (includes large color map).

Matley, Ian M. 1976. "Demographic Trends and Assimilation among the Finnic-speaking Peoples of North-western Russia." *Ural-Altaische Jahrbücher* 48:167–185.

Mellor, Roy. 1963. "A Minority Problem in Germany." *Scottish Geographical Magazine* 79:49–53.

Murphy, Alexander B. 1988. *The Regional Dynamics of Language Differentiation in Belgium: A Study in Cultural-political Geography*. Chicago, USA: University of Chicago, Geography Research Paper No. 227.

Mycklebost, Hallstein. 1989. "Armenia and the Armenians." *Norsk Geografisk Tidsskrift* 43:135–154.

Nash, Catherine. 1999. "Irish Placenames: Post-colonial Locations." *Transactions of the Institute of British Geographers* 24:457–480.

O'Luain, Cathal. 1989. "The Irish Language Today." *Europa Ethnica* 46 (1): 1–10.

Orton, Harold, and Nathalia Wright. 1974. *A Word Geography of England*. London, GB: Seminar Press.

Pryce, W.T.R. 1975. "Migration and the Evolution of Culture Areas: Cultural and Linguistic Frontiers in North-East Wales, 1750 and 1851." *Transactions of the Institute of British Geographers* 65:79–108.

Renfrew, Colin. 1988. *Archaeology and Language: The Puzzle of Indo-European Origin*. Cambridge, GB: Cambridge University Press.

———. 1989. "The Origins of Indo-European Languages." *Scientific American* 261 (4): 106–114.

Ryan, William, and Walter Pitman. 1998. *Noah's Flood*. New York, USA: Simon & Schuster.

Sanguin, André-Louis, ed. 1993. *Les minorités ethniques en Europe*. Paris, F: Harmattan.

Schultze, Joachim H. 1941. "Zur Geographie der altgriechischen Kolonisation." *Petermanns Geographische Mitteilungen* 87:7–12 (includes map).

Schwartz, Lee. 1991. "USSR Nationality Redistribution by Republic, 1979–1989." *Soviet Geography* 32:209–248.

Sopher, David E. 1955. "Arabic Place Names in Spain." *Names* 3:5–13.

Straka, Manfred. 1979. *Karte der Völker und Sprachen Europas unter besonderer Berücksichtigung der Volksgruppen.* Graz, A: Akademische Druck- u. Verlagsanstalt.

Wilkinson, Henry R. 1951. *Maps and Politics: A Review of the Ethnographic Cartography of Macedonia.* Liverpool, GB: University Press.

Withers, Charles W. J. 1984. *Gaelic in Scotland, 1698–1981: The Geographical History of a Language.* Edinburgh, GB: Donald.

———. 1988. *Gaelic Scotland: The Transformation of a Culture Region.* London, GB: Routledge.

Wixman, Ronald. 1980. *Language Aspects of Ethnic Patterns and Processes in the North Caucasus.* Chicago, USA: University of Chicago, Department of Geography, Research Paper No. 191.

———. 1981. "Territorial Russification and Linguistic Russianization in Some Soviet Republics." *Soviet Geography* 22:667–675.

———. 1984. "Demographic Russification and Linguistic Russianization of the Ukraine, 1959–1979." In *Geographical Studies on the Soviet Union,* ed. George J. Demko and Roland J. Fuchs. Chicago, USA: University of Chicago, Department of Geography, Research Paper No. 211.

Zaborski, Bogdan. 2000. "Europe Languages" (map). In *Goode's World Atlas.* 20th ed. Ed. John C. Hudson and Edward B. Espenshade Jr. Chicago, USA: Rand McNally, 152–153.

CHAPTER 5

Geogenetics

While far less important than religion and language in defining the European culture area, *race*—here defined as the *genetic* characteristics of people—does represent one of the three basic traits. The **Europoid** (or *Caucasian*) race distinguishes Europeans from *Negroid* Africans and *Mongoloid* Asians.

European Racial Self-Identity

Why should race, acultural rather than cultural, inherited rather than learned, play a role in the definition of the European culture area? Also, geneticists long ago discarded as false the concept of race—the division of humankind into physical types, based on supposedly covarying traits. Why, then, should we pay attention?

The answer is that the Caucasian race is a part of European self-identity. Asians and Africans, different in physical appearance, have a difficult if not impossible task in becoming accepted as Europeans when they immigrate. In short, many if not most Europeans feel that Europe is properly the homeland of white people. Such perceptions and biases help shape the phenomenon of we-versus-they that underlies perceived Europeanness. Recently, for example, swarthy vendors from the Caucasus region faced possible expulsion from the public markets in Moskva because of racial prejudice, and Africans have been attacked by skinheads in Germany and certain other countries. Simply ignoring the issue of race as popularly perceived will not make neo-Nazis and skinheads disappear, nor will it expunge widely held racial views. Inexorably bound up with the very concept of Europe, race became part of culture when it entered the European self-image.

In fact, Christianity long lent apocryphal support to this racial identity of Europeans. The three sons of the biblical Noah—Ham, Shem, and Ja-

141

pheth—supposedly fathered, respectively, the African, Asian, and European races. We should not hide behind "political correctness" and pretend that European self-identity is unconnected to racism. Nazism did not arise through immaculate conception nor did the skinheads.

Racially Exotic Immigration

Large numbers of racially exotic immigrants came to Europe after about 1950. Most came from the extensive, collapsing colonial empires of the British, French, Portuguese, and Dutch. Darker-skinned people from the tropics formed the bulk of these racially distinctive immigrants. They immediately tested the racial aspect of European self-identity.

In the United Kingdom, the principal groups are South Asians, derived mainly from India, Pakistan, and Bangladesh, including many persons who lived in East Africa prior to migrating to Britain. These Asians number about 1.5 million in the United Kingdom, forming over 2% of the national population. They live mainly in major industrial and commercial centers, such as London, Bradford, Birmingham, and Coventry. This selective urban concentration means that South Asians often form a substantial part of the city population. They are sufficiently dark complected to be regarded by the indigenous British as "coloured," and one can easily distinguish them from the tall, fair Britons. Chinese, almost all from Hong Kong, form the other major Asiatic group in the United Kingdom, numbering about 150,000. The Chinese generally do not live in urban ghettos, and in fact only half live in the large cities. They have scattered through the country and achieved considerable economic success.

The other major racial minority in Britain consists of Negroid, or black, immigrants. Afro-Caribbeans form the large majority of Britain's black population, about 77%. Blacks now number over 600,000. Their migration, like that of the South Asians, was facilitated by the fact that they hold British citizenship, a legacy of the empire. The tiny Caribbean island of Montserrat, for example, sent nearly one-third of its total population to Britain between 1955 and 1961. While exceptional in proportion, the emigration from Montserrat symptomized the economic troubles in the West Indies. Much larger and more populous Jamaica sent nearly one in every ten of its citizens to Britain in the 1953–1961 period, forming by far the largest West Indian contingent.

Residential segregation, far less intense than in the United States, characterizes both South Asian and black elements in British cities (see chapter 8). In the words of geographers T. P. Jones and D. McEvoy, "the ghetto must be recognized as an established feature" of British inner cities. In spite of civil rights legislation, most notably the Race Relations Acts of 1968 and 1976, racial discrimination persists in the United Kingdom. Occasionally, the racial ghettoes erupted in violence, as in Birmingham, England, in 1985.

These racial minorities, particularly the blacks, continue, as geographer Ceri Peach put it, to fill "gaps at the lower end of the occupational and residential ladders." On a far more encouraging note, Peach found a profound decrease in racial residential segregation in Britain between 1981 and 1991 (fig. 5.1). Only 2.6% of Caribbean blacks and 1.4% of Pakistanis still lived in ghetto neighborhoods by 1991, though one-fourth of Asian Indians and a third of the Bangladeshis did. The 1991 census of the United Kingdom also showed that 40% of all Afro-Caribbean males under the age of 35 had white spouses or partners, as contrasted to 22% of those aged 35 to 60. This does not mean that racism has vanished. As black British author Caryl Phillips stated about the Jewish holocaust, "if white people could do this to other white people, then what the hell would they do to me?"

France, similarly, is currently home to 300,000 Afro-Caribbeans who are French citizens due to France's continuing rule of its West Indies departments and Guiana. An additional 183,000 blacks in France come from former colonies within the French economic community in sub-Saharan

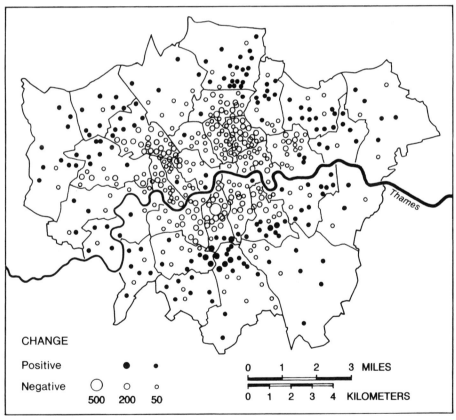

Figure 5.1. Distributional change of Caribbean-born population in London, 1981 to 1991. Older ghettoes are emptying and the residents scattering. (*Source:* Adapted from Peach 1996.)

Africa. They remain largely confined to racial neighborhoods and work at or near the bottom of the occupational ladder in semi- or unskilled manual labor jobs vacated by the increasingly prosperous native French.

The Netherlands absorbed 180,000 Eurasians and 35,000 Moluccans from Indonesia, as well as about 200,000 Afro-Caribbean immigrants from Surinam and the Dutch Antilles. In Rotterdam by 1972, some 12,000 Surinamese and lesser numbers from the Antilles formed about 2% of the population, a proportion accounted for by Moluccans alone by 1995. Following the British and French models, the Rotterdam racial minorities generally live in older residential sections adjacent to the city center. Amsterdam, 's Gravenhage, and Utrecht display similar patterns.

Portugal, too, inherited a sizable Negroid population from its former slave trade and African empire, a total of about 100,000 persons. In nearby Andalucía Province, in southern Spain, black African slaves introduced during Moorish rule remained common centuries later. Over 7% of the population of the city of Sevilla consisted of African slaves in the early 1500s. While most of these Africans were sent to the American colonies, a racial legacy survived in Andalucía, where a few villages still have populations displaying partially Negroid traits.

Germany also has immigrant racial minorities, though not on the scale of the former empire-ruling countries, and it acquired a small population of mulattoes as a result of the American military presence. About 95,000 Vietnamese reside in Germany, mainly in the eastern part of the country, where 15,000 natives of Mozambique in southern Africa also live. Some 57,000 Asian Indians and Sri Lankans had come to western Germany by 1990. Iceland forbade residence by non-Caucasians, even excluding black military personnel at the U.S. base at Keflavík. On a brighter note, numerous Swedes and other Scandinavians have adopted dark-skinned children from impoverished Third World countries. Reared in northern affluence and thoroughly assimilated, these children often find it difficult to gain full acceptance into society as adults.

Europeans of many nationalities have established so many ties to the rest of the world since the Age of Discovery that virtually every racial strain has found its way into Europe. Indeed, such infusions go back at least to Roman times, when black slaves were introduced. The immigration of the Roma (Gypsies) in the late Middle Ages represented the earliest infusion of darker-complected peoples from the Indian subcontinent, long predating the more recent influx. Clearly, European racial purity or homogeneity has always been a myth. That does little to alter the European racial self-image.

Traditional Europoid Subraces

The racial perceptions of Europeans also include internal subdivisions or *subraces* of the Caucasian people. These are based in the fact that human physical differences exist from region to region within the European culture area.

Before about 1960, when concepts such as race and subrace were abandoned by geneticists, researchers measured certain visible human traits, in particular skin, eye, and hair color; height; and the shape of the head. They discovered that people living around the shores of the North and Baltic Seas tend to be fairer in complexion and taller than most other Europeans and to have elongated heads. The central and eastern Europeans, by contrast, are roundheaded. Head shape is measured as the *cephalic index*, the ear-to-ear dimension as a percentage of the nose-to-back figure. Northern Europeans have cephalic indexes lower than 79, while those in central and eastern Europe range from 83 to 87. Scholars suggested that the broader heads of the central and eastern Europeans represented a legacy of repeated Asiatic invasions, since Mongoloid peoples have round heads and their incursions into Europe occurred along the east–west axis where high cephalic indices are found. Southern Europoids are darker in complexion and shorter in stature. The tallest people live along the eastern Adriatic coast and the shortest of all proved to be the Sami of the Arctic north.

From these findings it was a short leap to declaring the existence of regional Europoid subraces. These acquired names and immediately took on a life of their own, entering the European self-perception. Five Europoid subraces achieved popular recognition (fig. 5.2). The **Nordic** subrace, as the name implies, is centered in northern Europe, especially southern and central Scandinavia, the British Isles, and Iceland. Nordic people tend to be light complected and tall, with long heads. Overall, the Nordics are a big-boned people, physically larger than most of their southern neighbors.

In the southern extremities of Europe, the **Mediterranean** subrace forms a group characterized by relatively short stature, low to very low cephalic index, and dark complexion. Most often, Mediterranean people have a slender body build, narrow face, straight and prominent nose, small jaw, and small to medium head size. The form of the hair varies but is often curly, and in most cases the upper face is relatively long in proportion to the total face height. Sculpture from the period of classical Greece and the Roman Empire most often portrays individuals with Mediterranean traits. They have been portrayed as ancient bearers of technology from Mesopotamia, Anatolia, and Egypt, who established the first high civilization in the European culture area.

Much of the central section, wedged between the Nordic and Mediterranean zones, belongs to the **Alpine** subrace. The name is misleading, for members of this reputed subrace appear all the way from Bretagne on the Atlantic coast of France to the interior provinces of Russia. The principal distinguishing trait of the Alpines is a high cephalic index. They are of medium stature and stocky build, with short arms and legs, and large hands and feet. The face is broad or round, and the nose usually has a low bridge.

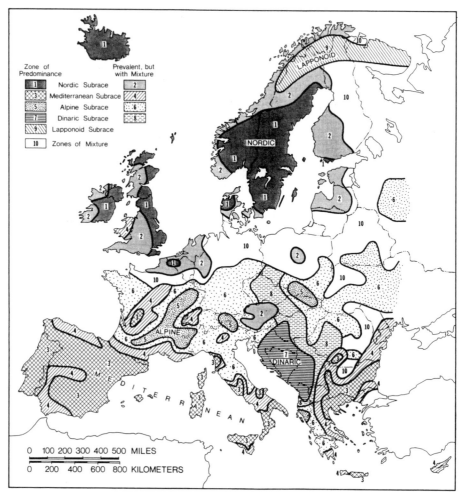

Figure 5.2. Caucasian subraces. This classification no longer enjoys scholarly acceptance, but many Europeans still believe these subraces exist and even exhibit different behavioral patterns. (*Sources:* Biasutti et al. 1967; Coon 1939; Ripley 1899.)

The **Dinaric** subrace consists of mountain-dwelling people. Their home lies principally the Dinaric Range along the eastern shore of the Adriatic Sea. Their face is usually somewhat triangular in shape, with a broad forehead, narrow jaw, and long, narrow, convex nose. Still more distinctive is the tall stature of the Dinarics, the major trait that distinguishes them from neighboring Mediterraneans and Alpines. Dinaric types have lived in the mountains of Albania for at least 2,500 years, and similar people dwell far to the east in the Caucasus.

The **Lapponoid** subrace lives in the northern parts of Sweden, Norway, Finland, and the Kola Peninsula in Russia. These people, the Sami, are of short stature, with small hands and feet and short arms and legs. Roundheaded, they have broad faces, widely separated eyes, pointed chins, small teeth, straight hair, and snub noses. Their complexion is somewhat darker than that of the Nordics to the south, and they have some projection of the lower face.

No sooner had this classification of subraces appeared about 1900 than Europeans began attaching *behavioral* images to each group, so repeatedly that the images became stereotyped. The Nordics supposedly possessed genius for leadership and were work-loving, efficient, and militaristic, while the Mediterraneans were labeled as artistic, lazy, inefficient, and hot-blooded. The Alpines were said to be unimaginative, plodding, and reserved.

These stereotypes have no more basis in scholarship than the subraces themselves, but they nevertheless appear again and again, and their imagined truth and importance reached absurd and tragic proportions in Nazi Germany. Nordic persons were favored, while people displaying the "wrong" physical traits, such as dark-complected Gypsies, faced slavery, imprisonment, or extermination. To a degree, German nationalism became identified with a specific subracial type, and persons who did not fit the "ideal" Nordic stereotype found it difficult to be accepted as rightful citizens of the Nazi state. Strangely, the most influential advocates of Nordic supremacy, Adolf Hitler and his propaganda minister, Josef Göbbels, were both short and dark complected.

After about 1960, the concept of race and subrace was discarded by geneticists. Races, they concluded, do not exist. Their objection centered on the lack of geographical concordance in the traits measured. Pigmentation, for example, does not match the distribution of head shape. Each physical trait varies areally in a unique way. Races and subraces, in short, are merely arbitrary classifications. Depending upon which specific traits are chosen for inclusion and what numerical breaking points are set for measurements, the racial groupings change. One classifier may choose to emphasize pigmentation and stature, while another prefers cephalic index. One might set 79 as the cephalic figure separating races or subraces, while another chooses 81 or 76.

Moreover, some traits thought to be genetic turned out to have cultural causes. Stature can be influenced by nutrition, while cephalic index could be altered by the use of infant cradle boards. As a result, scholarly attention shifted to genetic traits that are invisible to the eye and cannot be culturally altered.

Blood Chemistry

Today, instead, much geogenetic research focuses upon **blood chemistry**, which has proven to be highly complex, regionally varied, and enormously revealing. Initially, most findings involved 3 blood "factors," or *agglutino-*

gens: A, B, and Rh. Presence or absence of factors A and B led to the designation of four *blood types:* **type A,** containing only factor A; **type B,**
containing only factor B; **type O,** in which neither factor A nor B is present;
and **type AB,** containing both factors.

Each factor varies geographically. Blood type A, which accounts for
26.5% of all Europeans, occurs most commonly in western Iberia, Scandinavia, Finland, and scattered regions elsewhere (fig. 5.3). Factor A is rarest in
Sardegna and the northwestern insular fringe of Europe, but local exceptions abound, making the pattern very complicated. For example, factor A
is rare in Ireland, but in the Aran Islands, just off the coast of Ireland, 40%
of the people have type A blood, one of the highest rates in Europe. Note
how the geographical distribution of factor A appears unrelated to the 5
traditional Europoid subraces (compare figs. 5.2 and 5.3).

Blood factor B is uncommon in Europe, accounting for only 8.5% of the
population. The highest frequencies coincide with the East European Plain,
particularly the steppes, suggesting a link to Asiatic invasions (fig. 5.4).
Factor B appears least commonly in western Europe.

Most Europeans, 65%, have type O, meaning they have neither factor A
nor B in their blood. This is most common in the insular northwest and
occurs less frequently in eastern Europe. Many experts feel that type O
blood represents the most ancient population, a type never overwhelmed
by later invasions, but even so it is most common in remote refuge locations
(fig. 5.5). In this context, residents of Wales who have Welsh rather than
English surnames have a considerably higher frequency of type O blood.

The third blood factor is Rh, and its presence or absence is indicated by
a plus or minus sign. Together with factors A and B, it determines whether
blood can be transfused from one person to another. In Europe, 65% of the
population is **Rh+** and 35% **Rh–,** but the geographical pattern is pronounced (fig. 5.6). Rh– is most common in the Pyrenees, clearly linked to
the Basque people. Almost certainly, Rh– represents pre-Indo-European
ancestry and is an ancient blood characteristic linked to the hunters and
gatherers who originally colonized Europe. It is also almost exclusively a
European genetic characteristic (including overseas descendants), occurring virtually nowhere else in the world. Rh– appears least frequently
among Mediterranean peoples and the Uralic speakers of the far north.

Blood chemistry is far more complicated than factors A, B, and Rh.
Some 39 blood factors have been studied geographically by L. Luca Cavalli-
Sforza, Paolo Menozzi, and Alberto Piazza using a multivariate analysis
that seeks spatial covariations among different blood factors—that is,
among genes that may be inherited together. Using this *principal components
analysis,* they took blood samples from 400 locations in Europe, reduced
them to weighted means that summarized all gene frequencies at each
given place, and mapped the results.

The most common pattern that emerged was a southeast–northwest
gradient. This would seem to commemorate the spread of the Indo-European

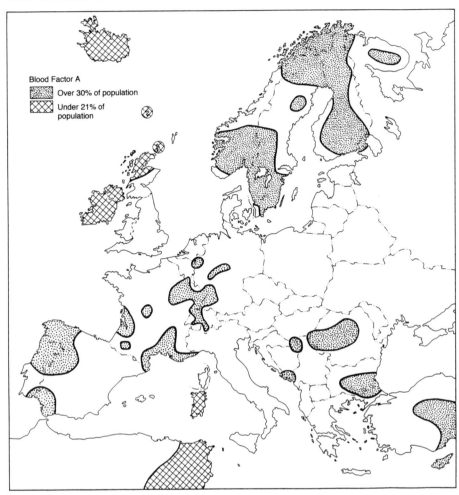

Figure 5.3.   Blood factor A in Europe. (*Sources:* Vallois and Marquer 1964; Cavalli-Sforza, Menozzi, and Piazza 1994; Mourant, Kopec, and Domaniewska-Sobczak 1958; Bunak 1974.)

peoples into Europe, bearing agriculture with them (compare figs. 5.7, 4.2, and 11.1). The pattern may instead simply reflect the fact that the far more ancient immigration waves also proceeded from southeast to northwest. The second most common geographical pattern (not shown in fig. 5.7) separated northern Scandinavia and Finland from the rest of Europe and probably can best be interpreted as the refuge of Uralic speakers, especially the Sami. A third cluster, an east–west gradient, reveals ancient migration from Asia across the steppe corridor, and a fourth suggests migration from southwest–northeast, moving from Africa through Iberia (fig. 5.7).

This geogenetic multivariate blood chemistry analysis also revealed 5 ethnolinguistic groups to be the most genetically distinct. In rank order,

Figure 5.4.   Blood factor B in Europe. (*Sources:* Vallois and Marquer 1964; Cavalli-Sforza, Menozzi, and Piazza 1994; Mourant, Kopec, and Domaniewska-Sobczak 1958; Bunak 1974.)

these were the Basques, Sardegnans, Sami, Maltese, and Icelanders. Geographical isolation clearly plays a role, since 3 of the 5 are island people and the other 2 enjoy, respectively, the protection of a mountain range and a subarctic climate. The Basque distinctiveness, in other words, is far more profound than merely a higher Rh– frequency and involves multiple blood genes. This strengthens the likelihood that the Basques are an ancient people who lived in Europe long before the arrival of the Indo-Europeans.

Blood chemistry studies, then, seem to establish a link between genetics and language. *Genetic boundaries*—lines along which multiple blood genes change—often parallel modern language borders. Robert R. Sokal, Guido Barbujani, and others studied 63 genetic elements, gathered from blood samples collected at 3,119 localities in Europe. They identified 33 genetic

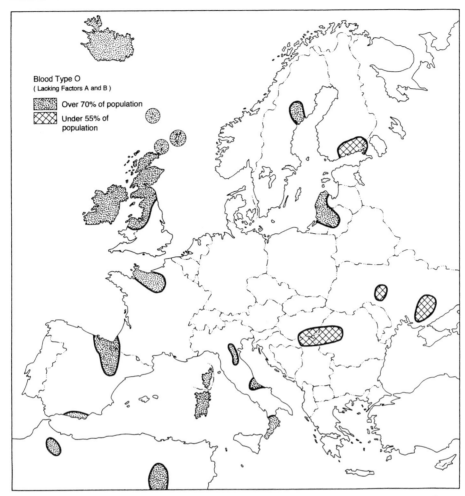

Figure 5.5.   Blood type O in Europe. (*Sources:* Vallois and Marquer 1964; Cavalli-Sforza, Menozzi, and Piazza 1994; Mourant, Kopec, and Domaniewska-Sobczak 1958; Bunak 1974.)

boundaries, 28 of which coincided with language borders (fig. 5.8). The most profound genetic changes occurred along the boundaries between the Sami and their neighbors, confirming the validity of the traditional concept of a Lapponoid subrace.

DNA Research

The latest geogenetic research involves *deoxyribonucleic acid* (**DNA**), the master genetic molecule that determines what a cell is and does. Of particular interest is the work done with *mitochondrial* DNA (*mtDNA*), which is inherited from the mother. Some 133 types of mtDNA have been discovered. Samples can be taken from blood, hair roots, or placentas.

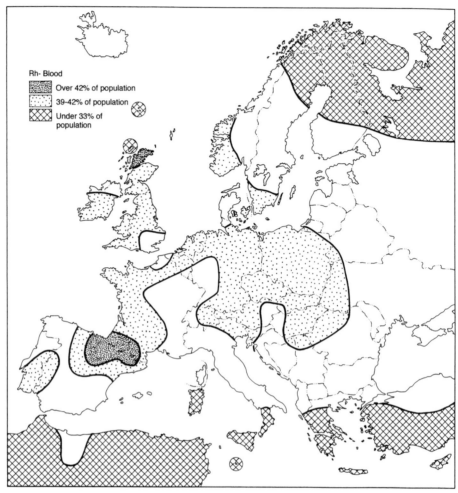

Figure 5.6.   Rh– blood frequency in Europe. (*Source:* Adapted from Cavalli-Sforza, Menozzi, and Piazza 1994.)

This molecule genetically mutates, or changes, at the constant rate of 2% to 4% per million years, providing the basis for a very rough chronology and prehistorical geography of populations. Martin Richards, Bryan Sykes, and their colleagues built upon the famous *Eve hypothesis*—that the earliest woman, from whom all humans descend, lived in Africa about 200,000 to 225,000 years ago, based on mtDNA evidence. Mutations of mtDNA that exist today in Europe, but not in Africa, allow informed speculation on European ancestries. These find support in parallel research on **male** DNA, rather than mtDNA.

The collective geogenetical work on DNA suggests that modern Europeans descend from immigrants who arrived from the Middle East and Central Asia beginning 40,000 to 50,000 years ago, and that they had earlier

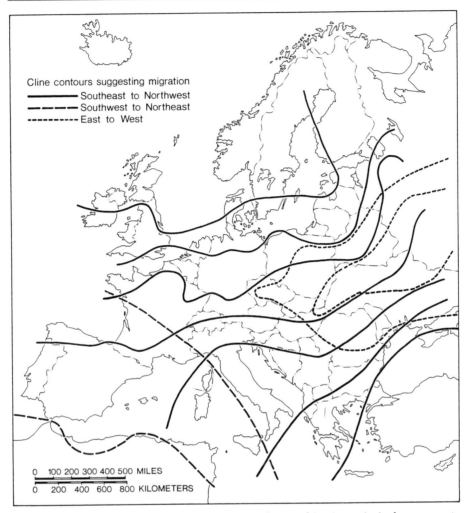

Figure 5.7.   Selected blood chemistry clines. Based on multivariate principal components analysis of thirty-nine blood gene forms at 400 sites, these clines, or spatial gradations, suggest migrations, some of which are quite ancient, from southeast to northwest, east to west, and southwest to northeast. (*Sources:* Ammerman and Cavalli-Sforza 1984, 105–107; Menozzi, Piazza, and Cavalli-Sforza 1978, 788–790, plus cover illustration.)

roots in Africa. DNA evidence of several different genetic lineages can be detected in modern Europeans. Here, then, are the true Europoid subraces.

The oldest of these, **Group 1,** revealed in mtDNA, arrived via the Bosporos crossing from Anatolia about 45,000 years ago. Their modern descendants are most common among the Basques and in the western peripheries of the British Isles, accounting for only about 6% of all Europeans. **Group 2,** indicated in male DNA, seems to have come from Central Asia, passing north of the Caspian and Black Seas and arriving about 35,000 years ago. Their descendants, too, are relatively few and appear most fre-

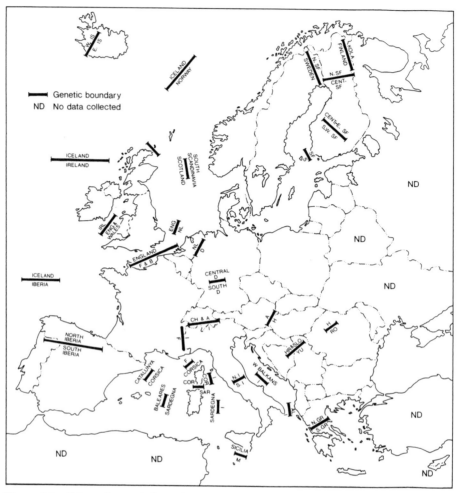

Figure 5.8. Selected genetic boundaries, based on 33 blood gene frequencies. The length of each bar is proportional to the magnitude of change at the boundary. Nearly all parallel language borders. (*Source:* Barbujani and Sokal 1990, 1817.)

quently in northern Scandinavia, especially among the Sami. **Group 3,** accounting for 80% of modern Europeans, apparently arrived about 25,000 years ago, moving from the Middle East in two prongs of migration separated by the Black Sea. **Group 4** immigration apparently accompanied the spread of agriculture and the Indo-European languages from Anatolia into Europe, about 8,000 to 10,000 years ago, branching as the languages did into Mediterranean and Danubian subgroups. They are well represented in France and northwestern Atlantic Europe, but poorly in Iberia and Sardegna. Oddly, the enormously important introduction of farming and Indo-European speech, so crucial to the development of European culture, seems to have had a rather minimal genetic impact on Europe.

Neandertals and Moderns

Geogenetic DNA research has also addressed the intriguing *Neandertal* question, joining the more traditional analysis of fossil remains. Hominids believed by some experts to be ancestral to modern humans lived in Europe as far back as 800,000 years or even earlier. About 1.7 million years ago, an early hominid, *Homo erectus*, lived in the Caucasus, as a recent fossil discovery in Georgia by geographer Reid Ferring revealed. This far periphery of Europe may have been the home of the first hominids to leave Africa. By 400,000 years ago, a type known as *archaic Homo sapiens* lived in France, and later fossils have also been found in Spain and Germany. About 230,000 years ago, probably in southwestern Europe and during an isolation of 100,000 years caused by glacial advance and climatic cooling, these archaic people evolved into **Neandertals** (*Homo neanderthalis* or *Homo sapiens neanderthalis*).

Most of the great Ice Age in Europe belonged to the Neandertals, who colonized widely (fig. 5.9) and seemed well adapted to life in the bitter cold conditions near the continental glaciers. Neandertals made stone tools,

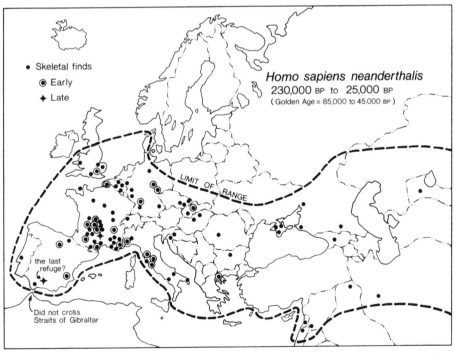

Figure 5.9.   Neandertal finds and range. *Homo sapiens neanderthalis* apparently originated in Europe and also eventually went extinct there, living in the period between 230,000 and 25,000 years ago. (*Sources:* Stringer and Gamble 1993; Dobson 1998; Hublin 1996.)

including thrust-spears, had fire in hearths, perhaps could speak, placed floral decorations in funerals, possessed brains larger than those of modern humans, and engaged in cannibalism. They differed from us in having a brow ridge on their skulls, in lacking a pointed chin, and in chewing more to the front of their mouth, using massive facial muscles. Neandertals had stocky bodies with short limbs—a good adaptation to severe cold—and possessed greater strength than we do. They lived hard lives in a difficult habitat. Lacking the bow and arrow and other projectile weapons, they had to move in close when killing game, using thrust-spears. Their skeletal remains reveal bone trauma that most closely resembles those suffered today by professional rodeo cowboys! The average Neandertal life span was only about 30 years, and the oldest remains discovered are of individuals in their 40s. Their "golden age," if such a term is appropriate, occurred between about 85,000 and 45,000 years ago. They disappeared from the scene, apparently going extinct, about 25,000 years ago, in their final refuge, Iberia. They proved incapable of crossing the narrow strait of Gibraltar, which might have led them to another refuge in North Africa.

Are Neandertals among the ancestors of modern Europeans? This is a hotly debated question, but DNA evidence seems rather conclusive. DNA extracted from several Neandertal fossils suggest that no genetic link exists. This, coupled with the admittedly imprecise migration chronology derived from DNA studies, which traces the departure of anatomically modern humans from Africa and their arrival in Europe no more than 50,000 years before the present, apparently relegates Neandertals to oblivion. Their existence probably coincided almost exactly with the duration of the Ice Age, to which they were well adapted.

Or have we completely misinterpreted them? Geographer Jerome Dobson recently theorized that Neandertals owed most of their distinctive physical characteristics to severe dietary iodine deficiency. He argues that they were merely modern humans deformed by iodine deprivation, a condition known as *cretinism* and still observable in some parts of the world today.

Whatever the character or fate of the Neandertals, Europe was destined to belong to **modern human beings** (*Homo sapiens sapiens*). Emerging from Africa, these people—our ancestors—reached the Middle East between 100,000 and 60,000 years ago, spread across Anatolia, and entered Europe at the Dardanelles about 45,000 years ago. Within only 5 millennia, they had completed the colonization of Europe, right up to the edge of the glaciers (fig. 5.10). Remarkably, they shared Europe with the Neandertals for 20,000 years, without demonstrably mixing with them genetically.

Almost simultaneous with their arrival in Europe, these modern humans achieved a cultural blossoming that, in a very real sense, can be said to mark the beginning of European civilization. Anatomically, modern humans became *behaviorally* modern. This Upper Paleolithic blossoming represented the most fundamental change in human culture in prehistory.

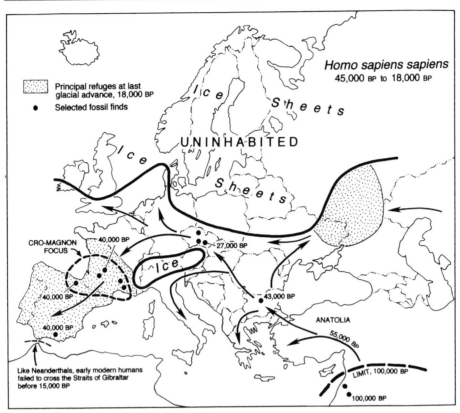

Figure 5.10. Early modern humans (*Homo sapiens sapiens*) in Europe. These people, the ancestors of the present-day Europeans, spread rapidly across the ice-free part of Europe after about 45,000 years ago, creating the first European culture area.

With it came new, refined tools and blades, needles, weaving, lamps, projectile weapons, art, sculpture, boats or rafts, complex dwelling structures, and more efficient fire hearths. The new culture spread rapidly, even suddenly, reaching Iberia and the Urals and providing the boundaries for the first European culture area. By 20,000 years ago it had yielded the exquisite cave paintings of southern France and the Cantabrian Mountains attributed to the Cro-Magnon people, the likely linguistic and genetic ancestors of the modern Basques.

About 18,000 years ago, after the demise of the Neandertals, the continental glaciers made a final southward advance, driving these early modern Europeans into 2 principal refuges—in the southwest and in the southern reaches of the East European Plain (fig. 5.10). At the abrupt end of the Ice Age, some 12,000 years ago, perhaps a few tens of thousands of them inhabited Europe. From that small base, the demographic development of modern Europe began, providing us a point of departure for a study of geodemography in the next chapter.

Sources and Suggested Readings

van Amersfoort, J.M.M., and C. Cortie. 1973. "Het Patroon van de Surinaamse Ves- tiging in Amsterdam in de Periode 1968 t/m 1970." *Tijdschrift voor Economische en Sociale Geografie* 64:283–294.

Ammerman, Albert J., and L. Luca Cavalli-Sforza. 1984. *The Neolithic Transition and the Genetics of Populations in Europe*. Princeton, N.J., USA: Princeton University Press.

Barbujani, Guido, and Robert R. Sokal. 1990. "Zones of Sharp Genetic Change in Europe Are Also Linguistic Boundaries." *Proceedings of the National Academy of Sciences, USA* 87:1816–1819.

Biasutti, Renato, et al. 1967. *Le Razze e i Popoli della Terra*. Vol. 2, *Europa–Asia*. 4th ed. Torino, I: Unione Tipografico-Editrice Torinese.

Bunak, V. 1974. "Genetic-geographical Zones of Eastern Europe by ABO Blood Groups." In *Soviet Ethnology and Anthropology Today*, ed. Y. Bromley. The Hague, NL: Mouton, 331–358.

Candella, P. B. 1942. "The Introduction of Blood Group B into Europe." *Human Biology* 14:413–444.

Cater, John, and Trevor Jones. 1979. "Ethnic Residential Space: The Case of Asians in Bradford." *Tijdschrift voor Economische en Sociale Geografie* 70:86–97.

Cavalli-Sforza, L. Luca, Paolo Menozzi, and Alberto Piazza. 1994. "Europe." Chap. 5 in *The History and Geography of Human Genes*. Princeton, N.J., USA: Princeton University Press, 255–301.

Condon, Stephanie A., and Philip E. Ogden. 1991. "Afro-Caribbean Migrants in France: Employment, State Policy and the Migration Process." *Transactions of the Institute of British Geographers* 16:440–457.

Coon, Carleton S. 1939. *The Races of Europe*. New York, USA: Macmillan.

Dobson, Jerome E. 1998. "The Iodine Factor in Health and Evolution." *Geographical Review* 88:1–28.

Drewe, P., G. A. van der Knaap, G. Mik, and H. M. Rodgers. 1975. "Segregation in Rotterdam." *Tijdschrift voor Economische en Sociale Geografie* 66:204–216.

Eaton, Martin. 1993. "Foreign Residents and Illegal Immigrants: os Negros em Por- tugal." *Ethnic and Racial Studies* 16:536–562.

Handt, Oliva, et al. 1994. "Molecular Genetic Analyses of the Tyrolean Ice Man." *Science* 264:1775–1778.

Hargreaves, Alec G., and Jeremy Leaman, eds. 1995. *Racism, Ethnicity and Politics in Contemporary Europe*. Aldershot, GB: Edward Elgar.

Hublin, Jean-J. 1996. "The First Europeans." *Archaeology* 49:36–44.

Jackson, Peter. 1992. "The Racialization of Labour in Post-war Bradford." *Journal of Historical Geography* 18:190–209.

Jones, Philip N. 1970. "Some Aspects of the Changing Distribution of Coloured Immigrants in Birmingham." *Transactions of the Institute of British Geographers* 50:199–218.

———. 1976. "Colored Minorities in Birmingham, England." *Annals of the Associa- tion of American Geographers* 66:89–103.

———. 1978. "The Distribution and Diffusion of the Coloured Population in En- gland and Wales, 1961–1971." *Transactions of the Institute of British Geographers* 3:515–532.

Jones, T. P., and D. McEvoy. 1978. "Race and Space in Cloud-Cuckoo Land." *Area* 10:162–166.

Kearsley, Geoffrey W., and Sheela R. Srivastava. 1974. "The Spatial Evolution of Glasgow's Asian Community." *Scottish Geographical Magazine* 90:110–124.

Lee, Trevor R. 1977. *Race and Residence: The Concentration and Dispersal of Immigrants in London*. Oxford, GB: Clarendon.

MacLaughlin, Jim. 1998. "Racism, Ethnicity and Multiculturalism in Contemporary Europe." *Political Geography* 17:1013–1024.

Menozzi, Paolo, Alberto Piazza, and L. Luca Cavalli-Sforza. 1978. "Synthetic Maps of Human Gene Frequencies in Europeans." *Science* 201:786–792.

Mourant, A. E., A. C. Kopec, and K. Domaniewska-Sobczak. 1958. *The ABO Blood Groups*. Oxford, GB: Blackwell.

Nilsson, Martin P. 1921. "The Race Problem of the Roman Empire." *Hereditas* 2:370–390.

Peach, Ceri. 1968. *West Indian Migration to Britain: A Social Geography*. London, GB: Oxford University Press.

———. 1996. "Does Britain Have Ghettos?" *Transactions of the Institute of British Geographers* 21:216–235.

Peach, G.C.K. 1966. "Factors Affecting the Distribution of West Indians in Great Britain." *Transactions and Paper of the Institute of British Geographers* 38:151–164.

Phillips, Caryl. 1993. *The European Tribe*. Winchester, Conn., USA: Faber & Faber.

Richards, Martin, et al. (37 authors). 2000. "Tracing European Founder Lineages in the Near Eastern mtDNA Pool." *American Journal of Human Genetics* 67: 1251–1276.

Richards, Martin, Bryan Sykes, et al. 1996. "Paleolithic and Neolithic Lineages in the European Mitochondrial Gene Pool." *American Journal of Human Genetics* 59:185–203.

Ripley, William Z. 1899. *The Races of Europe*. New York, USA: Appleton.

Robin, Nelly. 1996. *Atlas des migrations ouest-africaines vers l' Europe 1985–1993*. Paris, F: Eurostat.

Robinson, Vaughan. 1979. *The Segregation of Asians within a British City: Theory and Practice*. Oxford, GB: Oxford University School of Geography, Research Paper No. 22.

Semino, Ornella, et al. (17 authors). 2000. "The Genetic Legacy of Paleolithic Homo Sapiens in Extant Europeans: A Y Chromosome Perspective." *Science* 290:1155–1159.

Sokal, Robert R. 1988. "Genetic, Geographic, and Linguistic Distances in Europe." *Proceedings of the National Academy of Sciences, USA* 85:1722–1726.

Sokal, Robert R., et al. 1996. "Historical Population Movements in Europe Influence Genetic Relationships in Modern Samples." *Human Biology* 68 (6): 873–898.

Sokal, Robert R., Neal L. Ogden, and Barbara A. Thomson. 1988. "Genetic Changes across Language Boundaries in Europe." *American Journal of Physical Anthropology* 76:337–361.

Sokal, Robert R., Neal L. Ogden, and Chester Wilson. 1991. "Genetic Evidence for the Spread of Agriculture in Europe by Demic Diffusion." *Nature* 351:143–145.

Stringer, Christopher, and Clive Gamble. 1993. *In Search of the Neanderthals*. London, GB: Thames & Hudson.

Vallois, H. V., and P. Marquer. 1964. "Le Répartition en France des Groupes Sanguins A B O." *Bulletins et Mémoires de la Société d' Anthropologie de Paris* 6 (1): 1–200.

Wade, Nicholas. 2000. "The Origin of the Europeans." *New York Times*, 14 November, D1, D9.

CHAPTER 6

Geodemography

Europe possesses a highly distinctive demography, and various traits of its population help both to define and to differentiate the culture area. Numbers, densities, mobility, fertility, mortality, education, health, and living standards of the European people all reveal unique characteristics and geographical patterns. Religion, language, and geogenetics do not provide a full understanding of the human Europe; geodemography allows us to refine our view of the culture area.

Numbers

Europeans are very numerous, forming one of the largest population groups in the world. Within Europe (including Eurorussia, Armenia, and Georgia) live some 707 million people, a total surpassed only by Asia. About 1 of every 8 persons in the world is a European. If Eurorussia and the Caucasus states are subtracted, the remaining total, 582 million, is still more than double the population of the United States.

Six independent European states have populations in excess of 50 million, including Eurorussia with 116 million; Germany 82 million; Italy, the United Kingdom, and France, each with 59 million; and Ukraine 50 million. Eleven other European countries have at least 10 million inhabitants. European Russia, if separate, would form the ninth most populous country in the world.

Humankind did not originate in Europe, but prehistoric migration to Europe from ancestral Africa began very early. People multiplied slowly over many millennia. By the beginning of the Christian Era, about 33 million people lived in Europe, but the disruption associated with the collapse of the Roman Empire caused the total to fall to only 18 million by the year 600. The Medieval Age witnessed great population growth, to about 70 million by 1340, but then the ravages of the Black Death led to another major decline. Rebounding rapidly after about 1450, the European population reached 100 million by 1650, 200 million by shortly after 1800, 400 million by about 1900, and 600 million by 1960. During the last 2,000 years, the major center of population shifted northward from the Mediterranean to central Europe.

Density and Distribution

If the people presently living west of the Urals and north of the Mediterranean were evenly distributed over the land area of Europe, each square kilometer would contain about 72 persons. However, this figure conceals the fact that population density varies greatly from one part of Europe to another, ranging from the totally uninhabited glaciers of interior Iceland to more than 500 per square kilometer in some favored districts. Among independent states, densities range from Iceland's 2.6 persons per square kilometer to Malta's 1,200 and Monaco's 16,000.

The pattern of population distribution can even help provide boundaries for Europe. The culture area represents 1 of 4 major population clusters in the world, each of which is surrounded by areas of lower density. One way to display this pattern is through the concept of *continuous* and *discontinuous* settlement, the former including all areas in which habitations and transport routes form a dense network (fig. 6.1). Defined in this manner, Europe stands separate, bounded by sparsely settled deserts and subarctic wastes, which serve to isolate it from the peoples of sub-Saharan Africa and the great cultures of India and the Orient. To leave Europe requires passage through thinly peopled, harsh lands. Encapsulated in their separate "bubble" of continuous settlement, Europeans developed as a distinct people and culture.

Measured and mapped in another way, as the number of persons per square kilometer, the pattern of population density in Europe presents a core–periphery configuration (fig. 6.2). Most densely populated districts—those having 100, 200, or more persons per square kilometer—lie in or near the center of Europe, while regions of sparse settlement, with fewer than 25 or 50 persons per square kilometer, usually appear around the perimeter of the culture area, forming the transition into the deserts and boreal wastelands that border Europe. In the core, a corridor or axis of dense settlement reaches from England into Italy, including the Netherlands, Belgium, and Germany. In recent times, the core–periphery contrast grew even more pronounced in Europe, due to migration. In countries such as Sweden, for example, many people have abandoned the sparsely settled north to relocate in the more populous south.

Many causal forces interacted, over centuries, to produce the pattern of population distribution. Some of these forces reside in the physical environment. For example, most areas of densest population lie in the lowland

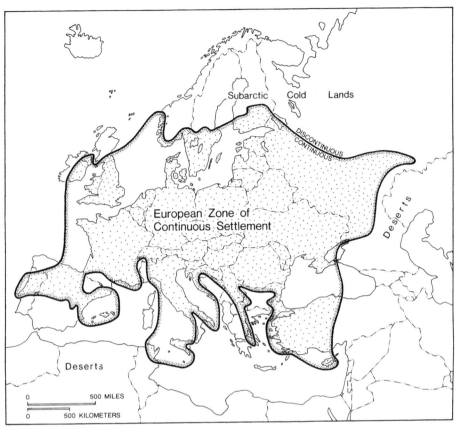

Figure 6.1.   Europe forms one of four major or "primary" clusters of "continuous" settle-ment in the world. "Continuous settlement" means that all habitations lie no more than 5 kilometers from other habitations in at least 6 different directions and that roads/railroads lie no farther than 16 to 32 kilometers away in at least 3 directions. In other words, the term describes a densely inhabited land, served by a transport network. (*Sources:* Adapted from Kirk H. Stone, 1993, personal communication; Stone 1978, 196; Stone 1962, 1966, 1971.)

plains regions, especially in the fertile, loessial parts of the Great European Plain, while European mountain ranges stand out as zones of sparser settle-ment. Also, Europeans have tended to avoid the colder climates, and the northern border of continuous settlement in Scandinavia follows very closely the line between humid continental and subarctic climate types.

Migration

The most potent force influencing population density is migration, and Europeans have always proven remarkably mobile, especially during the past 3 centuries. A great many "push" and "pull" factors work to prompt

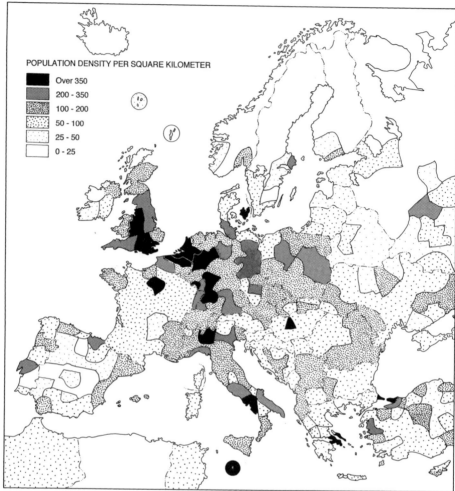

Figure 6.2. Population density in Europe. A distinct core–periphery pattern is evident. A core area of over 200 persons per square kilometer reaches southeast from the Anglican Plain through the Low Country and Germany to Sicilia, forming an English–Rhenish–Italian axis of dense population. Peripheral regions, especially the subarctic north, are far more sparsely settled.

the decision to leave one's home and seek another. From about 1500 to 1950, emigration from Europe constituted the dominant flow. During that period, many millions of Europeans departed for Anglo-America, Latin America, Australia, New Zealand, South Africa, Israel, Siberia, and Algeria. Iberians began the exodus in the 1500s. Between 1600 and 1880, this greatest emigration in all history involved mainly northwestern Europeans of Germanic and Celtic background seeking better economic opportunity abroad. After about 1870, the exodus spread to southern and eastern Europe.

Some countries lost substantial parts of their total populations in this manner, causing major changes in densities. The island of Ireland provides a good example. In 1841, the census listed more than 8 million Irish, a density of nearly 100 per square kilometer, and by the middle of the decade the Irish population had reached an all-time high of almost 8.5 million. Then came the great famine of the mid-1840s, bringing death to hundreds of thousands, and in its wake a massive and persistent out-migration to Great Britain and overseas. In a 5-year span from 1846 to 1851, some 800,000 Irish starved or perished from disease, and another million emigrated to foreign lands. Hardest hit was interior Ireland, where one county lost more than 20% of its population through emigration (fig. 6.3). A century later, a little more than half as many people resided in Ireland as in 1841. By the end of the twentieth century, 8.5 times as many persons claim-

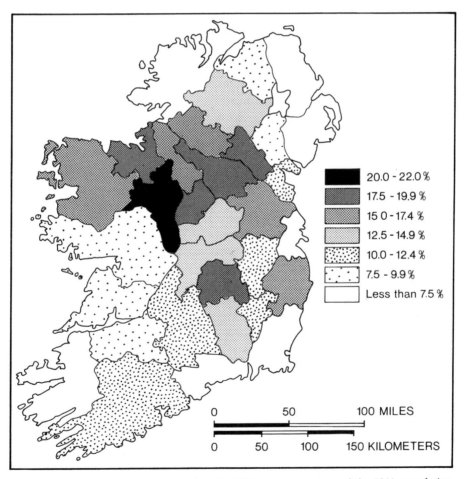

Figure 6.3. Emigration from Ireland, 1846–1851, as a percentage of the 1841 population. (*Sources:* After Cousens 1960, 121; see also Johnson 1988, 78–87.)

ing Irish ancestry lived in the United States as remained in Ireland, and even Canada had a fourth as many Irish as the home country.

Germans, too, departed their native land in enormous numbers, settling mainly in the United States but also in southern Brazil, Canada, and South Africa. Persons of German ancestry constitute the largest national origin group in the United States, numbering some 60 million in 1990, about 73% of the present population of Germany. Sweden and Norway experienced huge proportional losses. Between 20% and 25% of the total population of those two Scandinavian countries emigrated overseas in the nineteenth century.

Immigration

About 1950 Europe rather suddenly changed from a land dominated by emigration to one of immigration, and that pattern has prevailed to the present. A booming economy attracted foreign workers, and growing affluence left many Europeans unwilling to engage in menial jobs. Among the immigrants drawn into Europe to supply needed labor were the West Indians, Africans, and Asians mentioned in chapter 5, who came mainly to the United Kingdom, France, and the Netherlands.

Another major immigrant flow brought about 1 million Muslims from the formerly French-ruled **Maghreb** countries of North Africa—Morocco, Algeria, and Tunisia (fig. 6.4). Following on the heels of numerous ethnic French fleeing Algeria after that country overthrew rule by France in 1962, the Maghreb Muslims came mainly to France. In addition, many Moroccans went to Belgium and the Netherlands. The Maghreb immigration to France peaked in the 1970s, after which Italy and Spain became their major destinations. Paralleling the Maghreb immigration, another 2 million persons or more entered Europe from **Turkey** prior to 1990, three-quarters of them headed to Germany (fig. 6.4). Turks also became the largest non-European immigrant group in Switzerland and Sweden.

Since about 1990, this mass immigration has changed in character. The sources are now more diverse, reaching into sub-Saharan Africa and South Asia, though the Maghreb and Turkey remain important. In addition, most of the immigration in the past decade has been illegal, crossing into Europe at Gibraltar, at the waist of the Mediterranean, and at the Strait of Otranto. In 1996 alone, some 700,000 illegal immigrants reportedly escaped detection in Italy, and on the beaches north of Napoli thousands of sub-Saharan Africans live in makeshift shacks. The destination is almost always the EU countries, especially Germany. Switzerland is also a favored destination, and fully 20% of that country's population now consists of foreign born, over twice the proportion in the United States. Germany houses about 8 million foreign born.

An anti-immigrant backlash has developed in most of the major desti-

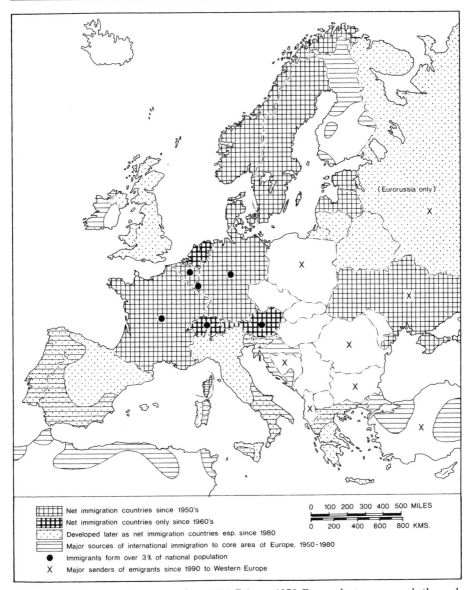

Figure 6.4.   Migration in Europe since 1950. Prior to 1950, Europe lost more people through migration than it gained, but since then the greater part of the culture area has become an immigration zone. (*Sources:* Adapted from King 1993b, 1993c, 24, 209.)

nation countries. Certain right-wing political parties, such as France's National Front, Austria's Freedom Party, and the Swiss People's Party openly oppose immigration, and in Austria this sentiment reached the highest levels of government in 2000. Some 500,000 illegal immigrants continue to enter the European Union each year. Many Europeans feel threatened today, fearing being overwhelmed by masses of poor people from the Third

World. Germans and Austrians have coined the word *überfremdung* ("over-foreignization") to describe this perceived threat.

Far less stigmatized is another type of immigration. After the collapse of the Soviet Union in 1991, ethnic Russians and Germans residing in the former Soviet Central Asian republics, particularly Kazakhstan, began moving to Russia and Germany, reversing a centuries' old diaspora and overwhelming the supply of jobs, housing, and social services. It differs from typical European immigration in that it involves the return of European-derived populations to Europe, rather than the intrusion of ethnically alien foreigners. As such, the migration can be compared to the movement of ethnic French out of Algeria in the 1960s.

Internal Migration

Equally profound mass migration occurs *within* Europe, a movement centuries old. One prevalent flow that began in the nineteenth century and still has not run its course everywhere is **rural–urban** migration. Other internal migration generally falls in the category of **periphery–core,** though several distinctly different flows can be detected. Perhaps the prototype for this sort of migration involved the large-scale movement of Irish to Great Britain in the nineteenth century, a movement that has greatly diminished. Of far greater magnitude in the periphery–core shift was the *south–north* migration in the period 1950 to 1975. Spain, Portugal, Italy, Greece, Croatia, and Slovenia became the major senders, with destinations lying mainly in France, Germany, Belgium, the Netherlands, and the Alpine countries (fig. 6.4). Some 5 million persons took part in this migration, including 1.7 million Italians, mainly from the impoverished southern part of that country, and 1.1 million Portuguese. They blazed a trail to the north in the 1950s and early 1960s that would later be followed by the Maghreb Africans and Turks. As late as 1970 in Germany, Yugoslavs and Italians ranked as the two largest immigrant groups. Portugal and Spain contributed disproportionately to France, and the Low Countries also received large contingents of Spaniards. Many Greek Cypriots came to the United Kingdom. Numerous southern European emigrants eventually returned to their native lands.

The northern periphery of Europe, far more thinly populated than the south, could not send mass migration to the core. Even so, a sizable proportion of the northerners went south, most notably Finns from subarctic districts who sought employment opportunities in central and southern Sweden.

At present, the largest periphery–core movement under way involves **east–west** migration. Long dammed up by the Iron Curtain and Cold War, this new avenue of mobility opened in earnest in the late 1980s. The former East Germany experienced a population decline of 1 million between 1989 and 1994. Dire predictions of uncontrollable mass migration from the east appeared, including speculation that as many as 40 million Russians desired to move west. The influx of 43,000 desperate Albanians to Italy in 1991 led a news weekly there to editorialize that "well-to-do Europe intends to defend itself from the invasion of the new barbarians who come from the East." In the same year, the French similarly recoiled at the sight of thousands of eastern Europeans camped in tents in the Bois de Boulogne Park in Paris, and the government acted to evict them. As early as 1989, about 1 million eastern Europeans, excluding emigrants from East Germany, resided in western Europe. About a third of these consisted of ethnic Germans from countries such as Romania, who enjoy the legal right to come to Germany.

Still, the predicted tidal wave of east–west migration has not materialized, in part because of more restrictive immigration policies. Only Germany, which housed one million eastern Europeans by 1990, and Austria, home to 600,000 foreigners by 1992, felt serious impacts, and many of their immigrants are Balkan War refugees or ethnic Germans. Berlin is now home to 100,000 Russians, many of them Jews, but migration from Russia and other former Soviet republics apparently peaked in 1990 at 454,000. Many eastern European states have a larger volume of immigration than emigration (fig. 6.4). Barring total economic collapse in the east, migration seems unlikely to get out of control. However, the great disparity in wealth and living standards between the 2 halves of Europe will continue to exert a powerful westward pull, and an even more profound contrast along Europe's Mediterranean frontier likewise produces continuing instability.

Zero Population Growth

One of the distinguishing human traits that sets Europeans apart has been their mastery over both fertility and mortality. A phenomenon known as the **demographic transition** originated in Europe in the nineteenth century. Prior to this far-reaching change, both birth rates and death rates remained high. Then, initiating the transition, Europeans lowered the death rate through improved health care and the elimination of famine, causing a major population explosion in the short run since birth rates stayed high.

The second stage of the demographic transition also began in Europe. It involved a gradual, persistent fall in the birth rate, leading to *sustained fertility decline* and to a situation in which both birth and death rates were low. The European population explosion had ended, ushering in a period of slow growth.

The transition initially revealed a vivid geography. Sustained fertility decline first appeared in France about 1820 (fig. 6.5). Ethnic minorities in France and people in other countries were initially slow to follow the French example, with the result that France fell behind major neighboring countries in size of population. In the 1700s, 1 of every 6 Europeans was

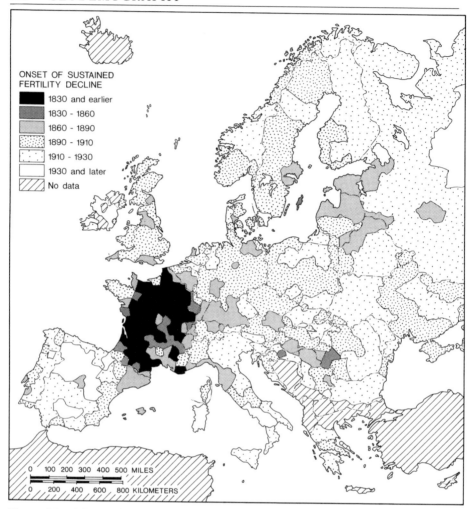

Figure 6.5. Advent of sustained fertility decline in Europe. The French-speaking part of France provided the prototype for diminished fertility. People in other countries were slow to emulate the French, but diffusion to the various peripheries of Europe eventually occurred. Today, all areas have birth rates far below the world average. (*Source:* Adapted from Coale and Watkins 1986, 484.)

French, and even as late as 1850, the French outnumbered the Germans, Italians, and British, but by 1970 they had become the smallest of these 4 nations.

Eventually, sustained fertility decline spread, following a **core–periphery** path. By 1900, about half of all European provinces had been affected (fig. 6.5), and today birth rates have become remarkably low throughout the culture area. In Europe as a whole, the annual rate of natural population change now stands at –0.1%, a startling contrast to Africa's 2.5% or even Turkey's 1.5%. In other words, Europe is the first sizable region in the world to attain *zero population growth*, with the number of births annually equal to the number of deaths.

Achievement of sustained fertility decline came last to the fringe areas of Europe, and some remnants of a core–periphery pattern can still be detected in the map of annual natural population change (fig. 6.6). Communist rule in eastern Europe and governmental encouragement of large families retarded the decline of birth rates, especially in Romania, but a major decline in fertility began in the east after 1990. In Russia, for example, the annual birth rate fell from 17.2 per thousand inhabitants in 1987 to only

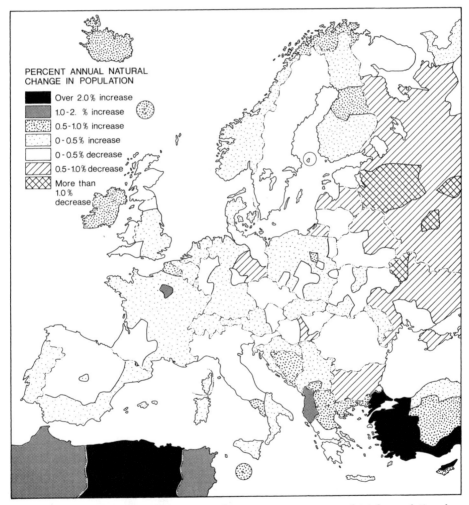

Figure 6.6. Annual natural population change, as a percentage of total population, by province. This rate is achieved by comparing the number of births and deaths in a year, calculating the difference (either plus or minus), and taking it as a percentage of population. Faint core–periphery and east–west patterns can be detected. Gains or losses through migration are not reflected here.

8.9 in 1996. Eastern Germany's birth rate declined from 11.1 in 1990, at the time of reunification, to only 5.1 as early as 1993. Some peripheral European areas remain anomalous in fertility, as, for example, Iceland, the Arctic fringe, and Muslim sections of the Balkans. The southern and eastern borders of the European culture area, where it touches the Islamic world, stand out very clearly on the map of annual population change. Today, perhaps this sharp contrast provides our elusive boundary for the European culture area.

Demographic Collapse?

Europe, in fact, has experienced the *second demographic transition,* in which birth rates fall below death rates, causing population decline. A most revealing measure is the *total fertility rate* (TFR), meaning the number of children born to the average woman during her lifetime. A TFR of 2.1 is required to maintain zero population growth. As the present millennium dawned, Europe's TFR stood at only 1.4, assuring substantial natural population decrease in coming decades. Western Germany provided the prototype, quickly followed by Austria and Hungary. Fertility dropped below replacement level there about 1965, with natural population decline setting in by 1980. The TFR in Europe as a whole had fallen to 1.69 as early as 1985 and in western Germany to 1.28. Russia experienced the second demographic transition with surprising rapidity; deaths exceeded births by 200,000 there in 1992 and by 800,000 the following year, by which time the TFR had declined to only 1.4. Today, Russia's TFR stands at 1.2. Even lower rank Bulgaria and Czechia at 1.1. Not one single European country today except Albania has a TFR as high as 2.1—the replacement level. Terms such as "demographic collapse" or "demographic crisis" are heard today in describing Europe. A greater contrast to the Third World, with its exploding populations, could not be imagined.

Clearly, most Europeans have decided that children are more of a liability than an asset. They achieved this remarkably low level of fertility through diverse techniques. In the formative stage in early nineteenth-century France, *infanticide*—the killing of the newborn—occurred widely. *Abortion,* early achieved with various folk medicines and later at modern, state-supported clinics, remains another favored European method, though now in decline. Abortion is disproportionately an *eastern* European birth control technique, and the annual number of abortions exceeds live births in Russia, Ukraine, Bulgaria, Belarus, Romania, Estonia, and Latvia (fig. 6.7). In the Homyel' District of Belarus, the area most severely doused with radioactive fallout in the Chornobyl nuclear disaster, 3 abortions are performed for every 1 live birth. In most of Europe, sterilization and diverse modern contraceptive techniques are preferred over abortion.

Or is there more than simply a desire for fewer children or a fear of

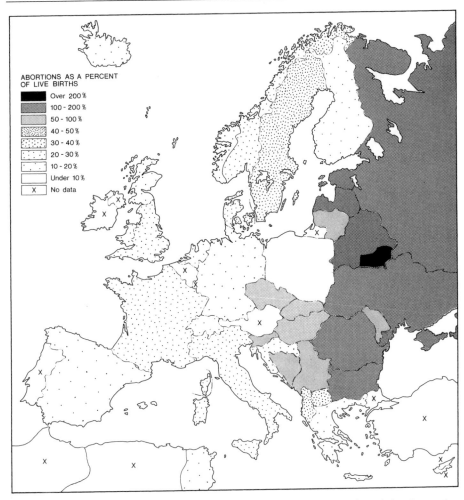

Figure 6.7.   Abortions as a percentage of live births, ca. 1990. The legality of abortion varies within Europe, as does its application. It appears to be the principal device for fertility control in eastern Europe. Poland instituted very restrictive abortion laws after 1990, and in the former East Germany, the abortion rate fell by 40% between 1989 and 1992. Internal differentiation is shown only for BY, N, and GB.

birth deformities at work in Europe's demographic decline? A study of European males revealed that their sperm count per milliliter of semen had fallen from 113 in 1938 to 66 by 1990. Perhaps severe environmental pollution has had an adverse effect on reproductive ability. In any case, if it were not for substantial immigration from Africa and Asia, the population of Europe would already be in sharp decline.

The result of both of these demographic transitions has been a rapid decline of the European proportion of the world population. In the year 1900, Europe accounted for 25% of the world total, but a century later in

2000, only just under 12% of all humans lived in Europe, and the proportion continues to decline. Should the present trend continue, Europeans will constitute an insignificant part of the world population by the year 2025, making the culture area an even more enticing goal of mass immigration from the impoverished Third World.

Age Structure

Because of fertility control and the reduction of the death rate, Europe's population is the world's oldest. All but 1 of the 20 countries in the world having the greatest proportion of people aged 65 or older lie in Europe, led by Sweden, Italy, and Monaco. Many provinces, especially in the European Union, have an aged population forming 16% or more of the total; a few even exceed 20% (fig. 6.8). With each passing year, these proportions grow higher. In 1999, Italy became the first country in the world having more people over the age of 65 than under 15, a status that is now shared with Germany, Greece, and San Marino. Major problems concerning provision of health and welfare services to an older population loom, since such a large demographic sector has reached retirement age. The later onset of profoundly diminished fertility in eastern Europe and most peripheral areas yields noticeable east–west and core–periphery patterns. The most obvious contrasts, however, separate Europe from North Africa, Turkey, and the Middle East.

The more affluent among Europe's elderly often migrate to selected provinces, helping to shape the map of aging. Many retired people seek to escape cities and colder regions. In Great Britain, for example, southern England's coast remains a preferred destination for retirees; the south of France enjoys popularity within that country; and the south coast of Norway lures many of the aged Norse. Some even leave their native country and migrate to the sunny Mediterranean, at least for part of the year. By the middle 1980s, for example, some 2,500 elderly Norwegians resided in the Benidorm District south of Valencia in Spain. In eastern Europe, by contrast, the elderly usually move to the cities, where their children live and health care amenities are better. Poland has such a migration pattern.

Education

Another distinctly European demographic trait is a high level of formal education. By any measure, Europe possesses the best-schooled population of any sizable area in the world. To understand the enormous global impact Europe has had, we must recognize that we deal here with skilled, educated people, not with poorly schooled or illiterate masses.

Access to basic education for the great majority of Europeans devel-

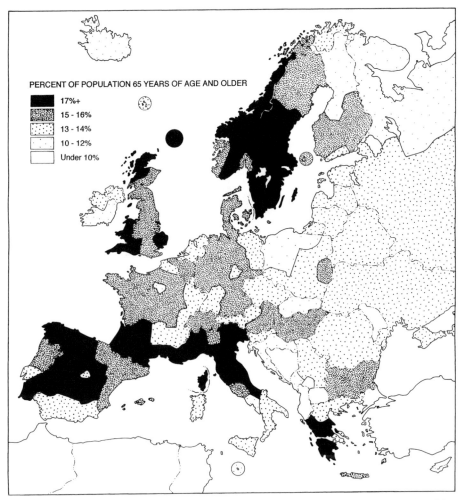

Figure 6.8.   Percentage of population aged 65 or older. Europe's population is far older than the world average. Undifferentiated sizable countries are BG, BY, CZ, H, RO, and Ua.

oped in the nineteenth and early twentieth centuries, beginning in north-western Europe and spreading southward and eastward. German peasants learned to read and write in the first half of the 1800s, while most Russians, Italians, and other Mediterranean and Slavic farm folk remained illiterate. Only after the Communist takeover did education become available to the average Russian. In most of Europe, education spread to the masses be-cause of ambitious government-supported education plans. European cen-tral governments direct the operation of schools.

The literacy rate offers a crude but still revealing measure of basic edu-cation. The overwhelming majority of Europeans above the age of 15 can read and write, and in most countries, from Ireland to Russia, the propor-tion stands at 99% or even higher. Only in Portugal, Albania, and Macedonia does the level fall below 90%. The Mediterranean forms an educational fault line along Europe's southern boundary, beyond which literacy rates are far lower, as in Morocco, at 44%, Algeria 59%, Turkey 82%, and Syria 70%.

More revealing than basic literacy is the level of reading proficiency. A recent survey, done in the late 1990s, found that the proportion of adults reading at the lowest of 5 levels stood at only 7% in Sweden, 11% in the Netherlands, 14% in Switzerland, and 15% in Germany. Surprisingly, 40% of adults in France ranked in this lowest reading category, comparable to Poland's 43%.

Other measures of education also prove revealing, as for example book readership. Northern Europe leads in the number of book titles published each year. Germany ranks first, followed by the United Kingdom, France, Spain, and the Netherlands. The high position of Spain results in part from the demands of a huge overseas Spanish-speaking population. On a per capita basis, Iceland, Denmark, Finland, and Switzerland lead. The Icelandic, Danish, and Finnic achievements are made even more remarkable by the fact that little or no foreign demand exists for books in the languages of those nations. Lowest levels of book production per capita occur in Ukraine, Romania, Belarus, and Albania, but even these countries compare favorably to bordering non-European states.

A testing of 13-year-old students in 40 countries and provinces worldwide in math and science skills is also revealing (fig. 6.9). The results were surprising, as for example in the relatively low ranking of countries such as Germany, France, and Sweden. The Dutch-speaking part of Belgium ranked much higher than French-speaking Wallonia. Among the top 4 countries in math skills, all lay in Asia, as was true of 3 of the top 4 in science.

Health

If Europeans are "wise," they are also usually healthy and wealthy. Access to high-quality affordable medical care remains the rule; doctor–patient ratios are low; the typical European consumes abundant, nutritional food; the traditional epidemic and endemic diseases have been banished; and life expectancy, with some eastern European exceptions, exceeds 70 years. Only Russians and Moldovans, whose life expectancy is 67 years, Belorussians and Ukrainians at 68, and Romanians at 69 fall below this level. Iceland, Sweden, Andorra, and Switzerland rank highest, at 79 years. These remarkable achievements in human health emanated from the core area of Europe and spread to the peripheries, a diffusion completed in fairly recent times. In Greece, representative of the European periphery, male life expectancy rose from 49 to 70 years in the half-century between 1930 and 1980. Only parts of eastern Europe in which the collapse of communism led to a

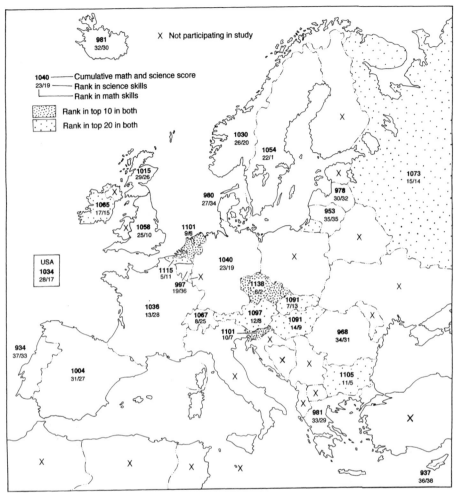

Figure 6.9.   Math and science skills of 13-year-old students. Rankings are shown worldwide among 40 selected countries. Separate scores and totals are shown for England, Scotland, Vlaanderen, and Wallonia in GB and B. (*Sources:* Third International Math and Science Study; *Economist,* 29 March 1997, 21.)

rapidly deteriorating level of health care and nutrition after 1990 depart substantially from the prevalent high standards.

The most revealing single indicator of health standards is the **infant mortality rate.** Indeed, this index, which shows the number of infants per thousand that die before reaching the age of 1 year, is widely regarded as the best single measure not just of health, but of the overall standard of living (fig. 6.10). Within Europe, a pronounced east–west contrast in the infant mortality rate exists. Romania, Macedonia, and Albania have the highest rates in Europe, ranging between 17 and 25. But even in eastern Europe, the rate remains good by world standards. In much of Africa and

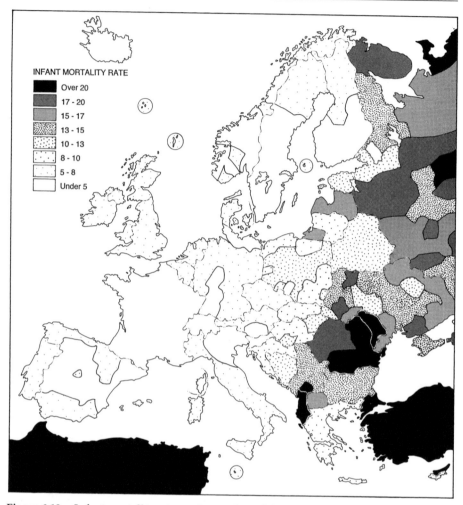

Figure 6.10. Infant mortality rate, or the number of deaths of children under 1 year of age per 1,000 live births. Many experts feel that this rate provides the single best index of the standard of living. The east–west and Europe–Africa contrasts are startling.

Asia, the infant mortality rate stands well above 100, and just across the Mediterranean and Aegean, one encounters rates such as 43 in Turkey, 44 in Algeria, and 52 in Egypt.

The major illnesses that still plague Europeans are those of the modern, industrial world: cancer, circulatory diseases, respiratory maladies, and, of course, Acquired Immune Deficiency Syndrome (AIDS). Environmental pollution can perhaps be blamed for many of these disorders. Respiratory diseases, for example, occur most frequently in the core countries of Europe, including the United Kingdom, Belgium, the Netherlands, Germany, Poland (which has the highest incidence in the world), and Czechia, where atmospheric pollution is most severe. In other cases, diseases seem to occur selectively in certain ethnic groups. Stomach cancer rates, for example, are highest in northern Wales and among the Dutch-speaking Belgians, suggesting a link to culturally based dietary preferences.

The AIDS epidemic reached Europe rather early, apparently diffusing from both Africa and North America. The disease took root initially in the southwest, especially in France and Spain, and the incidence remains highest there. No corner of Europe has escaped AIDS, but the countries of eastern Europe still report very low incidences, with the notable exception of the Kaliningrad exclave of Russia.

Wealth

On the average, Europeans remain far wealthier than the greater part of humanity, but conditions vary substantially within the culture area. Personal income is a poor measure of wealth, due to the variability of benefits received from governments in various countries and greatly differing inflation rates. More revealing is the **gross domestic product** (GDP), a measure of all goods and services produced within a country or province within a given time span, particularly when calculated on a *per capita* basis. The GDP per capita in the more prosperous countries exceeds $25,000, and this elite group includes Switzerland, Austria, Denmark, Germany, Iceland, Liechtenstein, Luxembourg, Norway, and Sweden. The per capita GDP for the 15 member countries of the European Union is $22,000.

The map of per capita GDP, measured by province, provides a startling picture of Europe's internal contrasts in wealth. A core–periphery pattern visually competes with an east–west component (fig. 6.11). The poorest areas, where economic conditions are bad and not improving, stretches from the Balkans into the East European Plain.

Such profound internal regional differences in wealth produce an inherent instability in Europe. Can so many live in such profound affluence next door to relative deprivation? Can Europe's "haves" and "have-nots" peacefully coexist? The European Union has long recognized the problems inherent within its own 15-nation member group, actively investing in poorer peripheral areas. But the economic distress of the Balkans and eastern Europe is of such great magnitude that the wealthy countries probably could not correct the problem even if they tried. Add to these internal contrasts the economic disparity between the prosperous half of Europe and adjacent North Africa, and the geographical position of the affluent, Europeans become insular, rendering their prosperity fragile and imperiled.

Europe, then, reveals vivid, ever-changing geodemographic contrasts, both internally and in comparison to bordering non-European countries. In part, these and other human patterns are rooted in the political geography of Europe, a topic dealt with in the next chapter.

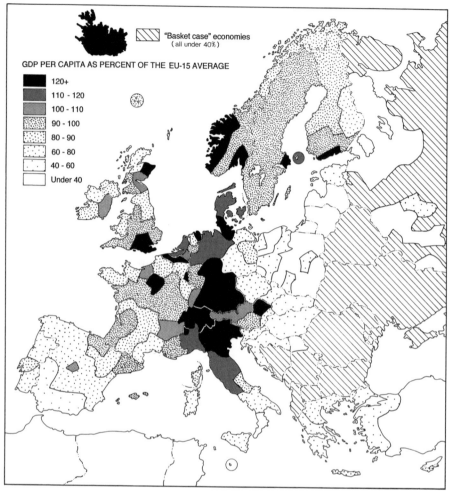

Figure 6.11. Distribution of wealth in Europe. The gross domestic product (GDP) is the value of all goods and services combined and should reveal the total output of the economy. Here, GDP per capita is the measure, shown as a percentage of the average GDP of all 15-member countries of the European Union (see fig. 7.17), of the wealthiest in the culture area. "Basket case" economies are those at the lowest level that are worsening or not improving markedly. Both core–periphery and east–west contrasts are evident.

Sources and Suggested Readings

Almagia, Roberto. 1929. "The Repopulation of the Roman Campagna." *Geographical Review* 19:529–555.

Berentsen, William H. 1996. "Regional Population Changes in Eastern Germany after Unification." *Post-Soviet Geography and Economics* 37:615–632.

Borgegård, Lars-Erik, Johan Håkansson, and Gunnar Malmberg. 1995. "Population Redistribution in Sweden." *Geografiska Annaler* 77B:31–45.

Breuer, Toni. 1986. "Changing Patterns of the Population Distribution in Spain." *GeoJournal* 13:75–84.

Carter, Francis W., R. A. French, and John Salt. 1993. "International Migration between East and West in Europe." *Ethnic and Racial Studies* 16:467–491.

Carter, Francis W., and W. Maik. 1999. *Shock-shift in an Enlarged Europe: The Geography of Socio-economic Change in East-central Europe after 1989*. Aldershot, GB: Ashgate.

Coale, Ansley J., and Susan C. Watkins, eds. 1986. *The Decline of Fertility in Europe*. Princeton, N.J., USA: Princeton University Press.

Cole, John P., and Igor V. Filatotchev. 1992. "Some Observations on Migration within and from the Former USSR in the 1990s." *Post-Soviet Geography* 33:432–453.

Coleman, David A. 1993. "Contrasting Age Structures of Western Europe and of Eastern Europe and the Former Soviet Union." *Population and Development Review* 19:523–555.

Compton, Paul A. 1976. "Religious Affiliation and Demographic Variability in Northern Ireland." *Transactions of the Institute of British Geographers* 1:433–445.

Cousens, S. H. 1960. "The Regional Pattern of Emigration during the Great Irish Famine, 1846–51." *Institute of British Geographers, Transactions and Papers* 28:121.

Demko, George J., Grigory Ioffe, and Zhanna Zaionchkovskaya, eds. 1999. *Population under Duress: The Geodemography of Post-Soviet Russia*. Boulder, Colo., USA: Westview.

Eberstadt, Nicholas. 1994. "Demographic Shocks in Eastern Germany, 1989–93." *Europe–Asia Studies* 46:519–533.

Fielding, Tony, and Hans Blotevogel. 1997. *People, Jobs, and Mobility in the New Europe*. New York, USA: Wiley.

Grigg, David. 1995. "The Nutritional Transition in Western Europe." *Journal of Historical Geography* 21:247–261.

Haliczer, Josef. 1934. "The Population of Europe, 1720, 1820, 1930." *Geography* 19:261–273.

Hall, Ray. 1993. "Europe's Changing Population." *Geography* 78 (1): 3–15.

Hall, Ray, and Paul White, eds. 1995. *Europe's Population: Towards the Next Century*. London, GB: University College Press.

Hamilton, Kimberly A. 1994. *Migration and the New Europe*. Boulder, Colo., USA: Westview.

Haub, Carl. 1995. "Population Changes in the Former Soviet Republics." *Population Bulletin* 49 (4).

Heilig, Gerhard, Thomas Büttner, and Wolfgang Lutz. 1990. "Germany's Population: Turbulent Past, Uncertain Future." *Population Bulletin* 45 (4): 1–45.

Hillmann, Felicitas, and Thomas Krings. 1996. "Einwanderer aus Entwicklungsländern nach Italien." *Die Erde* 127:127–143.

Hooimeijer, Pieter, et al., eds. 1994. *Population Dynamics in Europe: Current Issues in Population Geography*. Utrecht, NL: Netherlands Geographical Studies, No. 173.

Johnson, James H. 1988. "The Distribution of Irish Emigration in the Decade before the Great Famine." *Irish Geography* 21 (2): 78–87.

———. 1990. "The Context of Migration: The Example of Ireland in the Nineteenth Century." *Transactions of the Institute of British Geographers* 15:259–276.

Jones, P. N., and M. T. Wild. 1992. "Western Germany's Third Wave of Migrants: The Arrival of the Aussiedler." *Geoforum* 23:1–11.

Joshi, Heather, ed. 1989. *The Changing Population of Britain*. New York, USA: Basil Blackwell.

van de Kaa, Dirk J. 1987. "Europe's Second Demographic Transition." *Population Bulletin* 42 (1): 1–57.

King, Russell. 1993a. "Italy Reaches Zero Population Growth." *Geography* 78:63–69.

———, ed. 1993b. *Mass Migration in Europe: The Legacy and the Future.* London, GB: Belhaven.

———, ed. 1993c. *The New Geography of European Migrations.* New York, USA: Wiley.

———. 1996. "Migration and Development in the Mediterranean Region." *Geography* 81:3–14.

Korcelli, Piotr, and Alina Potrykowska. 1988. "Redistribution of the Elderly Population in Poland." *Geographia Polonica* 58:121–138.

Krings, Thomas. 1995. "Internationale Migration nach Deutschland und Italien im Vergleich." *Geographische Rundschau* 47:437–442.

Leitner, Helga. 1997. "Reconfiguring the Spatiality of Power: The Construction of a Supranational Migration Framework for the European Union." *Political Geography* 16:123–143.

Lesthaeghe, Ron. 1983. "A Century of Demographic and Cultural Change in Western Europe." *Population and Development Review* 9:411–435.

Lora-Tamayo D'Ocon, Gloria. 1996. "Extranjeros en España en 1991." *Estudios Geográficos* 57:67–92.

Löytönen, Markku. 1991. "The Spatial Diffusion of Human Immunodeficiency Virus Type 1 in Finland, 1982–1997." *Annals of the Association of American Geographers* 81:127–151.

Malkhazova, Svetlana M., et al. 1997. "Public Health and Environmental Pollution in Russia." *Bulletin, International Geographical Union* 47 (1): 5–16.

Mead, William R. 1951. "The Cold Farm in Finland, Resettlement of Finland's Displaced Farmers." *Geographical Review* 41:529–543.

Myklebost, Hallstein. 1989. "Migration of Elderly Norwegians." *Norsk Geografisk Tidsskrift* 43:191–213.

Noin, Daniel, and Robert Woods, eds. 1993. *The Changing Population of Europe.* Oxford, GB: Blackwell.

Oberhauser, Ann M. 1991. "The International Mobility of Labor: North African Migrant Workers in France." *Professional Geographer* 43:431–445.

Ogden, Philip E., and Paul E. White. 1989. *Migrants in Modern France.* London, GB: Unwin Hyman.

Pounds, Norman J. G., and Charles C. Roome. 1971. "Population Density in Fifteenth Century France and the Low Countries." *Annals of the Association of American Geographers* 61:116–130.

Preusser, Hubertus. 1976. "Entwicklung und räumliche Differenzierung der Bevölkerung Islands." *Geografiska Annaler* 58B:116–144.

Range, Peter R., and Joanna B. Pinneo. 1993. "Europe Faces an Immigrant Tide." *National Geographic* 183 (5): 94–125.

Salt, John, and Hugh Clout, eds. 1976. *Migration in Post-war Europe: Geographical Essays.* London, GB: Oxford University Press.

Samers, Michael. 1998. "Immigration, Ethnic Minorities, and Social Exclusion in the European Union." *Geoforum* 29:123–144.

van Selm, Bert. 1998. "Economic Performance in Russia's Regions." *Europe–Asia Studies* 50: 612–613.

Siirilä, Seppo, Lauri Hautamäki, Jorma Kuitunen, and Timo Keski-Petäjä. 1990. "Regional Well-being Variations in Finland." *Fennia* 168:179–200.

Stone, Kirk H. 1962. "Swedish Fringes of Settlement." *Annals of the Association of American Geographers* 52:373–393.

———. 1966. "Finnish Fringe of Settlement Zones." *Tijdschrift voor Economische en Sociale Geografie* 57:222–232.

———. 1971. "Regionalizing Spain's Continuous and Discontinuous Settlement." *Geoforum* 8:9–14.

———. 1978. "The World's Primary Settlement Regions." *GeoJournal* 2 (3): 196.

Thorarinsson, Sigurdur. 1961. "Population Changes in Iceland." *Geographical Review* 51:519–533.

Thumerelle, Pierre-Jean. 1992. "Migrations internationales et changement géopolitique en Europe." *Annales de Géographie* 101:289–318.

Usher, Abbott P. 1930. "The History of Population and Settlement in Eurasia." *Geographical Review* 20:110–132.

Velikonja, J. 1958. "Postwar Population Movements in Europe." *Annals of the Association of American Geographers* 48:458–481.

Volkers, Kees. 1991. "Selective Migration in the Netherlands: The Case of the Northeast Polder." *Hommes et Terres du Nord* 2/3:181–188.

Walsh, James A. 1991. "The Turn-around of the Turn-around in the Population of the Republic of Ireland." *Irish Geography* 24:117–125.

CHAPTER 7

Geopolitics

Devotion to personal freedom and democracy appeared in chapter 1 as among the cardinal traits that define Europe, adding a political dimension to the characterization of the culture area. As always, however, Europe defies such facile description. Democracy has deep roots in some countries, particularly in the West, while in others it forms merely a thin, fragile veneer over the face of a totalitarian heritage.

Fragmentation

A more compelling argument can be made for *fragmentation* as the defining political trait of Europe. Quite simply, the most distinctive aspect of European political geography, or *geopolitics,* is the splintering of the culture area into no fewer than 46 independent states (fig. 7.1). These countries, in turn, contain many autonomous regions and territories, some of which harbor separatist sentiments. Geographer Richard Griggs has counted 130 "nations" in Europe that presently lack independence. Spain alone houses 17 of these.

To gauge the magnitude of the fragmentation, consider that Europe contains almost exactly the same amount of territory as the United States. Imagine the complexity that would exist if every state within the United States were independent! At the Russian border this fragmentation abruptly gives way to the largest independent state in the world, suggesting to some that Europe ends at that boundary. This provides us another candidate in our unfinished quest to draw a line marking the eastern limit of the European culture area.

So severe is the political splintering of Europe that a number of *ministates* exist, some so small as to be invisible on a map of the culture area. These include Andorra, Liechtenstein, Monaco, San Marino, and Vatican City. Most ministates have turned their size into advantage, offering ser-

Figure 7.1.   The independent countries of Europe with selected dependent territories. Excluding Turkey, Europe now houses 46 independent states.

vices not always available in their larger neighbors, as for example the gambling casino in Monaco, the duty-free shops of Andorra, the postage stamp sales of San Marino, and the corporate headquarters lured to Liechtenstein by tax inducements.

Not only is Europe politically fragmented, but the level of internal division increased markedly during the twentieth century. In the year 1900, Europe exclusive of Turkey had 23 independent states; in 1930, 31; in 1985, 34; and by 1993, 46, double the total at the beginning of the century. The breakup of several great imperial states as a result of World War I, most notably the Austro-Hungarian and Ottoman Turkish empires, yielded many new countries. The collapse in 1991 of Europe's last surviving empire, the Soviet Union, coupled with the almost simultaneous disintegration of two smaller multiethnic states, Yugoslavia and Czechoslovakia, produced 13 more independent European states. Against this trend, the reunification of Germany offered the only anomaly.

Separatism

Nor has fragmentation necessarily run its course. Separatist movements of widely differing levels of intensity continue in Europe (fig. 7.2). Within Russia, Chechnya proclaimed its independence, prompting intermittent warfare. With Russian assistance, Abkhazia, the westernmost province of Georgia, won de facto statehood on the battlefield, and two other Georgian regions—Adzharia and South Ossetia—seized autonomy. Serbs in Bosnia–Herzegovina carved out a self-governing rebel republic, as did Slavs in the Transdnistrian region of Moldova and ethnic Albanians in Kosovo. Catalunya, Crna Gora, northern Italy, and Scotland, among others, toy with the notion of independence or seek full autonomy. Since 1945, political conflict in Europe has shifted increasingly from the *inter*national to the *intra*national scene.

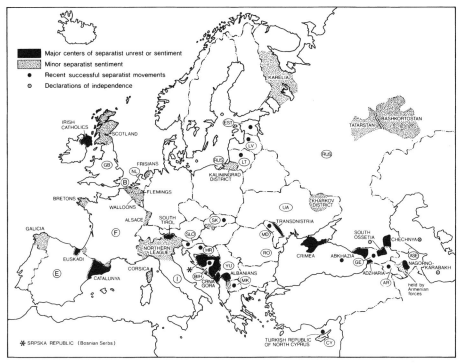

Figure 7.2.   Separatist unrest in Europe, since 1980. Twelve new recognized independent states have appeared as a result of such movements, and several others, such as Turkish North Cyprus and Abkhazia, have achieved de facto independence. Most, but not all, separatism is ethnically based and occurs in peripheral regions within states.

The recent proliferation of new states has occurred entirely in the east-ern half of Europe. By contrast, western Europe meanwhile moved signifi-cantly toward unification, within the framework of the European Union, as will be discussed later in this chapter. Even in the west, however, no sover-eign nation has been extinguished, and separatism grips many provinces (fig. 7.2).

Separatism almost invariably occurs in *peripheral* areas of the countries involved. Such fringe regions often lag behind in economic development and suffer neglect by the central government, or, conversely, are more prosper-ous than the rest of the country and lament their tax monies being spent on poorer provinces. Also, most successful separatist movements in twentieth-century Europe have involved peoples who had, previously in history, en-joyed independence.

The Ethnic Mainspring

Separatism in Europe is not only usually peripheral in location but also *ethnic* in nature. Groups seeking independence most often form an ethnic minority within a larger state. They differ linguistically and/or religiously from the country's majority. Compare the map of separatist unrest (fig. 7.2) to those showing language and religion (look back to figs. 1.8, 3.1, 3.17, and 4.1). Geographers Vladimir Kolossov and Andrei Treivish have identified some 200 compact ethnic districts, or homelands, within Europe.

We were not supposed to enter the twenty-first century faced with eth-nic problems. Marxist ideology instructed us that ethnic minorities would spontaneously melt away in the new socialist order, as class struggle ended, while western capitalism promised to extinguish ethnicity beneath a tide of pervasive popular culture. Both ideologies were flawed, for ethnic groups and ethnic-based separatism remain as strong as ever—or even more potent—on the threshold of the new millennium. Nowhere is that more evident than in Europe, that "land of ghosts" where nothing is ever forgotten.

If a country's population is relatively homogeneous linguistically and religiously, as in Denmark, Greece, Portugal, Czechia, Germany, and Aus-tria, separatism will not likely arise, but most European states house siz-able, regionally concentrated ethnoreligious or ethnolinguistic minorities rooted in ancient homelands. As geographer Alexander B. Murphy has noted, the map of independent states in Europe does not closely resemble the map of "nations"—that is, peoples possessing a group identity.

In spite of Europe's largely secularized nature, religion—or at least reli-gious heritage—often provides the distinguishing trait of ethnic groups that seek and win independence. Ireland and Croatia provide successful examples, and religious heritage also motivated the Serb rebels in Bosnia. Language even more commonly serves as the basis of ethnicity and separatism, as exemplified by the Catalans, South Tirol Germans, Frisians, Welsh, Flemings, Walloons, and Bretons. When language and religion *both* underlie ethnic identity, separatist tendencies can become even more potent. Examples include the secessions of Armenian Christians, Chechen and Abkhazi Caucasic Muslims, and Lithuanian Baltic Catholics.

Not all, or even most, ethnic minorities pursue separatism in Europe. Switzerland, as we will see later, successfully joins 4 linguistic and 2 religious groups, none of which seek to depart the Swiss Confederation. To spark separatism, ethnicity must be linked to some grievance. If minority status means persecution, attempted ethnocide, forced assimilation, domination, lack of autonomy, or denial of access to the country's power structure, grievances develop. Europeans possess long memories, and even abuses that occurred generations ago are rarely forgotten. If the peripheral location of an ethnic homeland causes it to be poorer economically than the country at large, then class struggle is added to ethnic grievance—a potent combination. Ireland provided a fine example at the time of its independence in the 1920s. If, by contrast, the ethnic periphery becomes richer than the rest of the state, then the minority group chafes at the diversion of their wealth to poorer regions. Croats, Slovenes, and Catalans found themselves in this position.

It also matters whether an ethnic group enjoyed independence in some previous era, especially if that freedom was involuntarily relinquished. Memories of past statehood and greatness can be very powerful. Greeks, Poles, Lithuanians, Bulgarians, Irish, Czechs, Croats, Norwegians, Serbs, Albanians, Armenians, and Bosnians all harbored such memories and went on to achieve renewed independence, in some cases more than once. The former boundaries of their vanished empires sometimes lead newly independent states into territorial conflicts in efforts to retrieve their lost golden age. The boundaries of medieval Serbia, for example, overlap so profoundly with those of modern Macedonia, Albania, Bosnia, Crna Gora, and even Greece, and memories of their former greatness remain so vivid among Serbs, that future Balkan peace might be endangered. Many Russians, too, look longingly toward the former frontiers of their recently collapsed empire.

Nonethnic Separatism

Not all secession movements in Europe have an ethnic basis. Other reasons can cause people to identify more closely with their province than with the central state, and the resultant sectionalism often becomes sufficient to fuel separatist sentiment. Sometimes ethnic separatism within a state prompts other, nonethnic components of the population to seek a similar goal. In Spain, where Catalans, Basques, and Gallegans won far-reaching autonomy, a mild separatist contagion spread to other provinces, where Castilian is spoken. By the middle 1980s, signs spray-painted on walls—a favored European way to express grievances—proclaimed that "Andalucía is a nation" or admonished people to vote "united Extremadura." Some Leónese even object to being part of Castilla y León Province and deface official signs with reference to the "pais leónes."

The Scottish separatist movement perhaps falls into the nonethnic category because the major bases of former Scottish identity—the Gaelic language and the clans—are moribund today. Nevertheless, a separatist movement exists in Scotland. Often, an *ethnic substrate* underlies seemingly nonethnic separatism. The people are no longer ethnic, but an echo of it survives to help form a special regional identity. Scotland, with its dimmed Celtic heritage, and Andalucía, still bearing the impress of Arabic identity, both exemplify ethnic substrates.

Separatism can develop, however, in the complete absence of ethnicity or ethnic substrates. Geographers recognize that nationality can derive as much from region and place as from cultural affiliation. Attachment and loyalty to regions must be considered in studying nationalism, especially in Europe, where people typically live in areas inhabited by their ancestors for centuries or even millennia. Dramatic and mundane things happen in places over the centuries, lending them nationalistic meaning. We should not be surprised, for example, when the inhabitants of many German-speaking regions seek no connections with Germany, as is true of the German Swiss, or when many northern inhabitants of the Po–Veneto Plain desire to secede from Italy.

In this context, very large states exhibit more nonethnic regional tensions than small ones. The sheer size of Russia, even after the loss of its empire, perhaps encourages regional separatism, as does the existence of an exclave, separated from the main body of Russian territory, around Kaliningrad on the Baltic. In Italy, the Northern League advocates separatism in order to break free of the poverty-plagued, crime-ridden south. As a general rule, nonethnic separatist movements stand less chance of success, though the secession of Slovakia, based mainly in economic and historic contrasts, provides an exception. The Slovaks, who differ only in dialect from the Czechs, nevertheless broke away, along a border that had long ago separated the empires of the Austrians and Hungarians. Their grievance lay partly in a tradition of regional poverty and neglect by the central government in Czech Praha, in spite of the fact that recent Czechoslovakian policy had addressed, with meaningful results, the issue of economic disparity. Also, Slovakia possessed many noncompetitive, inefficient manufacturing plants and stood to suffer greatly from Czech-led privatization following the demise of communism. Again, European memories are long, and the we versus they mindset remains almost indelible.

Types of States

To the complicated political mosaic of independent European states and restive provinces, even greater complexity is added by major political differences among the various countries. For example, age varies greatly. Most western European states are old, having maintained their independence for 500 years or more (fig. 7.3). Some others, especially in eastern Europe, acquired statehood only in the 1990s, though in many cases these countries had enjoyed independence in earlier centuries and represent revivals of extinct states.

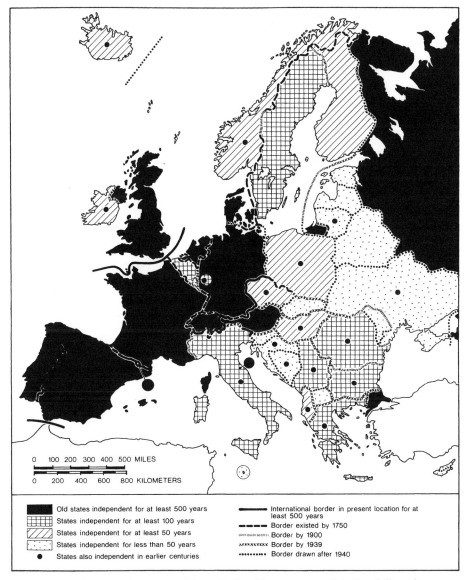

0   100 200 300 400 500 MILES

0   200   400   600   800 KILOMETERS

■ Old states independent for at least 500 years	━━━ International border in present location for at least 500 years
▦ States independent for at least 100 years	▬ ▬ ▬ Border existed by 1750
▨ States independent for at least 50 years	▥▥▥ Border by 1900
⋰ States independent for less than 50 years	××××××× Border by 1939
● States also independent in earlier centuries	••••••••• Border drawn after 1940

Figure 7.3.   The age of states and boundaries. The greater political stability of western Europe is reflected in the greater age of independent countries and borders there. Some states briefly lost their independence, such as Austria (1938–1945) and Portugal, and some durable borders likewise disappeared for short intervals.

Most older states originated in small **core areas** and grew outward over the centuries into surrounding territory (fig. 7.4). Such core areas generally possessed some measure of natural defense against the encroachments of rival political entities, a fairly dense population, at least in comparison to surrounding regions, and a prosperous agricultural economy that produced a surplus capable of supporting a sizable military establishment. Perhaps most important of all, the core area required a government headed

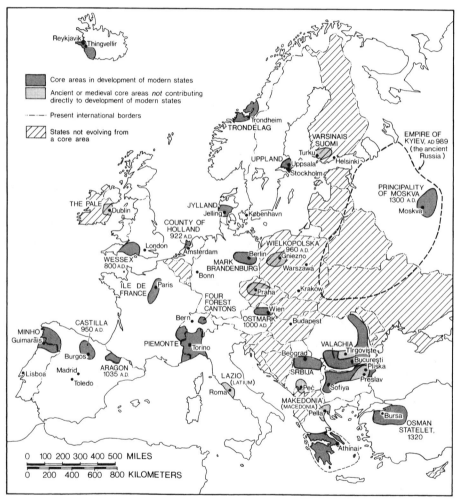

Figure 7.4. Core areas and the evolution of European states. Most modern independent countries evolved gradually from core areas, though many in eastern Europe did not. Certain others possess ancient or medieval core areas that did not contribute directly to the birth of the modern state, but nevertheless belong to the collective national memory. The Osman statelet was the core area of the Ottoman Empire and modern Turkey. The Kiyev Russian state collapsed and fragmented, but its memory aided the rise of the later Moskva-based Russia. (*Sources:* Based in part upon Pounds and Ball 1964; McManis 1967.)

by ambitious leaders skilled in the military and diplomatic arts, bent on territorial aggrandizement. During the process of accretion, the core often retained its status as the single most important area in the state, housing the capital city and the cultural and economic heart of the nation. The core area may be roughly centered in the national territory, or, if growth occurred mainly in one direction, it may be peripheral. Paris and the Île de France, the capital and core area of the French state, lie nearly in the middle of France, but Wessex, the nucleus of the United Kingdom, is eccentric. Spain also has a peripheral core, as do Italy, Russia, and Germany.

The typical core area contains the capital of the state, which is sometimes a *primate city*, one that contains by far the largest population and greatest concentration of economic and cultural functions. Paris and Athínai are core capitals enjoying national urban primacy. Not infrequently, the capital was removed from the original core, a relocation prompted by any one of several factors. In some instances, the political headquarters were relocated to the frontier of most active territorial expansion, in which case it is referred to as a *forward-thrust* capital. Sofiya succeeded earlier, more eastern capitals with Bulgarian expansion south and west at the expense of the Turks, while Lisboa and Madrid displaced northern capitals as the Portuguese and Spaniards pushed the Moors southward in Iberia. Similarly, a *head-link* capital is one thrust onto the periphery of most active commercial and cultural contacts. Peripheral St. Petersburg for a time replaced Moskva as the Russian capital when the czars desired closer cultural contacts with Europe, and Oslo replaced Trondheim in Norway as a result of its greater proximity to Sweden and Denmark, which ruled and dominated Norway for centuries.

Instability can result if states have no core areas or if multiple, competing cores are present. In the former category are Belgium, Belarus, and Albania, all born full-grown as children of power politics. Spain is plagued by the regionalism associated with two major northern medieval cores in Aragon and Old Castilla, both now identified with linguistic groups. The competition is between Barcelona in Catalunya and Castilian Madrid. As the capital city, Madrid has never quite succeeded in dominating the state, in part because of the sparse population and low productivity of its surroundings.

Many older European states represent the remnants of former empires that once ruled much larger parts of the culture area. The United Kingdom, Russia, Sweden, Denmark, Germany, Austria, and Turkey all fit this description. A great many other countries escaped colonial or imperial rule to become independent (fig. 7.5). Tensions typically exist between remnant empires and their former dependencies, especially in the Balkans and eastern Europe.

We should also differentiate **nation-states** from multinational countries. In nation-states, the people share a common heritage, culture, and homeland. Patriotism and independence represent very potent reflections

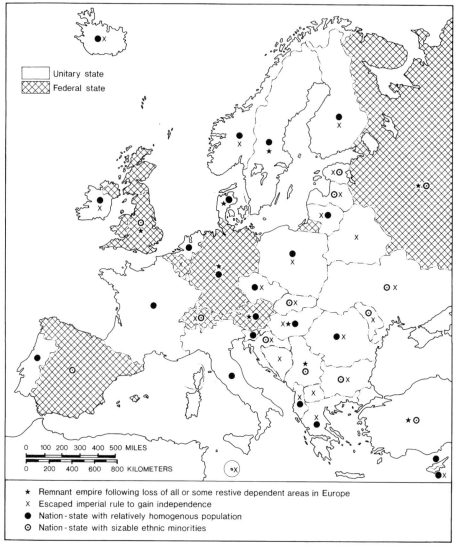

Figure 7.5.   Types of independent states, based upon unitary versus federal governments, nation-state status, and imperial versus colonial origin. Some of these classifications are necessarily arbitrary or even debatable. Is Moldova, for example, a nation-state or merely a temporarily detached part of the Romanian nation-state?

of the common culture and experience. The ideal nation-state possesses a homogeneous population, in which the large majority of the people—90% or more—have the same national identity. Many European countries fit this description, as, for example, Germany, Poland, Czechia, and Greece (fig. 7.5). Some other nation-states face instability because of sizable regional ethnic minorities who do not share the nationality that defines and dominates the state. Typically, such ethnic groups do not participate fully or at all in the political functioning of the state, and separatism can flourish in these situations. Most eastern European nation-states face such problems, including the remnant Yugoslavia, Estonia, Ukraine, and Bulgaria. Multinational states, an increasingly less common type in Europe since the collapse of the various empires, join peoples of different cultural background, and national identity does not rest upon a particular linguistic or religious group. Switzerland and Belgium, both astride the Germanic–Romance linguistic border, provide examples of multinational states. Bosnia–Herzegovina seeks in vain to be such a country.

With the notable exceptions of Germany and Austria, culturally homogeneous nation-states are **unitary** in administrative structure, with power concentrated in the central government (fig. 7.5). Most European countries are unitary, perhaps in part because of their small size. In **federal** states, by contrast, the individual provinces retain considerable power or even autonomy. Federalism often results from a desire to accommodate otherwise restive minority groups, as in Spain, Belgium, Russia, and the United Kingdom. Switzerland represents perhaps the purest example of a federal state, and that country did not even have a national capital until the mid-nineteenth century.

Finally, European countries differ greatly in the strength of that most admirable indigenous virtue, democracy. The tradition of freely elected governments remains strongest and oldest in western Europe, while the east has only the shallowest and most fragile democratic experience. Germany, on the east–west interface, fluctuated wildly between totalitarianism and federal democracy in the twentieth century.

Boundaries

International borders vary in diverse ways. All are marked in some way, but some contain barriers and cleared strips that can be clearly seen from the air. Oddly, even the peaceful, uncontested Sweden–Norway frontier is marked by a swath cut through the forest and by diverse official signs of varying age (fig. 7.6). The first acts of newly independent Estonia and Latvia included severing many connecting rural roads with trenchers, erecting street barriers within border towns, and establishing manned crossing points complete with booms. Their mutual border, previously a largely invisible line between Soviet republics, sprang vividly into the landscape.

The policies and legislation of independent states often have a homogenizing effect within their borders, with the result that a steplike effect appears along international boundaries. An example is the Rhine River border between France and Germany. On the French side lies the province of Alsace, and on the German side, Baden. Both Alsace and Baden are, by tradition, German-speaking and predominantly Roman Catholic, and yet significant differences developed between the 2 provinces. Prosperous

Figure 7.6. Swedish–Norwegian border near Torsby, Sweden. The border is clearly marked by a strip cleared through the Finnskog, or "Finns' Forest." (Photo by T.G.J.-B. 1985.)

Baden underwent rapid industrialization after 1945, absorbing numerous refugees from ceded eastern German territories, while Alsace stagnated economically. In part, the economic malaise of Alsace was caused by repeated boundary changes when the province passed back and forth from German to French rule in 1871, 1918, 1940, and 1945, but the highly centralized government of France also bears part of the blame for the depressed condition of peripheries such as Alsace. Baden, as part of a much less centralized federal state, has fared better and wields more influence. Federal funds generously assisted resettled refugees in Baden, causing a boom in housing construction and renovation. Rural population density is now much lower on the Alsatian side, and the prosperity of Baden causes many French citizens to commute to jobs on the German side of the Rhine. The 2 provinces also differ in the configuration of rural village suburbanization, a process under way in both due to the growth of nearby cities such as Strasbourg and Freiburg. Partly as a result of differences in national planning legislation, the suburbs being added to villages in Baden tend to be compact, with apartment dwellings most common, while Alsatian villages sprawl loosely across the countryside due to the dominance of freestanding, single-family suburban houses.

This differentiating effect of borders extends to those that no longer exist. Even archaic borders, vanished more than a millennium ago, leave their trace. One of these can be detected in the German province of Hessen, through which, in ancient times, ran the northern border of the Roman Empire. The Roman system of law required that inheritances be divided among all heirs, in contrast to the tradition of the neighboring German tribes, which favored primogeniture. After the empire collapsed and the political border ceased to exist, the boundary separating the different inheritance systems persisted. As a result, the degree of fragmentation of rural land parcels even today clearly reveals the ancient Roman border (fig. 7.7).

France: A Successful Unitary State

With these considerations of boundaries, separatism, and types of independent state as background, we turn now to a geopolitical analysis of selected European countries. An old and stable state, *France* in many ways offers a model for the development of a viable, successful independent country. Though linked by language and religion to the Mediterranean, France owes both its origin and name to a Germanic tribe, the Franks, who built a large

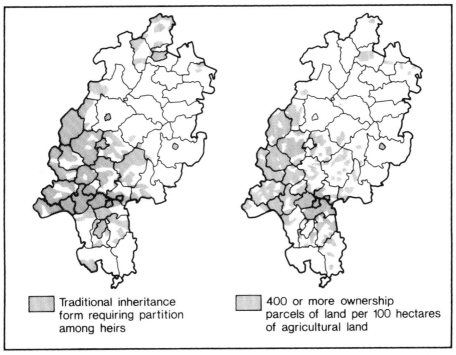

Traditional inheritance form requiring partition among heirs

400 or more ownership parcels of land per 100 hectares of agricultural land

Figure 7.7.   Inheritance systems and land fragmentation in the German province of Hessen, 1955. In the southern and western parts of Hessen, the tradition, dating to Roman times, was to divide the farms among the various heirs. As a result, the farms there became ever smaller over the centuries, with excessive fragmentation of the holdings. Northern and eastern Hessen, by contrast, clung to the ancient Germanic custom of primogeniture, by which the farm passes intact to the eldest son. (*Source:* Adapted from Ehlers 1977, 124.)

state in the power vacuum following the collapse of the Roman Empire. When this short-lived Frankish empire fragmented in A.D. 843, the western-most part—a loose feudal federation known as the Kingdom of the West Franks—became the embryonic France.

After about A.D. 1000, the kings of France, based in Paris, began a program of conquest and annexation to convert the federation, over which their rule was largely ceremonial, into a unitary state under royal domination. In this process, the so-called *Île de France*—the original, small domain of the kings in the center of the Paris Basin—served as the core area of the evolving unitary state (fig. 7.8). The Île de France enjoyed splendid natural defensive advantage, sheltered behind cuesta escarpment walls. Initial expansion within the basin continued to benefit from these outward-facing cuesta rings (see chapter 2).

From their Paris Basin fortress, the French kings undertook 3 prolonged campaigns of expansion: southward to reach the Mediterranean and the Pyrenees; westward to dislodge the English from the Atlantic coast, where they ruled Normandie and Aquitaine; and eastward at the expense of Bourgogne and other German states to the banks of the Rhine. By 1650, France had reached more or less its present territorial limits. The city of Paris, the Île de France, and the Paris Basin never lost their early dominance. A unitary state with a powerful central government based in Paris has always characterized France.

The boundaries achieved in French expansion had 2 advantages. First, belts of mountains and hills parallel the border in many places, including the Pyrenees, Alps, Jura, Vosges, and Ardennes (fig. 7.8). These provide some measure of natural defense. Second, the territory of France, after its expansion, has a hexagonal shape—the perfect configuration for an independent state, since its compactness shortens lines of communication as well as boundaries.

Still, the resultant France had problems. It was no nation-state. As late as 1790, half the population spoke a language other than the preferred Parisian form of French. In 1793, the government mandated elimination of regional languages and dialects, a policy continued into the late twentieth century. This policy had considerable success, but still today every tip of the French hexagon on the peripheries of the state houses an ethnic minority (fig. 7.8). These include the German-speaking Alsatians in the east, the Dutch speakers around Dunkerque in the north, the Celtic Bretons of Bretagne, the Basques of the western Pyrenees, the Catalans of the south, and the Italian-speaking Corsicans.

In addition, France had the task of uniting a Germanized north with a Mediterranean south. The northern French, occupying the Paris Basin, descended in large part from Germanic tribes—not only the Franks, but also Normans (Vikings), Burgundians, and others. While these tribes abandoned their ancestral languages and adopted French, they remained Germanic in many other ways. Their houses, villages, and farm field patterns

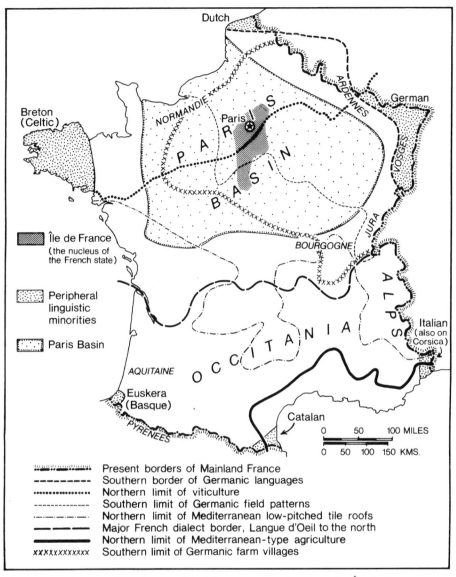

Figure 7.8. France: selected geopolitical features. Growing from the Île de France, a core area in the Paris Basin, France attained an optimal hexagonal shape and "natural" borders such as the Alps and Pyrenees, but annexed numerous peripheral ethnic areas in the process, as well as the more Romanized south.

are Teutonic in appearance and origin; their Germanic diet relies heavily on bovine dairy products, including butter for cooking; and their dialect of French, *langue d'oïl*, is distinctive.

The lands annexed in the south, sometimes called Occitania, retain a much stronger Roman and Mediterranean imprint, with minimal Germanic influence. We can detect this, for example, in the cultivation of grapes for wine, the use of olive oil in cooking, and the separate language known as *langue d'oc*. These are merely symptoms of a deeply rooted, distinctive southern regional culture.

The French reaction to these challenges of ethnic peripheries and regional culture has been to develop an all-powerful unitary state, based in Paris, and to impose the will and culture of the north on both the south and the restive peripheries. This strategy succeeded. France is a stable, firmly unified country. No province possesses enough power or will to seriously challenge Paris.

Germany: Federalism in the European Core

Just as France represents the legacy of the collapsed Frankish empire in the west, *Germany* descends from the *east* Frankish kingdom of A.D. 843. For the initial millennium of its existence, this German First *Reich,* unlike France, remained a loose federation of feudal states whose emperor had little authority outside his home statelet. Federalism, verging on virtual disunity, has been the normal German tendency, especially in the thousand years of the First Reich. Potential core areas, from which ambitious emperors might have forged a unitary state, certainly existed, such as the fertile *Börde* beyond the Ruhr River on the North European Plain, or the hill-ringed Upper Rhine Plain between Frankfurt am Main and Basel (see fig. 2.1), but no such process developed. By the 1600s, the First Reich housed some 300 virtually independent states.

The loose-knit First Reich did succeed in expanding eastward, into ancestral Slavic tribal lands, following the path of German agricultural colonists and forest clearers spreading east on the North German Plain and along the Danube. In each of these two lobes of eastern expansion, within the territory of the First Reich, a powerful state and ambitious royal family arose—*Prussia* (German *Preussen*) in the North European Plain, which grew from a core area in Brandenburg, and *Austria,* which expanded from the Ostmark (Eastern March) around Wien. These two new states both continued to function as part of the First Reich, even though some of the territories they annexed lay beyond its bounds. Once they consolidated their holdings in the colonial east, Prussia and Austria (by then called Österreich, or the "Eastern Empire") began competing with one another for control of the original, politically fragmented western part of the First Reich, each attempting to create a unitary German-speaking state under their rule. This contest lasted for centuries, but Prussia eventually emerged victorious in 1866. Five years later the Second Reich was born, a union of Prussia and western Germany. The Prussian capital, Berlin, was named the imperial capital and the Prussian kings became the German kaisers. Federalism persisted in the Second Reich, and member states such as Bayern and Sachsen retained their own monarchs and postal systems (fig. 7.9). Austria, the defeated rival, found itself excluded from Germany. The Third Reich grew out of the second, as the Nazis seized power and imposed the first dictatorship Germany had known. Unitary rule quickly replaced the traditional federalism, and not merely Germany but all of Europe felt the dire consequences. Nearly a half-century, marked by defeat and foreign military occupation, passed before the unified, federal Germany could be reestablished. The modern Germany emerged only in 1990, when the Federal Republic, which had arisen in the military occupation zones of the Americans, French, and British, annexed the German Democratic Republic, the old Russian occupation zone. In 1999, Berlin regained its status as the capital of Germany.

The essential problem of the German state—a problem that helps explain its federalism and repeated fragmentation—is that while it occupies the core of Europe, it also straddles the east–west and north–south divides that characterize Europe. The north–south divide is ancient, going back 2,000 years to the time when southern Germany was part of the Roman Empire, while the north was controlled by various Teutonic tribes. Roma placed its cultural imprint on the south, and such influences never completely disappeared, even after many centuries. Thus the German south

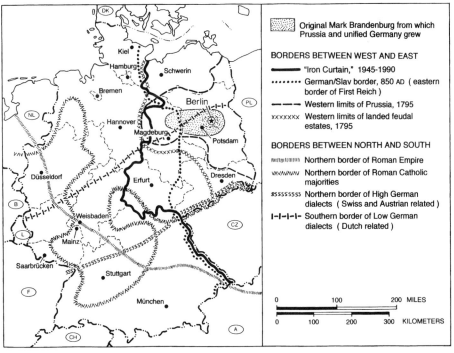

Figure 7.9. Germany, occupying much of the European core, has always struggled to unite north and south, east and west, lying astride these 2 European cultural fault lines.

remains Roman Catholic, while the north is Protestant. The country is home to 27,398,000 Protestants and 27,383,000 Catholics—about as even a split as could be imaginable! The ancient Roman practice of divisible inheritance survives in the south while the old Germanic custom of primogeniture—inheritance passing to the first-born child—prevails in the north (fig. 7.7). Dialects of the German language are also arranged in belts separating south from north.

The east–west division within Germany is also ancient and deeply rooted. A thousand years ago and more, German peoples lived only in lands west of the Elbe and Saale Rivers. Slavic tribes possessed eastern Germany, and only gradually did the Teutonic peoples spread east, absorbing the Slavs. In the process, they became considerably Slavicized. This colonial eastern German culture remained feudal, its landless peasants working on manorial estates owned by the aristocracy. Prussia, the political expression of eastern German culture, remained entirely confined to the east as late as the 1790s. When Prussia finally annexed western Germany to create the Second Reich, the east–west contrast did not weaken.

The distinctiveness of eastern Germany was powerfully reinforced between 1945 and 1990 when it was a communist country under Russian domination while western Germany belonged to the free, democratic, capitalist part of Europe. In spite of reunification in 1990, the old "Iron Curtain" border has far from disappeared. *Ossis* ("easterners") and *Wessis* ("westerners") still differ sharply in standard of living and political ideology. The prosperity divide between the 2 parts of Germany remains profound. The east, with 19% of the population, generates only 8% of Germany's tax revenues and has twice the level of unemployment. In an effort to mitigate this problem, the German government annually transfers $65 billion into the troubled eastern provinces. Some 83% of east Germans continue to think of themselves as having a separate identity. In Berlin, an "invisible wall" continues to divide the politically unified capital, influencing shopping patterns and even inner-city residential moves.

The German state has struggled, then, to create a political core in the culture area where perhaps none was meant to exist. The modern Germany pursues this task by structuring itself as a *federal* state, in which considerable powers are vested in the individual provinces and the central government is relatively weak.

The United Kingdom: Joining European Core and Periphery

If Germany's quixotic task has been to bridge east, west, north, and south, the United Kingdom has struggled to link Europe's core and periphery. Ultimately, this union proved untenable, and the Republic of Ireland broke away in the 1920s, culminating a revolt that had endured for centuries. The Irish secession occurred along one of several natural and cultural dividing lines that cut across the country's territory (fig. 7.10).

The United Kingdom was the creation of Germanic tribes, particularly the Saxons, Angles, and Normans, who came as waves of invaders from across the North Sea and English Channel, eventually mixing with indigenous groups and each other to become the English people. Their new state,

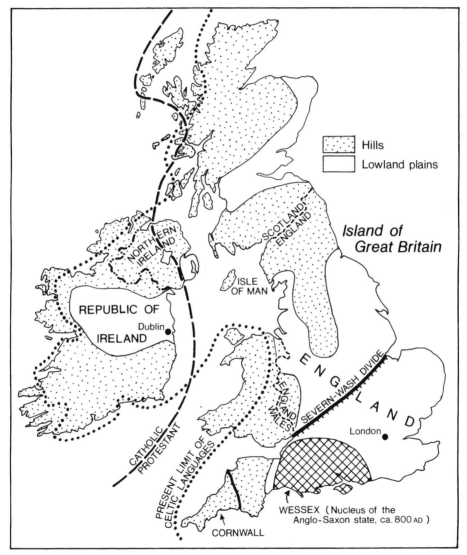

Figure 7.10.   The United Kingdom, originating as the Saxon state of Wessex, early united the English Scarplands as England and began the conquest of Celtic refuges. At its peak, the United Kingdom ruled all the British Isles, but ultimately it failed to hold together this part of the European core and periphery.

England, arose in Wessex, in the lowland plains that form the southeastern part of the island of Great Britain (fig. 7.10). Once the English had unified the lowlands, they turned to the second great task—conquering and annexing the hilly lands on the west and north, inhabited by the Celts. One by one these Celtic refuges—Cornwall, Wales, and Scotland—fell to the English. Even before these conquests were completed, the English began their third, and final, major expansion—in Ireland, another Celtic land, lying across a narrow sea to the west. The two British Isles, in this way, came to be a single country, the United Kingdom, ruled by the English from their base in the lowlands and London.

While outwardly successful, the expanded United Kingdom never fully absorbed the conquered Celts. Cultural and natural borders snaked through the country's territory, always threatening a rift. These included not only the environmental divide between fertile lowlands and barren hills and the separation into two major islands, but also the borders between Anglo-Saxons and Celts; Protestants and Catholics; rich and poor; and industrial and rural. It was along the Protestant–Catholic divide that the United Kingdom fragmented, though some Catholic counties in Northern Ireland remained under English control. The "troubles" that have plagued Northern Ireland for decades suggest that the borders of independent Ireland were not wisely drawn. Irish separatists there want the entire island to be part of the Irish Republic.

On the larger island, Great Britain, other divides continue to be troublesome to the United Kingdom. The independence movement in Scotland has many supporters, and the Scots in 1999 established their own separate parliament, as did Wales. "Rise up and be a nation again," implore bumper stickers in Scotland, a message carried forward by the Scottish Nationalist Party. Among other grievances, the Scots complain that England has never built an expressway to link the two provinces or provided a high-speed rail connection, failures seen as a deliberate effort to marginalize Scotland.

Another fissure opened up as deindustrialization struck the United Kingdom after about 1960. The older coal and steel districts—the English "Black Country"—fell into decay as factories and mines closed. As the United Kingdom emerged from this episode into the prosperity of the high-tech, postindustrial, service-dominated era (see chapters 9 and 10), the older decayed industrial districts were left behind economically. The *Severn–Wash Divide* developed, separating prosperous southeastern England from the rest of the country. Voting patterns now typically reveal this north–south division, and socioeconomic tensions are great.

The future of the United Kingdom remains uncertain. Will Northern Ireland be lost? Will Scotland opt for independence? Can the Severn–Wash Divide be closed? The United Kingdom is an ancient and largely stable state. Its citizens remember their common history and the great worldwide empire once ruled by Britain. Further disintegration seems unlikely. Only 26% of Scots in a 1999 public opinion poll favored secession from the

United Kingdom. More likely is the eventual withdrawal of Northern Ireland to become an independent state, perhaps the only way to resolve the Catholic–Protestant feud.

Italy: Roman Legacy

Like the United Kingdom, Italy struggles to unite segments of the European core and periphery. Unlike Britain, Italy is a relatively new state, by European standards, but resting upon the memory of vanished ancient greatness. The Roman Empire collapsed 1,500 ago and Italy fell into political fragmentation, but the memory of Roman glory and unity persisted. In the nineteenth century, a unification movement arose that reassembled Italy from an array of weak, small states ruled by feudal lords, princes, and popes. Although the unification movement originated in the north, in Piemonte, the ancient legacy demanded that Roma be the capital (fig. 7.11).

The major unifying factor for the new Italy, aside from the Italian language (fragmented into many dialects) and the ancient Roman legacy, was the country's natural framework—a large freestanding peninsula fringed by great mountains, the Alps, in the north. Italy, you might conclude, was designed by natural forces to be a single country. In truth, however, this peninsula was very diverse in the cultural sense and had been so even in Roman times. To unify Italy over 2,000 years ago, the tribes of Latium (modern Lazio)—a district surrounding Roma and the origin of the world "Latin"—had to conquer in the north both the Etruscan peoples of Toscana and the Celts of the Po–Veneto Plain, then called Cisalpine Gaul. Then they had to annex the Greek-inhabited lands of south Italy.

These ancient minorities never completely vanished. In Europe, perhaps nothing ever does. To complicate matters even more, new invaders settled the peninsula after the fall of the Roman Empire. Germanic tribes, especially the Lombards, seized the Po–Veneto Plain, while Arabs and crusaders ruled much of the south, including the large island of Sicilia. Then, in the 1400s and 1500s, northern Italy gave birth to a great awakening of culture—the Renaissance—and with it an era of propriety based in trade and manufacturing, while the south—the Mezzogiorno—remained mired in impoverished feudal bondage.

The modern Italian state has struggled to hold the north and south together. We can sum up northern Italy today as "European"—that is, prosperous, secularized, democratic, cosmopolitan, innovative, and capitalistic. The Mezzogiorno, by contrast, remains poor, devout, feudalistic (the Mafia being a classic feudal survival), traditional, corrupt, and provincial. Some of the resultant internal pressure was relieved by the mass migration of poor southerners to factory jobs in the north after 1950. In addition, the central government transfers enormous amounts of northern wealth to the south as subsidies, relief, and developmental funds.

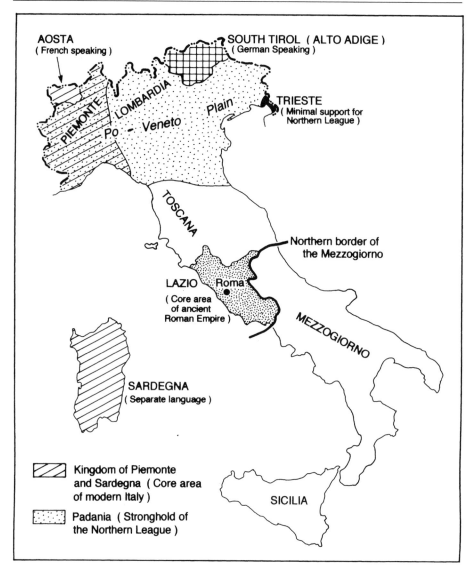

AOSTA
(French speaking)

SOUTH TIROL (ALTO ADIGE)
(German Speaking)

PIEMONTE

LOMBARDIA

Po - Veneto Plain

TRIESTE
(Minimal support for
Northern League)

TOSCANA

Northern border of
the Mezzogiorno

LAZIO Roma
(Core area
of ancient
Roman Empire)

MEZZOGIORNO

SARDEGNA
(Separate language)

Kingdom of Piemonte
and Sardegna (Core area
of modern Italy)

Padania (Stronghold of
the Northern League)

SICILIA

Figure 7.11. **Italy,** though provided with a natural framework by the peninsula and the Alps, consists of very different regions. A prosperous north contrasts with the Mezzogiorno.

Still, tensions persist. The prosperous northerners have disdain for southern Italians, and some even speak of *Padania*—an independent northern Italy (fig. 7.11). A political party, the *Northern League,* favors secession. In addition, inhabitants of the German-speaking part of Alpine Italy—the South Tirol or Alto Adige—have agitated for a half-century for autonomy or even to be joined to adjacent Austria. Corruption and inefficiency in Italy's central government have made matters worse.

Spain: A Multiethnic State

Spain, in common with Italy, has historically struggled to hold together north and south, but in fact its internal stresses are far more complicated than this simple twofold division. The Spanish state had its beginnings in far northern Iberia in the Christian resistance against the Muslim Arabs, who had invaded from Africa in the A.D. 700s. In particular, two Christian statelets, Castilla and Aragon, led the resistance, and when they united in the 1400s, Spain was born (fig. 7.12). The defining deed of Spanish national identity was successful warfare against the Arabs, pushing them southward back into Africa, a process completed only after 700 years, in 1492.

The resultant Spanish state included the far greater part of the Iberian

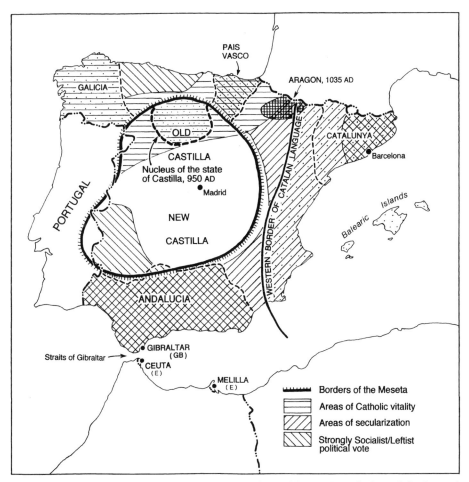

Figure 7.12. Spain, though a very old state, is plagued by restive ethnic peripheries and other internal contrasts.

Peninsula, excluding only Portugal in the far west, and the peninsular structure, coupled with the Pyrenees Mountains in the northeast, provided a natural framework for the state, just as it had in Italy. But also in common with Italy, the peninsula housed diverse peoples, speaking different languages and possessing strong regional allegiances. Portugal was one of these and succeeded in escaping Spanish rule. Others were incorporated, more or less against their will. The Castillans—the people of central Meseta—built and ruled Spain, establishing the capital city Madrid in the center of the elevated interior plains. Ethnic minorities in the peripheries—Basques, Catalans, and Gallegans—were dominated by the Castillans in a unitary state. Also, the cultural legacy of the Moors and Africa remained strong in southern Spain, particularly in the province of Andalucía. Southern regionalism today finds its expression in poverty, aristocratic landed estates, secularism, and socialist political leanings (fig. 7.12).

These tensions almost tore Spain apart in a civil war in the 1930s, but the outcome was a Castillan-run fascist dictatorship that endured into the 1970s, perpetuating the traditional strong-handed rule from Madrid and the Meseta. In a radical shift, Spain then adopted a federalist democracy and extended sweeping freedoms to the provinces and ethnic minorities. This has not proven entirely successful, as both the Basques and Catalans now exhibit strong separatist sentiments. The Spanish state is core versus periphery in miniature.

Switzerland and Belgium: Astride a Language Divide

The most important language frontier in western Europe separates Romance speech in the south from the Germanic tongues of the north. Switzerland and Belgium both straddle this cultural border and are in certain other respects similar, but only the Swiss achieved stability and long-term internal harmony.

Switzerland, one of the most viable European states, has enjoyed considerable success in joining different linguistic and religious groups in a multinational country. About two-thirds of the Swiss speak German, 17% French, and 10% Italian, in addition to a tiny Romansh minority. Religiously, Switzerland is 47.6% Catholic and 44.3% Protestant (fig. 7.13). The Alps provide additional disruption, cutting directly through the country, dividing much of Switzerland into separate valleys, each with its own identity and sense of autonomy. Ideally, according to political geographers, the population distribution within a state should be denser in the central regions, especially the core area, and sparse in the border peripheries, but Switzerland's terrain pattern helped produce precisely the opposite ar-

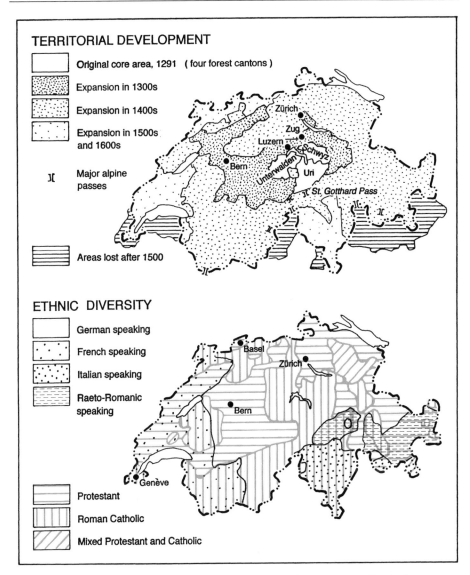

Figure 7.13.   Switzerland: Territorial development and ethnic diversity. The Swiss state is a classic example of gradual expansion from a core area. It includes a mixture of Roman Catholics and Protestants and four linguistic groups. (*Sources:* Fleure 1941; Schib 1965–1970, 21)

rangement. In spite of these problems, Switzerland has existed for over 700 years as an independent state.

The origins of the Swiss state can be traced to a core area in the 1200s around the eastern shores of the Vierwaldstätter See (Lake of Four Forest Cantons or Lake Luzern), at the northern approach to St. Gotthard Pass, the principal land route between Italy and central Europe in the Middle Ages. Feudal lords there banded together in 1291 for mutual defense and gradually over the centuries increased their autonomy within the loose-knit German First Reich, strengthened by their control of the strategic pass (fig. 7.13). The people of Canton Schwyz assumed an early leadership role and gave their regional name, Schweizer-land, to the country at large. As time passed, neighboring cantons and towns were annexed by conquest, purchase, or voluntary association. In its formative stage, the state remained wholly German in speech, Catholic in faith, and centered on the lake that afforded easy communication among the member cantons. From the first, Switzerland formed a very loose federal state, or *confederation*, a framework that successfully accommodated subsequent linguistic–religious diversity as the country continued to grow from its tiny core area.

In the 1400s and 1500s, the confederation seized control of other strategic Alpine passes and also Rhine River crossings, annexing in the process Italian- and French-speaking districts. In more recent times, Switzerland achieved prosperity and demonstrated an isolationist ability to avoid wars, accomplishments that greatly enhanced the value of Swiss citizenship and fostered nationalism.

Switzerland has faced its share of internal problems over the centuries, including at least five civil wars and, recently, ethnic tensions that led to the French-speaking part of Canton Bern to break away and form *Jura*, a new Francophone canton. But all things considered, Switzerland must be regarded as an astounding success in an improbable setting.

Belgium, also astride the Germanic–Romance linguistic border, joins the Dutch speakers of Vlaanderen in the north with French of Wallonia in the south and also rules a German-speaking area in the east (fig. 7.14). It has an advantage in that its population is religiously uniform, adhering to Roman Catholicism. The Belgian state, with about the same territorial size of Switzerland, sought to duplicate the Swiss success in establishing neutralism and uniting diverse ethnic groups. The Belgians largely failed in this attempt, and their state became plagued by internal strife.

Belgium, a much newer state than Switzerland, dates only from 1830, when its Catholic population, with approval and encouragement from the Great Powers of Europe, broke away from the Protestant-dominated Netherlands. The crucial mistake came when the newly independent Belgium was constituted as a unitary state under Walloon French domination, in effect excluding the Dutch-speaking majority from the power structure. Only very gradually did the Dutch attain equal cultural rights, as in 1891 when their language first appeared alongside French on the country's postage stamps and currency or in 1898, when a regulation requiring that laws be published in Dutch first took effect. As a result, the Dutch, also called *Flemings*, and Walloons developed a deep-seated mutual antagonism. Virtual partition came in 1963, with the drawing of an official language border within Belgium, north of which the Dutch tongue enjoys preference (fig. 7.14).

The Fleming–Walloon rivalry flared into violence in the 1960s with

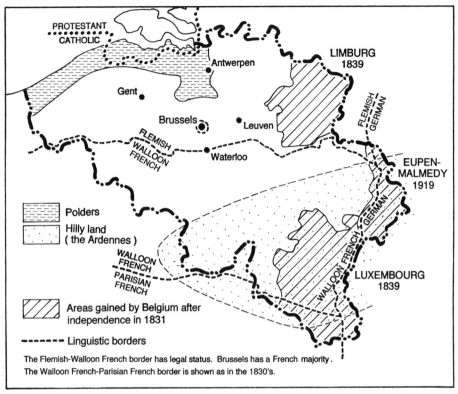

Figure 7.14.   Belgium. In addition to the problems caused by the Fleming–Walloon conflict, Belgium occupies the natural invasion route between Germany and France.

street fighting in the capital city, Brussels, which has a French majority but lies north of the linguistic border. Students at the traditionally French University of Leuven, in Flemish territory, rioted in successful support of demands that instruction be in the Dutch tongue and that French faculty be dismissed. Tension persists between the 2 groups, though in recent decades violence has ceased. Reflecting this tension, the government has not enumerated linguistic groups since 1947. Federalist reforms have made Belgium much more like Switzerland. In effect, Belgium now has separate, ethnic-based governments.

Yugoslavia: A Balkan Tragedy

Belgium's problems astride a major cultural divide pale in comparison to the geopolitical fate of Yugoslavia, the "land of the South Slavs." Formed following World War I when peacemakers appended various territories to previously independent Serbia, the new Yugoslavia straddled profound human fault lines. It joined shards of diverse former empires—Roman, Byzantine, Turkish, Austrian, and Hungarian—each of which had left indelible cultural residues. While largely Serbo-Croatian in speech, Yugoslavia inherited 3 major mutually antagonistic faiths—Catholicism, Orthodoxy, and Islam; 2 alphabets; and, physically, an awkward joining of the Adriatic coast and rugged Dinaric Range to the Hungarian Basin.

Making matters worse, the Serbs dominated Yugoslavia from the first, regarding it in effect as their reborn empire, a unitary Greater Serbia. Beograd, the Serb capital, became the national capital, and street signs there remained exclusively in the Cyrillic alphabet. No meaningful steps toward federalism came until far too late. Serbs saw themselves both as defenders of the Orthodox faith and of European civilization at large against the Turks. Catholic Slovenes and Croats, as well as the Muslim Bosnians, though fellow south Slavs, became second-class Yugoslav citizens. Croats took advantage of the German occupation during World War II to commit various atrocities against the temporarily weakened Serbs.

Also, major economic disparities developed among the various provinces of Yugoslavia, with Slovenia and Croatia becoming relatively prosperous while Macedonia and parts of Serbia fell behind (fig. 7.15). Add to this the fact that both Croatia and Bosnia–Herzegovina harbored memories of medieval independence. The rise to power of an uncompromising Serbian nationalist leader in Yugoslavia sealed the doom of the state. In 1991 and 1992, 4 provinces seceded from Yugoslavia and achieved independence— Slovenia, Croatia, Macedonia, and Bosnia–Herzegovina (fig. 7.15).

The tragedy of Yugoslavia centered on the fact that ethnonational identities had coalesced around religion and language in the nineteenth and twentieth centuries. In a region of thoroughly mixed peoples, this was particularly unfortunate. Traditionally in the Balkans, people had identified with *territories,* regarding themselves as "Bosnians," "Kosovars," "Herzegovians," "Dalmacians," and such. In other words, they had *regional* rather than ethnic identities. Embedded in this mosaic of regions were scattered small areas of ethnic homogeneity. Srbija Proper was one of these (fig. 7.15). In those nuclei, nation-states developed beginning in the late nineteenth century, and as each expanded, ethnically mixed populations were annexed. As identity shifted from region to ethnicity, a volatile situation developed, dooming Yugoslavia. Political boundaries rarely matched ethnic borders, and most districts had a high degree of mixing. The nation-state principle, applied to such a situation, made ethnic cleansing almost inevitable.

Of the successor states to the former Yugoslavia, the most viable would seem to be *Slovenia,* which stood aside from the subsequent troubles and, in any case, had only a tiny Serb minority. *Croatia,* plagued by an awkward shape, made matters worse by opting for a French-style unitary state that could not easily accommodate minority rights. Even some ethnic Croatian districts have grown restive. In Istra, the westernmost part of Croatia, many people feel a greater loyalty to province than to state. Istrians will tell the

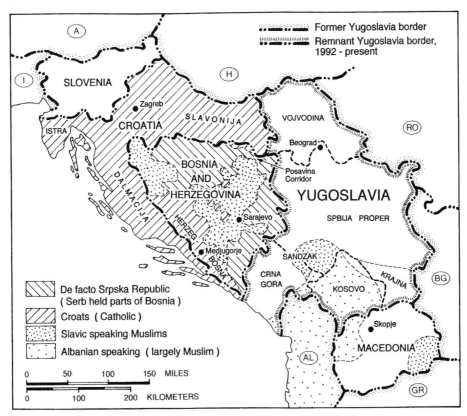

Figure 7.15.   The ongoing disintegration of the former Yugoslavia. Five successor states emerged in the 1990s—Slovenia, Croatia, Bosnia and Herzegovina, Macedonia, and the remnant Yugoslavia. The latter includes Crna Gora, a restive republic, and Kosovo, now effectively detached from Yugoslavia by foreign invaders. Troubled multiethnic Bosnia and Herzegovina retain most the problems that destroyed the former Yugoslavia.

visitor that "we have an identity of our own" and "Zagreb seems far away." Croatia expelled hundreds of thousands of ethnic Serbs from its territory in the mid-1990s.

Landlocked *Macedonia* is a mere fragment of the former territory by that name, which laps over into Greece and Bulgaria and once housed a population of Bulgars, Pomaks, Turks, Greeks, and Albanians. Even the remnant independent Macedonia retains sizable Albanian and other Muslim minorities.

Bosnia–Herzegovina was, upon becoming independent, almost as diverse as the former Yugoslavia at large, a microcosm of that failed state. Even massive ethnic cleansing and genocide have not destroyed its ethnic diversity. Civil war produced the de facto *Srpska Republic,* now populated and ruled predominantly by Serbs, who desire reunification with the remnant Yugoslavia. Its territory is very awkwardly shaped, with 2 areas barely joined at the strategic Posavina Corridor (fig. 7.15). The remainder of Bosnia and Herzegovina is made up of the "Muslim–Croat Federation," but in fact the Croat districts form the shadow "Herzeg–Bosna" Republic, whose people would happily be annexed to Croatia. Lying in Herzeg–Bosna is the major Croat religious pilgrimage town of Medjugorje, a place possessing enormous emotional importance to all Croats (fig. 7.15).

The condition of the remnant *Yugoslavia* is also unstable. It consists today of only 2 federated states, *Srbija* (Serbia) and *Crna Gora* (Montenegro) (fig. 7.15). Crna Gora, itself formerly independent, did not secede in the early 1990s when the other republics of the former Yugoslavia broke away, but a strong secessionist movement now exists. Were Crna Gora to become independent, Yugoslavia would cease to exist. Both Serbs and Montenegrins are mainly Eastern Orthodox Christians and speak dialects of the same language. These ties may suffice to hold Yugoslavia together. Still, the Montenegrins' loyalty is, in keeping with Balkan tradition, much stronger to their region than to Yugoslavia.

Srbija itself has begun to disintegrate. *Kosovo*, a dominantly Albanian–Muslim region, is now under foreign military occupation, precipitated by Serb atrocities, and its seems unlikely that it can be rejoined to Srbija. *Vojvodina*, the northernmost province of Yugoslavia, has a mixed population including many ethnic Hungarians, whose loyalty to a Serb nation-state would be weak. Also potentially troublesome is the *Sandzak* region on the border with Crna Gora, peopled predominantly by 250,000 Slavic-speaking Muslims. In a worst-case scenario, Srbija could be reduced to a remnant nation-state encompassing only Srbija Proper and Krajna, a border territory in the south (fig. 7.15).

Russia: Nation-State or Empire?

In most respects, Russia presents a political anomaly in Europe. It is the only state to establish enduring unity over a sizable section of the culture area within the last millennium, causing eastern Europe to assume a very different political character from the west. Even in its greatly diminished post-Soviet size, Russia remains by far the largest independent state in Europe and the entire world, retaining the aspect of empire long after the other great imperial states collapsed.

Early Russian attempts at state building, centered in Ukrainian Kyiv, were destroyed by Asiatic invaders (fig. 7.4). Sheltered by extensive forests from the Tatar hordes and favored by a radial pattern of navigable streams, Muscovy—the environs of Moskva—developed in the late Middle Ages as the new political focus of Russia (fig. 7.16). Growing from the Muscovy core area, the Russian state grew to dominate the East European Plain, a terrain unit that has ever since provided structure to the state. From a

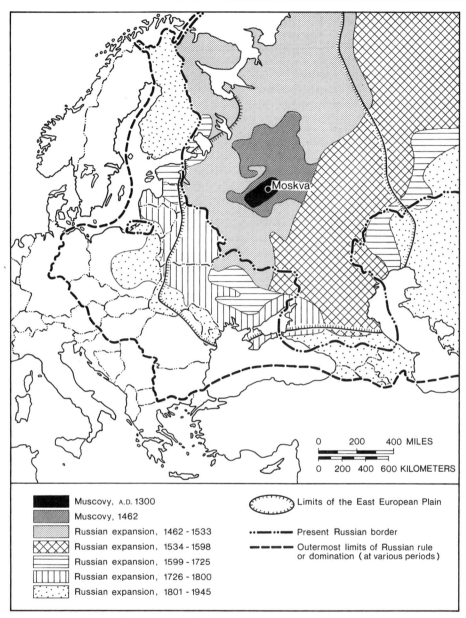

■ Muscovy, A.D. 1300	⬭ Limits of the East European Plain
▨ Muscovy, 1462	
▧ Russian expansion, 1462 - 1533	••—••—•• Present Russian border
⧄ Russian expansion, 1534 - 1598	— — — Outermost limits of Russian rule
▤ Russian expansion, 1599 - 1725	or domination (at various periods)
▥ Russian expansion, 1726 - 1800	
⋰ Russian expansion, 1801 - 1945	

Figure 7.16.   Territorial evolution of Russia in Europe. Russia grew from a core area, the Principality of Muscovy around Moskva, to encompass a huge empire that only collapsed in 1991. Its influence has at times extended deep into Europe and even more profoundly into Asia, but the East European Plain has always provided the spatial and physical focus of Russia.

European perspective, Russia *is* the East European Plain, and the huge Siberian appendage beyond the Urals possesses little population or importance. To Russians, too, the "real" Russia lies in the great western plain.

When the Soviet Union disintegrated in 1991, Russia faced a difficult transition. An empire traditionally under despotic, unitary rule and far more like China than Germany, Russia evolved painfully and perhaps abortively toward nation-state status and federalism. In the Russia that emerged from the collapsed empire, about 82% of the people spoke Russian, and no single ethnic minority claimed as much as 4% of the population. Since 1991, the Russian proportion has increased slightly as a result of international migration among the countries of the former Soviet Union. Increasingly, Russian nationalists regard the country as a nation-state and emphasize its *Eurasian*—as opposed to *European*—character.

Federalism accommodates the ethnic minorities in autonomous republics, some of which have secessionist goals. Various Turkic, Caucasic, and Muslim minorities seek, with greater or lesser fervor, to dismantle the nested doll "empire within the empire" (fig. 7.2). *Chechnya*, a "breakaway rogue state" in the Caucasus on the borders of Georgia, declared independence in 1991 and has since been intermittently at war with Russia (figs. 1.8 and 7.2). *Ichkería* is the native name for Chechnya. No other Caucasic peoples openly pursue independence from Russia, perhaps mainly because the northern Caucasus is such a shatterbelt ethnically, with few groups possessing adequate population size or territory to be viable independent states. Russia's role here might be to provide the shelter of a larger state, thereby preventing tribal warfare, but the heavy-handed tactics employed by the Russians in the recent Chechen war undermine such a role.

Tatarstan, a Turkic Muslim republic lying on and beyond the Volga, in the southeastern reaches of the East European Plain, declared "sovereignty" in 1992 and enjoys considerable autonomy. So does neighboring *Bashkortostan*, also Turkic and Muslim (fig. 7.2). Oil-rich, the Tatars and Bashkiris, who are closely related linguistically, cooperate in diverse ways to loosen the control of the Russian government over their republics. Their territories adjoin, forming a "Greater Tatariya," but they will not likely unite. The Tatars are racially and culturally more Europeanized, a dominantly city-dwelling people, while the Bashkiris, even in physical appearance, remain more Asian.

Few other republics or districts are likely to try to leave the Russian Federation. *Karelia*, in the northwest, is a nominally Finnish republic, but ethnic Russians form the large majority of the population (fig. 7.2). Separatist tendencies in Karelia have much more to do with criminal Mafia control of the government than with ethnic unrest. The *Kaliningrad District*, on the Baltic Sea, presents a special problem to Russia (fig. 7.2). This territory was never a part of Russia before 1945, when it was taken from Germany, nor did any Russians live there. The German population was expelled and replaced by Russians. Moreover, Kaliningrad is an exclave, separated from the rest of Russian territory. In many ways, Kaliningrad is beginning to function like a separate Baltic republic, based on its status as a free-trade zone and smugglers' paradise.

Another issue facing Russia is the status of *Belarus*, one of the former Soviet republics that became an independent state in 1991 (fig. 7.1). Belarus did not actively seek independence, achieving that status by default when the Soviet Union's central government was abolished. Many or most Belorussians regard themselves as Russians, and they have never before been an independent country. There is a basis of Belorussian ethnicity. A minority of them speaks a separate dialect of Russian, and their name, meaning "White Russians," derives from a light complexion, reputedly the result of never having mixed with Tatars or other Asiatic invaders, isolated in their marshy homeland. Poverty-stricken, with huge areas too poorly drained for farming or laid waste by Chernobyl radiation, and burdened with a corrupt, strong-armed dictator, Belarus would be a liability for Russia. Indeed, Russians disparagingly call Belorussians "potato eaters"—a people so poor they survive on potatoes. A recently proclaimed federation of the 2 countries lacks any real substance, but at the same time no noteworthy nation-building has occurred, nor is public support for continued independence strong.

Geopoliticians try to adopt the long-term view in assessing the evolution of independent states. From this perspective, we can predict that the Russia emerging from the present period of flux, whether nation-state or renewed empire, whether federal or unitary, will almost certainly perpetuate the ancient Slavic unification of the huge East European Plain and continue to present an anomaly in an otherwise politically fragmented culture area.

Ukraine: From Border Province to Independent State

Ukraine, the second largest country in Europe in geographical area and the sixth largest in population, resembles Belarus in some ways (fig. 7.1). Its independence occurred in the same manner and not as the result of a separatist movement, and many Ukrainians, especially the 12 million or so who are ethnic Russians, remain ambivalent about its independence.

Unlike Belarus, Ukraine contains huge areas of fertile chernozem soils and large mineral deposits, especially coal. It is a potentially rich country, and its present poverty is more the result of mismanagement. Although "Ukraine" means "border province," commemorating its position along the battle lines between Russians and their historical enemies, the Tatar–Mongols, Turks, and Poles, the country has a proud history. The initial unification and Christianization of Russia emanated from Ukraine and its capital, Kiyev (fig. 7.4).

The strongest nationalist sentiment in Ukraine is found in the western half of the country, sometimes referred to as the "European" part. Long ruled by Poland and Austria–Hungary, the western Ukrainians came under the influence of Roman Catholicism, giving rise to the *Uniate* Church (see chapter 3), a hybrid of Catholic and Orthodox faiths. The revived Uniate Church provides one major basis of Ukrainian nationalism today.

The eastern part of Ukraine, more heavily Orthodox and Russian, does not share this nationalism. The peninsula of *Krym*, jutting into the Black Sea and peopled dominantly by Russians and Crimean Tatars, recently was granted the status of autonomous republic, in an effort to defuse separatist sentiment. The most heavily Russian district north of the peninsula, *Kharkov* (now renamed Karkhiv by Ukraine), is also restive (fig. 7.2). The western-most part of the country, the Zakarpats'ka District, lies west of the Carpa-thian Mountains and has no history prior to 1945 of belonging to Ukraine. There, too, Ukrainian nationalism has not taken root, though no separatist sentiment has arisen.

A potential problem for Ukraine also exists in *Transdnistria*, a fertile, dominantly Slavic sliver of adjacent Moldova (fig. 7.2). A separatist move-ment exists there, but Transdnistria is too small to become a viable state. Were it to secede from Moldova, the area would logically join Ukraine, but such a transfer might lead to a major boundary dispute, involving also Romania, which regards itself as Moldova's protector, given the 2 countries' shared language and Latinized, wine-drinking culture.

The European Union

Partly to present a more united front to the Soviet Union, some countries in politically fragmented western Europe began moving in the 1950s toward a supranational federalism. This initiative began in the economic sphere with agreements reducing coal and steel tariffs, and the greatest success so far has been in the realm of free trade. The multinational organization, since 1993 called the *European Union*, began with 6 countries in the heart of Eu-rope and has since expanded to 15 (fig. 7.17). So successful has this move-ment been that some experts now speak of "post-sovereign Europe."

Most nonmember European countries have applied for admission into the European Union, though 3—Iceland, Norway, and Switzerland—as well as the Faeroe Islands, a dependency of Denmark, declined invitations to join (fig. 7.17). On the "fast track" for entry are the formerly communist countries of Estonia, Czechia, Hungary, Poland, and Slovenia, as well as Malta and Cyprus. Six others have been placed on a "slow track" to entry, including Turkey, which has been kept waiting for a decade or more and must expect an additional lengthy delay.

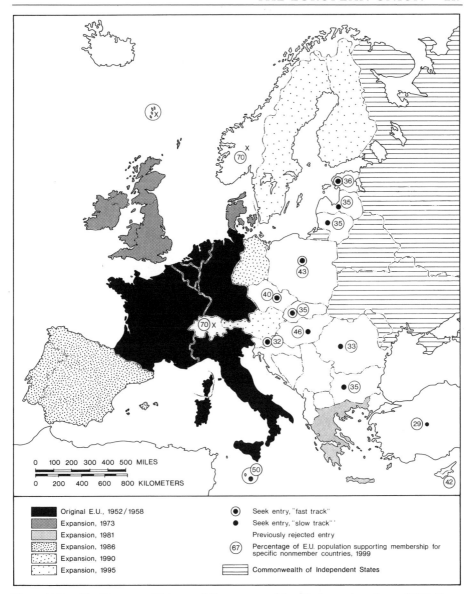

Figure 7.17.   The European Union and Commonwealth of Independent States (CIS). From a 6-country nucleus in the 1950s, the European Union has grown to include nearly all of western Europe and seeks to impose federalism upon a part of the culture area long plagued by political fragmentation. Expansion will continue. The CIS is the shadow of the former Soviet Union.

Turkey's application raises old and new questions. Is the European Union only for Europeans? Is Turkey a European country? The Turks once threatened Europe's very existence, conquering the Balkan Peninsula and 3 times laying siege to Wien, a city that is the very epitome of Europe. They destroyed the Greek empire, annexed all of its lands, and built a mosque atop the Parthenon in Athínai, the very symbol of classical Greece. Can Europeans forget these old memories? Forget that Turks speak an alien language and adhere to an alien religion—Islam? Forget the centuries of warfare required to drive Turks back to the small foothold they now hold in Europe around Istanbul, the former Greek Constantinople? Forget the genocide committed by the Turks against Christian Armenians in 1915? Forget the Turkish invasion of the dominantly Greek island nation of Cyprus in the 1970s and their continued military presence there? Can Europe forgive the ongoing brutal suppression of the Kurds, a separatist minority in Turkey? As one EU diplomat recently said, "if you want to kill support for EU expansion and enlargement, just talk of Turkey, Ukraine, and Belarus." Only 29% of the population in the present 15-country European Union favors Turkish admission. Turkey would need to institute major internal reforms, sacrificing considerable sovereignty, to gain admission. Many Turks oppose such changes.

Whatever the pace and geographical extent of its expansion, the European Union is a vital movement counteracting Europe's political fragmentation. The union, with a parliament that meets in Strasbourg, is envisioned as a loose federation with common foreign policy and military force. Most member states have now adopted EU currency, the *euro*. Growing cross-border connectivity characterizes the European Union, especially in investments, business mergers, labor mobility, and other economic-related matters. Clearly, the economic impetus is toward increased unity, a trend now under way for 4 decades, though union progress politically and culturally has come more slowly. Within the zone called the *Schengen Group*— Germany, France, Italy, Spain, Portugal, the Netherlands, Belgium, and Luxembourg—all passport checks at border crossings have been eliminated. Greece will soon join this group.

Increasingly, and largely as a result of the European Union, Europeans are identifying themselves with the union or Europe, instead of only with their individual country (fig. 7.18). The most "European-minded" include the Italians, Luxembourgers, Romanians, French, and Albanians, while the strongest nationalism occurs in the United Kingdom, Russia, Portugal, Scandinavia, and Finland. When asked whether their country's membership in the European Union was "a good thing," the highest positive responses came from Ireland, the Netherlands, Italy, Luxembourg, and Greece (fig. 7.19). As Tom Moring, a Finnish academician said, "being a citizen of Europe is still rather vague, rather abstract as an identity." In effect, the union offers a pragmatic federal identity based on peace, pros-

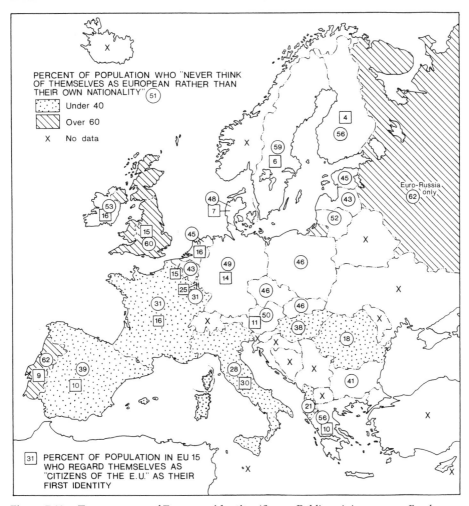

Figure 7.18. Two measures of European identity. (*Source:* Public opinion surveys *Eurobarometer* 1998.)

perity, and democracy, a "Fortress Europe" perhaps most closely resembling the Swiss micromodel.

Within the European Union, the power of the member independent states is being eroded or bypassed on 2 fronts. While the master plan of the union envisioned decision making only at national and federation levels, many regions and provinces within the various countries now exert considerable power, linked to the issue of separatism discussed earlier. Spain, for example, has lost aspects of sovereignty both to the union and to autonomous provinces such as Catalunya. Increasingly, one hears of a federalized "Europe of the regions" or "Europe of the fatherlands," implying a federal structure linking a mosaic of ethnic homelands in which the formerly independent states have been doubly demoted. The homelands would presum-

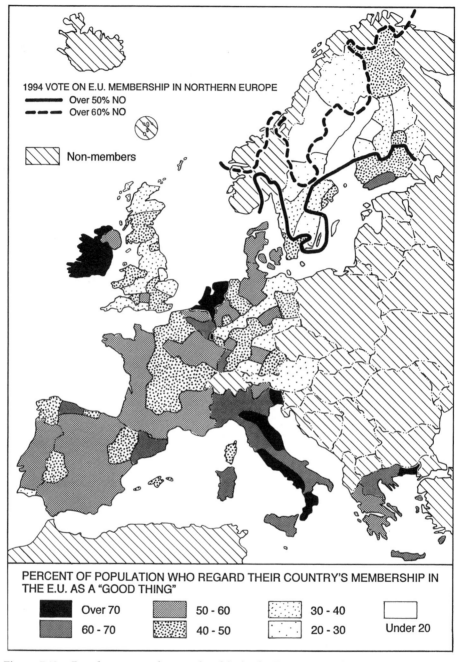

1994 VOTE ON E.U. MEMBERSHIP IN NORTHERN EUROPE
——— Over 50% NO
- - - Over 60% NO

▨ Non-members

PERCENT OF POPULATION WHO REGARD THEIR COUNTRY'S MEMBERSHIP IN THE E.U. AS A "GOOD THING"

■ Over 70   50 - 60   30 - 40

60 - 70   40 - 50   20 - 30   Under 20

Figure 7.19.   Popular support for membership in the European Union. In recently admitted countries, such as A, S, and SF, support remains weak. The 1994 vote in northern Europe revealed a core–periphery pattern, with the peripheries voting "no" on entry to the union. In S and SF, the populous south voted these countries into the union, but in N the nays had the majority.

ably offset the excess and sheer size of EU integration, allowing Europe's diverse regional cultures to survive and flourish.

A related development, the *Euregio,* erodes borders. All across Europe, especially within the union, these regional associations that link districts across international boundaries have been formed. They vary greatly in level of success, but all have the impact of weakening the existing borders that separate peoples. Examples include *Egrensis* Euregio, spanning the Germany–Czechia border, and *Saar–Lor–Lux* Euregio, joining Luxembourg to parts of Germany and France. Within Euregios, meetings are held to discuss common problems, student exchanges are arranged, regional planning coordinated, and the like.

Further complicating the pattern is the fact that not all member countries are moving toward EU integration at the same rate. "Europe at two speeds" describes the rapid meshing under way in the central core countries as contrasted to peripheral laggards. Scandinavia and the United Kingdom, in particular, often seem out of step. The Schengen passport control area is not the only example. When the euro goes into circulation in 2002, replacing national currencies, the United Kingdom, Sweden, and Denmark will not participate. The union seems to be fragmenting into inner and outer tiers.

The eventual level of federalism and sacrifice of national sovereignties that will occur even in the inner tier remains unclear, particularly now that military confrontation with Russia has ended. A highly centralized and powerful EU government will not be created, but at the same time the member states will probably never regain their former level of sovereignty.

Eastern Europe has nothing comparable to the European Union. Given Russia's enormous size, perhaps none is needed. Russia did establish the Commonwealth of Independent States (CIS), an economic union of 12 of the former 15 republics of the Soviet Union. Only the 3 Baltic states— Estonia, Latvia, and Lithuania—rejected CIS membership. A very different enterprise, far less ambitious than the European Union, the CIS has an uncertain future, tainted by Russian domination and memories of Soviet imperialism.

NATO and Beyond

The European Union developed beneath the military-strategic shield of the *North Atlantic Treaty Organization* (NATO). Founded in 1949, NATO has been dominated from the first by the United States. During the 4 decades of the Cold War, NATO formed a military alliance confronting the Soviet Bloc, which controlled the eastern half of Europe (fig. 7.20). Weakened by World War II, Europe had become merely a zone of confrontation between the United States and the Soviet Union. Under the protection of America

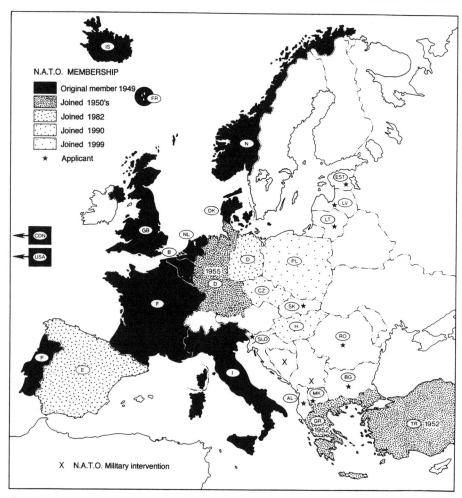

Figure 7.20.   NATO expansion, 1949 to present. Dominated by the United States, NATO is a holdover from the Cold War. Many applicant countries fear a revival of Russian imperialism.

and NATO, western Europe prospered and gradually, through the European Union, federated.

With the collapse of the Soviet threat after 1990, NATO expanded into the former Soviet satellite states. Poland, Czechia, and Hungary joined NATO in 1999, and a long list of other eastern European applicants has formed (fig. 7.20). The purpose of NATO also changed. It became a military force employed to intervene in local and regional conflicts. In Bosnia–Herzegovina, NATO forces serve as peacekeepers, but in Kosovo, the alliance attacked Yugoslavia in an act of war. Increasingly, the European members of NATO chafed at American domination.

In response, the European Union is now creating a 60,000-soldier force to replace NATO in dealing with European crises. The United States is not included, nor is Turkey. When this force is deployed in 2003, NATO will, in effect, become obsolete. More important, Europe will have reassumed strategic control over its territory, marginalizing both the United States and Russia. The Cold War will truly have ended.

Electoral Geography

As if the fragmentation into scores of independent states and autonomous regions were not complicated enough, additional political complexity is revealed by voting patterns. A free vote of the people on some controversial issue can be one of the purest expressions of culture. Free elections occur in almost every European country, and a vivid electoral mosaic exists, adding another revealing dimension of political and cultural geography.

In the accompanying map of voting behavior and ideology, a simple threefold classification has been employed—leftist, rightist, and centrist (fig. 7.21). Rightists, in this classification, include people who support the free enterprise market system, are nationalists, and conservative. Leftists favor government-sponsored socialism and European federation, while centrists work toward some middle way or compromise.

Viewed in this manner, Europe reveals a core–periphery configuration. As a general rule, rightist sentiment is strongest in the core region, especially south Germany (where Nazism arose) and adjacent parts of Alpine Europe. Northern Iberia, southern Great Britain, and the Polish–Ukrainian borderlands also form noteworthy rightist bastions. In prosperous western Europe, rightist ideology has experienced a notable upswing, often tied to issues such as the fate of resident foreign laborers from Third World countries.

Leftist sentiment remains strongest in the former communist countries and in northern Europe, where collectivism runs deep in the cultural tradition. Western Christianity tended to foster individualism, while the Eastern Church retained a more collectivist outlook, and the leftist tendencies of the eastern European peripheries thus have roots far older than communism. Surveys concerning approval of a market economy regularly reveal steadily diminishing support as one progresses eastward across Europe. Ukraine, for example, is divided between a leftist eastern part and a rightist western area. In Eurorussia, however, a north–south divide is evident. The "Red Belt" of strongest leftist sentiment lies in the southern half of Eurorussia, while support for market economy reforms is greatest in the northern half (fig. 7.22). Leftist politics also prevail in declining manufacturing districts of the west, such as the British Midlands and northern France, and in troubled rural regions like southern Iberia (fig. 7.23). Again, much of the voting pattern can be understood as the reflection of a prosperous European core pitted against a problem-ridden periphery.

In some European regions, ethnic politics play a larger role than left–

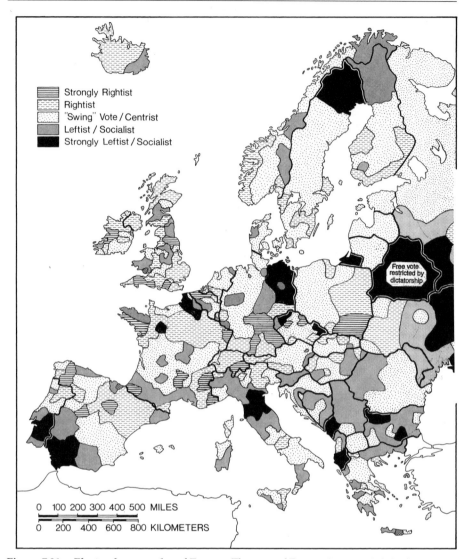

Figure 7.21.   Electoral geography of Europe. The core of Europe is more rightist/conserva-
tive and the peripheries more leftist/socialist. (*Sources:* Vanlaer 1984, 1991, 155; Sallnow,
John, and Webber 1982; O'Loughlin and van der Wusten 1993; Passchier and van der Wusten
1990; Agnew 1997; Craumer and Clem 1999; McFaul and Petrov 1997; Sarramea 1985.)

right–centrist ideologies. Groups such as the Hungarians in Slovakia,
German-speaking Tirolers in Italy, and Turks in Bulgaria strongly support
such parties. Separatist movements almost always find expression in ethnic
political parties.

Political geography, then, whether reflected in the crazy quilt of independent states or in the intricate mosaic of voting patterns, vividly reveals

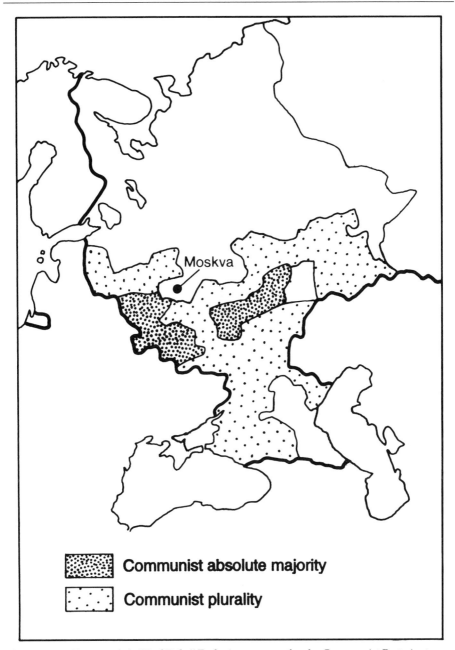

Figure 7.22.   Eurorussia's "Red Belt." Enduring support for the Communist Party is strongest in a belt across southern Eurorussia. The Red Belt extends over into Belarus and eastern Ukraine (see fig. 7.21). (*Source:* McFaul and Petrov 1997.)

Figure 7.23.   Communist election graffiti in Lisboa, Portugal. Impoverished southern Iberia continues to be a center of leftist sentiment. (Photo by T.G.J.-B. 1999.)

European internal diversity. East versus west and core versus periphery are both vividly evident.

Sources and Suggested Readings

Agnew, John. 1995. "The Rhetoric of Regionalism: The Northern League in Italian Politics, 1983–94." *Transactions of the Institute of British Geographers* 20:156–172.

———. 1997. "The Dramaturgy of Horizons: Geographical Scale in the Reconstruction of Italy by the New Italian Political Parties, 1992–95." *Political Geography* 16:99–121.

Arbós, Xavier. 1987. "Central versus Peripheral Nationalism in Building Democracy: The Case of Spain." *Canadian Review of Studies in Nationalism* 14:143–160.

Bunkse, Edmunds V. 1999. "Reality of Rural Landscape Symbolism in the Formation of a Post-Soviet, Postmodern Latvian Identity." *Norsk Geografisk Tidsskrift* 53:121–138.

Burghardt, Andrew F. 1962. *Borderland: A Historical and Geographical Study of Burgenland, Austria.* Madison, USA: University of Wisconsin Press.

Carter, Francis W., Peter Jordan, and Violette Rey, eds. 1996. *Central Europe after the Fall of the Iron Curtain: Geopolitical Perspectives, Spatial Patterns and Trends.* New York, USA: Peter Lang.

Chinn, Jeff, and Robert Kaiser. 1996. *Russians As the New Minority: Ethnicity and Nationalism in the Soviet Successor States.* Boulder, Colo., USA: Westview.

Cornish, Vaughan. 1923. *The Great Capitals: A Historical Geography.* London, GB: Methuen.

Craumer, Peter R., and James I. Clem. 1999. "Ukraine's Emerging Electoral Geography." *Post-Soviet Geography and Economics* 40:1–26.

Dawson, Andrew H. 1993. *A Geography of European Integration: A Common European Home.* New York, USA: Wiley.

Douglas, Neville, and Peter Shirlow, eds. 1998. "Special Issue: Space, Place and Politics in Northern Ireland." *Political Geography* 17:125–249.

Ehlers, Eckart. 1977. "Land Consolidation and Farm Resettlement in the Federal Republic of Germany." In *Man, Culture, and Settlement,* ed. Robert C. Eidt et al. New Delhi, IND: Kalyani.

Ettema, W. A. 1980. *Spanish Galicia: A Case Study in Peripheral Integration.* Utrecht, NL: Utrechtse Geografische Studie No. 18.

Fleure, H. J. 1941. "Notes on the Evolution of Switzerland." *Geography* 26:169–177.

Gómez-Ibáñez, Daniel A. 1975. *The Western Pyrenees: Differential Evolution of the French and Spanish Borderland.* Oxford, GB: Clarendon.

Gorenburg, Dmitry. 1999. "Regional Separatism in Russia." *Europe–Asia Studies* 51:245–274.

Griggs, Richard. 1994. "Ethnicity and Nationalism—the European Nations." *National Geographic Research & Exploration* 10:259–265.

Habermas, Jürgen. 1996. "The European Nation-state: Its Achievements and Its Limits." In *Mapping the Nation,* ed. Gopal Balakrishnan. London, GB: Verso, 281–294.

Harris, Chauncy D. 1991. "Unification of Germany in 1990." *Geographical Review* 81:170–182.

Heffernan, Michael. 1997. *Twentieth-century Europe: A Political Geography.* New York, USA: Wiley.

———. 1998. *The Meaning of Europe: Geography and Geopolitics.* London, GB: Arnold.

Heslinga, Marcus W. 1962. *The Irish Border as a Cultural Divide: A Contribution to the Study of Regionalism in the British Isles.* Assen, NL: van Gorcum.

Hilde, Paal S. 1999. "Slovak Nationalism and the Break-up of Czechoslovakia." *Europe–Asia Studies* 51:647–665.

Hooson, David, ed. 1994. *Geography and National Identity.* Oxford, GB: Blackwell, containing chapters on D, E, F, GB, PL, SLO, and UKR.

Hough, Jerry F. 1998. "The Political Geography of European Russia: Republics and Oblasts." *Post-Soviet Geography and Economics* 39:63–95.

Jones, Alun. 1994. *The New Germany: A Human Geography.* Chichester, GB: Wiley.

Kaiser, Robert J. 1994. *The Geography of Nationalism in Russia and the USSR.* Princeton, N.J., USA: Princeton University Press.

———. 1995. "Prospects for the Disintegration of the Russian Federation." *Post-Soviet Geography* 36:426–435.

Klemencic, Vladimir, and Rado Genorio. 1993. "The New State of Slovenia and its Function within the Frame of Europe." *GeoJournal* 30:323–333.

Kliot, N., and Y. Mansfield. 1997. "The Political Landscape of Partition: The Case of Cyprus." *Political Geography* 16:495–521.

Kolossov, Vladimir, and Andrei Treivish. 1998. "The Political Geography of European Minorities, Past and Future." *Political Geography* 17:517–534.

Korsmo, Fae. 1996. "Claiming Territory: The Saami Assemblies as Ethno-political Institutions." *Polar Geography* 20:163–179.

Leimgruber, Walter. 1981. "Political Boundaries as a Factor in Regional Integration: Examples from Basle and Ticino." *Regio Basiliensis* 22:192–201.

Leitner, Helga. 1997. "Reconfiguring the Spatiality of Power: The Construction of a Supranational Migration Framework for the European Union." *Political Geography* 16:123–143.

Lundén, Thomas. 1981. "Proximity, Equality and Difference: The Evolution of the Norwegian–Swedish Boundary Landscape." *Regio Basiliensis* 22:128–139.

McFaul, Michael, and Nikolai Petrov. 1997. "Russian Electoral Politics after Transition: Regional and National Assessments." *Post-Soviet Geography and Economics* 38:507–549.

McManis, Douglas R. 1967. "The Core of Italy: The Case for Lombardy–Piedmont." *Professional Geographer* 19:251–257.

Morris, A. S. 1971. "The Medieval Emergence of the Volga–Oka Region." *Annals of the Association of American Geographers* 61:697–710.

Murphy, Alexander B. 1988. *The Regional Dynamics of Language Differentiation in Belgium: A Study in Cultural-political Geography.* Chicago, USA: University of Chicago Geography Research Paper No. 277.

———. 1990. "Electoral Geography and the Ideology of Place: The Making of Regions in Belgian Electoral Politics." In *Developments in Electoral Geography*, ed. R. J. Johnston, F. M. Shelley, and P. J. Taylor. London. GB: Routledge, 227–241.

Murphy, Alexander B., and Anne Hunderi-Ely. 1996. "The Geography of the 1994 Nordic Vote on European Union Membership." *Professional Geographer* 48:284–297.

O'Loughlin, John, and Herman van der Wusten, eds. 1993. *The New Political Geography of Eastern Europe.* London, GB: Belhaven.

Paasi, A. 1996. *Territories, Boundaries and Consciousness: The Changing Geographies of the Finnish–Russian Border.* Chichester, GB: Wiley.

Parker, Geoffrey. 1988. *The Geopolitics of Domination: Territorial Supremacy in Europe and the Mediterranean from the Ottoman Empire to the Superpowers.* London, GB: Routledge.

Passchier, N. P., and Herman van der Wusten. 1990. "The Electoral Geography of the Netherlands in the Era of Mass Politics, 1888–1986." In *Developments in Electoral Geography,* ed. R. J. Johnston, F. M. Shelley, and P. J. Taylor. London, GB: Routledge, 39–59.

Penrose, J. 1990. "Frisian Nationalism: A Response to Cultural and Political Hegemony." *Environment and Planning D: Society and Space* 8:427–448.

Pounds, Norman J. G. 1954. "France and 'Les Limites Naturelles' from the Seventeenth to the Twentieth Centuries." *Annals of the Association of American Geographers* 44:51–62.

Pounds, Norman J. G., and Sue Simons Ball. 1964. "Core-areas and the Development of the European States System." *Annals of the Association of American Geographers* 54:24–40.

Raffestin, Claude. 1985. "Langues et pouvoir en Suisse." *L'Espace Géographique* 2:151–155.

Rokkan, Stein, and Derek W. Urwin. 1982. *The Politics of Territorial Identity: Studies in European Regionalism.* London, GB: Sage.

Rugg, Dean S. 1994. "Communist Legacies in the Albanian Landscape." *Geographical Review* 84:59–73.

Sallnow, John, Anna John, and Sarah K. Webber. 1982. *An Electoral Atlas of Europe, 1968–1981: A Political Geographic Compendium.* London, GB: Butterworth Scientific.

Sanguin, André-Louis. 1983. *La Suisse: Essai de géographie politique.* Gap, F: Éditions Ophrys.

Sarramea, J. 1985. "Géographie électorale de la France." *L'Information Géographique* 49 (3): 95–108.

Schib, Karl. 1965–1970. "Territoriale Entwicklung der Eidgenossenschaft." In *Atlas der Schweiz.* Wabern-Bern, CH: Verlag der eidgenossischen Landestopographie.

Schöller, Peter. 1987. "Die Spannung zwischen Zentralismus, Föderalismus und Regionalismus als Grundzug der politisch-geographischen Entwicklung Deutschlands bis zur Gegenwart." *Erdkunde* 41:77–106.

Shaw, Denis J. B., and Michael J. Bradshaw. 1992. "Problems of Ukrainian Independence." *Post-Soviet Geography* 33:10–20.

Smith, Graham. 1999. "Russia: Geopolitical Shifts and the New Eurasianism." *Transactions of the Institute of British Geographers* 24:481–500.

Spooner, D. J. 1984. "The Southern Problem, the Neapolitan Problem, and Italian Regional Policy." *Geographical Journal* 150:11–26.

Stanislawski, Dan. 1959. *The Individuality of Portugal: A Study in Historical-political Geography.* Austin, USA: University of Texas Press.

Thomas, Peter. 1990. "Belgium's North–south Divide and the Walloon Regional Problem." *Geography* 76:36–50.

Unwin, Tim. 1999. "Contested Reconstruction of National Identities in Eastern Europe." *Norsk Geografisk Tidsskrift* 53:113–120.

Vandermotten, Christian. 1991. "La résurgence des nationalismes en Europe centre-orientale et en Union Soviétique." *Revue Belge de Géographie* 115:87–101.

Vanlaer, Jean. 1984. *200 millions de voix: une géographie des familles politiques européennes.* Brussels, B: Société Royale Belge de Géographie et Laboratoire de Géographie Humaine de l'Université Libre.

———. 1991. "Les premières élections libres en Europe de l'Est: systèmes de partis et clivages régionaux." *Revue Belge de Géographie* 115:140–157.

Wild, Trevor, and Philip N. Jones. 1988. "Rural Suburbanisation and Village Expansion in the Rhine Rift Valley: A Cross-frontier Comparison." *Geografiska Annaler* 70B:275–290.

———. 1994. "Spatial Impacts of German Unification." *Geographical Journal* 160:1–16.

Williams, Allan M. 1991. *The European Community: The Contradiction of Integration.* 2nd ed. Oxford, GB: Basil Blackwell.

Williams, Colin H. 1980. "Ethnic Separatism in Western Europe." *Tijdschrift voor Economische en Sociale Geografie* 71:142–158.

Wise, Mark, and Richard Gibb. 1993. *Single Market to Social Europe: The European Community in the 1990s.* Harlow, Essex, GB: Longman.

Wixman, Ronald. 1991. "Ethnic Nationalism in Eastern Europe." In *Eastern Europe: The Impact of Geographic Forces on a Strategic Region.* Washington, D.C., USA: Central Intelligence Agency, 36–47.

CHAPTER 8

Cities

A city may be defined as a relatively large, permanent settlement containing a dense cluster of socially heterogeneous people engaged in specialized, primarily nonagricultural types of work. Much that we regard as "European" has its roots in the city. The innovations, changes, and great ideas used in chapter 1 to epitomize Europe sprang, with few exceptions, from the urban population of Europe. In some provinces and countries, more than four-fifths of the population live in cities and towns, and the proportion in Belgium has reached 97% (fig. 8.1).

The Mercantile City

Though the city epitomizes European civilization and represents an ancient, vital institution there, its origins lie elsewhere. In fact, the diffusion of urbanism followed the same northwestward path from the Near East that brought the Indo-European languages, Christianity, agriculture, and the political state to Europe (fig. 8.2). Many of these innovations were interrelated in that agriculture greatly increased food production per capita, freeing a portion of the population to engage in urban activities, such as trade, crafts, the military, and political administration. These occupations all became centered in cities and in fact provided the very reason for urban existence. Trade represented the most important single function, and the term **mercantile city** best describes European urban centers prior to the 1700s and 1800s.

Cities thrive in peace, law, and order, conditions best produced when organized political states replaced tribal governments. In turn, cities serve as centers of administration. Rulers found cities convenient bases from which to rule. Symbiotically, then, cities housed the very governments that fostered them. Some early cities probably arose as religious sites, centered on temples, and the priestly class also formed an influential part of urban

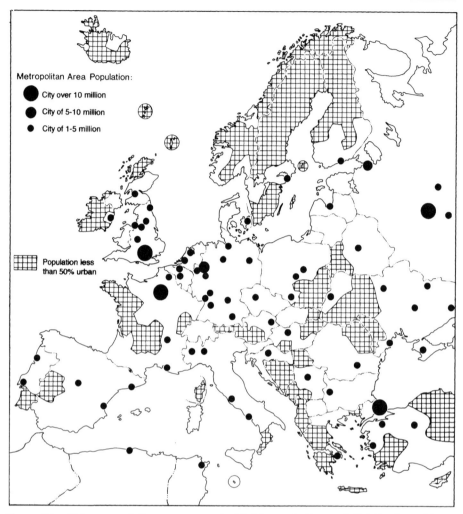

Figure 8.1. Urban population as a percent of total population and distribution of large metropolitan areas. Countries differ somewhat in their definition of *urban* and *metropolitan area,* but the figures are roughly comparable. *Urban* is defined as settlements of 10,000 or more population. The core of Europe is more highly urbanized, in general, than the peripheries.

population from the very first. Scholars, artists, and philosophers early joined the merchants, artisans, rulers, soldiers, and clerics as urbanites, making the city a center of learning and creativity. Human heterogeneity and crowding energized the urban population, leading to new ideas and inventions. Not the least of these was democracy, the noblest of all European ideas and born of its cities.

The first Europeans to receive urbanism from the Near East and Anatolia, about 2000 B.C., were the Greeks. Within 7 centuries, small city-states, each ruling a small tributary rural territory, dotted the Pelopónnisos and

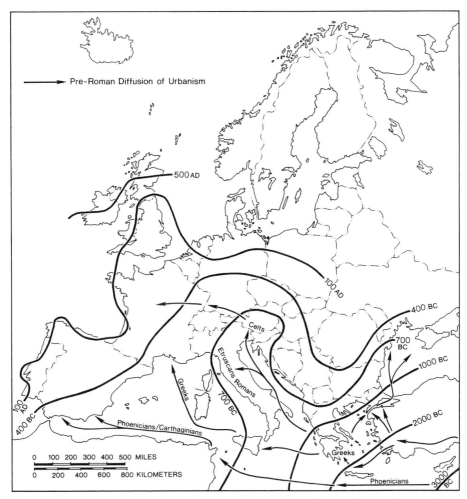

Figure 8.2.   Diffusion of the city. The source and paths of diffusion show striking similarities to the diffusionary routes of the Indo-European languages, agriculture, the political state, and Christianity. Just as was probably true in the spread of agriculture and languages, Iberia received its first urban impulse from Afro-Asiatic peoples by way of North Africa. (*Source:* Pounds 1969, with modifications.)

Aegean shores, forming the basis of the Greek *heroic* age, which ended about 1200 B.C. After a brief dark age, the Greeks began their greatest era of city founding some three centuries later, culminating in the Hellenic golden age. Greek colonists carried urbanism as far afield as the Black Sea coasts, southern Italy, and the south of France. Siracusa on Sicilia and Marseille in Languedoc represent their work. By about 500 B.C., some 600 cities existed in peninsular Greece and the Aegean. The Phoenicians, a Mediterranean people of the Near East, also founded some cities as trading colonies in Europe, especially in southern Iberia.

Most of these early Mediterranean cities remained small in size and rather unimpressive in appearance. Unlike farm villages, they were surrounded by walls and often boasted a temple, a palace, a theater, and a marketplace. Rarely did they exceed 5,000 in population, though Athínai may have had as many as 300,000 residents in the peak of its classical glory and Kórinthos perhaps 90,000. Only the larger acquired importance beyond their local areas. Even at the apex of classical urban development, as little as one-quarter of the Greek population lived in cities. As in the heroic age, the city-state dominated the classical Hellenic world.

The idea of urbanism spread quickly in Europe. Beginning about 800 B.C., Celts established a number of small cities in the Alpine peripheries, most notably at Hallstatt in Austria, and the Etruscans of Italy became active city builders in the same period. Romans, destined to become the greatest of all European city founders, were influenced by both Greeks and Etruscans. They eventually replaced the concept of the city-state and their troublesome small wars with empire and the *pax Romana*. At the dawn of Roman greatness, the imperial core districts of Latium (modern Lazio) and Etruria (modern Toscana) contained some 42 cities; by midpoint in the empire's life span under Augustus, 430 new cities existed in Italy alone (fig. 8.3). In its classical grandeur, Roma may have boasted a population of a half-million, packed into an area of barely 23 square kilometers.

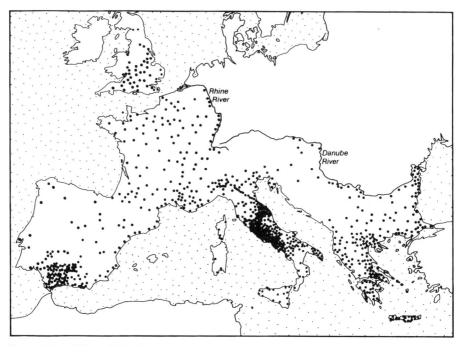

Figure 8.3.   Cities of the Roman Empire by the third century A.D. Note the clusterings in central Italy, southern Spain, and Greece. (*Source:* After Pounds 1969.)

Romans speeded the diffusion of urban life through Europe by founding new cities in France, Germany, Britain, interior Iberia, and along the Danube. Some new towns grew around military barracks or camps, an origin suggested by the British town suffixes -caster and -chester, as in Lancaster or Winchester, derived from the Latin word castra ("military camp"). Three areas stood out as centers of urban development under Roman rule—central Italy, Greece, and Andalucía in Spain (fig. 8.3). Most of these cities remained small by modern standards. In France, the Roman towns ranged from about 600 to 35,000 in population, while in the British periphery of the empire the size varied from 500 or less up to the 17,000 inhabitants of London.

The heritage of Roman urbanization is considerable. Many sites have been continuously occupied since Roman times, as, for example, the city of Trier in Germany, and other sites were reoccupied after a period of abandonment. Even names are often corruptions of the original Latin form, as for example Köln (Latin Colonia Agrippinensis) and London (Londinium). One of the most interesting names, Zaragoza, began as the Roman Caesarea Augusta and was corrupted by the Arabic Moorish conquerors to Zarakusta and again by the Christian liberators of Spain to its present form.

Following another dark age after the fall of the Roman Empire, during which urban population shrank and some towns became totally abandoned, Europe entered its last great age of city founding in the Middle Ages, taking advantage of the security provided by the feudal system. Germanic peoples established most of the new cities during this era. Europe's urban focus shifted to new regions, allowing the Po–Veneto Plain and the Low Country–Rhinelands to replace the earlier southern concentrations (fig. 8.4).

Most Germanic towns grew from fortified preurban cores, sites dominated by the stronghold of a feudal lord. The A.D. 800s and 900s had been a major period of castle construction by feudal landowners as they sought to secure the surrounding countryside. The catalysts in changing most preurban cores to towns were itinerant traders, who initially made use of secure marketplaces adjacent to strongholds along transport routes. In time, the desire for safe winter quarters led the traders to establish permanent residence at the preurban cores, creating merchant colonies. Artisans were attracted by the presence of merchants, and the town population grew steadily. In an early stage of development, a "town" often consisted of several distinct nuclei: the feudal fortress; one or more marketplaces; scattered, fortified houses of merchants; a church; and some farmhouses (fig. 8.5). The German city of Braunschweig, for example, originated in 1269 through the union of 5 distinct nuclei, each of which had its own name. In an earlier era, Roma had arisen in a very similar manner as the union of adjacent hilltop villages.

The three essential attributes of the medieval Germanic city included the charter, the town wall, and the marketplace. The charter, a governmen-

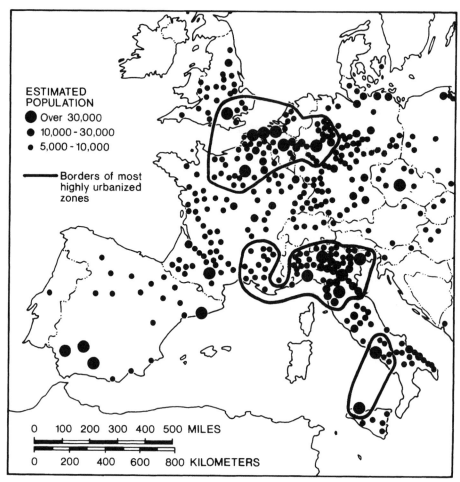

Figure 8.4.   Distribution of important cities, about A.D. 1500. Northern Italy and the Low Country had become the new urban centers in Europe. Thousands of smaller towns do not appear on the map. (*Source:* Pounds 1989, 260.)

tal decree from an emperor or lesser ruler granting political autonomy to the town, freed its populace from the manorial restrictions of the rural areas. The city became self-governing and responsible for its own defense. Charters were typically requested by colonies of well-to-do merchants, who found that manorial restrictions hindered the mobility and exercise of personal initiative so vital in trading activities. Many cities date their founding from the granting of a charter, though most existed prior to that time. City-states similar to those of classical Greece, legitimized by charter, appeared throughout most of central and western Europe.

Self-government demanded self-defense, and the castles and fortified houses gave way to city walls (fig. 8.6). All important parts of the city lay inside the wall, including the mercantile and manufacturing establishments,

Figure 8.5.   The medieval center of Moskva retains its ancient fortress—the Kremlin; its first marketplace—Red Square; and St. Basil's, a venerable church. Moskva, situated on the river of the same name, commanded the water trade route leading from the Baltic to the Black and Caspian Seas. (Photo by T.G.J.-B. 1999.)

Figure 8.6.   Avila, on the Castilian Meseta of interior Spain. The city retains its splendid ring of medieval walls. (Photo by T.G.J.-B. 1986.)

the fortress, the church, and the homes of the majority of the population. Urban expansion often required the construction of new, more inclusive walls, and some larger cities eventually needed 3 or 4 rebuildings. In the period before gunpowder came into widespread use, city walls adequately repelled invaders.

The marketplace, often supplemented by a bourse, or trading hall, served as the focus of economic activity in the town, for the mercantile function remained dominant throughout the medieval period. Larger places held annual trade fairs, some of which began in the days of itinerant traders before permanent settlement had transformed the preurban cores into towns. Some of the more famous of these fairs survive to the present day, as at Leipzig, Frankfurt am Main, Milano, and Lyon. In size, the towns of the Middle Ages closely resembled their classical ancestors. Few exceeded 100,000 in population. Gent, the famous textile center of Vlaanderen, had only 56,000 inhabitants in the mid-1300s. Paris, the largest European city, and Napoli were the only 2 with more than 100,000 by the year 1400.

After about 1500 the founding of new cities declined markedly, except in the far north. City-states gave way to larger, more powerful kingdoms. Tiny San Marino represents one of the very few surviving European city-states, clinging to its independence in the Appennini Mountains. Urbanization continued to affect a small part of the European population. In 1600, only 4 million of the 85 million Europeans lived in towns of 15,000 population or more, about 5% of the total. The Netherlands and Italy, the most highly urbanized countries, could claim only about 12% or 13% of their populations as urban, while only 2% of the Germans, French, and English lived in large towns at that time.

The Industrial City

European cities changed rapidly after about 1800 as a result of the Industrial Revolution. Manufacturing became the dominant function of many urban centers, putting an end to the age of mercantile cities (see chapter 9). The hallmark of the industrial phase was the great increase in city size, prompted by the gravitation of the majority of the European population to urban, industrial areas. England and Wales urbanized more than half their population by the 1850s. A half-century later, more than three-quarters of the English and Welsh lived in cities, and Germany had become the second nation to have over half of its population urban. Many other countries, especially in northwestern Europe, reached this level by 1930, and the trend continues to spread toward the peripheries of the culture area (fig. 8.1).

The Industrial Revolution produced the first European cities to have more than a million inhabitants. London passed the million mark in the first decade of the nineteenth century and exceeded 2 million by 1850. Paris claimed more than a million by 1846 and by the turn of the century, Berlin, Wien, St. Petersburg, and Moskva had reached this level. Today, about 70 metropolitan areas west of the Urals and south to the borders of Christendom claimed more than a million inhabitants. Scores more have populations of between 500,000 and 1 million. A core–periphery pattern appears in the geographical distribution of these large cities (fig. 8.1).

Counterurbanization

In the late twentieth century, particularly after about 1965, a new trend called *counterurbanization* began to influence Europe. Counterurbanization is the deglomeration or decentralization of population, as sizable numbers of people leave cities and move to semirural fringes or even to fully rural peripheries. Larger cities stagnate or decline in population due to net migratory losses, while villages and smaller urban places grow. Improved transportation and communications networks permit fairly long-range commuting, and many jobs can be performed at home. As a rule, the movement away from cities is limited to the more affluent segment of the population, and it often occurs in stages, beginning with the acquisition of a second home for vacation purposes. An author, data processor, or designer comes to realize that his or her job can be performed just as well in locations remote from the urban office. The products of his or her work can be shipped, mailed, or electronically transmitted to the city.

The aging of the European population, with 15% or more of all persons now over 65 years old in many regions, also contributes to counterurbanization because affluent retired people often relocate to rural areas. The sudden, rapid decline of such traditional manufacturing industries as textiles and steel also caused many overspecialized cities to lose population. Among the hardest hit by manufacturing decline were Glasgow, Manchester, Belfast, Torino, and many cities in the formerly communist east. Equally important, waves of foreign immigrant guest workers began arriving in the cities, causing many natives to flee. In addition, large numbers of Europeans embraced *antiurbanism,* a perception based in urban problems, crowding, and stress, as well as the attractive counterimage of the countryside as a place of harmony, civility, and sociability.

The United Kingdom, the first country to urbanize massively, also became the first to feel the effects of counterurbanization in the 1960s. Western Germany experienced an almost simultaneous onset of the phenomenon, followed by the Low Countries, France, and Denmark. The period 1975–1982 in France saw the rural population grow more rapidly than the urban for the first time in well over a century. France's Atlantic coastal, Mediterranean, and Alpine provinces gained population most rapidly.

Counterurbanization slowed in most countries in the 1980s, leading some urban geographers to label it as a temporary and inconsequential shift. France experienced a resurgence of growth in the largest metropolitan areas by 1990, and only the decaying heavily industrial cities exhibit long-term population losses. Germany, too, saw a slowing down of counterurbanization in the late 1980s, following 15 years during which the trend intensified. Most western European countries now invest heavily in urban redevelopment, making the cities more attractive places to live. These improvements, coupled with the ancient, traditional prestige of urban living in European culture, have apparently blunted any further large-scale counterurbanization, at least in the west.

Today, counterurbanization is occurring most profoundly in eastern Europe. The cities of the southern Urals region in Russia are among the most severely impacted.

Urban Site

Geographers study diverse spatial and ecological aspects of urbanization. Perhaps none is more fundamental than an analysis of the specific physical location, or **site.** Decisions that determined the sites of most European cities rested heavily upon the need for defense and access to trade routes. An easily defended site was particularly important to feudal lords who built strongholds during the insecure period after the Roman Empire fell. Romans themselves rarely chose protected sites for their army camps and other settlements, because their military force enjoyed superiority to that of neighboring tribes. Roman camps typically possessed *offensive* advantage, along roads and navigable streams rather than on high points. Still, episodes of piracy in the classical and preclassical Mediterranean influenced the defensive siting of Athínai and Roma, both of which lie a short distance inland from the coast.

Many types of defensive sites exist. The *river-meander site,* with the city located inside a loop where the stream turns back upon itself, leaves only a narrow neck of land unprotected by the waters. Besançon on the Doubs River in far eastern France provides an example of a river-meander site. *Incised* meanders proved particularly popular because the river loop became permanent by cutting down to form a steep-sided valley. The city of Bern, capital of Switzerland, on the Aare River, offers a splendid example of an incised river-meander site, as does Toledo in Spain (fig. 8.7).

Similar to the river-meander site but even more advantageous, the *river-island site* combined a natural moat with an easier river crossing, the latter an advantage for the merchant trade. Paris began as a town on the Île de la Cité, or "island of the city," in the middle of the Seine River, as did Wrocław on the Odra (Oder) in Poland, Limerick in Ireland, and others. Stockholm, the capital of Sweden, occupies a *lake-island site,* originating on a dozen or so small islands in the area where Lake Mälaren joins the Baltic

Figure 8.7.   Toledo, in the central Meseta of Spain, an example of a river-meander urban site. The original settlement, now the core of the city, lay inside the loop of the incised meander of the Tajo River. Such a location provided natural defense on three sides. (Photo by T.G.J.-B. 1986.)

Sea. Perhaps even more satisfactory, the *offshore-island site,* combined defense with a port facility. The classic example, Venèzia, rests on wooden pilings driven into an offshore sandbar, which separated a coastal lagoon from the open Adriatic Sea. Larch wood imported from Russia serves as Venèzia's foundations. The same category includes the famous town and abbey of Mont-Saint-Michel, situated on a rock off the coast of Normandie in France (fig. 8.8). At high tide, the rock and town become insular, while at low tide, tidal flats formerly made access difficult. A causeway changed this situation in modern times. Danger from the direction of the sea often prompted *sheltered-harbor sites,* where narrow entrances could be easily defended. Oslo, at the head of a fjord in Norway, and the Portuguese capital of Lisboa both occupy sheltered harbors.

High points offered obvious defensive advantages. Many towns lie at the foot of a fortified high point (fig. 8.9). Such cities often derived their names from the stronghold, as is indicated by many place names ending or beginning in *-burg, -bourg, -borg, castelo-, -grad,* and *-linna,* all of which mean "fortress" or "castle" in various European languages. Scottish Edinburgh ("Edwin's fort"), dominated by the impressive Castle Rock, provides a good example, as do Salzburg in Austria and Castelo Branco in Portugal. Other cities sited adjacent to fortified high points include Praha, Vaduz in Liechtenstein, Sion in Switzerland, and Budapest.

Figure 8.8.   The town and abbey of Mont-Saint-Michel, France, an example of the offshore-island urban site. At low tide, as in this picture, the town is connected to the nearby Normandie mainland by an expanse of sand, but at high tide it is an island. In modern times, a causeway was built to the mainland. Such a site offered obvious defensive advantages. (Photo by T.G.J.-B. 1999.)

Closely akin are those towns and cities that, in their formative stage at least, lay entirely on high ground, often adjacent to the stronghold. Examples include Beograd ("white fortress"), on a high bluff overlooking the confluence of the Danube and the Sava; Segovia and Zamora in Spain; Laôn in France; Shaftesbury, a Saxon hill town in England; and Castelo de Vide in Portugal. Often, such hill towns in Romance-language lands bear the place name prefix *Mont-* or *Monte-*, as in Monte Corno, Italy.

Merchants, largely responsible for the development of cities from pre-urban cores, generally selected stronghold sites that lay on *trade routes*. Numerous types of sites possessed advantages for the merchants. In the early medieval period, before bridges became common, *river-ford sites,* where the stream was shallow and its bed firm, offered good sites. Some cities bear names that indicate the former importance of fords, including the German and English suffixes *-furt* and *-ford.* Frankfurt ("Franks' ford") in Germany lies at an easy crossing of the Main River, where the ancient trade route from the Upper Rhine Plain passes northward toward the Great European Plain. Upstream on the Main from Frankfurt we find the towns of Ochsen-furt ("ford for oxen"), Schweinfurt ("swine-ford"), Hassfurt ("Hessians' ford"), Trennfurt, and Lengfurt. The English cities of Oxford on the

Figure 8.9.   The city of Sion/Sitten, in the Swiss canton of Valais/Wallis, an example of the high-point urban site. Sion developed at the foot of not 1, but 2 fortified high points, secular and ecclesiastical. The beautifully preserved fortresses still dominate the skyline of the city. Merchants who were responsible for creating the original urban nucleus chose to locate adjacent to the fortresses for reasons of security. (Photo by T.G.J.-B. 1978.)

Thames, Hertford on the Lea, and Bedford on the Ouse again suggest the former importance of river shallows in urban siting. The Latin word for "ford," *trajectus,* also survives in corrupted form in the town names such as Utrecht (*trajectus ad Rhenum,* or "ford on the Rhine") in the Netherlands.

A similar function was served by *bridge-point sites,* where streams narrowed down and possessed firm banks and beds. Town names including *pont, bridge, brück,* and the like indicate that the site was originally chosen for bridge construction. The Romans, great bridge builders, founded many towns that derive both their site and name from the Roman structure, as for example Les-Ponts-de-Cé ("bridges of Caesar") on the Loire River in France, and Paunton (from the Latin *Adpontem* ["at the bridge"]) in Lincolnshire, England. Historic London Bridge, of which several have existed through history, originally stood at a point on the Thames just upstream from the marsh-flanked estuary, at a site where the banks were firm and the stream narrow. It served as an important river crossing on the Roman route from the Strait of Dover to the interior of England. Examples of other bridge-point cities named for their function include Cambridge ("bridge on the Cam River") and Brigham ("bridge settlement") in England, Pontoise ("bridge on the Oise River") near Paris, Bersenbrück ("broken bridge") in northwestern Germany, Bruchsal ("bridge over the Salzbach") in the German province of Baden, Innsbruck ("bridge on the Inn River") in Austria, and Puente-la-Reina ("queen's bridge") in Spain.

Many city sites north of the Alps are riverine because navigable streams have long served as trade routes. *Confluence sites,* where two rivers meet, are common. The German city of Koblenz, at the juncture of the Rhine and the Mosel, actually derived its name from the Latin word for confluence, while Passau in the German province of Bayern may be the only city where three rivers—the Danube, Inn, and Ilz—meet at precisely the same point. The rise of Paris was facilitated by the convergence of the Marne, Oise, and Seine Rivers in the general vicinity of the city, and Lyon profited from its position at the confluence of Rhône and Saône. *Head-of-navigation sites* serve as transshipment points, such as Basel on the upper reaches of the navigable sector of the Rhine River in Switzerland. In countries such as Finland, where an intricate network of lakes and rivers provided the major trade routes, fortifications built at strategic narrows sometimes provided urban nuclei, as at Savonlinna ("castle in Savo Province") and Hämeenlinna ("castle in Häme Province") (fig. 8.10).

Crossroad sites occur throughout Europe. One of the more famous is Wien, the Austrian capital, located where an east–west route connecting the Hungarian Plain with southern Germany along the Danube Valley met

Figure 8.10.   The castle that gives a name to the Finnish city of Savonlinna. It was founded by the Swedes to command the narrows between Lakes Pihlajavesi and Haukivesi. Even today, Russian and Finnish ships pass beside the fortress as they ply a major trade route. (Photo by T.G.J.-B. 1985.)

the ancient north–south route, which skirted the eastern foot of the Alps and passed through the Moravian Gate to Poland and the Baltic. Hannover in Germany stands at the juncture of an old route that runs along the southern edge of the North German Plain and the road that follows the course of the Leine River through the Hercynian hills south of the city.

Seaport sites occur in two basic types. Those at or near the juncture of navigable rivers or estuaries and the coast include such cities as London, Hamburg, Bordeaux, and Gdansk. In southern Europe, however, the seasonality of precipitation and short length of many streams rendered rivers less useful for transportation. Great ports usually developed at the juncture of highways and the coast rather than at the marshy, shallow river mouths. Cádiz lies some 30 kilometers south of the mouth of the Guadalquivir, and Marseille is well to the east of the Rhône delta marshes in southern France. Other Mediterranean rivers such as the Po and Tevere also have no major ports at their mouths, in part because of silting.

Mercantile activity was by far the most significant of the economic functions served by the preindustrial city. However, other economic factors were occasionally determinant in siting, in particular mining and the operation of health resorts. Extraction of iron ore, copper, salt, silver, and other minerals or metals often gave rise to mining towns. In Germany and Austria, place names including *Salz* or *hall* ("salt"), *Eisen* ("iron"), *Gold*, and *Kupfer* ("copper"), as in *Salzburg* (Austria) and *Kupferberg* (Germany), indicate the present or former importance of mining. The German city of *Halle* still has a saline spring in its very center, where the settlement began in Celtic times. *Spa sites* include towns that developed around mineral or hot springs, long sought by Europeans for relief from any number of ailments. Spa towns often date to Roman times. These places typically bear names indicative of their function, including elements such as *bains, Bad(en),* or *bagni,* all of which mean "bath." Examples are *Bad Pyrmont* and *Wiesbaden* in Germany, *Bagnoli* ("bath") near Napoli in Italy, and *Luxeuil-les-Bains* in eastern France. The English city of *Bath*, known to the Romans as Aquae Sulis, has an ancient resort tradition. In the Slavic lands, the name elements *-vody* ("waters"), as in *Mineralny Vody* ("mineral waters") a city near the Caucasus Mountains, and *-vary* ("hot springs"), as in *Karlovy Vary*, Czechia, describe resort towns.

Cityscapes

Europe's urban places reveal a distinctive morphology, or "cityscape," differing markedly from cities in North America and other overseas areas colonized by European emigrants. The urban *street pattern* represents one easily observable element of the cityscape.

In most European cities, the street pattern exhibits irregularity and a lack of planning. Streets meet at odd angles and seem to run every which way. Blocks take on the shape of parallelograms or triangles, and the visitor easily becomes disoriented. Automobile traffic moves with great difficulty, for thoroughfare avenues are rare (fig. 8.11). In parts of southern Europe, particularly Iberia, Arabic influence in street pattern produced a twisted maze with numerous dead ends, as in the old quarters of Toledo, Lisboa, and Sevilla.

Further complicating the irregularity of street pattern is the common practice of giving several different names to an avenue or street along its short, sinuous course. Often, the name changes at almost every intersection. Over a length of only six blocks in München, for example, one reasonably straight street bears the names Maxburgstrasse, Löwengrube, Schäfflstrasse, Schrammerstrasse, and Hofgraben. Additional confusion comes from an unsystematic and unpredictable numbering of the houses and buildings.

Europeans have in general resisted recent attempts to modify the crazy-quilt pattern of streets and render it more suitable for motorized traffic flow. Wartime destruction leveled as much as 80% of the buildings in some German cities, providing an opportunity to revise street patterns in the

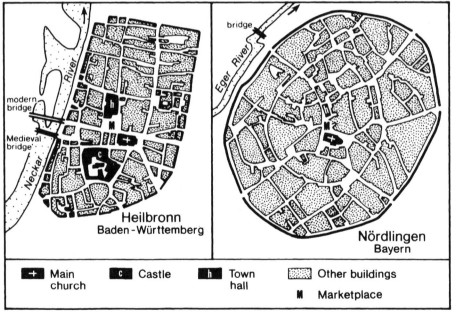

Figure 8.11. Examples of medieval towns in Germany. In Heilbronn, the Deutschherren-hof, a castle-fortress, was the successor to an ancient Frankish fortress. The church, town hall, and marketplace shared the center of the city with the fortress. Heilbronn was heavily damaged in World War II. Nördlingen, where the old outer wall is still intact, has the maze of the streets typical of medieval towns. An earlier wall that was outgrown is clearly traced by the circular street. The overall street pattern is of the type referred to as *radial concentric*. (*Sources:* Gutkind 1964–1969; Dickinson 1945.)

central portions. Urban planners wanted to lay out broader and straighter streets, but few western German cities actually acquired thoroughfares in the process of rebuilding. In contrast, the Dutch and British reconstruction of Rotterdam and Coventry produced cities better adapted to the needs of the automobile. Even earlier, in the 1700s and 1800s, authorities in some larger cities created grand, straight ceremonial avenues or boulevards. Thousands of Parisians, for example, lost their homes through royal decree to make way for the Avenue des Champs-Élysées. These impressive avenues provide a marked contrast to the remainder of the street pattern.

The traffic problems created by the irregularity of street patterns become more critical because of the narrowness of thoroughfares and the scarcity of parking space. In the German city of Bremen, 84% of the total street mileage is less than 7 meters wide, a minimum width for handling heavy 2-way traffic. Even so, Bremen is better off than the German cities of Lübeck, with 91% less than 7 meters, and Oldenburg, in which only 1% of all street mileage measures wider than that. Averages for 141 German cities indicate that 77% of the total urban street mileage remains too narrow for safe and efficient 2-way traffic of any considerable volume. In consequence, most central-city streets carry only 1-way traffic. Sizable districts have been designated as pedestrian zones, with automobiles banished. Pedestrians in the central section of a typical European city no longer feel intimidated by traffic or repelled by the visual blight of "machine space." Things seem drawn on a human scale and aesthetically pleasing.

In marked contrast to such an irregular street pattern are those European cities laid out on a grid or checkerboard pattern. Some of these are quite ancient, for the Greeks, Etruscans, and Romans sometimes used the grid pattern, particularly in colonial towns. The Roman plan featured two axial thoroughfares that met in the center of the town at the market, flanked by lesser avenues that completed the grid. One can still see traces of the ancient pattern today in cities such as Pavia and Napoli in Italy, Köln in Germany, Zaragoza in Spain, and Chester in England (fig. 8.12). In later times, the gridiron plan experienced a revival and served as the model for new towns founded by the Germans in east-central Europe, by the French kings in southern France, by the Swedish empire in northern Europe, and by Renaissance town builders in northern Italy. Some of the planned cities display a striking radial pattern (fig. 8.13). Often the gridiron layout remains confined to the original part of the town, and suburbs added later reveal the more typically chaotic European street pattern. Irregularities also often developed later in the original grid of Roman-founded towns, as at Pavia (fig. 8.12).

Another morphological measure of the European city is the *degree of compactness*. In comparison to North American and Australian urban centers, Europeans cities of comparable population cover much less geographical area (fig. 8.14). A foreign visitor often gains the impression that European cities seem smaller than they actually are in terms of population.

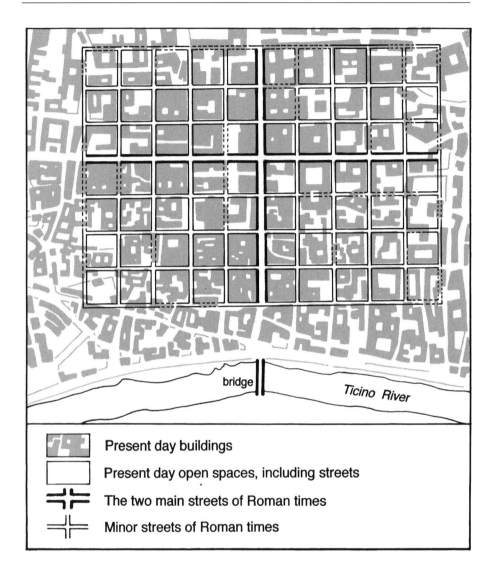

Figure 8.12. Survival of the Roman grid pattern in Pavia, Italy. To walk in the central section of modern Pavia (Roman Ticinum) is to be guided in the footsteps of the ancient Romans. The degree of survival of the Roman checkerboard pattern is quite remarkable, for most of the original streets are still in use after 20 centuries. The 2 main intersecting streets of Roman times have even maintained their dominance. Note how much less regular the streets are outside the old Roman core. Pavia is on the Ticino River south of Milano. (*Source:* After Gutkind 1964–1969.)

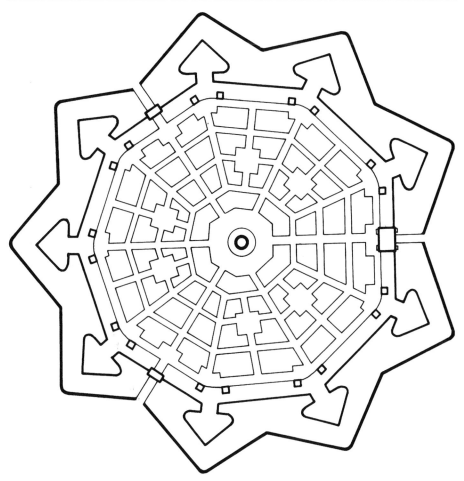

Figure 8.13.   Central part of Palmanova, Italy, in the far eastern Po–Veneto Plain. Founded in 1593 during the Renaissance era, Palmanova displays a highly planned street pattern, as did most of the cities established after the end of the Middle Ages.

In 1960, for example, single-family detached homes accounted for only 16% of all urban residences in western Germany. Since then, detached housing has risen dramatically in the cities of western Europe, but without completely sacrificing compactness. Suburban lots tend to be considerably smaller than in Canada or the United States, and front yards are generally absent. Eastern European cities retain a low percentage of single-family homes. Throughout Europe, many urbanites prefer to live close to the center of town, where the old city core serves as a place to gather after work, to stroll, and to dine. Apartment housing allows proximity to the central city, and most urban cores suffer little blight, decay, and crime. Even suburban housing, in countries as diverse as Iceland, Spain, Czechia, and Latvia, often takes the form of high-rise apartment complexes. On the periphery of

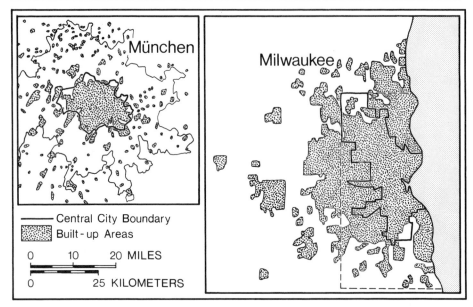

Figure 8.14. München, Germany, and Milwaukee, Wisconsin, metropolitan areas drawn to the same scale. The 2 urban areas each have about 1.5 million inhabitants, but notice how much more compact the built-up area of München is. (*Source:* After Holzner 1986, 18.)

most European cities lie garden allotments for the apartment dwellers, serving in effect as their "backyards." In eastern Europe, *dachas*—summer houses, often very substantial second homes—are built on these allotments. In smaller towns, privately owned, detached housing appears much more commonly than in the cities (fig. 8.15). In European cities, the medieval custom of combining residence and place of work survives to a surprising degree. Bakers, butchers, or restaurant owners often live above their shops. Most city dwellers reside at least within walking or cycling range of their place of employment, though commuting is now common in western Europe.

The *skyline* or visual profile of the European city also presents a distinctive appearance. North Americans, accustomed to a skyline dominated by huge high-rise buildings, or skyscrapers, at the center of the city, with progressively lower structures toward the suburbs, find the European city inverted (fig. 8.16). The urban skyline of Europe features a central skyline still dominated by church spires, the venerable hilltop fortress, or some special landmark such as the Eiffel Tower. The central cities of Europe typically contain historic buildings of considerable age, erected before modern structural technology permitted great height. Edifices of more than 5 or 6 stories remain uncommon.

Even when catastrophes destroy the old urban cores, Europeans generally rebuild them as before. World War II, for example, altered few skylines. A comparison of photographs of prewar and postwar München, 80% of

Figure 8.15.   Single-family detached private housing in the small Swedish mill town and service center of Torsby, in Värmland Province. Surrounded by a well-kept, fenced lawn and garden, this home is typical of smaller urban centers in Europe. (Photo by T.G.J.-B. 1985.)

which was destroyed by bombing, reveals a striking similarity. As in the reestablishment of the old, preautomobile street patterns, Europeans simply revived the vanished cities of prewar times. Perhaps the most remarkable re-creation took place in the former German Baltic port city of Danzig, present-day Gdansk, part of Poland, since 1945. The German population of the severely damaged city was expelled, but the Poles then proceeded to spend huge sums of money to produce a duplicate of the old German Hanseatic city. Their attention to detail in reconstruction was simply astounding. The end product is a museum town from another age, but Poland solidified, with time, effort, and money, a valid claim to a city that Germans and Russians destroyed.

Beyond the central city, with its low skyline profile, lie rings of taller buildings, including huge apartment blocks. High-rise commercial skyscrapers have appeared in some urban peripheries, presenting precisely the opposite arrangement than one finds in an American city. Taller buildings form a doughnut-shaped rim in the European city, surrounding the low-profile center (fig. 8.16).

Urban Zones

The preceding section on urban morphology implies a distinctive zonation within European cities. Age, continued growth, governmental policy, and

Figure 8.16. Paris, looking westward from the Eiffel Tower. An American would mistake this as a view toward the center of the city, whereas in reality the modern high-rise buildings stand in Paris's outer ring. (Photo by T.G.J.-B. 1978.)

city planning produced a compartmentalization unique to European urbanism.

As suggested earlier, the center of the European city consists of the *preindustrial core,* the mercantile city of past times, including all districts that formerly lay within the ramparts and walls. Remnants of these walls often survive, marking the outer limits of the core. The famous Porta Nigra ("Black Gate") in the German city of Trier is a Roman survival, while the Holstentor ("Holstein Gate") at Lübeck survives as a remnant of medieval walls. In some instances, the entire circuit of city walls remains to enclose the old core. Lugo in Spanish Galiza retains its Roman walls and Ávila, in the Castilian heartland of Spain, boasts a medieval ring of walls and gates that ranks among Europe's finest (fig. 8.6). Óbidos in Portugal, Carcassonne in France, Dinkelsbühl in Germany, and Ródhos in Greece offer other examples of surviving or rebuilt town walls. More often, the walls no longer exist, their place taken by a ring street and a string of parks. Riga in Latvia and Frankfurt am Main fit this description, as do many other places.

Within the old preindustrial core, a number of venerable buildings and squares survive, including an impressive cathedral, bearing witness to the extraordinary importance and vitality of Christianity in the Middle Ages. Even as early as the era of classical Greece, municipal pride in public buildings and religious edifices was one of the principal traits that distinguished townsfolk from residents of farm villages, and citizens bore the large expense involved in cathedral construction with little complaint. Many of these churches, such as Notre Dame on the Île de la Cité in Paris, San Marco in Venèzia, the Köln Cathedral, St. Stephans in Wien, the magnificent cathedral at Chartres, southwest of Paris, and Santa María in Burgos, Spain, rank among the great architectural treasures of the world.

If the city served as the residence of a royal family, the urban core usually includes a palace or fortress. Examples include the Louvre in Paris, the Hofburg in Wien, Edinburgh Castle, and the Palazzo Ducale in Venèzia. In some cities, the royal residence in the medieval core was identical with the feudal stronghold on high ground, which had originally attracted urban settlement. In many instances, royalty abandoned these residences in the central city to build splendid new palaces in the suburbs. Versailles supplanted the Louvre in Paris and set the standard for other European royalty. The Hapsburgs of Austria built Schönbrunn Palace on the outer fringe of Wien and the Wittelsbachs of Bayern in southern Germany ordered the construction of the beautiful Nymphenburg Palace on the western outskirts of München.

The urban core area centers on the old marketplace, which often lies in front of the cathedral (fig. 8.17). These public squares are often very impressive, ringed with arcades, as at the Plaza Mayor in Salamanca, Spain, and decorated with plantings or fountains, as at the Prato della Valle in Padova, Italy. Most cities have several such fine squares, each with a distinctive character and function. Near or on one of these squares stands the town hall, housing the city government.

In an economic sense, the urban core serves a number of purposes, retaining the multifunctional character of medieval times. It houses a variety of small retail stores, cafés, restaurants, multifamily residences, and workshoplike factories of craftsmen workers. The distinction between residential, industrial, and commercial zones is rather weak, with a great deal of areal interweaving. Gild houses of the medieval crafts still stand in many preindustrial urban cores, as does the bourse, a trading hall for merchants. Institutional functions also remain common in the central city, including governmental agencies and museums. Some well-preserved urban central areas have become virtual outdoor museums, bypassed by economic activity and increasingly depopulated, though this trend seems to be reversing. Some central-city dwellers complain they cannot be expected to live in an unchanging, romanticized setting of past times. The crumbling architectural heritage of the past is expensive to maintain and difficult to adjust to the modern age. Venèzia's core area, largely a historic district, provides an extreme example. Plagued by flooding, decay, and pollution, Venèzia's central area population has declined from 137,000 in 1961 to only 85,000 today. *Façadism* has provided another increasingly popular solution. Outwardly, buildings look much as they did 500 years ago, preserving the historic appearance of the preindustrial city, but inwardly a thoroughly

Figure 8.17.   The arcaded town square is the pride of Novy Jicín, in Morava Province, Czechia. Commanding the strategic Moravian Gate trade route, Novy Jicín, founded by Germans as Neutitschein, retains much of its preindustrial core. (Photo by T.G.J.-B. 1982.)

modern remodeling has occurred. As a result, these buildings are rarely what they seem to be.

Though some European central cities remain choked by automobile traffic, perhaps most notoriously Roma, most others have taken major steps to restrict motorist access. Pedestrian zones have proliferated since about 1970, parking space has been drastically reduced, bicycle routes provided, and mass transit upgraded. Zürich eliminated 10,000 central-city parking spaces, and voters in Amsterdam a decade ago approved a plan to eliminate most automobile traffic in the entire old quarter of the city. In Freiburg, Germany, a leader in the pedestrian zone movement, the use of cars for intracity trips dropped from 60% in 1975 to 46% by 1993. In nearby Heidelberg, nearly a quarter of all nonpedestrian traffic now moves by bicycle.

Surrounding the preindustrial core in the European city lies the *inner ring*. It began as a slum outside the city walls—in French the *faubourg* ("false city"). In time, these slum hovels gave way to more substantial buildings as the city grew, and some fine neighborhoods developed. In function, the inner ring remains predominantly residential, as opposed to the retail–institutional focus of the city center. This zone is sometimes called the "preindustrial suburb." The inner ring frequently contains the railroad stations, which ring the periphery of the old medieval core. The tight clustering of venerated old structures made it impossible for railroad lines to penetrate the interior. Such large cities as Paris and London have a circle of rail terminals, and the stations typically bear the name of the major city that lies on their rail route: In Paris, one finds the Gare de Lyon ("station of Lyon") at the terminus of the rail line leading out to that city in the Rhône–Saône Valley, the Gare St. Lazare, the Gare d'Orléans, and so on. In many instances, one suburban railroad station serves as the main one, where trains for all destinations may be taken, but sometimes the traveler must choose correctly among five or more stations to find the right train.

The Industrial Revolution added a *middle ring* to the European city, mainly in the 1800s. A dingy halo of factories, huge workers' apartment blocks or row houses, and railroad yards, the middle ring is often called the "industrial suburbs." It became by far the largest part of the typical European city, dwarfing the older core and inner ring. It housed the burgeoning population that made Europe dominantly urbanized, as commoners finally became urbanites. A controlled-access perimeter highway now often marks the outer limits of the middle ring. Today, many European cities are renewing and rebuilding the middle-ring district, converting it to nonindustrial uses and gentrified housing.

Since about 1950, many European cities, especially in the west, added an *outer ring* or "postindustrial suburb." It consists of a loose assemblage of low-density residences dominated by detached single-family houses, modern factories devoted to high-tech industry, and firms specializing in data gathering and processing. Some planned satellite towns also appear in the outer ring, as do the garden plots and dachas of the inner-city population. In spite of the low density of building, the outer ring often contains American-inspired glass-and-steel high-rise commercial structures (fig. 8.16). Access to the city center by mass transit is normally available. Typically, the outer ring developed in segments and usually remains incomplete. In London, where the outer ring lies beyond a zoned, largely open "greenbelt," a high-class residential fringe began taking shape in the western periphery by the 1950s and has since spread clockwise around to the northeast. In East Anglia, where much of London's outer belt growth is now centered, the urbanized area increased by 15% between 1970 and 1990.

In other words, *suburbanization* is occurring in Europe. Though it began later than in North America, due in part to a lag in accepting the private automobile to commute to work, suburb development is bringing urban problems very similar to those in the United States, especially sprawl on the peripheries of cities and decay in the center. Stockholm provides a good example of these problems.

The suburban *shopping mall*, another symptom of urban Americanization, made its appearance in Europe's outer rings in the 1980s. France now has over 600 such malls, the United Kingdom nearly 800, Italy 226, and Germany 204. Budapest's Duna Plaza, in the northern suburb, opened in 1996, as the shopping mall invaded the formerly communist east. Several countries passed legislation to control the proliferation of malls, but not before the retail patterns of most sizable cities had already been Americanized.

Human Patterns

At best, a study of urban site, morphology, and zones reveal the mere skeleton of the European city. We must now flesh out the urban image by considering vivid human patterns, the mosaic of neighborhoods. The European city is decidedly heterogeneous culturally, racially, and socially. That has been true since the time of ancient Greece, when the first European urbanites segregated themselves along tribal lines.

Religion long acted as one of the most powerful forces segregating people within the towns of Europe. In Roman cities, evidence strongly suggests that Christians occupied certain neighborhoods early in the diffusion of their faith. The term *ghetto*, to designate a Jewish neighborhood, derives from medieval Venèzia, and most European towns of the Middle Ages had separate Jewish districts, reminders of which are still seen in names such as the German *Judengasse* ("Street of the Jews") or Sevilla's *Judaría* ("Jewish Quarter"). Even today, residential segregation along religious lines can be seen in Belfast and Londonderry, Northern Ireland, where one finds Catholic and Protestant neighborhoods (fig. 3.13). The level of denominational segregation rose sharply in the 1970s and more gently in the 1980s and 1990s in Belfast, ghettoizing the city's Catholics, who make up a third of the population. Muslims live in segregated neighborhoods in many cities of mainland Europe. Jews in the United Kingdom have formed suburban concentrations in some cities.

Linguistic differences also traditionally separated people within European cities, a practice most common in areas of speech diversity. Brno, in the Czech province of Morava, had a medieval residential pattern in which Germans lived in the northern part of the city and Czechs in the south. Towns such as Armagh and Downpatrick in Northern Ireland developed distinct quarters in the seventeenth century, as is indicated by the survival of English Street, Irish Street, and Scotch Street. In medieval Caernarvon, Wales, the portion of the town enclosed by walls housed the English, while Welsh clustered in the faubourg just outside the walls.

The huge immigration of foreigners to European cities since about 1950 greatly increased cultural diversity and potential for ethnic and racial neighborhoods. Some 15 million foreigners lived in northwestern Europe by 1980, nearly all concentrated in cities. Frankfurt am Main had a population over 20% foreign by 1990, as did Wien. Most of these immigrants found homes in the decaying residences of the preindustrial core and inner ring, often occupying apartments abandoned by natives who moved to the periphery.

Oddly, few ethnic neighborhoods and ghettoes developed from this influx. True, when viewed on a citywide perspective, European urban centers do reveal an ethnic patterning. In Paris, for example, foreigners cluster in the northeastern quadrant, including parts of both the inner and middle rings (fig. 8.18). However, a closer look at almost any western European city shows that foreign ethnic segregation normally occurs at the level of individual apartment houses, rarely at the scale of city blocks, and never at a district level. In Brussels, for example, no area the size of a census tract has a majority consisting of a single foreign group (fig. 8.19). Tiny, multiple concentrations of individual foreign ethnic groups remain the rule. Ethnic residential segregation is on the decline in most European cities (fig. 5.1).

Clearly, forces other than ethnicity today underlie most human patterning in Europe's cities. Socioeconomic class appears to be far more important in determining where people live. Traditionally, the most expensive and prestigious residences lay nearest the city center, and, as suggested earlier, the early peripheral faubourgs began as slums. In other words, the European city displayed a geographical pattern precisely the reverse of what would seem normal to Americans.

Within the better sections of the preindustrial city, segregation often occurred along occupational lines. Surviving street names again provide clues. In München, for example, we find the Ledererstrasse ("Street of the Leather workers"), Färbergraben ("Street of the Cloth-dyers"), Sattlerstrasse ("Street of the Saddlers"), and others. Such names referred to the artisans' places of work and usually also their residences. In medieval Lü-

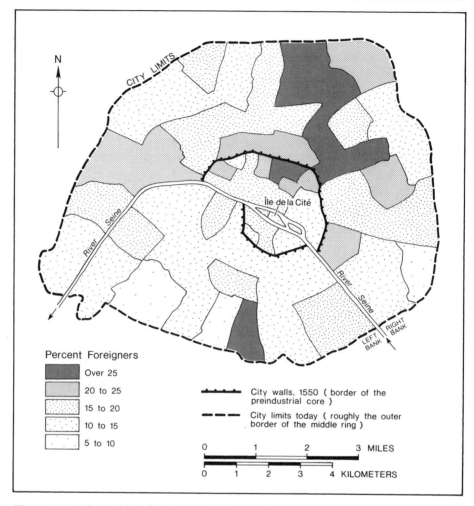

Figure 8.18.   The resident foreign population within the city limits of Paris in the 1980s, by city district and shown as a percentage of total population. At this map scale, European cities such as Paris seem to have ethnic neighborhoods, but the appearance is misleading. The city limits of Paris include only the preindustrial core plus the inner and middle rings. The Île de la Cité is the original nucleus of Paris and the walls of 1500 mark the limits of the preindustrial core. (*Source:* Modified from White 1987, 193.)

beck, merchants lived to the west of a main north–south street, while artisans resided to the east. Ordinary laborers lived outside the town walls.

Residential neighborhoods in European cities today remain rooted in class. The clustering of foreign laborers in certain districts speaks of their socioeconomic status rather than their ethnic background, and that explains their near-chaotic mixing. After World War II, a more Americanlike pattern began to emerge, in which prestigious neighborhoods developed in the outer ring. For example, in present-day Liverpool, England, persons

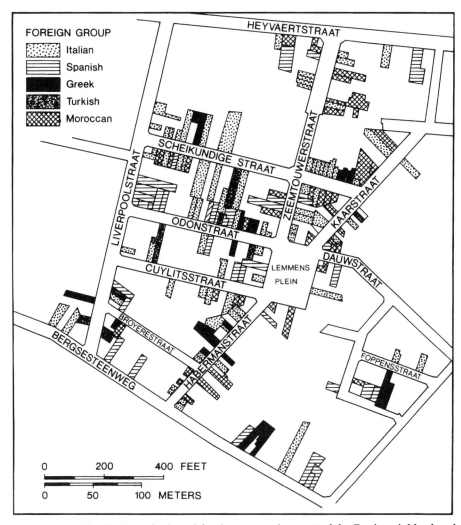

Figure 8.19. Distribution of selected foreign groups in a part of the Rosée neighborhood, Brussels, by apartment house, in the middle 1970s. Unshaded units were either nonresidential or inhabited by other groups, including Belgians. Note that the foreign groups lived mixed on every street, rather than in ethnic neighborhoods. This pattern remains typical of cities in northwestern Europe. (*Source:* Adapted from Kesteloot 1987, 228.)

engaged in artistic endeavors, business owners, and administrators live in residential areas farthest from the city center, while unskilled and semi-skilled laborers reside in and near the preindustrial core.

Still, *gentrification*—the upgrading of older, decaying central-city and inner-ring residential areas for occupancy by upper-income people—is common in Europe. Rather than continuing to explode spatially into surrounding rural areas while the inner city goes to ruin, many of Europe's city dwellers are turning inward and "recycling" older neighborhoods.

Gentrification acts to displace the lower classes. Conflicts inevitably result. Perhaps the group most adversely affected consists of urban squatters—homeless people who illegally take up residence in derelict, empty buildings. Called *kraakers* in the Netherlands and *squats* in Britain, this preponderantly young, antiestablishment group began seizing abandoned central-city buildings in the 1960s. Amsterdam, London, Hamburg, West Berlin, and København became the major scenes of urban squatting. The movement peaked in the 1980s and has since largely succumbed to police pressure and gentrification. Some squatters relocated to formerly communist cities after 1990, especially East Berlin and Praha.

Types of Cities

Preceding sections of this chapter perhaps led you to believe that a European type of city exists, and to a certain degree that is true. Some features occur widely, such as the presence of a preindustrial core and the prestige attached to the old town market square. Still, each European city possesses its own distinct character and personality. Many aspects of European urbanism vary regionally, and we can discern different types of cities. The classification presented here consists of 5 regional types: British, Mediterranean, central European, Nordic, and east European cities (fig. 8.20).

The **British city type,** more than others in Europe, resembles the urban centers of the United States, though major differences also exist. A high rate of owner-occupied housing and detached or semidetached, single-family residences, as well as flight to the suburbs of the outer ring characterize both British and American cities. Inner urban decay and blight, coupled with poverty, diminishing services, and crime, afflict all the major British conurbations. Britons devote less attention to the preservation of inner-city historic structures than do most Europeans. Some experts now speak of urban "decline" and "crisis" in Britain. Journalist and former Londoner Peter Kellner said the "downward spiral of decay" caused him to leave the city, and he and others lament the pollution, filth, eroding tax base, decaying infrastructure, rat infestations, "squats," and widespread vagrancy. As a result, counterurbanization and suburbization have worked more vigorously in Britain than the rest of Europe. This dispersal also feeds upon the British perception that the "real" England lies in the countryside and that the city is an anomaly and aberration. Suburban expansion causes the British city to be less compact than normal for Europe and produces a steep population-density gradient from core to periphery. Americans find all these British conditions familiar, but continental Europeans regard them as odd and generally undesirable. Clearly, the British city represents a distinctive urban type within Europe.

At the same time, the British city has experienced far more inner-area gentrification than its American counterpart, and the government is quite

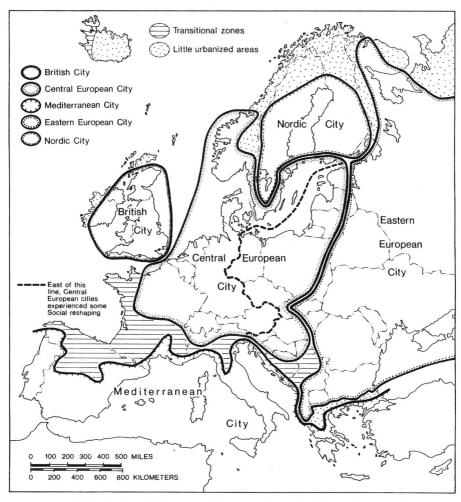

Figure 8.20.   Distribution of European city types. Considerable overlapping of city types occurs but is not shown, as for example where socialist influences partially reshaped many central European cities in the communist era. (*Sources:* Leontidou 1990, 4; Hamilton 1978; Ford 1985; Gritsai 1997a, 1997b; Argenbright 1999; Pacione 1997; Sabelberg 1986.)

active in the effort to stem decay. In Belfast, for example, the proportion of "unfit" housing declined from 25% to 8% between 1978 and 1992, largely as a result of public expenditures on urban regeneration. The walled inner city of Londonderry (or Derry, as Irish separatists prefer), has undergone refurbishing, the once-blighted East End district of Glasgow became transformed in the 1980s, and many similar projects are presently under way. In urban regeneration, the British city occupies an intermediate position between those of the United States and western Europe.

The **central European city type,** sometimes called the *Germanic* type, characterizes the core of the culture area (fig. 8.20). In origin, the central

European city reflects mainly the period of urban genesis led by the Germans during the feudal Middle Ages. The early attainment of city-state status, which allowed a quasi-democratic form of government to take root in the Germanic cities while the countryside remained under feudal despotism, fostered a profound sense of urban superiority and a strong antirural bias. One is either a burgher or a *bauer* ("farmer"). City governments, visually represented by the town hall, or *Rathaus,* retain considerable importance. Some cities even preserve a vestige of their former independent city-state rule, as for example Hamburg and Bremen, which enjoy provincial status within Germany, and Luxembourg, which remains in effect a free city-state. Central European citizens attach great importance to the preindustrial core, the root of urban self-government and democracy, and as a result central-city decay has never approached the British levels (fig. 8.21). The preindustrial core, wreathed by parks and remnant walls, remains a prestigious place to live, and historic preservation and renewal projects, including abundant façadism, typify the central European city. The central public square retains great importance. In World War II, many German preindustrial cores were destroyed by bombing, but these old districts, so prized by the citizenry, were lovingly rebuilt, a process still under way today in cities such as Dresden (fig. 8.22).

Figure 8.21.   The preindustrial core of the small Hessian city of Weilburg, on the Lahn River in Germany. A typical central European city, Weilburg perches on an incised meander of the river and the urban core retains its royal palace, cathedral, and town hall. Many people still reside in the central city, though new suburbs appear in the distance. Little evidence of urban decay can be found in such places. (Photo by T.G.J.-B. 1991.)

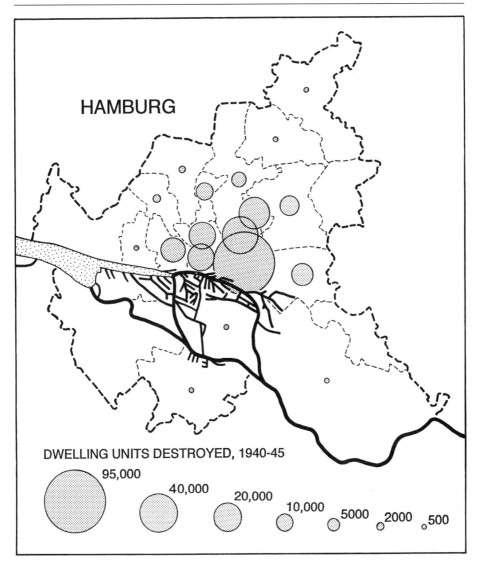

HAMBURG

DWELLING UNITS DESTROYED, 1940-45

95,000

40,000

20,000

10,000

5000   2000   500

Figure 8.22.   **War damage to housing in Hamburg, Germany.** Destruction was most pro-found in the old preindustrial core, but the visitor today will not find much evidence of the damage. Central Europeans prize very highly their medieval urban cores. (*Source:* City of Hamburg 1951, 6.)

Counterurbanism and suburbanization, blunted by the appeal and snobbery of the city and the antirural bias, proved weaker than in Britain. In housing density, the central European city falls between the extremes of the British urban area, dominated by single-family residences, and the cities of southern and eastern Europe, where apartment housing prevails. Urban planning and land use zoning enjoy popular support and have greatly contributed to the renewal, aesthetic appeal, and livability of Germanic cities. The pedestrian zone movement began here and still enjoys its greatest acceptance in central Europe.

In some areas, the problems associated with British cities have taken root in central Europe, but they are aggressively combated. Economically depressed industrial cities in Germany's Ruhr and the coalfields of the Belgian–French border region offer examples of blight and decay, as do many cities in the east that long remained under communist rule.

Some central European cities experienced a half-century or more of communist rule, which imposed rigid socialist control over what had been a capitalistic urban structure. Warszawa, Budapest, Leipzig, Praha, and Riga provide examples. These cities all bore the earlier imprint of central European urban culture, reflecting a long tradition. They were fully developed cities at the time of the communist takeover. Socialist ideals and planning never completely transformed them, though change did come. In Warszawa, for example, an early communist-directed residential mixing of social groups after 1945 steadily gave way during the following 40 years to a reemergence of class-based neighborhoods. Budapest became an odd amalgamation of central European and communist urbanism (fig. 8.23). Most of these cities have rapidly regained their central European character and identity since the fall of communism in the early 1990s.

In the **Mediterranean city type,** a greater spontaneity of growth and

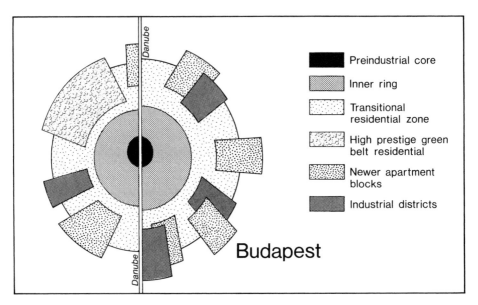

Figure 8.23.   A stylized scheme of modern Budapest. A central European type of city in heritage, Budapest reflects that tradition in its preindustrial core and inner ring. A socialist city from the late 1940s until 1990, Budapest accordingly has peripheral apartment blocks located adjacent to industrial complexes. The high-prestige greenbelt represents an anomaly for a communist city and reflects the significant new inroads made by capitalism in Hungary, beginning even as early as 1970. (*Source:* Enyedi and Szirmai 1992, 99.)

development occurred, with minimal attention to urban planning or zoning (fig. 8.20). The Germanic rural–urban dichotomy is absent in Mediterranean civilization, and the transition from the city to the countryside appears more gradually. Since classical times, many farmers and rural laborers have resided in Mediterranean cities, prompting many such places to be labeled *agrotowns*. Less social segregation occurs, and juxtaposition of good and bad districts is common. A diversity of social classes is found in most parts of the Mediterranean city, in mixed neighborhoods, though squatter slums and low-income apartment high-rises dominate the outer peripheries.

Small workshops of self-employed artisans are scattered through the city, and mixed land use reflects the lack of zoning, or, more exactly, widespread disregard for zoning regulations. Owners more typically live above their place of business than in the British or central European cities, and most other people live close to their place of work. Inhabitants tend to view the city rather than the home as the principal venue for life, and as a result more people are to be seen in the streets, plazas, and shops. A central business district in the British–Germanic sense does not exist, and small shops appear even in the finer residential neighborhoods. To the Germanic eye, the Mediterranean city seems disorderly, but the people of the south see their cities instead as places of "light, heat, and spontaneity," a welcome contrast to the "cold, disciplined" cities beyond the Alps.

Mediterranean cities represent the most compact type in Europe, with very high residential densities and virtually no development of an outer ring. High-status residential areas lie instead in the inner ring, adjacent to the preindustrial core and linked to it by a fine boulevard (fig. 8.24). While the old walled part of the town retains great prestige and swarms with life, it is often largely given over to institutional functions, especially schools, museums, churches, and convents. A failure to restrict automobile access to the center creates a nightmare of traffic congestion, noise, and air pollution in the preindustrial core, and the pedestrian zone concept remains in its infancy here. The periphery of the Mediterranean city is the most stigmatized section, in contrast to the British model. Industries are concentrated there, as are poor people living in spartan high-rise apartment blocks or illegal squatter slums of self-built huts reminiscent of Third World countries.

Geographers have distinguished different subtypes of Mediterranean cities, and some feel the larger category is too inclusive to be very useful. One expert argues for the existence of the "south Italian city," while another presents a case for the "Spanish city." All such proposals have merit and remind us again of the great internal diversity of the European culture area (fig. 8.24).

Change comes, if often slowly, to the Mediterranean cities, eroding their distinctiveness. In Lisboa, for example, the old hilltop Moorish-built core, Alfama, still houses rich and poor alike, but a walk by the coauthors through that neighborhood at the dawn of the new millennium revealed a

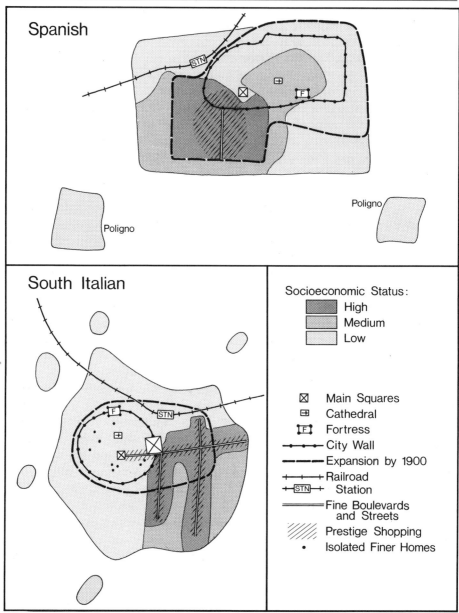

Figure 8.24.   Models of the typical Spanish and southern Italian city both are examples of the Mediterranean city type, but they are sufficiently distinctive to be considered regional subtypes. The outlying clusters, called *polignos* in Spain, are recent laborer apartment blocks or squatter settlements. In the southern Italian type, the core has a maze of dead-end streets and remains largely residential, while in the Spanish type, most of the core is now institutional and has connecting streets. (*Sources:* Ford 1985, 268; Sabelberg 1986; Fusch 1994; Pacione 1987.)

vigorous, pervasive gentrification under way that was rapidly displacing African immigrants and others in the poverty class. Very soon Alfama will belong to the affluent. Increasingly, across all of the Mediterranean region, poor people are being pushed out to the peripheral slums.

The **east European city type** bears the residual imprint of socialism and communism (fig. 8.20). In fact, this urban type was formerly called the *socialist* city and later *postsocialist*. Eastern Europe was very weakly urbanized prior to the communist era. In the Soviet Union in 1926, for example, only 18% of the population lived in cities, but by 1989 the proportion there reached 66%. In such countries, socialist doctrine shaped urban development in diverse ways, and the legacy will persist long into the future. Under communism, the government controlled urban development, including the demand for and supply of housing. Land, in effect, had no monetary value.

The ideal socialist city would have abolished socioeconomic residential segregation; guaranteed availability of public services such as child care; provided abundant public-green space; offered equal, if rudimentary, access to all consumer goods; and created self-sufficient, small neighborhoods where residents lived, worked, and shopped. In many respects, east European cities still reflect these socialist goals, particularly in Russia, Ukraine, Belarus, and the Balkans. The east European city resembles a collection of separate towns tied together. Population densities remain remarkably high in comparison to cities in most of the remainder of Europe, and the normal gradient toward lesser densities on the urban periphery is retarded and in some cities even reversed, with an outer rim of higher concentration of people (fig. 8.25). All of Moskva has a population density comparable to that of *central* London. A far less marked spatial difference of function occurs within the city than in the west, including a much more even spread of industries throughout the urban area, a phenomenon associated with the former absence of cash values for land. Social, economic, and ethnic segregation by districts or sectors is diminished. Workers in a particular industry might be segregated in response to a desire to minimize the journey to work. Public mass transportation prevails and the automobile remains a less important means of moving about the city than in western countries. Even those workers who inhabit the characteristic belt of prefabricated high-rise apartments, grouped in neighborhoods of 2,000 to 5,000 people, enjoy easy access to the city center. In comparison to the west, a higher proportion of the urban workforce finds employment in manufacturing, construction, and transportation, with lower percentages in trade, administration, and services.

Sinister forces also helped shape the east European city and will long leave a visible legacy in these postsocialist times. Authorities sought to convey the power of the state and the insignificance of the individual person. Governmental buildings of overwhelming size, reflecting monumentality in architecture, provide one example. Oversized public squares, in which

Figure 8.25.   The northern periphery of Moskva. Huge complexes of high-rise apartments produce dense concentrations of population even on the outer margins of the city, a typical phenomenon in the east European city type. Even so, much green space is preserved, catering to the Russian love of the forest. (Photo by T.G.J.-B. 1997.)

mass political rallies could be held, appear gargantuan, cold, and empty at other times. Worst of all, the cult of personality associated with some communist dictatorships, most notoriously in Romania and Albania, allowed megalomaniacal leaders to massively reshape cities, often destroying much of the beauty from earlier eras. The precommunist city disappeared from central Bucuresti, and the imprint of a personality cult will long linger there.

At the same time, infrastructure decays alarmingly in many east European cities. Shoddily constructed and inadequately maintained buildings abound. The east European cities inherited these deficiencies from the socialist era, and the cost of correcting them lies beyond their means in most cases.

Still, pervasive change has come to the east European city since the fall of communism. Moskva, the Russian capital, provides an example, if somewhat atypical. A July 1991 decree provided for privatization of apartments in Russian cities. In Moskva, some 25% of all housing had been privatized by 1993, as had nearly 5,000 businesses, mainly those engaged in consumer services. The socialist city had few shops, but in Moskva today retail outlets abound, from upscale boutiques to makeshift sidewalk markets. One finds more automobiles—Moskva now has legendary traffic jams;

more light, including neon signs; more litter; more color; outdoor advertising; and more crime. By contrast, many communist monuments have toppled and the socialist slogans that formerly festooned public places have all vanished. Numerous factories closed and the proportion of the urban workforce employed in manufacturing plummeted. Service-sector jobs multiplied rapidly, involving everything from clerks and fast-food workers to realtors, banks, lawyers, and stockbrokers (fig. 8.26). The proportion of Moskva's labor force engaged in service activities passed 50% as early as 1993 and is today substantially higher.

A minor type, the **Nordic city**, occurs in Scandinavia and Finland. More recent in origin and usually founded under Swedish rule, these cities generally date from the 1600s and 1700s, the era of the Swedish empire. A grid pattern of streets invariably characterizes the core of the Nordic city, though often that pattern breaks down in the suburbs (fig. 8.27). A waterside site was unfailingly chosen for the Nordic city, whether marine, riverine, or lakeside. Of the various European urban types, the Nordic city is the least compact, with broad avenues, abundant freestanding single-family residences, and spacious open areas. In fact, some Nordic cities consist of several different clusters separated by green space or even farmland, heightening the dispersed urban character (fig. 8.28). Trees grow more abundantly along the urban streets, revealing the strong northern love of forests. The Nordic city is modest in size, usually having less than 100,000 inhabitants, and the local industries typically consist of small firms manufacturing high-quality, even luxury products. In spite of their size, Nordic cities offer an impressive array of amenities, from museums, sport complexes, and hospitals to symphony orchestras and bicycle paths. Surely, these rank among the most appealing and livable cities in the world.

The Urban Network

Site, morphology, and internal cultural and economic patterning, while essential geographical attributes of cities, do not complete the spatial analysis of urbanism. The distribution of cities must also be considered, especially their location relative to each other in an **urban network.**

In spite of the fact that Europe forms the most highly urbanized culture area in the world, *megalopolis* development remains uncommon there. A megalopolis forms when adjacent cities grow until they coalesce, forming a polynucleated urban complex. The region between Boston and Washington, D.C., in the United States is a megalopolis. In Europe, because of better land use planning and greenbelt preservation, megalopolis formation remained less common. Among the few examples are *Randstad Holland* (fig. 8.29), with a collective population of close to 7 million; the *Rhein–Ruhr* in western Germany, containing about 12 million inhabitants; the *Flemish Diamond* of northern Belgium; *Lancs–Yorks* in the old, declining industrial heart

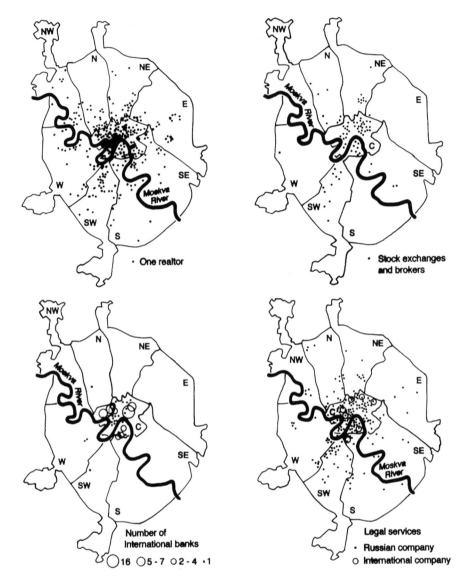

Figure 8.26.   Moskva: selected service enterprises, 1995. A scant half-decade into its transformation from a socialist to an east European city, Moskva already had sizable numbers of realtors, brokers, stock exchanges, banks, and lawyers. Increasingly, its labor force is employed in these and other service-sector jobs. (*Source:* Gritsai 1997a, 368, 369.)

of England; and *Donbas* in eastern Ukraine (fig. 8.30). These megalopolises retain more open space than would be expected, due to rigorous zoning policies. The Randstad Holland, for example, remains doughnut shaped, due to a largely successful plan to keep the center, called the "Green Heart," open (fig. 8.29).

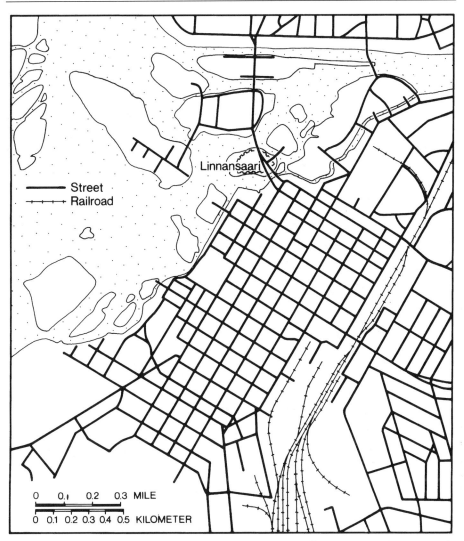

Figure 8.27.   Oulu, a Nordic city of Finland. Clearly preserved in its central section is the gridiron plan and public squares laid out by its Swedish founders. The city dates from 1605 and was originally protected by the island fortress on Linnansaari.

Some urban geographers suggest that the first 3 megalopolises—Randstad, Rhein–Ruhr, and Flemish Diamond—have now coalesced into a single supercity. Others would combine even more urban areas, forming the "urban banana," stretching from Lancs–Yorks to Roma (fig. 8.30). The "banana" stretches the concept of megalopolis, as it is far from contiguous and is interrupted by the Alps.

Other urban geographers reject the concepts of megalopolis and big banana, arguing that *service* functions, which have surpassed manufacturing as the main urban activity in Europe (see chapters 9 and 10), work to

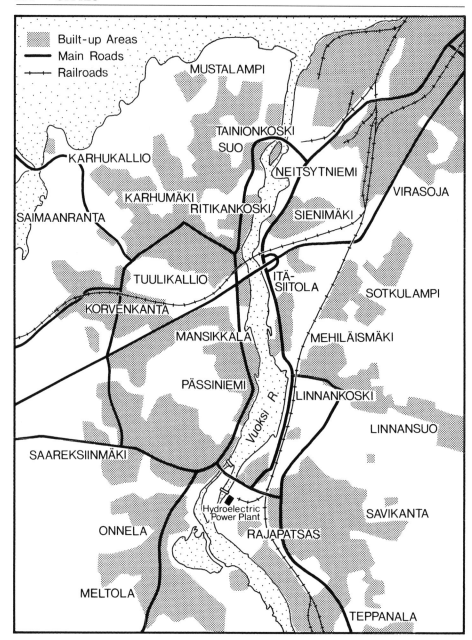

Figure 8.28.   Imatra, a Finnish city consisting of scattered clusters. The clusters are loosely focused on the hydroelectric plant at the famous Imatra rapids, where the waters of the Finnish Lake Plateau escape through the Salpausselkä moraine wall. Imatra is a small city of about 35,000 people.

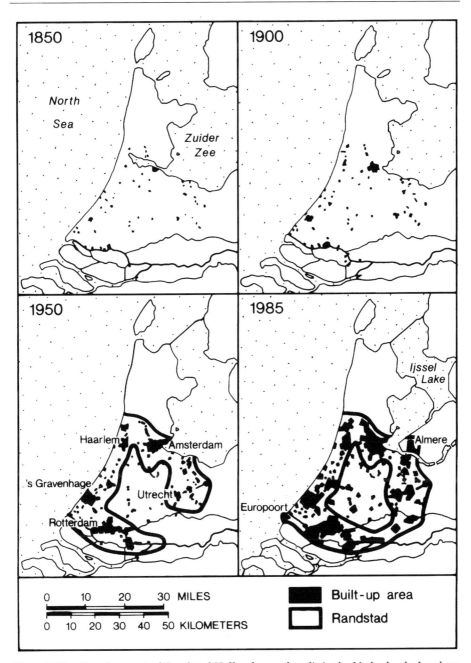

Figure 8.29.   Development of Randstad Holland, megalopolis in the Netherlands. Land use planning and zoning are being employed to keep the central area, or "doughnut hole," open, but suburban development is encroaching. Note the use of some reclaimed Zuider Zee polderland for expansion of the Randstad. (*Sources: Randstad Holland* 1980, 14; van Wessep, Dieleman, and Jobse 1993.)

LANCS-
YORKS

RANDSTAD

RHEIN-
RUHR

FLEMISH
TRIANGLE

The
Urban
"Banana"

DONBAS

0   100 200 300 400 500   MILES

0   200   400   600   800   KILOMETERS

Figure 8.30.   European megalopolises and the "Urban Banana" dominate Europe's core. (*Sources:* After van Wessep, Dieleman, and Jobse 1993; Dieleman and Faludi 1998.)

produce an orderly network of regularly spaced urban places. These services include a variety of governmental, educational, medical, retail, and related activities.

The German geographer Walter Christaller proposed **central place theory** to explain the spatial networks of cities generated by service functions. He defined a "central place" as any settlement that served as the center of its rural hinterland and the economic mediator between its surroundings and the outside world. Crucial to the theory is the fact that different goods and services vary (1) in range, the maximum distance or radius from the supply center at which the goods and services can reach the consumers, and (2) in the size of population required to make provision of services economically feasible. For example, it requires a larger number of people

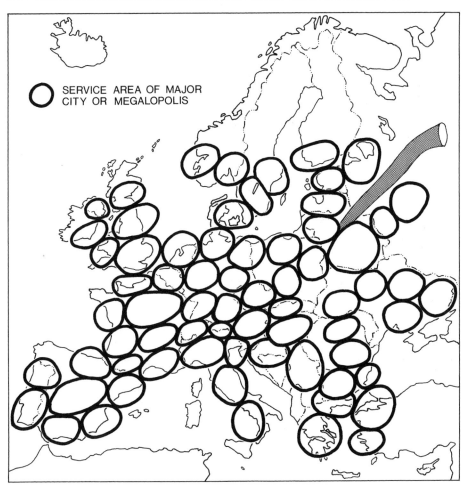

Figure 8.31.   The European urban "grape bunch." A network of major cities, with tributary service areas, resembles quite another fruit from the one depicted in figure 8.30! (*Sources: After Kunzmann and Wegener 1991; Christaller 1966.*)

to support a hospital, university, or department store than to support a gasoline station, post office, or grocery store. Similarly, consumers will travel a greater distance to consult a heart specialist, record a land title, or purchase an automobile than they will to buy a loaf of bread, mail a letter, or fill their automobile with gasoline. People spend as little time and effort as possible in making use of the services of central places, but they must travel farther to use services that require a large market.

The range variance of different central goods and services produces a hierarchy of central places in terms of the size of population and the number of goods and services available. At the top of the hierarchy stand regional metropolises, which offer all services associated with central places and have very large tributary hinterlands. These are often national capitals, or at least the political centers of sizable regions. Europe's urban system, then, will consist of a series of major cities, each with a tributary region.

When mapped, these cities and their service regions more closely resemble a messy bunch of grapes rather than a banana (fig. 8.31). So, pick which fruit appeals to you most, banana or grapes! Either model reveals a pronounced core–periphery pattern within Europe, with the center heavily urbanized and the margins rural (figs. 8.30 and 8.31).

While service functions today dominate Europe's urban structure, the great era of city growth coincided with the rise of mining and manufacturing industries. The following chapter deals with these industrial activities.

Sources and Suggested Readings

Agnew, John, and Calogero Muscarà. 1993. *Rome*. London, GB: Belhaven.

Argenbright, Robert. 1999. "Remaking Moscow: New Places, New Selves." *Geographical Review* 89:1–22.

Basovsky, O., and B. Divinsky. 1991. "The Development of Modern Urbanization in Slovakia and Its Present Problems." *Revue Belge de Géographie* 115:265–277.

Beaujeu-Garnier, Jacqueline. 1986. "Urbanization in France since World War II." In *World Patterns of Modern Urban Change*, ed. Michael P. Conzen. Chicago, USA: University of Chicago, Department of Geography, Research Paper No. 217–218.

Benevolo, Leonardo. 1993. *The European City*. Trans. Carl Ipsen. Oxford, GB: Blackwell.

Beynon, Erdmann D. 1943. "Budapest: An Ecological Study." *Geographical Review* 33:256–275.

Book, Tommy. 1995. "The Urban Field of Berlin." *Geografiska Annaler* 77B:177–196.

Bowes, Alison, Jacqui McCluskey, and Duncan Sim. 1990. "The Changing Nature of Glasgow's Ethnic-minority Community." *Scottish Geographical Magazine* 106:99–107.

Burdack, Joachim. 1993. "Jüngere Tendenzen der Bevölkerungsentwicklung im Städtesystem Frankreichs." *Erdkunde* 47:52–60.

Burtenshaw, David, M. Bateman, and G. J. Ashworth. 1981. *The City in West Europe*. New York, USA: Wiley.

Byfuglien, Jan. 1995. "Urbanisation and Centralisation in Norway." *Norsk Geografisk Tidsskrift* 49:35–44.

Carter, Francis W. 1972. *Dubrovnik (Ragusa): A Classic City-state*. London, GB: Seminar Press.

Cherry, Gordon E. 1994. *Birmingham: A Study in Geography, History and Planning*. Chichester, GB: Wiley.

Christaller, Walter. 1966. *The Central Places of Southern Germany*. Trans. Carlisle W. Baskin. Englewood Cliffs, N.J., USA: Prentice Hall.

City of Hamburg. 1951. "Hamburg in Zahlen." *Statistisches Landesamt* 29: 6.

Clark, David. 1989. *Urban Decline: The British Experience*. London, GB: Routledge.

Claval, Paul. 1984. "Reflections on the Cultural Geography of the European City." In *The City in Cultural Context*, ed. John A. Agnew, John Mercer, and David E. Sopher. Boston, USA: Allen and Unwin, 31–49.

Clout, Hugh D., ed. 1994. *Europe's Cities in the Late Twentieth Century.* Utrecht, NL: Royal Dutch Geographical Society.

Cooke, Phil. 1989. *Localities: The Changing Face of Urban Britain.* Winchester, GB: Unwin Hyman.

Cornish, Vaughan. 1923. *The Great Capitals: A Historical Geography.* London, GB: Methuen.

Cross, D.F.W. 1990. *Counterurbanisation in England and Wales.* Aldershot, GB: Avebury, Gower.

Danta, Darrick R. 1993. "Ceausescu's Bucharest." *Geographical Review* 83:170–183.

Dematteis, G. 1986. "Counter-urbanization in Italy." In *Progress in Settlement Geography,* ed. L. S. Bourne et al. Milano, I: Franco Angeli, 161–193.

Dennis, Richard. 1986. *English Industrial Cities of the Nineteenth Century: A Social Geography.* Cambridge, GB: Cambridge University Press.

Dickinson, Robert E. 1945. "The Morphology of the Medieval German Town." *Geographical Review* 35:74–97.

Dieleman, Frans M., and Andreas Faludi. 1998. "Randstad, Rhine–Ruhr and Flemish Diamond as one Polynucleated Macro-Region?" *Tijdschrift voor Economische en Sociale Geografie* 89:320–327.

Doherty, Paul, and Michael A. Poole. 1997. "Ethnic Residential Segregation in Belfast, Northern Ireland, 1971–1991." *Geographical Review* 87:520–536.

Dunford, Mick, and Grigoris Kafkalas, eds. 1992. *Cities and Regions in the New Europe: The Global–local Interplay and Spatial Development Strategies.* New York, USA: Wiley.

Enyedi, György, and Viktória Szirmai. 1992. *Budapest: A Central European Capital.* London, GB: Belhaven.

European Urban and Regional Studies. 1994–present. A major scholarly journal devoted largely to European cities.

Fielding, A. J. 1982. "Counterurbanisation in Western Europe." *Progress in Planning* 17 (1): 1–52.

Ford, Larry R. 1978. "Continuity and Change in Historic Cities: Bath, Chester, and Norwich." *Geographical Review* 68:253–273.

———. 1985. "Urban Morphology and Preservation in Spain." *Geographical Review* 75:265–299.

Fusch, Richard. 1994. "The Piazza in Italian Urban Morphology." *Geographical Review* 84:424–438.

Gallois, Lucien. 1923. "The Origin and Growth of Paris." *Geographical Review* 13:345–367.

Gaspar, Jorge, and Allan M. Williams. 1994. *Lisbon.* London, GB: Belhaven.

Glebe, Günther, and John O'Loughlin, eds. 1987. *Foreign Minorities in Continental European Cities.* Stuttgart, D: Franz Steiner.

Gritsai, Olga. 1997a. "Business Services and Restructuring of Urban Space in Moscow." *GeoJournal* 42:365–376.

———. 1997b. "The Economic Restructuring of Moscow in the International Context." *GeoJournal* 42:341–347.

Gutkind, Erwin A. 1964–1969. *International History of City Development,* New York, USA: Free Press.

Hall, Peter. 1993. "Forces Shaping Urban Europe." *Urban Studies* 30:883–898.

Hamilton, F. E. Ian. 1978. "The East European and Soviet City." *Geographical Magazine* 50:511–515.

Hoggart, Keith, and David R. Green, eds. 1991. *London: A New Metropolitan Geography.* London, GB: Edward Arnold.

Holzner, Lutz. 1986. *Research Profile* (Milwaukee, USA: University of Wisconsin, Milwaukee Graduate School), 9 (2): 18.

———. 1970. "The Role of History and Tradition in the Urban Geography of West Germany." *Annals of the Association of American Geographers* 60:315–339.

Hoyle, B. S., and David A. Pinder, eds. 1992. *European Port Cities in Transition.* London, GB: Belhaven.

Illeris, Sven. 1990. "Counter-urbanization Revisited: The New Map of Population Distribution in Central and North-western Europe." *Norsk Geografisk Tidsskrift* 44:39–52.

Ioffe, Grigory, and Tatyana Nefedova. 2000. *The Environs of Russian Cities.* Lampeter, Wales, GB: Edwin Mellen.

Jobse, Rein B. 1987. "The Restructuring of Dutch Cities." *Tijdschrift voor Economische en Sociale Geografie* 78:305–311.

Jones, Emrys. 1960. *A Social Geography of Belfast.* London, GB: Oxford University Press.

Kearns, Gerry, and Charles W. J. Withers, eds. 1991. *Urbanising Britain.* Cambridge, GB: Cambridge University Press.

Kesteloot, Christian. 1987. In *Foreign Minorities in Continental European Cities,* ed. Günther Glebe and John O'Loughlin. Stuttgart, D: Franz Steiner.

Kontuly, Thomas, and Roland Vogelsang. 1988. "Explanations for the Intensification of Counterurbanization in the Federal Republic of Germany." *Professional Geographer* 40:42–54.

Kunzmann, K. R., and R.-M. Wegener. 1991. "The Pattern of Urbanization in Western Europe." *Ekistics* 350/351:282–291.

de Lannoy, W. 1975. "Residential Segregation of Foreigners in Brussels." *Bulletin, Société Belge d'Études Géographiques* 44:215–238.

Lentz, Sebastian. 1997. "Cityentwicklung in Moskau: Zwischen Transformation und Globalisierung." *Zeitschrift für Wirtschaftsgeographie* 41:110–122.

Leontidou, Lila. 1990. *The Mediterranean City in Transition: Social Change and Urban Development.* Cambridge, GB: Cambridge University Press.

Lichtenberger, Elisabeth. 1993. *Vienna: Bridge between Cultures.* Trans. Dietlinde Mühlgassner and Craig Reisser. London, GB: Belhaven.

MacLaran, Andrew. 1993. *Dublin: The Shaping of a Capital.* London, GB: Belhaven.

Maloutas, Thomas. 1993. "Social Segregation in Athens." *Antipode* 25:223–239.

Medvedkov, Olga. 1990. *Soviet Urbanisation.* London, GB: Routledge.

Mik, Ger. 1983. "Residential Segregation in Rotterdam: Background and Policy." *Tijdschrift voor Economische en Sociale Geografie* 74:74–86.

Murphey, Rhoads. 1954. "The City as a Center of Change: Western Europe and China." *Annals of the Association of American Geographers* 44:349–362.

Murphy, Alexander B., ed. 1993. *Brussels.* London, GB: Belhaven.

Noble, Allen G., and Frank J. Costa. 1990. "The Growth of Metro Systems in Madrid, Rome, and Athens." *Cities* 7:224–229.

Noin, Daniel, and Paul White. 1993. *Paris.* London, GB: Belhaven.

Ogden, Philip E. 1985. "Counterurbanisation in France." *Geography* 70:24–35.

Özüekren, A. Sule, and Ronald van Kempen, eds. 1997. *Turks in European Cities: Housing and Urban Segregation.* Utrecht, NL: European Research Centre on Migration and Ethnic Relations.

Pacione, Michael. 1987. "The Socio-spatial Development of the South Italian City: The Case of Naples." *Transactions of the Institute of British Geographers* 12:433–450.

———. 1995. *Glasgow: The Socio-spatial Development of the City.* New York, USA: Wiley.

———. 1996. "Ethnic Segregation in the European City: The Case of Vienna." *Geography* 81:120–132.

———, ed. 1997. *Britain's Cities: Geographies of Division in Urban Britain*. London, GB: Routledge.

———. 1998. "The Social Geography of Rome." *Tijdschrift voor Economische en Sociale Geografie* 89:359–370.

Pounds, Norman J. G. 1969. "The Urbanization of the Classical World." *Annals of the Association of American Geographers* 59:135–157.

———. 1989. *Hearth and Home*. Bloomington, USA: Indiana University Press.

Price, Edward T. 1964. "Viterbo: Landscape of an Italian City." *Annals of the Association of American Geographers* 54:242–275.

Randstad Holland. 1980. Utrecht, NL: Centre for the Geography of the Netherlands.

Regulska, Joanna, and Adam Kowalewski. 1993. *Warsaw*. London, GB: Belhaven.

Roseman, Curtis C., et al., eds. 1996. *EthniCity: Geographic Perspectives on Ethnic Change in Modern Cities*. Lanham, Md., USA: University Press of America.

Rowland, Richard H. 1995. "Declining Towns in Russia, 1989–1993." *Post-Soviet Geography* 36:436–445.

———. 1998. "Metropolitan Population Change in Russia and the Former Soviet Union, 1897–1997." *Post-Soviet Geography and Economics* 39:271–296.

Sabelberg, Elmar. 1986. "The South-Italian City—a Cultural-genetic Type of City." *GeoJournal* 13:59–66.

Thomas, David. 1963. "London's Green Belt: The Evolution of an Idea." *Geographical Journal* 129:14–24.

Vance, James E., Jr. 1990. *The Continuing City: Urban Morphology in Western Civilization*. Baltimore, Md., USA: Johns Hopkins University Press.

van Wessep, Jan, Frans M. Dieleman, and Rein B. Jobse. 1993. *Randstad Holland*. London, GB: Belhaven.

White, Paul. 1987. In *Foreign Minorities in Continental European Cities*, ed. Günther Glebe and John O'Loughlin. Stuttgart, D: Franz Steiner.

White, Paul D., and Daniel Gutting. 1998. "Berlin: Social Convergences and Contrasts in the Reunited City." *Geography* 83:214–226.

William-Olsson, W. 1940. "Stockholm: Its Structure and Development." *Geographical Review* 30:420–438.

Williams, Allan M. 1981. "Bairros Clandestinos: Illegal Housing in Portugal." *Geografisch Tijdschrift* 15:24–34.

CHAPTER 9

Primary and Secondary Industries

Europeans are an urban people because, preponderantly, they find employment in industrial pursuits. Geographers distinguish 3 types of industrial livelihood: primary, secondary, and service. The present chapter deals with the first 2 types. Primary industries are those involved in extracting resources from the earth and seas. Mining, fishing, and lumbering (see chapter 2) provide the principal examples of primary industry. Agriculture is also a primary activity (see chapter 11). Secondary industry is the processing stage, commonly called *manufacturing*, in which the materials collected by primary industries are converted into finished products. Ore is converted to steel, fibers made into cloth, steel and textiles become clothing, automobiles, machines, and the like. The number and proportion of the European workforce employed in primary and secondary industries have declined markedly since about 1960 but still remain large (fig. 9.1).

Historical Geography

European culture has been closely intertwined with primary and secondary industries since the time of the Bronze and Iron Ages, the origins of which lie in prehistory in the same Near Eastern culture hearth that gave Europe agriculture, Christianity, Indo-European speech, the city, and the political state. Over the centuries, many geographical changes occurred in primary and secondary industries within Europe, and centers of political power and cultural flowering shifted spatially with the rise and fall of industrial activity. Ultimately, Europe placed its highly distinctive mark upon industry in a great wave of innovations that form the basis of modern European civilization.

Initially, primary and secondary industries were centered in Mediterra-

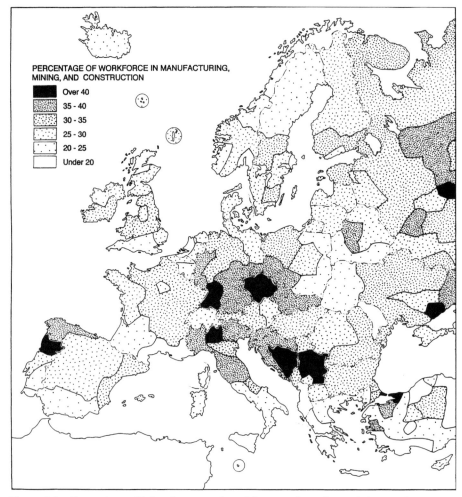

Figure 9.1.   Percentage of labor force employed in manufacturing, mining, and construction—the principal primary and secondary industries. Manufacturing tends to be most important in the core of Europe and in the east.

nean Europe, particularly in Greece. By the golden age of Greece, the cities of Athínai and Kórinthos led in manufacturing, boasting cloth makers, dyers, leather workers, potters, weapon makers, jewelers, metalworkers, stonemasons, and shipwrights to keep the great Greek merchant fleets and navies afloat. The Hellenic leadership in artisanry passed temporarily to the Romans, only to return to the Byzantine Greeks. Constantinople (modern Istanbul) was in time rivaled by Moorish Spain, where Toledo developed a reputation for high-quality steel and Córdoba produced fine leather goods.

Then came the rise of northern Italy to industrial leadership. Above all, the Italian blossoming resulted from the dominant position achieved by its merchants, who ranged from China to England. Cities such as Genova,

Milano, Firenze, and Venèzia acquired widespread fame for their silks and other textiles, cloth dying, brassware, weaponry, glass, and shipbuilding. At its peak, Venèzia housed 16,000 shipwrights, who turned out an average of 1 galleon per day, using prefabricated parts in an early-day assembly line production. By 1300, artisans of the city of Firenze fabricated 100,000 pieces of cloth per year, and Milano became the chief European center of weaponry manufacture. A system of free, prosperous craftsmen facilitated the northern Italian achievement, a major departure from the classical tradition of slave artisans.

The industrial–commercial leadership next shifted north to Belgium, Switzerland, and southern Germany in particular, where Italian skills were in some instances transplanted. Other Italians founded the silk industry of Lyon, in France. The most important industrial district of the north lay in Vlaanderen, where the first major developments occurred in the 1100s. Vlaanderen, like northern Italy, acquired its industrial importance partly as a result of a favorable trade location. A fortunate concentration of river, road, and marine trade routes allowed the Flemings to achieve the same dominance in northern Europe that the Italian towns had in the Mediterranean. Cloth making was centered at Ypres, Gent, Brugge, and Douai, which drew on the wool of England and Spain as primary raw material. In the 1400s, linen joined wool as a major product of the Flemish towns and attained an importance that persisted into the nineteenth century.

Carried by emigrant artisans, the influence of Vlaanderen was instrumental in the industrial development of the Netherlands beginning in the 1400s. Flemish tradesmen skilled in woolen textile manufacture also migrated to England, particularly Yorkshire, as early as the 1300s. The Netherlands rose to industrial dominance in the seventeenth century, and northern Germany also experienced growth.

The gradual northward shift of industrial activity and corresponding decline in southern Europe meant that manufacturing became increasingly identified with Germanic, Protestant areas and less with Roman Catholic, Romance-language countries. Some writers have suggested that certain social characteristics of Protestantism, including approval of change and veneration of work, proved more conducive to industrial development. Persecution and expulsion of Huguenot merchants and artisans by the Catholic-backed French government and similar pressure on Protestant Flemings by the Spanish rulers contributed materially to the industrial rise of the Netherlands, northern Germany, and England. The most important European manufacturing lay in Protestant lands by the 1700s.

Traditional Manufacturing Systems

Traditional European manufacturing was carried on in 2 different systems: *gild* and *cottage* industry, the former based in towns and cities, the latter largely rural. The gild was a professional organization of free artisans skilled in a particular craft. The skills passed from generation to generation through an apprenticeship system. A boy served as apprentice, for example, to a cooper, potter, mason, ironworker, glassblower, silversmith, sculptor, or master weaver and worked for years as a helper. At the end of apprenticeship, the young man demonstrated his skill before an examining board composed of members of the particular gild. Approval allowed the apprentice to be a member of the gild and begin practicing the trade on his own. In larger cities, each major gild had a house on the main municipal square, and some of these survive today in well-preserved towns such as Gent, Brugge, and Antwerpen in Belgium.

Many relics of the gild system remain today, and craft shops are still surprisingly numerous, even in the more advanced countries such as Germany. In that nation scores of registered crafts still exist, represented by thousands of local gilds, including tailors, bakers, knifesmiths, sausage makers, and others. The same high standards for membership typical of medieval times survive to the present day.

A much more common traditional system of manufacturing, cottage industry, remained confined to European farm villages, generally practiced as a sideline to agriculture. A village might have a cobbler, weaver, miller, and blacksmith, who spent part of the time farming and the remainder, during slack periods in the fields, working at the household trade. The abundance of people today with surnames such as Smith, Miller, Potter, Weaver, Weber, and the like suggest the former abundance of village crafts. Little formality surrounded the passing on of skills, and sons most commonly learned from fathers and daughters from mothers simply by observing the work being done. Cottage trades survive today in some parts of Europe, particularly if they attract buyers from beyond the village community. On islands off the west coast of Scotland, for example, women still weave the famous Harris Tweed on looms in their individual cottages.

The Industrial Revolution

In Britain during the 1600s, some skilled craftsmen began moving to rural areas to escape the confining, formal character of the urban gilds, which acted to keep membership and production low, while the quality of goods and prices remained high. By fleeing to villages and small towns, they acquired the freedom to increase output and cheapen products, thereby enlarging the market. Simultaneously, some workers engaged in cottage industry began increasing their output and selling wares in a larger territory, abandoning farming altogether. Among such protoindustrial villagers—fugitive gildsmen and, particularly, cottagers—in a small corner of England, a series of revolutionary manufacturing innovations occurred in the 1700s, forever changing England, Europe, and the entire world.

Both primary and secondary industry, both gild and cottage manufacturing systems, were fundamentally altered by this **Industrial Revolution.** Collectively, the associated inventions represent the most rapid and pervasive technological change in the history of the human race. Two fundamental modifications accompanied the revolution. First, machines replaced human hands in extracting primary resources and in fashioning products. The word *manufacturing* ("made by hand") became technically obsolete. No longer would the weaver sit at the hand loom and painstakingly produce each piece of cloth; instead, huge mechanical looms were invented to do the job faster and more economically. In many industries, the machine made possible the use of interchangeable parts and the assembly line. A second change involved the rise of inanimate power, as humans harnessed water, steam, and eventually electricity, petroleum, and the atom. The new technology did not appear overnight but in bits and pieces over many decades and centuries. Nearly all of the interconnected developments of the formative stage of the Industrial Revolution, from about 1730 to 1850, occurred in back-country Great Britain. That is, the Industrial Revolution arose in a peripheral part of Europe, in a small and previously insignificant kingdom. Innovations often occur in such peripheries, where orthodox thinking and behavior are weaker. Europe offers numerous examples (fig. 1.9).

The *textile* industry first felt the effect of the Industrial Revolution. Beginning in the 1730s, major advances led to mechanical spinning and weaving devices driven by waterpower and operated by semiskilled labor. These technological breakthroughs occurred in village and small town areas, where cottagers and the antigild mood had long favored quantity of goods over quality and low price over high. The lower price of goods expanded the market available for manufactured cloth. The textile revolution did not occur in London, Bristol, or Edinburgh—the great gild cities of Britain—but instead in the small towns and villages of dominantly rural areas in England such as *Lancashire, Yorkshire,* and the *Midlands* (fig. 9.2). New mechanized factories soon appeared wherever waterfalls and rapids could power the machine looms, particularly on the eastern and western sides of the Pennines, where some traditional textile making had long been centered. In Yorkshire, on the eastern flank, a woolen textile center since late medieval times, the same streams that had long provided the soft water for cleaning wool now turned the waterwheels that drove the new machine looms. Lancashire, on the western Pennine flank, applied the power loom to cotton textile manufacture. To a lesser extent, the Midlands and, somewhat later, the *Scottish Lowlands* shared the water-powered textile boom. By 1830, Britain produced 70% of the world's cotton textiles.

Waterpower dominated the early textile phase of the Industrial Revolution, but not for long. James Watt and others perfected the steam engine in the 1760s, and the first steam-powered cotton textile mill went into operation shortly thereafter. General acceptance followed in the 1790s. The steam

Figure 9.2.   The concentrations of primary industry and traditional heavy manufacturing, about 1960. Major manufacturing districts: 1. Lancashire; 2. Yorkshire–Humberside; 3. English Midlands; 4. Scottish Lowlands; 5. South Wales; 6. Newcastle–Tyneside–Tees; 7. Greater London; 8. Sambre–Meuse–Lys; 9. Ruhr; 10. Upper Slask; 11. Bohemian Basin; 12. Saxon Triangle; 13. Saar–Lorraine; 14. Lower Sachsen; 15. Randstad Holland; 16. Upper Rhine Plain; 17. Greater Hamburg; 18. Paris–Lower Seine; 19. Upper Po Plain; 20. Swedish Central Lowland; 21. Bergslagen; 22. Swiss Plateau–Jura; 23. Rhône–Alps; 24. Greater Moskva; 25. Greater St. Petersburg; 26. Donets Basin–Lower Don; 27. Kryvyy Rih–Dnipro Bend; 28. Ploësti; and 29. Kiruna–Gällivare. Key for the fishing areas: C = cod; F = flounder; H = herring; M = mackerel; O = oysters; S = sardines; Sp = sponges; St = sturgeon; and T = tuna.

engine required fuel, but Great Britain, an almost totally deforested land, had an inadequate supply of wood. The island fortunately possessed an even better fuel—coal. The *mining of coal* represented the second major industry to be affected by the Industrial Revolution. Coal had a problem: It was bulky and difficult to transport any great distance, especially at the turn of the nineteenth century, before the railroad, internal combustion engine, and bulk-carrying ships had been developed. Consequently, the industries that relied upon coal as fuel were drawn to the coalfields, just as the earlier factories had been attracted to waterfalls and rapids. The Midlands, Lancashire, and Yorkshire, as well as the Scottish Lowlands, possessed noteworthy coal deposits, allowing a smooth transition from water to thermal power with a minimum of factory relocation. In addition, substantial reserves of coal occurred along the coastal fringe of southern Wales and in the region of Newcastle on the North Sea coast near the Scottish border (fig. 9.2).

A distinctive trait of the Industrial Revolution had become evident: areal concentration of industries. True, certain towns and districts had been known for a particular product under traditional manufacturing systems, but many such industries lay dispersed through a large number of small towns over fairly large regions. In contrast, mechanized production focused on a small number of cities and districts, which attracted very large populations. Gravitation to the coalfields accelerated the areal focalization of industry, causing great increases in population in favored districts and substantial emigration elsewhere.

Metallurgical industries, including the making of *iron* and *steel,* also felt the effects of the Industrial Revolution. Throughout most of history, the smelting of iron remained a primitive process, and few who practiced it had any valid understanding of what happened chemically. Iron ore was simply heated over a charcoal fire, and the charcoal's carbon combined with the ore's oxygen to free the iron. Some carbon also combined with the iron to provide hardness, for pure iron is rather malleable and easily cut. Too much carbon resulted in brittle cast iron; a proper amount resulted in steel. Different varieties of steel could be produced by accidental or purposeful addition of various *ferroalloys,* metals such as nickel or chrome. Before the mid-1700s, much superstition, ritual, and ceremony were associated with steelmaking as the keepers of the forges sought to make good steel. Those towns that became famous for high-quality steel, such as Toledo or Solingen, more often than not owed their reputation to particular local ores that spontaneously produced fine steel when smelted. Iron processing had changed little in thousands of years, and the industry in Europe was thoroughly dispersed geographically, with small forges located wherever iron ore deposits occurred. The industry, more rural than urban, was often found in thinly populated hill districts. Charcoal remained dominant in the smelting process.

The Industrial Revolution brought major changes to the iron and steel industry. The pivotal early developments occurred in Coalbrookdale, a town and valley in the Midlands (fig. 9.2). There, in 1709, *coke* was first substituted for charcoal in smelting, a process that caused steelmaking to become cheaper and permitted the use of lower-grade ores. By 1790, Coalbrookdale produced almost 50% of Britain's iron. Coke, nearly pure carbon, burns at a higher temperature than charcoal and is derived by heating high-grade coal to draw off the gaseous constituents. In timber-poor Britain, the use of coke increased rapidly after the middle eighteenth century. By 1788, some 70% of all blast furnaces in England and Scotland relied on coke instead of charcoal, and by 1806 the proportion had reached 97%. Acceptance of coke drastically changed the areal distribution of steelmaking. The industry abandoned countless scattered small forges and, out of necessity, relocated in the coal districts, where coke could be obtained most cheaply. Iron and steel thus contributed to the accelerating nucleation of industries in small coalfield districts.

Other technological changes reshaped British steelmaking. The traditional hammer and anvil gave way to the rolling mill as the final processing stage, blast furnaces supplanted small ovens, and metallurgical science arose to replace superstition and ritual. Through such innovation and change, the steelmakers of Britain achieved world leadership in the nineteenth century.

Steelmaking initially remained concentrated in the Midlands because coal and iron ore both occurred there. Birmingham became as synonymous with steel as Toledo had been in a different age and culture. The Midlands meant to steel what Lancashire and Yorkshire did to textiles. In other developing British manufacturing areas where both ore and coal occurred, additional concentrations of steel mills soon developed, as in the *Newcastle–Tyneside–Tees* district, where the legendary coal of Newcastle supplemented iron ore from the nearby Cleveland Hills; in *South Wales;* and in the western part of the Scottish Lowlands (fig. 9.2).

Another industry forever changed by the Industrial Revolution was the ancient and honored craft of *shipbuilding.* Traditionally, ships had been small, wooden, and powered by wind or oars. The Industrial Revolution created demands for larger, faster ships to transport bulky raw materials and finished products and provided the technology needed to produce such vessels. Iron barges first appeared in the late 1700s, and experimental steam navigation began about the same time. Steam-powered steel ships arose in the 1830s, and wooden sailing vessels disappeared a generation later.

The major shipbuilding centers in Britain arose where coalfields and steel mills bordered tidewater. One such location was the Tyneside, but the major center developed on the *Clydeside* near Glasgow in the Scottish Lowlands. By the 1890s, British shipyards produced 80% of the world's seagoing tonnage, and Britannia ruled the waves.

Textiles, coal mining, steelmaking, and shipbuilding formed the core of the Industrial Revolution, but other industries were also involved. The shift to machinery gave rise to an entire new engineering industry specializing in the manufacture of machines and machine tools. Both the raw material of this industry—steel—and its market—other manufacturing industries—lay in the coalfields, and as a result the machine makers located there too.

As machines became more numerous and complex, the industry that supplied them grew steadily.

Another basically new industry arose, devoted to the large-scale manufacture and processing of various *chemicals,* including dyes, paints, fertilizers, drugs, explosives, soap, and, eventually, products such as synthetic
fibers. Many such items could be salvaged from by-products of the coking
process, and, partly for this reason, many chemical factories developed in
the coalfields. Other industries besides shipbuilding and machine making
used finished steel as a raw material, and these often located near steel
mills: manufacturers of cutlery, surgical instruments, locks, locomotives,
automobiles, and weaponry. Similarly, textile-using industries, such as the
making of clothing, found it advantageous to be situated near the textile
factories.

The snowballing accumulation of a great variety of industries in the
coalfield districts of Britain caused hundreds of thousands of people to
migrate there seeking factory employment. In short order, the British population massed in a small number of clusters. These concentrations in turn
attracted still other manufacturers, primarily those that needed to be close
to the consumers of their products, such as bakers, brewers, meatpackers,
and other food processors.

The importance of coal as a locational factor in the formative stages of
the British Industrial Revolution was so great that all but one of the major
industrial districts developed on the coalfields. *London* provided the only
exception (fig. 9.2). Remote from coal deposits, it had no significant natural
resources other than a navigable river; yet London developed into the
largest single industrial center in the United Kingdom. Its advantages were
several. First, London had already accumulated a large population before
the Industrial Revolution, reaching 700,000 in the late 1600s and accounting
for 1 out of every 10 Britishers. This population offered both market and
labor supply when industrialization came. Second, London served as the
center for commerce and trade of the country, handling in its harbor three-
quarters of the nation's overseas trade by 1700. As a result, a concentration
of banks, insurance firms, and shipping brokerage houses developed,
which in turn stimulated the process of growth. Industries that depended
on foreign areas either as suppliers of raw materials or as consumers of
finished products found advantage by locating in London. Third, the large,
well-to-do merchant class of the city controlled a huge amount of capital
needed for investment in industrial activities. Consequently, London
thrived in the Industrial Revolution. Its diverse industries eventually
ranged from clothing and food processing to oil refining, various engineering and electronic industries, printing, and automobile and aircraft manufacture.

On a far more modest scale, coastal *Northern Ireland*—the Protestant
part of the island—followed Greater London's example and industrialized

in the absence of coal (fig. 9.2). Linen textiles and shipbuilding became the principal industries of cities such as Belfast and Londonderry.

Diffusion to the Mainland

On mainland Europe, numerous industrial districts rose in imitation of the British in the nineteenth century. With some notable exceptions, the spread remained confined to Germanic areas, especially northern Germany. Through good fortune, the Germanic people found parts of their land much better supplied with coal than did the French, Iberians, and Italians.

As in Britain, manufacturing on the European mainland tended to localize in small coalfield districts. The first mainland area to feel the effects of the British innovations, the *Sambre–Meuse–Lys*, straddled the Belgian–French border (fig. 9.2). Long before the Industrial Revolution, textile manufacture was well established, especially in the basin of the Lys River. Even before 1800, British textile technology began to be adopted. Traditional metalworking industries had long lined the region's rivers, and in the Middle Ages, copper, brass, and iron came from towns such as Dinant, Namur, and Huy. Around Namur in the mid-1500s, 120 forges and furnaces supported the activities of 7,000 charcoal burners in the surrounding forests. A district of adjacent Brabant became known as the "forest of the charcoal makers."

Coal in the Sambre–Meuse area occurs on the Great European Plain at the foot of the belt of Hercynian Hills, in this case the Ardennes. Some use was made of the coal as early as the 1500s, but large-scale mining activities awaited the nineteenth century. The first major use of coke on the European mainland occurred in the Sambre–Meuse area. A coke-fired blast furnace operated at Liège by 1823, and within 2 decades 45 of 120 furnaces used coke. Expansion of coke production outstripped any other mainland industrial district. Sambre–Meuse craftsmen served as leaders in adopting British techniques, remaining ahead of better-endowed districts in Germany until the mid-1860s. Textile production became centered in Lille, France, known for cottons, linens, and woolens; in Verviers, Belgium, where woolens dominated; and the southern Netherlands. The Sambre–Meuse–Lys district departed from the nineteenth century European industrial norm in being only partially Germanic, although it included a northern projection into Dutch and German territory.

One mainland manufacturing district, the *Ruhr* in Germany, eventually surpassed all the others in importance and even eclipsed the British parent districts (fig. 9.2). Also situated at the juncture of the Great European Plain and the Hercynian regions to the south (Sauerland and Siegerland), it lies largely in one of the many fertile loessial *Börde* along the southern edge of the plains (fig. 9.3). Underlying the Börde, huge deposits of high-grade coal reached to the surface near the hills.

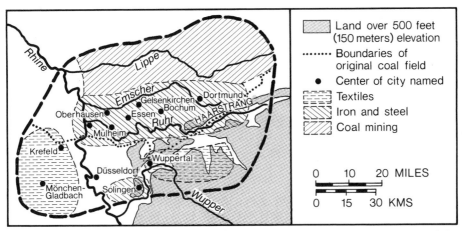

Figure 9.3.   The Ruhr industrial district, Germany, about 1950. The southern part of the coalfield had been largely mined out, and mining migrated steadily northward. Steel mills remained concentrated between the Ruhr and Emscher Rivers, while textiles were manufactured at Wuppertal and in the cities west of the Rhine. (*Source:* Pounds 1952.)

Development of the Ruhr District lagged considerably behind English or even Belgian efforts. Small amounts of coal had been chipped away from the surface outcroppings at least as early as the thirteenth century, mainly to provide heat for local houses. In medieval times, a significant iron and steel industry developed at the town of Solingen and elsewhere in the hilly Sauerland and Siegerland, based on local deposits of iron ore and the survival of large, charcoal-producing forests. Linen textiles made from locally grown flax by both gildsmen and cottagers were similarly well established in the area by the late Middle Ages. As late as 1800 the steelmakers continued to function in the traditional way, as did the textile weavers. Little or no suggestion of the Industrial Revolution sweeping Britain was visible in the Ruhr, though steam pumps installed in 1801 combated water seepage in some of the small coal mines. The towns remained small, confined within medieval walls, and functioning primarily as agricultural trade centers. A visitor from the thirteenth or fourteenth centuries would have felt at home in the Ruhr at the beginning of the 1800s. Even the next half-century brought few changes, and a traveler in 1847 described the Ruhr as "poetically rural." Coal mining was still carried on in hundreds of small rural mines, employing in total only some 13,000 men. Urban growth had not been rapid, and gilds still dominated the manufacture of steel at Solingen. Nevertheless, the first mark of the Industrial Revolution had been placed on this pastoral setting. Mechanized, steam-powered textile mills arose by 1850 in Krefeld and the twin cities of Mönchen–Gladbach, west of the Rhine. The textile gilds and cottage weavers rapidly gave way to the new technology. As in Britain, the textile industry led the way.

In the last half of the nineteenth century, the Ruhr underwent almost complete change, emerging by the end of the 1800s as the most important European industrial center. Annual coal production increased by 33 times in the last half of the century. The mines grew from small rural enterprises scratching at the surface of the earth to become sizable urban establishments employing hundreds of thousands of workers and utilizing sophisticated mining machinery. The manufacture of iron and steel shifted primarily to the coalfield, and large plants using coke supplanted the charcoal-burning gilds of Solingen. The small, local iron ore deposits proved inadequate to supply the demand, and the Ruhr reached out to Sweden, Spain, and Lorraine for additional ore, exporting in exchange large amounts of coking coal. The Rhine River forfeited much of its romantic character, steeped in German mythology, to become the major transport route linking the Ruhr to the rest of the world. Barges bearing coal and ore came to dominate the riverine scene at the foot of the Lorelei Cliffs, as progress shoved aside poetry. Industrial names such as Krupp and Thyssen joined Schiller and Goethe in the German pantheon.

The population of the Ruhr exploded, as towns became sprawling industrial cities. A line of urban centers developed from Dortmund in the east through Bochum, Essen, and Oberhausen to Duisburg on the Rhine in the west. Essen, which had a population of only 4,000 within its medieval town walls in 1800 and still only 10,000 at midcentury, became a city of 200,000 by 1900. The local agricultural population proved inadequate as a labor supply, and workers immigrated from other parts of Germany, as well as from Belgium, the Netherlands, Italy, and the Slavic lands of the east. A melting pot of peoples assembled, giving the Ruhr a distinctly different ethnic character from the rest of Germany. A gray pall of smoke settled over the district, blackening buildings and human lungs and blotting out the sun. With the smoke came a prosperous, powerful Germany, which assumed its place among the leading nations of the world.

Near the headwaters of the Wisla and Odra (Oder) Rivers in southern Poland, where the North European Plain joins the hills and mountains of central Europe in another of the loessial embayments, lies the *Upper Slask* industrial district (fig. 9.2). Though once German and formerly called Schlesien or Silesia, today it lies in Poland. A tradition of iron smelting, well established here by the 1700s, relied on abundant local forests for charcoal and on small amounts of iron ore found in the region. The large coal deposits remained very nearly untouched. Upper Slask lay on a remote frontier, the outermost tip of Prussian, and later German, territory, in an area far removed from markets and sparsely populated. The upper Odra River offered fewer possibilities for transport than did the mighty Rhine, and the sea lay far away. Furthermore, the coal deposits were smaller than those of the Ruhr. In spite of these shortcomings, Upper Slask underwent industrialization in the nineteenth century, in large part because the Prussian government desired it. Financial encouragements, including subsidies, went to the wealthy landlords who owned most of the area, and they responded with investments in industry. Because timber was more abundant than coking coal, the use of charcoal persisted longer in Upper Slask, even into the 1860s. Local iron ores were soon exhausted, and imports from Austria via the Moravian Gate rail route became necessary. After major improvements to the Odra waterway in 1895, allowing easier access to the Baltic Sea, Sweden became the dominant supplier of ore. The district never rivaled the Ruhr, but it did produce about 10% of Germany's iron by 1900. Before World War I, almost the entire district lay in Germany, with only a small part across the border in Austria–Hungary; after the war, half of the region was awarded to the new Polish state on the basis of a plebiscite. In 1945, the Poles seized the remainder, expelling most resident Germans. Poland, then industrially backward, in this way acquired an important manufacturing base.

Another of the coalfield industrial districts developed largely by the Germans, the *Saar–Lorraine,* straddles the present border between Germany and France, also including parts of southern Luxembourg (fig. 9.2). The German Saarland contains the greater part of the coal, while French Lorraine is one of the traditional centers of iron ore mining in Europe. Here, too, industrialization occurred rather late, lagging considerably behind the British districts. Coke, first used in 1838, gradually replaced charcoal. Major steel plants with blast furnaces appeared only in the 1850s. In fact, the major development of the district did not occur until after Germany annexed Lorraine in 1871. The principal hindrance to expansion was that most of the Saarland coal could not be coked, necessitating the import of Ruhr coals. The industrial value of the Saar–Lorraine areas prompted numerous boundary changes. Germany twice seized and lost part of the iron ore deposits, and France twice sought to detach Saarland from Germany. The peripheral border location of the Saar–Lorraine District long presented a problem, not unlike that faced by Upper Slask.

Another area of industrialization in nineteenth-century Europe lay in the northern part of the province of Cechy, until 1918 a part of German-ruled Austria but today the core of Czechia (fig. 9.2). Under encouragement from the Austro-Hungarian government, a well-rounded industrial area had developed by the 1870s, though this *Bohemian Basin* region faced the same problems of remoteness and poor water-transport facilities that plagued nearby Upper Slask. The coal deposits were also much smaller than in the more important industrial regions of Germany, Belgium, and Britain. Iron and steel manufacture, based on coal deposits northwest of Praha and ore from the nearby Krusné Hory (Ore Mountains) on the north, became centered in the cities of Kladno and Plzen and provided raw material for the Skoda armaments works. Other diverse industries of this district include cotton and linen textiles, especially around Liberec; heavy machinery and clothing manufacture at Praha; world-famous ceramics and glassware from Karlovy Vary; and food processing, including brewing at Plzen, which gave its name to the well-known Pilsner beers.

Another German industrial region of importance arising in the nineteenth century lay in the *Saxon Triangle*, with apexes at the cities of Plauen, Halle, and Dresden, an area traditionally part of the Kingdom of Sachsen (fig. 9.2). The local coalfield included only small, scattered deposits of a lower quality. Privileges and subsidies offered by the Saxon government, coupled with the presence of iron ore in the mountains to the south, stimulated industrial growth here as early as the 1600s. Immigrant artisans, mainly French Huguenot refugees and Dutch, greatly aided the establishment of porcelain, textile, and armament manufacture. Textiles clustered at Plauen and Chemnitz, where original use of waterpower gave way to coal as a fuel. Halle and Bitterfeld produced chemicals, based in part on potash deposits. The tradition of fine porcelain manufacture became established in the Dresden area; while printing and publishing gravitated to Leipzig.

The last European coalfield industrial complex to be developed lay far to the east, in Ukraine. Major coal deposits in the *Donets Basin*, combined with the huge iron ore deposits of nearby *Kryvyy Rih*, permitted development of one of Europe's most important centers of heavy industry. Most of this development occurred under early Soviet rule in the 1920s and 1930s, and by the time of World War II, Germans regarded the complex as a major military objective.

Spreading beyond the Coalfields

In most areas not gifted with coal deposits, the nineteenth century witnessed slow industrial growth, or even decline in the face of competition from the coal areas. Some urban centers with sizable populations in the pre–Industrial Revolution period imitated the success of London in attracting industries on the basis of a large, ready-made labor force and market. In this category were such districts as Paris, Hamburg, Wien, and Randstad Holland. *Paris* developed two basic industries: high-quality luxury items such as fashion clothing, cosmetics, and jewelry, distributed in small workshop factories around the city; and engineering industries, dominated in the present century by automobile manufacture and concentrated in the suburb towns. Most of the rest of France lagged behind industrially, not only because coal was absent, but also because of the slow French population growth rate, which affected both labor supply and market; a transport system so highly centered in Paris that outlying districts had difficult access to raw materials and market; and a lack of governmental encouragement of non-Parisian industrialization in the 1800s. The Rotterdam–Europoort section of the *Randstad Holland* industrial district has in recent decades developed a large oil-refining and petrochemical industry (fig. 9.2).

Another major district that developed in the nineteenth century lay in the *Upper Rhine Plain* of southwestern Germany and French Alsace, including cities such as Mannheim and Frankfurt am Main (fig. 9.2). This area lay on an ancient routeway between the Mediterranean coast and the North European Plain, and many cities had a heritage of gild industries. In the 1800s, new industries moved here, especially those producing textiles and chemicals. Ludwigshafen am Rhine, founded in the nineteenth century on the Rhine River, became the site of the famous Farben chemical works, and the Frankfurt suburb of Höchst developed a similar industry. In the twentieth century, the Upper Rhine and nearby Neckar Valley acquired important automobile factories, including the Daimler–Benz Works at Stuttgart and the Opel Plant at Rüsselsheim near Frankfurt. Early on, Alsace developed textile mills at waterpower sites along the foot of the Vosges.

Hydropower, converted into electricity, helped revive the former industrial greatness of northern Italy, particularly in the area between Milano and Torino in the upper reaches of the *Po Plain* (fig. 9.2). Milano became the first European city to have electric lights, in 1883. The government provided added subsidies and incentives to industrialization, and a sizable workforce of cheap labor was assembled from among the peasantry of the adjacent Alpine fringe and southern Italy. The diverse industries eventually included iron and steel, based on imported raw materials; automobile manufacture, including the Fiat Plant at Torino; and textiles. The district is served by the port of Genova, across the Appennini Mountains on the Mediterranean coast, a city that acquired sizable iron and steel mills and shipbuilding yards of its own. Once-proud Venèzia profited less than might be expected from the rise of the Po Valley industries, for the Adriatic Sea remained a backwater, leading away from the major markets and suppliers of raw materials, except for petroleum from the Middle East.

The industrial portion of Switzerland, lying to the north of the Alps on the *Swiss Plateau* and in the hilly *Jura*, developed industries adapted to a scarcity of raw materials (fig. 9.2). The Swiss relied on highly skilled labor to produce quality goods with a high value added in the manufacturing process. Hydroelectric power brought a major expansion of industry in the twentieth century. Watchmaking, concentrated in numerous small towns and cities of the Jura, is a typical Swiss industry, retaining a pre–Industrial Revolution areal dispersal and veneration for craftsmen. St. Gallen in the east became the major textile center, producing such items as luxury silks, laces, and ribbons, while Basel in northwestern Switzerland evolved into an important chemical center at the head of barge navigation on the Rhine. Other industries specialized in the production of various kinds of machinery or food processing, including milk chocolate.

Several small areas in northern Spain also felt the effects of the Industrial Revolution, particularly the Barcelona area on the Mediterranean shore and the Bay of Biscay coast around Bilbao and San Sebastián (fig. 9.2). In the latter area, major iron ore deposits and minor coalfields supported a local steel industry, which in turn provided raw material for shipbuilders.

Barcelona, whose rising industrial capacity presented a Catalonian challenge to the primacy of inland Madrid, became the scene of diverse manufacturing, including textiles.

Despite very early industrial beginnings, Sweden had become a poor country by the late 1800s. Though endowed with fine iron ore and copper deposits, which had been mined in the *Bergslagen* area since the Middle Ages, Sweden lacked coal deposits and could not share in the early Industrial Revolution (fig. 9.2). Its steelmakers, known for the high quality of their product, continued to use charcoal. Adoption of hydroelectric power finally permitted the modernization of Swedish industry around 1900, eventually creating an economic well-being unsurpassed in the world. Hydropower fueled electric furnaces employed in steelmaking, and while Sweden's output of steel never rivaled Germany or Britain, the quality was unsurpassed, including various steel alloys. When the Bergslagen ores played out, Sweden developed new iron ore mines in the far north, around *Kiruna* and *Gällivare* (fig. 9.2). A variety of local engineering industries rely on this steel, including manufacturers of machines, automobiles, ball bearings, electrical equipment, aircraft engines, bicycles, diesel motors, armaments, and ships. Steel production remained concentrated in the Bergslagen area, but the engineering industries scattered widely in the nearby *Swedish Central Lowland*, a belt between Stockholm and Göteborg, including such enterprises as the Volvo automobile industry and household appliance factories (fig. 9.2).

Finland, also late to industrialize, relied upon its abundant waterpower and forests to develop a manufacturing complex in the southwest and far-flung primary industry in the woodlands. On that precarious base, the Finns, too, achieved an enviable standard of living. Wood products remain a specialty in Finland.

The period 1900–1960 witnessed other efforts to industrialize the European peripheries. Ties to raw material sites weakened with improved transportation. Ports became favored new places for steelmaking because ore and coal could be shipped by sea. As a result, coastal steel mills developed at seaports such as Valencia in eastern Spain and Piombino, Genova, Taranto, and Napoli in Italy.

Deindustrialization

In the year 1900, all of the European industrial districts combined accounted for about 90% of the world's manufacturing output, an overwhelming dominance. The power and prosperity of the Germanic industrial core reached unprecedented heights, and European colonial empires ruled the far greater part of the Eastern Hemisphere. In spite of two highly destructive world wars, Europe remained the industrial heartland of the world in the middle twentieth century, though not as dominant.

Few, if any, experts viewing the industrial geography of Europe in 1960 anticipated the radical changes that lay immediately ahead.

Put simply, the most important mass-production industries, both primary and secondary, went into severe and irreversible decline, prompting use of terms such as *deindustrialization, industrial crisis,* and *industrial fallibility.* Once-prosperous industrial districts became, within no more than 2 decades, "derelict," "pauperized," and eligible for economic assistance. The blue-collar labor force in a single generation deteriorated into "a dispirited people who reflected a growing passivity to their plight," to use words of geographer C. Shane Davies. Entire working-class communities became devastated and dependent upon unemployment relief.

The statistical evidence of deindustrialization is both convincing and sobering. In the United Kingdom, birthplace of the Industrial Revolution, the labor force employed in manufacturing plummeted from 9.1 million in 1966 to 5.1 million by 1987 (fig. 9.4). In the English Midlands, where the modern coal and steel industry was born, manufacturing employment fell by 55% during that 2-decade span. In Wales, "its spirit and wealth now broken," employment in mining dropped from an all-time high of 270,000 to only 24,000 by 1982. All of Great Britain could claim only 31 coal mines, with 12,000 employees, by 1994. In the half-century after 1930, some 400,000 people emigrated from the South Wales industrial area. The Newcastle–Tyneside–Tees district of northeastern England saw its last operating shipyard and deep coal mine closed in 1994. Manchester in Lancashire and Belfast in Northern Ireland, once prosperous industrial cities, have suffered particularly severe decline. Even London has not been spared. Its manufacturing workforce declined by 40% in the brief period between 1975 and 1982, and an additional 300,000 industrial jobs were lost in greater London during the decade ending in 1991.

Western European mainland industrial districts fared little better. The peak year of coal production in the Saar–Lorraine was 1957, and 20 years later it had been labeled a "problem region," as had the Ruhr and Sambre–Meuse–Lys. In western Germany, the workforce employed in coal mining dwindled from 600,000 in 1955 to 95,000 by 1995. The Ligurian coast around Genova in Italy and the Bay of Biscay coast of northern Spain also joined the list of severely stricken industrial regions (fig. 9.4). Torino in the Po Valley suffered particularly severe manufacturing decline. In France, which had 190,000 coal miners in 1948, the number shrank to 6,000 a half-century later and the government ordered an end to all coal mining by 2005.

The crisis began in the primary sector, in particular coal mining. A steadily decreasing demand for coal, principally the result of a shift to alternative energy sources, especially petroleum, brought depression to mining. Also contributing to the decline of the mining sector was the depletion of minerals such as iron ore. Saar–Lorraine ore peaked in output in 1960, and even in Sweden, Europe's leading iron ore producer, the reserve is now

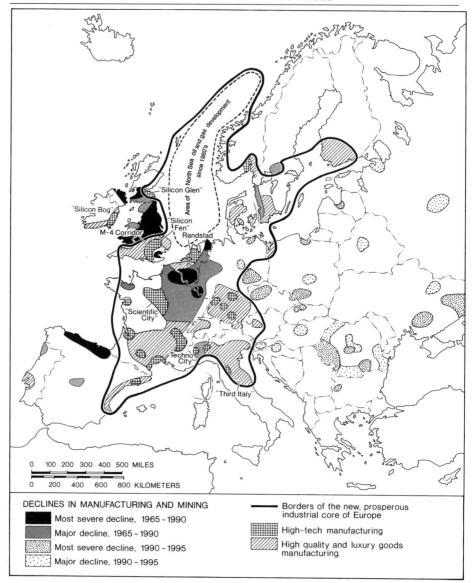

Figure 9.4.   Zones of deindustrialization and of new manufacturing growth 1960–2000.
Decline and growth remain largely separate geographically. The emerging new core of primary and secondary industries, based on high-tech, crafts, and, to a lesser extent, petroleum, is more confined areally than its predecessor and excludes virtually all of the formerly communist east.

small and the yield low. As a result, western European steel production has declined from its peak year in 1974.

Textile manufacture also suffered. Britain's position began to slip even in the nineteenth and early twentieth centuries, as its share of world cotton textile production dropped from 56% in 1870 to 38% in 1915. An extreme example of decline is provided by the linen industry of Northern Ireland. Between 1950 and 1970, the labor force and number of factories in the Belfast area fell by half, a critical decline in the local economy, since a fifth of the labor force had been employed in the linen industry. Shipbuilding declined even more catastrophically. As recently as 1948, the United Kingdom produced almost half of the world tonnage launched, but by 1980 its share had fallen to only 4%. The 1960s witnessed the most rapid decline. The plight of shipbuilding is illustrated by the Clydeside District in the Scottish Lowlands. Local shipyards began their rise to world importance in the 1830s, only to find prosperity arrested a century later. Clydeside ship tonnage peaked in 1913. Foreign competition, particularly from Japan, sent the Clydeside into severe depression after the middle 1950s. In short, deindustrialization struck hardest at the traditional mass-production enterprises that had formed the core of the Industrial Revolution—textiles, steel, coal mining, shipbuilding, and chemicals—and at the districts overspecialized in these pursuits. Textile towns such as Troyes in France and mining centers like South Wales suffered most.

In eastern Europe, traditional mass-production industries remained free of competition in the absence of a market economy before 1990. Their inefficiency did not lead to decline as long as the communist system of central planning survived and subsidized them. As a result, deindustrialization came both late and very abruptly to the east, largely running its course in a half-decade and causing massive economic problems and social dislocations (fig. 9.4). Industrial *collapse* better describes what happened in eastern Europe.

In Russia, oil production declined to 68% of the 1990 level by 1997 and iron ore output to 59%, while coal production similarly declined 66% in the 1990–1995 period. Russia retained 261 coal mines but has proposed closing 150 of them. Russian manufactures likewise plummeted, and by 1997, chemical production stood at 46% of the 1990 output, iron and steel at 59%, and machinery and metalworking at 40%. The declines have ended, and output in some industries has risen since 1997. Privatization of Russian metallurgy industries was largely completed by 1996, involving 398 out of 411 enterprises. In Ukraine, total industrial output in 1997 stood at only half the level of 1990.

Elsewhere in formerly communist eastern Europe, deindustrialization took a similar toll. In Romania, the labor force declined by 7% in just 2 years, from 1989 to 1991. The east German industrial city of Plauen in the Saxon Triangle lost a third of its total population between 1990 and 1994, and the east German textile workforce plummeted from 320,000 in 1990 to only 20,000 by 1999. The process is ongoing. Poland, which employed

237,000 coal miners in 1998, planned to cut the workforce to 120,000 by 2002, closing 24 of 65 mines.

In both eastern and western Europe, deindustrialization has led to rather high rates of unemployment, particularly in the old, decayed heavy industry districts (fig. 9.5). The most persistent governmental efforts have failed to correct the unemployment problem in many areas. Blue-collar workers are not easily retrained for other types of work.

Industrial Rejuvenation

Deindustrialization never became pervasive in Europe as a whole. While many major industries and districts declined into crisis, others retained stability or achieved impressive growth.

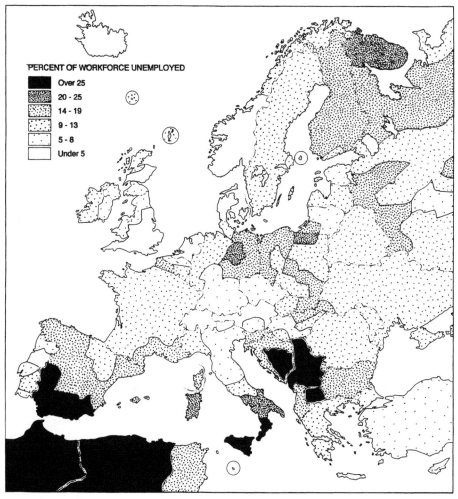

Figure 9.5.   Unemployment in Europe. Much joblessness was caused by deindustrialization.

In the primary sector, the collapse of coal mining and decline of iron ore production occurred simultaneously with the rise of the great North Sea oil and natural gas field, a submarine deposit shared by the United Kingdom, Norway, Denmark, Germany, and the Netherlands (fig. 9.4). The northern forests of Sweden, Finland, and Russia, a renewable primary resource, continued to yield their sizable harvests. These 3 northern European countries still provide about 21% of the world's sawn lumber exports and 16% of the wood pulp and paper.

Much more important than these primary industries to European rejuvenation has been the shift to the manufacture of high-quality goods requiring a skilled labor force, ongoing innovation, and/or sophisticated technology. Western Europeans have successfully moved from emphasis on mass-produced goods requiring large factories and minimally skilled labor to a focus on labor-intensive operations producing items of high value, often produced in small workshops. They have, in short, chosen to depend upon the cardinal virtues of European culture—education, individualism, and innovation.

The most glamorous of these new enterprises can be grouped under the much-used term *high-tech.* Properly speaking, these include industries manufacturing high-technology products such as electronic and microelectronic devices, data processing equipment, robotics, telecommunications apparatus, and the like. To these should be added firms that make preponderant *use* of such sophisticated products in the manufacturing process, such as pharmaceutical firms and pesticide makers. Central to the entire high-tech enterprise is the computer.

All such manufacturers invest heavily in research and development, in order to foster the innovations that drive the volatile high-tech industry, though these innovations more often than not spawn new companies. Research and development activity constitutes a *service industry* and as such will be considered in chapter 10. While much is made of high-tech manufacturing and several European countries have tied their industrial future to such activity, these firms employ far fewer people than the old, collapsed ones. Their rise has done little to address the problems associated with deindustrialization, and high-tech manufacturing will not likely achieve the century-long stability and prosperity of the older system.

Perhaps more promising for Europe's future is the manufacture of high-quality expensive luxury goods, mainly for export. These factories operate as *labor-* and *design-* (rather than technology-) intensive craft industries and represent, in fact, a revival of gildlike manufacturing. Indeed, the apprenticeship system has survived from gild times, under government protection in countries such as Germany. The highly skilled workforce enjoys high wages, job security, and the satisfaction of laboring in "a positive culture of work." Creativity, skill, and craftsman pride are all essential components. Factories tend to be small and the workplace pleasant. Typical products include ceramics, pottery, decorative glassware, fine clothing, jewelry, quality leather goods such as shoes, well-crafted wood products, and luxury automobiles. Such manufacturing survived in Europe even during the heyday of heavy industry, especially in noncoalfield districts such as the Swiss Plateau–Jura, but a major expansion has occurred since 1970. High-quality craft industries have one great potential weakness—their dependence upon a high level of prosperity among consumers, many of whom reside outside Europe. Any major worldwide depression would undermine such industries. Western Europe's continued prosperity and high standard of living are always at risk.

Geographically, deindustrialization and rejuvenation occurred in quite distinct European regions, with relatively little overlap (fig. 9.4). The districts characterized by high-tech and craft industries tend to lie outside the economically depressed, deindustrialized areas, in regions that had little heavy industry in earlier times. Geographer Allen J. Scott called these "new industrial spaces." Southern England, southern Germany, and southern France eclipsed the northern parts of those countries as the centers of manufacturing, while the eastern part of the Po–Veneto Plain has surpassed the older Milano–Torino focus.

High-tech industry, which tends to be drawn to universities, major airports, suburbs, small towns, and medium-sized cities, developed in places such as the "M-4 Corridor," a crescent-shaped area west of London; "Silicon Glen" in the Lothians near Edinburgh; "Scientific City," southwest of Paris; Mediterranean France; the Dutch Randstad; and the suburbs of München, Augsburg, Nürnberg, and several other south German cities (fig. 9.4). In some cases, the older, declining industrial centers have sought to claim a share of high-tech industry, as northeast of Milano and at Torino in Italy, where "Technocity" has been developed, but these efforts remain the exception rather than the rule. *Re*industrialization is a difficult process. The European high-tech industry lags far behind its American counterpart.

The regions devoted to craft-style manufacturing include, most notably, the "Third Italy," which as early as 1981 claimed 37% of all manufacturing employment in that country; the provinces of Bayern and Baden–Württemberg in south Germany, where conservative state governments fostered such development; the south of France; southern England; central Denmark; most of south-central Sweden; and southwestern Finland (fig. 9.4).

The Third Italy, typical of these new industrial spaces, produces a great array of goods, including luxury automobiles such as Alfa Romeo and Ferrari, silks from Como, jewelry from Vicenza, tiles from Modena, and fine woolen textiles from Biella. The district is also heavily engaged in manufacturing the precision machines and tools required to make some of these goods, including those used in the manufacture of gold jewelry.

Western Europe, then, contains an odd patchwork of decayed, distressed deindustrialized districts alongside booming centers of high-tech and craft manufacturing. Eastern Europe's condition is less fortunate, for deindustrialization there has not been accompanied by any noteworthy rise of new enterprises devoted to sophisticated technology, skilled crafts, or new discoveries of primary resources. The east–west industrial contrast has become vivid and alarming, given the social and political connotations. Decades of suppressed individualism and ideologically based education deprive eastern Europe of precisely the sort of people needed to develop such industries.

Still, not all is bleak in the east. Economic downturns reversed in 1995 in most countries. Many western firms have opened factories in the formerly communist countries, and some local manufacturers made the transition to a market economy. Poland's Szczecin shipyards have risen to world prominence, and the eastern German toy making town of Sonneberg in Thüringen has regained much of its former fame and vigor, after cutting the communist-era workforce of 18,000 down to a lean 1,200.

In Russia, small private businesses, each employing fewer than 200 workers, numbered about 900,000 by 1995, giving employment to nearly 9 million people. Enclaves of relative prosperity have developed in Eurorussia, most notably in Moskva, but also in St. Petersburg and even certain provincial towns, such as Novgorod—so successful that "the Novgorod model" has entered business jargon.

Core and Periphery

Both the old and new industrial order in Europe feature a core–periphery pattern (figs. 9.2 and 9.4). Under the geographical configuration that prevailed before deindustrialization, manufacturing districts lay mainly in the European core, with few exceptions, even though the Industrial Revolution began in a peripheral area. In that pattern, the European periphery housed mainly primary industries that supplied raw materials for the manufacturing core. These included forest products from the north; fishing in the peripheral oceans and seas; mining, as at Kiruna and Kryvyy Rih; and the extraction of petroleum and natural gas at places such as Ploësti in the Valachian Plain and in the hinter reaches of the East European Plain (fig. 9.2).

In the seas that flank Europe on the south, west, and north, a great variety of commercially valuable fish is found (fig. 9.2). These are exploited in part by peoples of the less-industrialized periphery of Europe, particularly Norwegians, Icelanders, Faeroese, Portuguese, Greeks, Dalmatian Croats, and Basques. Norway, with one of the smallest populations in Europe, accounts for 2.5% of the total world catch of fish each year, and Iceland is also a major fishing country. Fishing occupies a very sizable segment of the labor force in Iceland and the Faeroe Islands. A large number of fisherfolk generally live in lands poorly suited for agriculture; in Norway, for example, only 3% of the national territory is arable.

The types of fisheries vary from one peripheral sea to another in Europe. Mediterranean fisherfolk go after tuna, sardines—which are named for the Italian island of Sardegna—and sponges, found particularly in the Aegean. The Black and Caspian Seas yield sturgeon, from which caviar is obtained, while the North Sea, Arctic Ocean, and Norwegian Sea fisherfolk specialize in cod, herring, mackerel, and haddock. The less saline Baltic Sea is important for flounder and eels, in addition to cod and herring. Oysters and sardines provide the principal take in the Bay of Biscay and other Iberian Atlantic waters.

In Europe's new industrial order, the core has diminished in size and the periphery expanded (fig. 9.4). If the stricken manufacturing districts of Britain, northern Spain, and eastern Europe are excluded, then the new core, represented by high-tech and craft industry concentrations as well as North Sea petroleum, displays a thinner profile than the old one. Even so, the traditional pattern of a manufacturing core and primary industrial periphery remains intact.

Environmental Damage

Not surprisingly, the industrial core–periphery pattern in Europe has a sinister mirror image reflection in damage to water, land, and air. The Industrial Revolution and the prosperity it brought exacted a terrible price in environmental quality. No part of Europe has been exempt from this damage, but the highly industrialized core has suffered most, as suggested earlier, in the discussion of forest death in chapter 2 (fig. 2.9). The greatest concentration of environmental damage has occurred in the *Black Triangle*, the borderland between eastern Germany, Czechia, and southern Poland (fig. 9.6). Visits to ravaged industrial towns such as Eisleben and Bitterfeld in Germany provide a sobering experience for any sensitive person.

Nor was the damage limited to the natural environment. The graceful humanized landscapes of preindustrial Europe—the fine old towns and aesthetically pleasing rural landscapes—also suffered harm. Industrial activity has altered or obliterated many of the myriad places that endow Europe with its special human character, prompting geographer J. Douglas Porteous to coin the word *topocide*—the deliberate obliteration of a place—to describe the fate of his native Howdendyke in Yorkshire. The "Faustian bargain" that industrialized Europe made now exacts its price.

Such warnings came very early. After a brief initial period of optimism about industrialization in the period before 1775, the more sensitive Europeans—poets and artists—sensed that something was amiss. They expressed their alarm in the form of paintings and poems, beginning in the last quarter of the eighteenth century. The Scottish poet Robert Burns visited an iron foundry "lest we gang to Hell, it may be nae surprise," and many artists of the period left paintings of the industrialized districts that convey a sinister, foreboding landscape. Such warnings continued over the

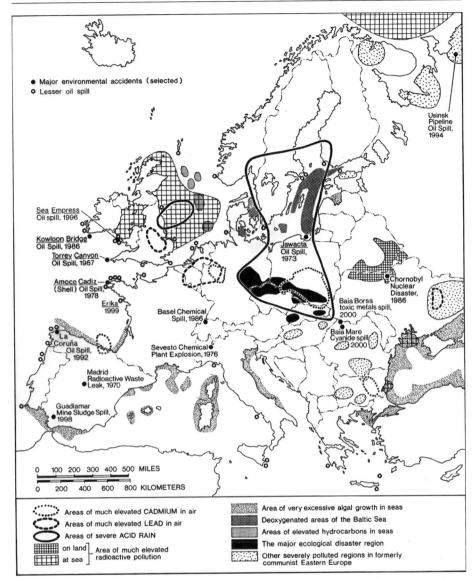

Figure 9.6.   Selected patterns of environmental pollution. The core of Europe has been most disastrously affected, but the peripheries have not escaped, due to the discharge of polluted rivers, the practice of dumping toxic wastes in the sea, and oil spills in the transport lanes. (*Sources:* Carré 1992, 142; *The Economist Atlas of the New Europe* 1992, 203, 210; Ionescu 1991, 20–25; Petrow 1968, frontispiece; *Concise Statistical Yearbook of Poland, 1991*, 1992, 25; Clout et al. 1989, 182; Thompson 1991, 45; Vilchek et al. 1996, 22–23.)

following centuries, and the Welshman Richard Llewellyn, in 1939, penned the poignant novel *How Green Was My Valley*, a classic lament of the economic oppression of his people and the ravaging of their countryside by industrialization. The European land today lies burdened with slag heaps, its soil poisoned by toxic waste, its streams and lakes polluted, its air darkened.

The ongoing environmental problems represent, in most cases, the consequences of deliberate, repeated, and habitual actions bound up in the processes of primary and secondary industry. Western Europeans have made some impressive strides in altering such behavior and in repairing some of the more visible damage, though the task at times seems impossible. In other cases, catastrophic industrial accidents, rather than deliberate action, causes environmental damage. Chemical factories have experienced several major disasters, most notably at Sevesto in northern Italy and at Basel in Switzerland. The most recent major disaster, at the Baia Mare gold mine in northern Romania, spilled huge quantities of cyanide into the Tisza and Danube Rivers, rendering them largely devoid of aquatic life for hundreds of kilometers (fig. 9.6).

The human consequences of these environmental problems and disasters are profound. For example, at Sevesto, where the chemical factory exploded, high rates of leukemia, lymphoma, and liver cancer rates plague the people exposed to the dioxin cloud; Bulgaria's fishing industry has been devastated by dieoffs of mackerel, sturgeons, and anchovies; at Bitterfeld in Germany, air pollution caused diminished lung capacity and impaired immune systems in children; and in Russia's Kola Peninsula, devastated by nuclear waste and nickel smelters, respiratory and genetic diseases proliferate.

Deindustrialization, especially in eastern Europe, led to greatly reduced levels of environmental pollution. Russia provides some revealing examples. Emissions of hazardous atmospheric contaminants decreased by 47% at Moskva, 56% at St. Petersburg, and 49% at Magnitogorsk in the Urals between 1992 and 1998. The situation in the Black Triangle is also much improved, but that only says that *additional* damage to the regional habitat has been cut back. A network of national parks and other nature preserves offers additional hope to eastern Europe.

The Green Movement

One European reaction to the problem of industrial pollution has been the rise of *Green* politics. Characterized by ecological platforms, skepticism of technology, opposition to the collusion of industry and government, rejection of consumerism, and a desire to change basic lifestyles, the Green movement arose mainly in the 1980s, centered in environmentally troubled yet wealthy countries such as Germany. In the most recent elections in

Luxembourg, the Greens carried over 10% of the popular vote. The combination of pollution and prosperity seems essential to Green success.

The Greens emerged as a major electoral force in the western European elections of 1989. In spite of their radical positions, they regularly achieve over a tenth of the vote in a sizable part of northwestern Europe, centered in northern France, parts of the Low Country, southwestern Germany, and England (fig. 9.7). In the severely polluted east, the Greens fare best in Czechia. In Norway, typical of the less polluted European periphery and

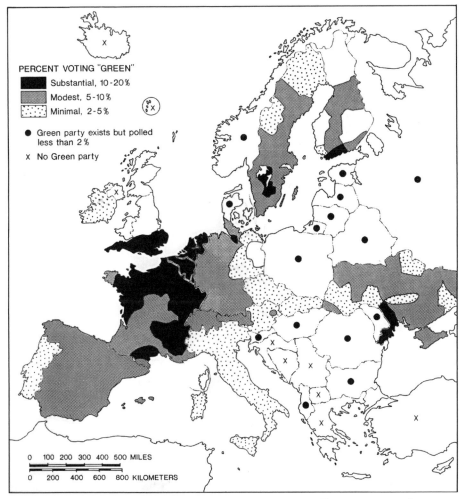

Figure 9.7.   The "Green" vote in selected elections, 1990s. The pattern reveals a core–periphery configuration, with a Green heartland in northern France, Belgium, Germany, and England south of the Severn–Wash line. This heartland coincides with prosperous areas experiencing major ecological problems. For Finland, the percentages shown are not votes but instead Greens as a proportion of elected representatives. (*Sources:* Dijkink and van der Wusten 1992, 7–11; Sallnow and Arlett 1989, 10–14; Vanlaer 1984.)

dependent upon enterprises such as whaling, the Greens have failed to poll as much as 1% of the vote in any province. In Greece, on the opposite periphery of Europe, they have been similarly unsuccessful.

The industrial geography of Europe, as we have seen, is in flux. New patterns and industries emerge as old ones decline. High-tech and craft industries form only part of the changing economic geography. To obtain a more complete picture, we must now turn to another category altogether— the so-called service industries. Chapter 10 is devoted to that growing sector of the economy.

Sources and Suggested Readings

Alfrey, Judith, and Catherine Clark. 1993. *The Landscape of Industry: Patterns of Change in the Ironbridge Gorge.* London, GB: Routledge.

Braun, Boris, and Reinhold E. Grotz. 1993. "Support for Competitiveness: National and Common Strategies for Manufacturing Industries within the European Community." *Erdkunde* 47:105–117.

Carré, François. 1992. "Aperçu sur la pollution de la mer du Nord." *Hommes et Terres du Nord* 3:142.

Carter, F. W., and W. Maik, eds. 1999. *Shock-shift in an Enlarged Europe: The Geography of Socio-economic Change in East-central Europe after 1989.* Aldershot, GB: Ashgate.

Clout, Hugh, et al. 1989. *Western Europe: Geographical Perspectives.* 2nd ed. Harlow, GB: Longman.

Concise Statistical Yearbook of Poland, 1991. 1992. Warszawa, PL: Central Statistical Office.

Cumbers, Andrew. 1995. "North Sea Oil and Regional Economic Development." *Area* 27:208–217.

Davies, C. S. 1983. "Wales: Industrial Fallibility and Spirit of Place." *Journal of Cultural Geography* 4 (1): 72–86.

———. 1984. "Dark Inner Landscapes: The South Wales Coalfield." *Landscape Journal* 3:36–44.

Dijkink, Gertjan, and Herman van der Wusten. 1992. "Green Politics in Europe." *Political Geography* 11:7–11.

Economist Atlas of the New Europe, The. 1992. New York, USA: Henry Holt.

Edwards, K. C. 1961. "Historical Geography of the Luxembourg Iron and Steel Industry." *Institute of British Geographers, Transactions and Papers* 29:1–16.

Evans, I. M. 1980. "Aspects of the Steel Crisis in Europe, with Particular Reference to Belgium and Luxembourg." *Geographical Journal* 146:396–407.

Fleming, Douglas K. 1967. "Coastal Steelworks in the Common Market Countries." *Geographical Review* 57:48–72.

Gatrell, Anthony C., and Andrew A. Lovett. 1986. "The Geography of Hazardous Waste Disposal in England and Wales." *Area* 18:275–283.

Gregory, Derek. 1982. *Regional Transformation and Industrial Revolution: A Geography of the Yorkshire Woolen Industry.* Minneapolis, USA: University of Minnesota Press.

Grotz, Reinhold E., and D. Wadley. 1987. "Economic and Spatial Change in German

Manufacturing, 1970–1986." *Tijdschrift voor Economische en Sociale Geografie* 78:162–175.

Hall, Peter. 1962. *The Industries of London since 1861*. London, GB: Hutchinson.

Hall, Peter, Michael Breheny, Ronald McQuaid, and Douglas Hart. 1987. *Western Sunrise: The Genesis and Growth of Britain's Major High Tech Corridor*. London, GB: Allen & Unwin.

Harrison, Richard T. 1985. "The Labour Market Impact of Industrial Decline and Restructuring: The Example of the Northern Ireland Shipbuilding Industry." *Tijdschrift voor Economische en Sociale Geografie* 76:332–344.

Hartshorne, Richard. 1934. "Upper Silesian Industrial District." *Geographical Review* 24:423–438.

Hudson, Pat, ed. 1989. *Regions and Industries: A Perspective on the Industrial Revolution in Britain*. Cambridge, GB: Cambridge University Press.

Ionescu, Dan. 1991. "Romania: The A to Z of the Most Polluted Areas." *Report on Eastern Europe* 2 (19): 20–25.

Jalabert, Guy, and Maïté Grégoris. 1987. "Turin: de la ville-usine à la technopole." *Annales de Géographie* 96:680–704.

Jones, Philip N. 1993. "On Defining a Western European Automobile Industry: Problems and Potentials." *Erdkunde* 47:25–39.

King, Russell L. 1985. *The Industrial Geography of Italy*. New York, USA: St. Martin's.

Langton, John. 1979. *Geographical Change and Industrial Revolution: Coalmining in South West Lancashire, 1590–1799*. Cambridge, GB: Cambridge University Press.

———. 1984. "The Industrial Revolution and the Regional Geography of England." *Transactions of the Institute of British Geographers* 9:145–167.

Lindkvist, Knut B. 1996. "Norwegian Fisheries and the Basis of Regional Development." *Norsk Geografisk Tidsskrift* 50:171–186.

Manners, Ian R. 1982. *North Sea Oil and Environmental Planning: The United Kingdom Experience*. Austin, USA: University of Texas Press.

Martin, John E., ed. 1966. *Greater London: An Industrial Geography*. London, GB: Bell.

Morris, John. 1987. "Global Restructuring and the Region: Manufacturing Industry in Wales." *Tijdschrift voor Economische en Sociale Geografie* 78:16–29.

Nefedova, T. G., V. Streletsky, and A. Treivish. 1992. "La Ruhr, la Haute Silésie et le Donbass dans la trajectoire historique des vieilles régions industrielles européennes du charbon et de l'acier." *Revue Belge de Géographie* 116:41–48.

North, J., and D. J. Spooner. 1978. "The Geography of the Coal Industry in the U.K. in the 1970s." *GeoJournal* 2:255–272.

Peterson, D. J. 1993. *Troubled Lands: The Legacy of Soviet Environmental Destruction*. Boulder, Colo., USA: Westview.

Petrow, Richard. 1968. *In the Wake of the Torrey Canyon*. New York, USA: David McKay.

Pickles, John. 1995. "Restructuring State Enterprises: Industrial Geography and Eastern European Transitions." *Geographische Zeitschrift* 83:114–131.

Pollard, Sidney. 1981. *Peaceful Conquest: The Industrialization of Europe, 1760–1970*. Oxford, GB: Oxford University Press.

Popescu, Claudia. 1993. "Romanian Industry in Transition." *GeoJournal* 29:41–48.

Porteous, J. Douglas. 1989. *Planned to Death: The Annihilation of a Place Called Howdendyke*. Toronto, CDN: University of Toronto Press.

Pounds, Norman J. G. 1952. *The Ruhr: A Study in Historical and Economic Geography*. London, GB: Faber.

———. 1957. "Historical Geography of the Iron and Steel Industry of France." *Annals of the Association of American Geographers* 47:3–14.

————. 1958. *The Upper Silesian Industrial Region.* Bloomington, USA: Indiana University Press.

Rodwin, Lloyd, and Hidehiko Sazanami, eds. 1991. *Industrial Change and Regional Economic Transformation: The Experience of Western Europe.* London, GB: HarperCollins.

Sadler, David. 1990. "Privatising British Steel: The Politics of Production and Place." *Area* 22:47–55.

————. 1995. "Old Industrial Places and Regions: The Limits to Reindustrialisation." In *Europe at the Margins: New Mosaics of Inequality,* ed. Costis Hadjimichalis and David Sadler. Chichester, GB: Wiley, 133–148.

Sadler, David, Adam Swain, and Ray Hudson. 1993. "The Automobile Industry and Eastern Europe." *Area* 25:339–349.

Sagers, Matthew J. 1996a. "The Iron and Steel Industry in Russia and the CIS in the Mid-1990s." *Post-Soviet Geography and Economics* 37:195–263.

————. 1996b. "Russian Crude Oil Production in 1996." *Post-Soviet Geography and Economics* 37:523–587.

————. 1997. "Turnaround in Russian Oil Production in 1997." *Post-Soviet Geography and Economics* 38:499–505.

Sallnow, John, and Sarah Arlett. 1989. "Green Today, Gone Tomorrow?" *Geographical Magazine* 61 (11): 10–14.

Scott, Allen J. 1988. *New Industrial Spaces: Flexible Production and Regional Development in North America and Western Europe.* London, GB: Pion.

Sjøholt, Peter. 1996. "The Norwegian North Sea Petroleum Industry." *Norsk Geografisk Tidsskrift* 50:225–242.

de Smidt, Marc, and Egbert Wever. 1990. *An Industrial Geography of the Netherlands.* London, GB: Routledge.

Smith, Adrian. 1994. "Uneven Development and the Restructuring of the Armaments Industry in Slovakia." *Transactions of the Institute of British Geographers* 19:404–424.

Steed, G.P.F. 1974. "The Northern Ireland Linen Complex." *Annals of the Association of American Geographers* 64:397–408.

Thompson, Jon. 1991. "East Europe's Dark Dawn: The Iron Curtain Rises to Reveal a Land Tarnished by Pollution." *National Geographic* 179 (6): 36–69.

Tuppen, John N. 1980. *France: Studies in Industrial Geography.* Boulder, Colo., USA: Praeger.

Vanlaer, Jean. 1984. *200 millions de voix: une géographie des familles politiques européennes.* Brussels, B: Société Royale Belge de Géographie et Laboratoire de Géographie Humaine de l'Université Libre.

Vilchek, G. E., et al. 1996. "The Environment in the Russian Arctic." *Polar Geography* 20:22–23.

Wabe, J. W. 1986. "The Regional Impact of De-industrialization in the European Community." *Regional Studies* 20:27–36.

Warren, Kenneth. 1970. *The British Iron and Steel Industry since 1840: An Economic Geography.* London, GB: Bell.

Wells, Peter, and Michael Rawlinson. 1994. *The New European Automobile Industry.* New York, USA: St. Martin's.

Williams, Allan M. 1987. *The Western European Economy: A Geography of Post-war Development.* London, GB: Hutchinson.

CHAPTER 10

Service Industries

Service industries involve neither the extraction of resources nor manufacturing but instead include a broad range of activities such as government, health care, education, transportation, energy production, banking, retailing, wholesaling, advertising, legal services, consulting, information processing, research and development, and tourism. Oddly, the term *postindustrial* denotes the rise to dominance of these service industries in modern Europe, coincident with the decline of primary and secondary industries. No general agreement exists on how to categorize these diverse enterprises. Some geographers prefer to distinguish *market*, or private, services from *governmental*, or public services. Others suggest that the primary distinction should be between *producer* and *consumer* services. Many label all service industries as *tertiary* economic activities.

The most outstanding fact concerning service industries in Europe is their disproportionate growth since about 1950. While most service activities have always been present, a marked increase has occurred, especially in recent decades and in the western part of Europe. Well over half of the labor force in many countries and provinces now finds employment in service industries (fig. 10.1). In Austria, for example, jobs in the services sector rose from 30% of the workforce in 1961 to 62% in 1998. Eastern Europe lags behind the western part of the culture area in this respect, but even there the proportion often exceeds 40%.

No service activity better epitomizes Europe than **transportation** and **communication**. European culture has for centuries thrived upon the most complex and complete network of any region of comparable size in the entire world. As suggested in chapter 1, the dense mesh of transportation facilities provides one defining trait for the European culture area (fig. 10.2). The resultant flow of trade goods and information can only be described as remarkable.

313

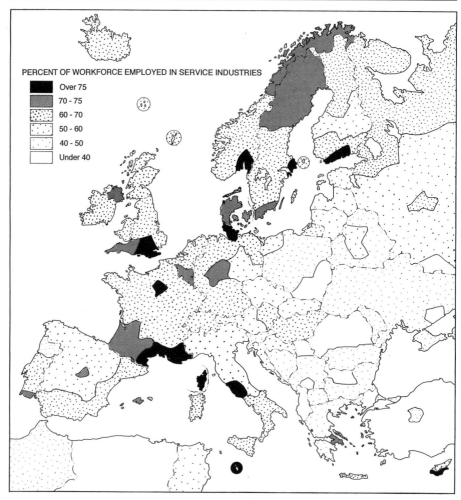

Figure 10.1.   Percentage of labor force employed in the service industries. These diverse activities include government, transport, trade, finance, retailing, energy supply, tourism, education, health, and other services. An east–west contrast can be detected within Europe.

Highways

Europe's roads have provided a crucial component of the service sector at least since the time of the Romans. Desiring to rule more than the Mediterranean shores, the Romans built a truly astounding network of stone-paved roads connecting all parts of their empire within Europe (fig. 10.3). They constructed some 320,000 kilometers of highway in the empire as a whole, and, astoundingly, some remain in use today. Construction on the oldest of these Roman roads—the *Appian Way* from Roma southeast to Brindisi on the Adriatic coast—began in 312 B.C. Laid out by surveyors in long, straight stretches where terrain permitted, the Roman highways offered a mobility

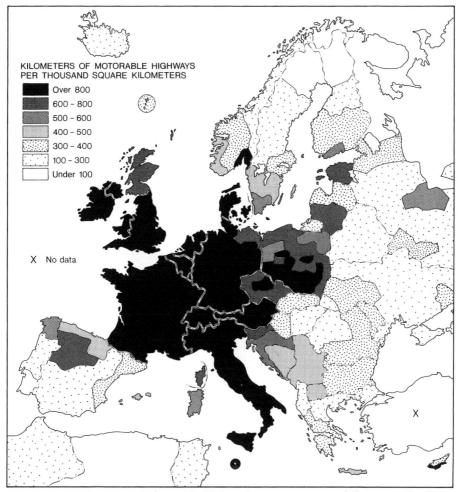

Figure 10.2.   Kilometers of motorable highways per 1,000 square kilometers. The European road density exceeds that of any other sizable part of the world. A pronounced core–periphery pattern exists.

KILOMETERS OF MOTORABLE HIGHWAYS
PER THOUSAND SQUARE KILOMETERS

Over 800
600 – 800
500 – 600
400 – 500
300 – 400
100 – 300
Under 100

X   No data

previously unknown to merchants, the military, and the common folk. Roman engineers bridged even major streams such as the Rhône, and some of these splendid stone spans remain in use today after 2,000 years of traffic, flood, and warfare. Among them are the bridges over the Tejo River at Alcántara and the Guadiana at Mérida, both in southwestern Spain. Contrary to the popular saying, not all roads led to Roma (fig. 10.3). The network had few major focal points.

The decline of trade during the Dark Ages curtailed the use of roads, as did political fragmentation. A rebirth of major mercantile activity in medieval times, coupled with the internal security provided by the feudal system, renewed the demand for roads. The new routes hardly rivaled their

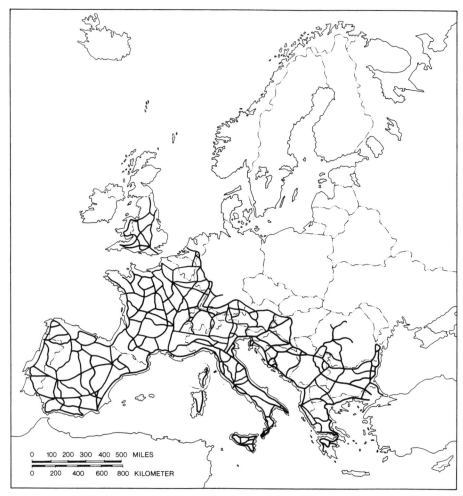

Figure 10.3.   The Roman roads in Europe. The political borders are modern. (*Source: Westermanns Grosser Atlas zur Weltgeschichte* 1956.)

Roman predecessors. Pavement was a rarity. Numerous streams remained unbridged, and as a consequence, river-ford sites typified many emerging towns. In time, new road patterns emerged. Regions that had undergone political unification, such as France and the United Kingdom, developed highly centralized road patterns by the eighteenth or nineteenth centuries, with the major routes radiating out from the national capital (fig. 10.4). Paris was the all-important hub of French roads, and Dublin served a similar function within Ireland. No transport focal point existed within the network of politically fragmented Germany, reflecting the lack of centralized organization. Some new routes unused in earlier times arose. St. Gotthard Pass through the Alps, ignored by the Romans, emerged as the great north–south route between Italy and the Rhine Valley in the Middle Ages, sup-

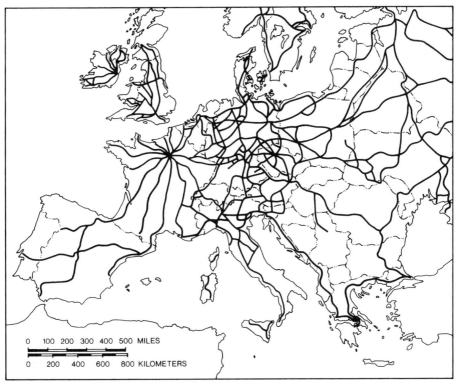

Figure 10.4.   Main post roads in Europe, 1850. Note the highly centralized pattern in France and the lack of a dominant focal point in central Europe; also note the core–periphery pattern of road density. Compare it to figure 12.6. The political borders are modern. (*Source:* Hoffman 1969, 107.)

planting Splügen Pass to the east. The importance of the Gotthard route survives to the present.

Improvements came very slowly. John McAdam, for whom *macadam* roads are named, built all-weather highways in England in the early 1800s, paved with several thin layers of tightly packed crushed rock set in place by the application of water. The dawn of the modern era of bridge building occurred in 1826 when the British constructed a steel suspension bridge linking the large island of Anglesey to the coast of Wales.

Continued improvement and elaboration of Europe's highway system occurred in the 1900s largely because of the automobile, and a pronounced west–east contrast developed. Western Europe's middle class gained the financial ability to purchase cars after the middle of the twentieth century. In 1950, only 6.1 million private automobiles existed in noncommunist Europe, about 1 for every 48 persons, but by 1970 the total had increased tenfold and by the middle 1980s to 112.4 million, so that 1 Westerner in 3 owned a car, a proportion that has remained fairly constant since (fig. 10.5).

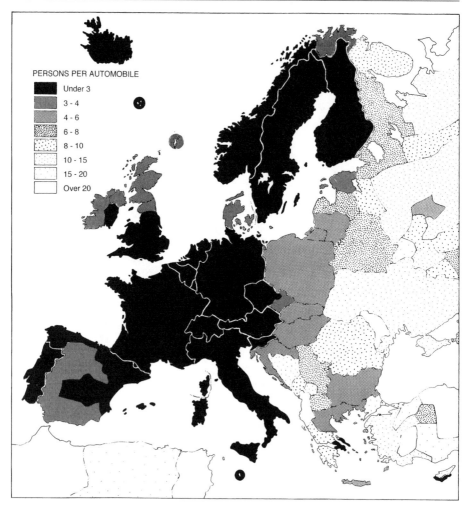

Figure 10.5. Persons per automobile. Private car ownership remains more common in western Europe, but it also distinguishes Europeans from non-Europeans in adjacent Africa and Asia.

Truck traffic also increased rapidly in Western Europe and by 1990 it carried 64% of all freight, as contrasted to less than half as late as 1970.

Eastern Europe long remained a region of far lower automobile ownership, much less truck usage, and sparser highway network (figs. 10.2 and 10.5). Private car ownership still today offers one of the contrasts between European east and west. Highway infrastructure deteriorated in much of the east since the 1970s, and one of the first major tasks undertaken by the German government after reunification in 1990 involved upgrading roads in its new eastern provinces. Automobile ownership has increased rapidly in eastern Europe, even in the poorest countries such as Albania, where the number of passenger cars rose from 3,000 to 70,000 between 1985 and 1997.

Private automobiles now account for 80% of all passenger-kilometers in western Europe and almost half in the east. Trucks and vans dominate goods transport, except in eastern Europe. This rise of private automobile and truck transport caused a major boom in highway construction that continues to the present in most parts of Europe, especially the west. An already dense network has become even denser. In the process, many new bridges have been erected, some of which rank as grand works of art (fig. 10.6). Controlled-access expressways proliferated greatly in the last 3 decades of the twentieth century, building upon the prototype of Germany's *autobahn* system, the first links of which date to the Nazi era (fig. 10.7).

While east–west contrasts remain in highway transportation, the more compelling and vivid contrast is that between European core and periphery (figs. 10.2 and 10.7). The densest network exists in the center, while peripheries have a sparser pattern. Some settlements in Norway, for example, remain unconnected to the country's highway system, though an ambitious, ongoing program of road, tunnel, and bridge construction is underway in that country, linking even some sparsely settled offshore islands to the road network.

Efforts to integrate Europe's highway system have progressed for decades, with the aim of more effectively meshing together the various national networks of roads. The "European highway" designation is one

Figure 10.6.   Recently constructed highway bridge over the lower Seine River in Normandie, France. Europe enters the new millennium with a superb road network, but one nevertheless congested by traffic. (Photo by T.G.J.-B. 1999.)

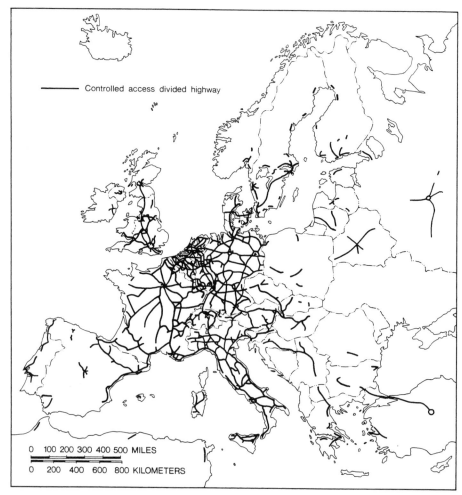

Figure 10.7. Controlled-access, divided highways. Germany built the prototype of such expressways in the 1930s and they remain a trait of the European core.

result. In addition to their national number, many routes also have a standard *E* designation. For example, the *E8* highway runs from 's Gravenhage eastward through Hannover, Berlin, Poznan, Warszawa, and Minsk to Moskva. The *E1* extends from Sicilia in the far south to Roma, Genova, Lyon, Paris, Le Havre, and, after a ferry connection, to London. New routes of this type include the *Via Baltica*, an upgraded highway from Tallinn to Riga, Vilnius, and into Poland.

Road Congestion

In spite of the ambitious programs of highway and expressway construction, the road network of the European core has become overwhelmed by the volume of automobile and truck traffic. Bottlenecks have formed at natural obstacles such as the Alps and sea channels, and traffic jams of enormous size develop even on many expressways. Germans regularly endure the *Autobahnstau* ("expressway dam") when freeway traffic comes to a halt even in the countryside. Many international borders also produce jams (fig. 10.8).

As John Whitelegg noted over a decade ago, high levels of motorization constitute a major source of "disturbance, nuisance, health hazards, landtake, and ecological disruption," not to mention an appalling death rate from accidents and frequent gridlock traffic jams on the freeways.

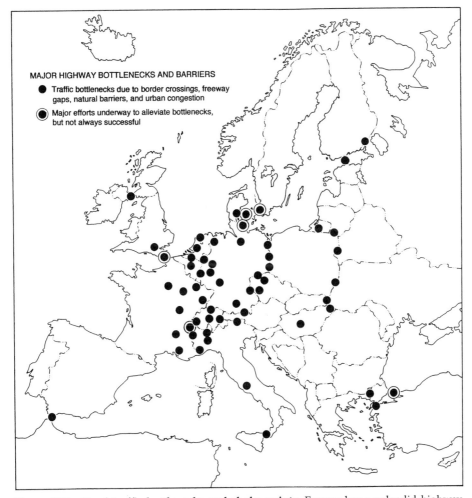

Figure 10.8.   Road traffic bottlenecks and choke points. Europe has a splendid highway network, but its large population, high automobile ownership rate, indented coastline, and numerous international borders, coupled with the position of the Alps in the central core, create many choke points.

Germany, the epicenter of these problems, has seen picturesque towns such as Idar–Oberstein mutilated by highway construction and watched forests die from automobile exhaust while suffering nearly 350,000 traffic accidents annually resulting in death or injury in its western provinces alone. Even so, public opinion has begun to turn against additional road building in Germany. Switzerland heavily taxes transit trucks to reduce traffic, noise, and pollution.

Efforts to relieve some of the bottlenecks have been partially successful. Perhaps most ambitious have been the bridge–tunnel between Denmark and Sweden and the English Channel tunnel, through which cars and trucks move by rail. In addition, the *Schengen* pact, in which the core countries of the European Union removed all internal border passport control, alleviated numerous choke points (fig. 10.8). In the final analysis, however, the road congestion problem cannot be solved. Europe has too many people, too many vehicles, too many barriers, and not enough space.

Railroads

Europeans invented the railroad, just as they did the all-weather highway, and Europe possesses almost one-third of the world's rail tracks by length. Railroad network density is greatest in central Europe, and a pronounced core–periphery pattern exists (fig. 10.9). Outlying islands such as Iceland, Faeroes, Shetlands, Baleares, Malta, Kriti, Åland, and Cyprus have no railroad lines nor do the northernmost provinces of Norway. European railroads are state-owned rather than private, with the result that relatively little duplication of routes developed.

The European railroad system derives from the English Industrial Revolution. In 1767, a British ironworks cast the first rails, initially for use by horse-drawn trams. A crude steam locomotive appeared by 1804 and ten years later a locomotive first pulled a train. By 1825, the British opened regularly operated railroad service connecting the industrial towns of Darlington and Stockton on the River Tees in northeastern England. The British invention, prompted by increased demands for bulk transport, spread rapidly to mainland Europe, reaching France by 1832, Belgium and Germany by 1835, Austria–Hungary by 1838, Italy and the Netherlands by 1839, and Switzerland by 1844. By midcentury, a railroad network had developed in England, and significant beginnings had been made in the Paris Basin, Belgium, and northern Germany (fig. 10.10). The great era of rail construction ended by 1900 in Europe, by which time nearly all of the present network existed. Albania, the final country to join the railroad age, built its first line in 1947.

Deindustrialization and the rise of motorized highway transport caused a notable shrinkage of the railroad network in the twentieth century, particularly in western Europe. As early as the 1920s, over 700 kilometers

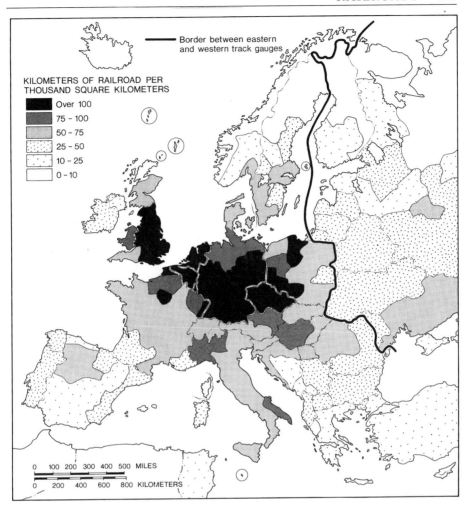

KILOMETERS OF RAILROAD PER
THOUSAND SQUARE KILOMETERS

- Over 100
- 75 – 100
- 50 – 75
- 25 – 50
- 10 – 25
- 0 – 10

Border between eastern
and western track gauges

Figure 10.9.   Railroad density and gauge. A core–periphery contrast is obvious, and the gauge difference adds an east–west component to the pattern. The western gauge is typically 1.64 meters and the eastern 1.74 meters.

of line had been abandoned in Great Britain. In western Germany, the number of passenger rail cars on the *Bundesbahn* (Federal Railroad) declined from 22,600 in 1958 to 18,700 as early as 1967, and the volume of riders decreased in almost every western country. Sweden in the 1990s terminated most passenger rail service in the northern two-thirds of its country. Freight movement by rail in western Europe dropped from 30% of all tonnage in 1970 to 18% by 1990.

The railroads lost ground to trucks as freight movers in part because of *dematerialization*—the need for smaller and more frequent deliveries. The shift away from heavy industries to those manufacturing high-quality and luxury goods brought this change. Another problem the railroads faced

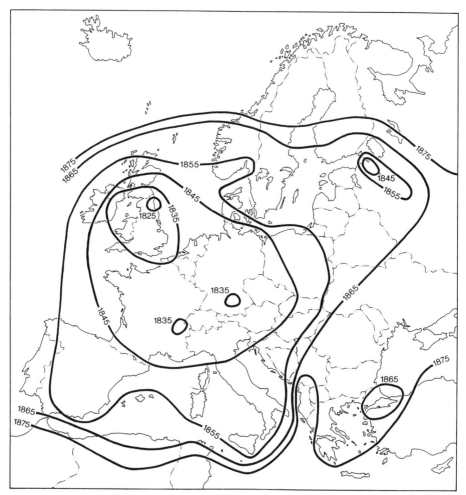

Figure 10.10. Diffusion of the railroad in nineteenth-century Europe. A striking core–periphery pattern appears. Political borders shown are modern.

was that no real European-wide network ever existed, but instead a series of patched-together national systems, due to the rarity of new line construction since 1900. Postindustrial Europe made transport demands that the railroads were poorly designed to meet.

Still, Europeans have by no means given up on rail transport, either freight or passenger. The international *Trans-Europ Express,* introduced in the 1960s, attracted business travelers by offering luxurious rolling stock and quicker service. Then, in the early 1980s, France led the way in ultra-high-speed passenger rail service (TGV), followed a decade later by Germany, with its ICE. The United Kingdom has followed more slowly. Expansion of high-speed passenger rail transport has top priority in the European Union, and enormous sums are being spent. A master plan for a Europe-wide network now exists (fig. 10.11). When completed, this high-speed system will extend to all corners of Europe, including the east, where railroads retained their traditional importance in spite of deteriorated track quality. High-speed trains operating in Europe today travel at 160 to 350 kph and obviously have no grade crossings. They compete successfully, time- and cost-wise, with many airline connections.

The most compelling evidence of Europe's future commitment to rail transport is provided by the recent completion of the 50-kilometer English Channel *Eurotunnel*, or "Chunnel," which links England and France by railroad (fig. 10.12). Trains move through the tunnel at speeds of up to 160 kph carrying freight, passengers, and ferried automobiles. Once a major

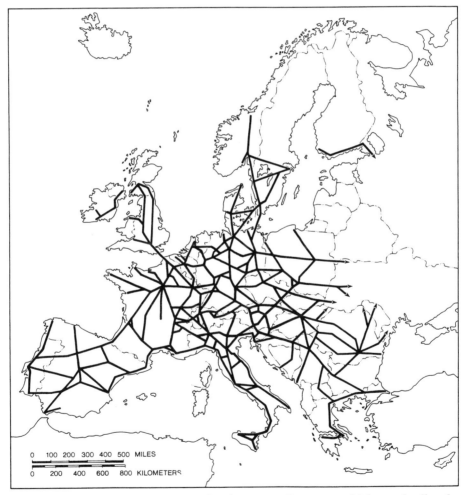

Figure 10.11.   The European master plan for twenty-first-century high-speed railroads. This plan will be difficult to implement, especially in the Balkans and eastern Europe. Part of the system, particularly in France, is already operational.

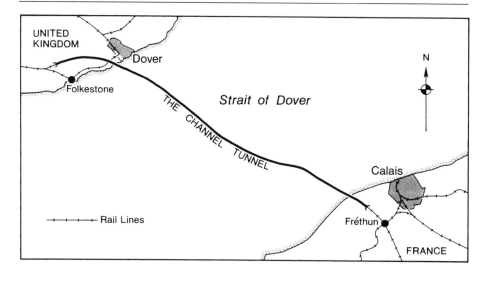

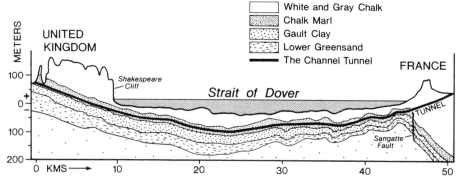

Figure 10.12. The Channel Tunnel, providing a railroad link between England and France. Completed in the 1990s, it links Britain directly to the ultra-high-speed rail system of the mainland. The Chunnel, or Eurotunnel, as it is also called, transports both passengers and automobiles.

hindrance to land transport, the English Channel can now be crossed in only 33 minutes, terminal to terminal. The ultra-high-speed system is totally electric and double-tracked.

Waterways

Complementing the road and rail systems is an intricate network of waterways. It consists of Europe's rivers and peripheral seas, connected by a series of canals (see fig. 2.20).

The interconnected oceans and seas flanking Europe on 3 sides provide a splendid opportunity for transportation. The outline of Europe shows deep indentations on all shorelines, with the result that no part of the culture area lies any great distance from the sea. Small wonder that Europeans have long taken advantage of the pattern of peripheral seas to move their commodities from place to place.

The Mediterranean, the first sea used extensively for transportation, proved admirably suited to early navigators who needed few advanced marine skills because ships could sail about its waters without ever losing sight of land. High, rocky coasts with promontories made even more visible by the erection of temples and shrines atop, guided the sailors of ancient Greece, as did the many mountainous islands (see fig. 3.2). By "coasting" parallel to the shore or keeping island landfalls in sight, the sailors overcame much of the danger of sea transport. At a remarkably early date, Mediterranean seamen ventured out beyond Gibraltar as far as Cornwall in Great Britain, attracted by tin mines. Still, at the time depicted in the Homeric epics, about 1200 B.C., the Greeks apparently remained ignorant of even the western part of the Mediterranean. Ulysses' relatively short voyage to western lands such as Malta and Tunisia placed him in unknown waters, where fear and imagination led him to people the shores with one-eyed cannibalistic giants and sorceresses who changed men to swine. In later centuries, the Greeks searched out every bay and cove around the Mediterranean and used the sea as the highway of their far-flung commercial empire. The Romans succeeded the Phoenicians and Greeks. They in turn gave way to other great Mediterranean seafaring peoples, including the Byzantine Greeks and Venetians.

The use of the North and Baltic Seas for trade came later. By the eighth century, a trade in furs, slaves, and amber developed in the Baltic, while merchants in the North Sea handled cloth, wine, and wool. The Middle Ages brought the *Hanseatic League,* or Hansa, a trading union of many towns, in countries around the shores of the North and Baltic Seas. With the Age of Discovery, the Atlantic assumed its present position as the major trade route of Europe.

Complementing the peripheral seas are numerous navigable rivers, improved through dredging, removing rapids, constructing locks, and digging connecting canals. The major use of rivers and canals for transportation began in the Middle Ages, for the classical Mediterranean peoples did not have navigable rivers at their disposal. Only after the commercial focus of Europe shifted north of the Alps did river traffic become important. The Great European Plain is drained by a series of parallel navigable rivers trending southeast to northwest, most of which rise in the hills and mountains south of the plain. Some achieved major use by the 1100s and 1200s, and feudal lords who resided along the banks of such streams as the Rhine collected tolls from ships passing beneath their strongholds. In modern times many rivers have been internationalized, and the countries through which they flow cannot charge unnecessary tolls or restrict traffic.

Early on, the navigable rivers of Europe became bound together by canals. The building of canals antedated railroad construction, beginning in earnest in the late 1700s and reaching a peak in the first half of the nineteenth century. Most canals connected the different rivers on the Great European Plain. The English led the way in canal building as well as railroads, and by 1790 they had established a good network. Some 8,000 kilometers of canals existed in the United Kingdom by the middle 1800s, and the Industrial Revolution experienced a "canal phase." Inland waterways became the prime carriers of bulky products with a low per-unit value, particularly raw or semiprocessed materials. Canals and rivers provided most of the important linkages for early industrial districts.

By the end of the great era of European canal building, barges could cross the entire Great European Plain, from France to Russia (fig. 2.20). The densest concentration of canals anywhere in the world lay in the region from the Seine and English Scarplands eastward to the Odra (Oder) River. That link remains open today, part of which is Germany's *Mittelland Canal*. Other major water linkages included the *Kiel Canal*, shortening the distance between the Baltic and North Seas, and the *Canal du Midi* through the Gap of Carcassonne. Russia long ago linked the headwaters of the Volga, Don, and Neva Rivers with canals to allow movement through the East European Plain.

After the great age of canals ended, many became derelict, bypassed by railroads and highways. Once-famous waterways such as the Göta Canal of Sweden became largely recreational routes used by vacationers. Canals experienced a decline even more profound than that afflicting the railroads. By 1948, some 6,500 kilometers of the British waterway system had been abandoned. Usage continues to decrease; inland waterways carried 12.5% of Europe's freight tonnage in 1970 but only 8% by 1990, though the actual tonnage decline was slight. Waterways are now used only for bulk transport, as well as for car ferries and tourism.

Even so, several European countries have continued to upgrade their waterways for transport use, most notably Germany and France. Canalization of the Moselle River with 14 locks between Thionville in Lorraine and Koblenz in Germany, where it joins the Rhine, greatly enhanced the navigability of the river in the 1960s, ironically just before deindustrialization struck hard at the Saar–Lorraine region. Romania opened the *Danube–Black Sea Canal* in 1984, shortening the route by avoiding the river delta, and in 1992 Germany completed the *Main–Danube Canal*, linking the Rhine River–North Sea with the Black Sea by way of Nürnberg. The latter canal, which parallels an outmoded predecessor, can accommodate huge "Eurobarges" carrying as much freight as 90 truck trailers or 60 rail freight cars.

The elaborate network of seas, rivers, and canals focuses on Europe's numerous port facilities, most of which lie at the transshipment points between inland waterways and the open ocean. A string of major ports lines the shores of the North and Baltic Seas, at the mouths or on the lower courses of the rivers of the Great European Plain. These include, from west to east, Bordeaux on the Garonne, Nantes on the Loire, Le Havre and Rouen on the Seine, London on the Thames, Antwerpen on the Schelde, Rotterdam–Europoort on the Rhine, Bremerhaven on the Weser, Hamburg on the Elbe, Szczecin on the Odra, Gdansk on the Wisla, Riga on the Daugava, and St. Petersburg on the Neva (fig. 2.20). In contrast, most major ports of southern Europe, including Barcelona, Genova, and Napoli, are generally not river-ine but instead lie some distance removed from the silted river deltas. An exception is Marseille, where a major port, Fos, operates west of the city at the mouth of the Rhône, at the southern access to the core of Europe. Traffic volume at Marseille–Fos increased enormously since World War II and it now ranks as Europe's second largest port. Europoort, serving Rotterdam and the rest of the Randstad Holland, as well as the European industrial heartland, ranks as the greatest port of Europe, reflecting the huge volume of traffic carried by the Rhine and Maas Rivers. Rotterdam began to grow rapidly in the last 3 decades of the nineteenth century, coincident with the rise of the Ruhr and other industrial areas along the Rhine. By 1938, the Dutch port ranked as the largest in Europe in terms of tonnage handled, and in 1962 it became the leading tonnage port in the world, surpassing New York City. Europe's seaports are all *containerized*, handling freight in standard-sized rectangular containers that are easily stacked in ships or moved by truck and railroad flatcar (fig. 10.13).

Pipelines

After 1950, as Europe shifted steadily away from coal as its primary energy source, adopting instead petroleum and natural gas, a system of pipelines was built. Most lines connect the European core area, where consumption is centered, to peripheral and external sources. One major supplier consists of oil and gas fields in the hinter reaches of Russia's East European Plain and beyond, in western Siberia and central Asia. Oil and gas pipelines operated by Russia's state-owned *Transneft* bring these fossil fuels westward to Europe (fig. 10.14). Much of the oil flows through the *Druzba* ("Friendship") Pipeline, which crosses southern Russia and Belarus to Lviv in Ukraine, home of a major pipeline depot, and on into the heart of Europe. This antiquated line can handle only about 1.25 million barrels of petroleum per day. Oil from Azerbaijan in the Caspian area is exported via pipelines across Georgia and the Russian Caucasus to ports on the Black Sea, most notably Novorossiysk. Plans for several major new pipelines in this part of Europe are underway in an effort to solve present problems of inadequate capacity.

North Sea oil flows to Great Britain, Denmark, Germany, and the Netherlands in a series of pipelines, some of which cross the floor of the sea. The Middle East remains the largest supplier of petroleum for Europe. To

Figure 10.13.   Containerized port of Bremerhaven, at the mouth of the Weser River in Germany. Ships are quickly loaded and unloaded, and the standardized containers can be put on trucks or railroad cars. (Photo by T.G.J.-B. 1999.)

accommodate this oil, pipelines lead northward from the Mediterranean, beginning at Trieste and Genova in Italy, Marseille in France, and Málaga in Spain. Two of these lines cross the Alps to the German city of Ingolstadt on the Danube River in the province of Bayern, a major refining center. The pipeline from Marseille passes north through the Rhône–Saône Corridor, Belfort Gate, and Upper Rhine Plain, reaching Karlsruhe in southwestern Germany and the Lorraine area of France. Since virtually all pipelines have been built since 1950, their routes reflect international planning. Cooperation within the European Union led to the selection of southern Germany as an oil-refining center, fed by the pipelines originating in France and Italy.

Air Transport

Europe has a dense network of air routes and a large number of airlines, including Lufthansa (Germany), Alitalia (Italy), Air France, Sabena (Belgium), Swissair, KLM (Netherlands), British Airways, Aer Lingus (Republic of Ireland), S.A.S. (Sweden, Denmark, and Norway), and others. The largest volume of traffic moves through London's Heathrow Airport, Rhein–Main near Frankfurt, Charles de Gaulle at Paris, Schiphol at Amsterdam, and

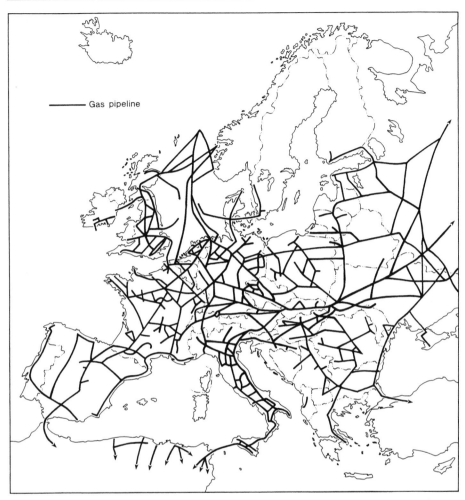

Figure 10.14.   Gas pipelines. The main sources lie in the east, in Siberia and central Asia, while the principal consumers are in the European core region. (*Source: International Petroleum Encyclopedia* 1999, 136–142.)

Leonardo da Vinci near Roma. Congestion at some of these airports, especially London Heathrow, caused additional ones to be built or enlarged. Competition has also arisen. München now rivals Frankfurt with its facility, situated in the virtual center of Europe.

When travel restrictions between east and west loosened after 1990, airlines proved better able than any other mode of passenger transport to exploit the demand for increased movement within Europe. Years will pass before the railroad and highway infrastructure in the east can be upgraded sufficiently to allow ease of movement, but airline connections are already in place. Even eastern cities formerly difficult to reach by air, such as Riga, now enjoy much enhanced airline linkages.

The main problem with airline transportation within Europe is that fares are kept artificially high. In 1996, a Roma–Brussels round trip ticket (about the same distance as Atlanta–Washington, D.C.) cost $1,600, while Oslo–København was priced at $300 (about the same distance as Houston–New Orleans, which cost $90). Adding to the problems are low airport capacities and antiquated air traffic control, neither of which kept pace with the rapid increase in demand that began after 1980. Many intercity air connections within the European core carry over 1 million passengers annually.

Communications

Much of Europe has excellent internal communications connections, especially telecommunications, including computer-to-computer data exchange, e-mail, fax, and telephone. The growth of the European telecommunications system was particularly rapid in the 1990s.

Both Germany and the United Kingdom surpassed the 3 million mark in number of persons having an online account or Internet access in 1997, though other countries of the European core area, most notably France and Italy, lagged far behind. Finland and the Scandinavian countries rank highest if Internet connections are measured on a per capita basis (fig. 10.15). The pattern reveals both north–south and east–west contrasts. Indeed, eastern Europe and Turkey hardly exist, from an Internet perspective. The still-developing Integrated Services Digital Network (ISDN), designed to replace existing telecommunications systems by simultaneously transmitting data, text, voice, and image messages, is being implemented. ISDN was available in a narrowband version as early as about 1990 in some major cities.

In general, however, Europe as a whole has failed to keep pace with the United States in telecommunications and is not known as a major center of innovation. This will almost certainly have a negative impact on industrial logistics, commercial transactions, and transport systems in the twenty-first century.

Euromobile

All of Europe's transport systems are in the midst of revolutionary change, leading to ever-increased mobility and exchange. The term *Euromobile*, used as the title of a recent book, perhaps best describes this evolving situation, as the movement of people, information, and commodities within and between all countries becomes intense. The inherent unity of the European culture area is vividly reflected in the system of transport and communications.

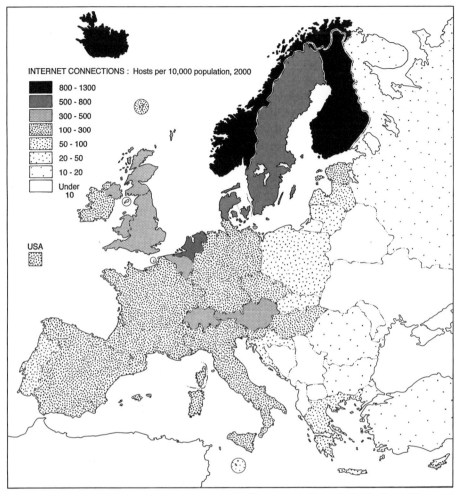

Figure 10.15.   Internet connections, proportional to population, 2000. Northern Europe is the most "wired" region and eastern Europe the least. Italy and France lag far behind the remainder of the European core. (*Source:* Internet Software Consortium, <www.isc.org> [last accessed: Dec. 2000].)

Still, major problems persist. The enhanced mobility benefits mainly the European core, though it has tied together east and west, separated by a half-century's Cold War. Euromobility—the more intensive transport–communications system—reflects a need for still more flexibility and reliability, still higher frequency deliveries, and even better-coordinated shipments. Multinodality is essential, though these nodes will all lie in the core region.

The desired system remains far from complete. In addition to the previously mentioned barriers and choke points (fig. 10.8), connections between core and peripheries remain rather poorly developed. Moreover, the transport system in the core region, good as it is, cannot at present handle the demand at peak times. Add to this system serious problems of infrastructure quality and density in eastern Europe and the difficulties mount. Unless the desired level of Euromobility can be attained, and soon, economic growth will be adversely affected.

Energy Production

Europeans consume vast amounts of energy in sustaining their high standard of living. In fact, a high per capita consumption of electricity and other forms of energy provides one defining trait to help us bound the European culture area (Figure 10.16). A sizable service industry exists to supply the needed power.

Traditionally, indigenously produced *coal* provided the greater part of Europe's primary energy, but after about 1950, when consumption levels in western Europe began rising beyond all expectations, coal gradually lost its dominance. Petroleum and natural gas soon surpassed coal in most of western and southern Europe, though most oil had to be imported, placing Europeans in a vulnerable position. The sharp oil price increase instigated by the Organization of Petroleum Exporting Countries in 1973 sent shock waves through western Europe, and the Russian turnoff of the subsidized oil flow to its former empire and sphere of domination in eastern Europe in the early 1990s had a similarly traumatic impact.

One European reaction to the rapidly growing need for energy and the problem of foreign dependency has been increased development of indigenous sources such as hydroelectric, wind, and geothermal power (fig. 10.16). Denmark pioneered the effort to harness the westerly winds for electric power generation, and tens of thousands of graceful, 3-bladed wind turbines now line the North Sea and Atlantic coast and river estuaries, from Denmark to France and Spain. Germany generates the greatest amount of aeolic power, followed by Spain, but Denmark ranks highest on a per capita basis and manufactures over half of the world's wind turbines. Iceland gets 7% of its electricity from geothermal power, tapping the island's superheated volcanic subsurface.

The far more controversial nuclear power industry also grew in response to rising consumption. The United Kingdom put the first nuclear power plant online in 1956, followed by France 2 years later and western Germany in 1961. Some countries, most notably France, now depend upon nuclear plants for the far greater part of their electricity (fig. 10.16). Certain others, under pressure from "Greens" or in the fear of terrorists, became disenchanted with nuclear energy, and curtailed production. Italy phased out its modest industry altogether and voters in Sweden demanded that their country follow suit, though that has not happened. By contrast, some newly independent eastern countries, including Lithuania and Slovakia,

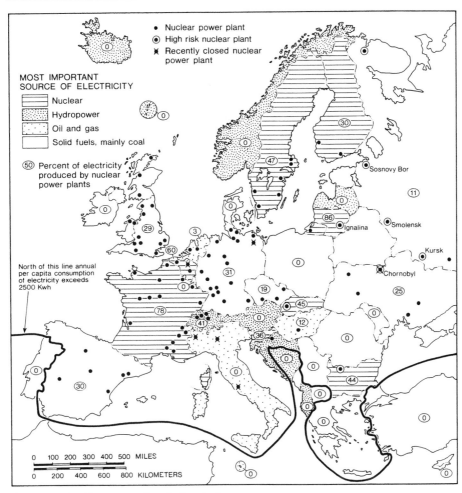

Figure 10.16.   The geography of electrical energy.

had to increase their nuclear dependence when cheap Russian oil ceased to flow. Regrettably, some eastern European power plants remain dangerous, due to obsolete design, inadequate maintenance, or poor management (fig. 10.16). Armenia, suffering acute power shortages, reopened an obsolete, earthquake-damaged nuclear reactor, and Bulgaria's power plants remain notoriously dangerous. The largest number of nuclear power reactors are in France, with 59, the United Kingdom 35, Russia 29, Germany 20, Ukraine 16, and Sweden 12.

These widely differing decisions at the national level produced a vivid geography of primary energy in Europe (fig. 10.16). This complex spatial pattern reflects the European quandary and lack of consensus concerning energy—how to provide an adequate supply safely, dependably, and at an affordable cost, while at the same time avoiding profound ecological damage. Europeans must find a solution to this pressing problem if their prosperity and high living standards are to survive. Stupidities proliferate. For example, pigs from the Netherlands go by truck to Italy for slaughter, in order that the prestigious label "Parma ham" can be affixed to the meat, yielding a higher price, while Bavarian potatoes journey to Italy for washing, only to be reshipped to Germany to sell, wasting fossil fuel and clogging Alpine highways in order to benefit from cheap Italian labor.

The Environmental Cost

On the eastern horizon lie the irradiated meadows and fields around Chornobyl, in northern Ukraine, the scene of the worst nuclear power accident in world history in 1986 (Chernobyl is the obsolete Russian form of the name). This meltdown, apparently caused by a low-intensity earthquake, spewed radioactive pollution over much of Europe, causing noteworthy contamination as far afield as northern Scandinavia. Closer to the site of the disaster, Ukraine permanently lost 5 million hectares of farmland and neighboring Belarus had to abandon 20% of its arable land (fig. 9.6). Over 1.6 million Belorussians today live in radioactive contamination zones, 80% of them in Homel Province, which experienced a 6% decline in population between 1989 and 1999. Belorussian children experience an elevated incidence of thyroid tumors as a legacy of Chornobyl, and perhaps 10,000 persons have died as a direct or indirect result of the catastrophe. The possibility of future nuclear power disasters remains great. Lithuania experienced an "event" at its Chornobyl-style Ignalina Plant in 1992, as did St. Petersburg at the Sosnovy Bor Plant and the Russian town of Balakovo near the lower Volga.

Europe's thirst for energy has also led to a series of catastrophic oil spills, both in petroleum-producing fields and from oil tanker accidents (fig. 9.6). The energy sector of the service industrial economy now regularly accounts for the most serious environmental problems in Europe.

Producer Services

Another sector of activity consists of higher-order services catering to large business enterprises. These *producer* services include banking, stock and bond exchanges, accounting, advertising, legal services, research and development, insurance, marketing and wholesaling, real estate brokerage, various types of consulting, and the processing and provision of knowledge and information. Such activities, as well as many corporate headquarters, cluster strikingly in the inner core of western Europe, revealing the dominant economic position of that small part of the culture area and of the "big three" members of the European Union—Germany, France, and the United Kingdom (fig. 10.17).

Early on, London and Paris became the financial centers of not just Europe, but the world, and in the twentieth century, and especially in the 1990s, London eclipsed its rival. Centered in "The City"—the central part of London—the financial service industry employs 600,000 workers today. London has over 550 banks, many of the world's largest insurance companies, and a famous stock exchange, and handles 30% of the world's currency trading. Deindustrialization hardly touched London's prosperity, due to this role as the world's financial leader. Dubbed the "Thames tiger," London is expected to gain 200,000 additional jobs in the 2000–2002 period.

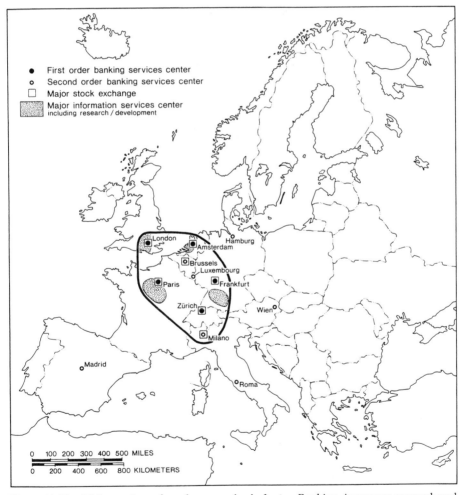

Figure 10.17.   Major centers of producer service industry. Banking, insurance, research and development, information processing, stock and bond exchanges, and other producer services are highly concentrated in an inner-core region of Europe.

If London, a city of 7 million, were an independent country, it would rank eighth among the nations of Europe in size of economy. Frankfurt, Zürich, and Paris also rank as major financial centers, but far behind London. The United Kingdom's rejection of the European Union's new currency, the *euro*—scheduled to go into general circulation in 2002—may erode London's position. The new European Central Bank will be in Frankfurt.

The service sector devoted to the generation, storing, and processing of diverse types of information forms a mainspring in this age of rapid technological change. It includes an institutionalized research and development component and subsidiary consultancy firms. This information sector tends to be clustered in the same European inner core that houses financial services (fig. 10.17). Locationally, the information services remain linked to the major centers of high-tech manufacturing, in particular the western suburbs of London, the southern and southwestern satellite cities of Paris, the Randstad Holland megalopolis, and southwestern Germany (figs. 9.4 and 10.17).

As Europe enters the twenty-first century, this striking concentration of producer services represents the most powerful statement of core–periphery contrasts. Even though producer services, in a time of instant communications, need not be concentrated geographically, the fact is that the core of Europe has grown smaller and more powerful in the postindustrial age. Increasingly, the European peripheries find it difficult to keep pace or maintain a status quo. Eastern Europe, in particular, faces well-nigh insurmountable problems in achieving prosperity given the dominant position of the inner-core region. Most of the decisions and innovations that shape and reshape the economy and future of Europe derive from the inner core, from a small, elite group engaged in the producer service industries.

Consumer Services

The remainder, and far greater, part of the service sector consists of, for want of a better term, *consumer* services. Among them we find governmental agencies, health care and welfare systems, educational facilities, retailing outlets, an elaborately developed industry serving tourism and recreational activities, and other enterprises serving social and individual needs.

Most Europeans employed in the service sector work in these consumer-oriented industries. They represent, in the main, a very different, far less elitist labor force than that engaged in providing producer-related services. Most consumer service jobs pay modest wages, usually lower than those recently lost in the primary and manufacturing industries. For many Europeans, the postindustrial age has brought diminished living standards.

The core–periphery contrast so evident in producer-oriented industries is absent in the consumer sector. Peripheral regions, in fact, often have a larger proportion of their total labor force engaged in service activities than does the European core (fig. 10.1). In Scandinavia and Iceland, the northern periphery of Europe, various benefit and welfare services typical of Nordic socialism find their richest development, causing unusually high levels of service-sector employment. A similar pattern prevails in regions reliant upon tourism, such as the Mediterranean isles. Instead of core–periphery, the greatest internal European contrast in consumer services involves west versus east (fig. 10.1). In the formerly communist countries, retailing and touristic services remain less abundant, accounting for most of the contrast in service-sector employment between the two halves of Europe.

Tourism

Tourism—the short-term movement to destinations away from the place of permanent residence for reasons unconnected to livelihood—forms an integral part of the European lifestyle. In the western half of Europe, tourism experienced very rapid growth after 1950 and especially in the two decades following 1965, during which the number of tourists doubled. Tourism constitutes an important growth sector in the economy and provides one of the main reasons why employment in consumer service industries has grown so large. Prior to World War II, tourism remained an elitist activity of the upper class, but today most Europeans participate. The large majority of tourists in Europe are Europeans, meaning that overseas visitors constitute the far lesser part of the industry.

Tourism displays a vivid geography in its sources, destinations, and flows. Most tourists come from the wealthy countries of northern and western Europe, and their vacation destinations most often lie to the south. Over half of all EU tourists seek out beaches for their holiday. Spain possesses the greatest concentration of southern seaside resorts, grouped in such coastal districts as the Costa del Sol and Costa del Azahar, as well as the Baleares Isles (fig. 10.18). Between 1959 and 1964, the number of tourists coming to Spain increased from 4 million to 14 million and the country's foreign currency earning grew tenfold, marking the beginning of the Iberian beach resort era. Today, 48 million foreign visitors come to Spain each year and a fifth of all cash receipts derive from tourism, making it the country's largest industry. As is generally the case with tourism, the economic impact in Spain remained highly localized, in a coastal corridor. Even today, the tourist infrastructure remains rather weakly developed in most interior areas, away from the beaches, in spite of the cultural richness of the country.

Many beach resorts also developed in Mediterranean France, northern Italy, the Dalmacija coast of Croatia, the Black Sea shore of Bulgaria, and

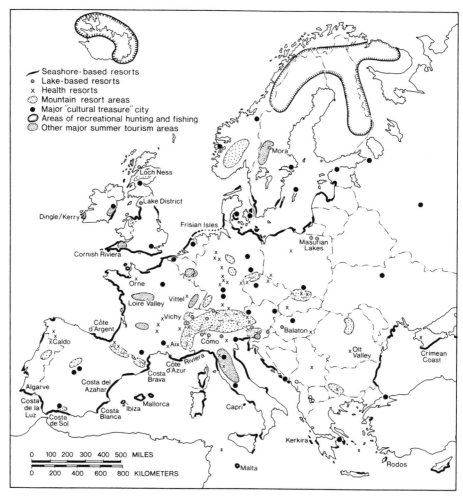

Figure 10.18. Major tourist destinations in Europe. The most important tourist flow is from north to south, favoring the Mediterranean beaches and Alpine mountain resorts. (*Sources:* Mayer 1975, 55, 98–99; Hoffman 1989, 184–185; White 1987.)

Ukrainian Krym. The tourist industry's main shortcoming is extreme vulnerability to economic downturns and political unrest. Tourist flows to beach resorts tend to be channelized. Two-thirds of the vacationers in Malta, where the tourist boom began in the 1960s, come from the United Kingdom, in part because the islands were once a British colony. Germans prefer the Italian beaches and also patronize Dalmacija heavily.

The second most common tourist flow is from lowland to highland. Mountain and hill areas attract abundant visitors in both winter and summer, and the Alps, benefiting from central location, dominate the highland tourist industry (fig. 10.18). Together, Switzerland and Austria receive annually twice as many visitors—27.2 million—as their combined resident population (fig. 10.19).

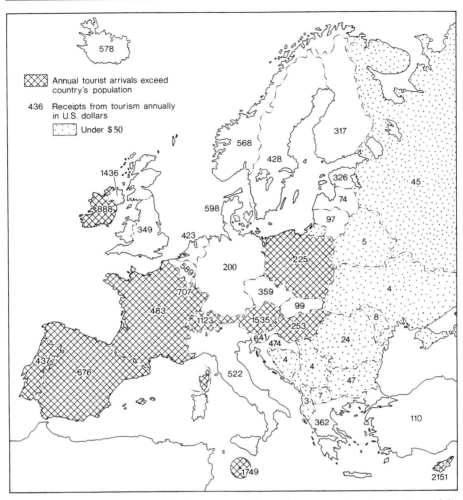

Figure 10.19. Tourism: 2 statistical measures. Dependence upon tourism varies widely within Europe, with both north–south and east–west contrasts.

At least a quarter of all EU tourists seek out rural areas for their vacations. Many farms in favored districts offer guest accommodations. A third of all farmers in Finland's Åland Islands house vacationers, as do about a fourth of those in the Austrian Alps and 16% of Scottish islanders and highlanders. In some Norwegian municipalities, the proportion runs as high as 40%.

Cultural tourism also ranks high in Europe, directed to places offering museums, well-preserved medieval or Renaissance quarters, theatrical and musical festivals, notable archaeological sites, and the like. Five million tourists visit Venèzia each year. Stonehenge in England became so overrun by visitors that protective measures became necessary, as also occurred at the Athínai Acropolis. The very names of certain cities—Paris, Wien, Firenze—

connote culture and refinement, attracting many tourists. More bucolic in message and appeal, the numerous open-air folk museums of Europe remind visitors of a romanticized, irrevocably lost rural past. Such outdoor museums, centered upon collections of traditional farmsteads relocated from the countryside, appeared first in Scandinavia, the prototype being Skansen in Stockholm, and the concept has spread through most of trans-Alpine Europe, from Kizhi Island in Russian Karelia to the Ulster Folk Museum in Northern Ireland and the Schweizerisches Freilichtmuseum in central Switzerland. Following the Skansen example, many of these open-air displays combine the appeals of folk museum and amusement park.

European tourists are less likely than their American counterparts to spend their vacations traveling to one place after another. A "tour" differs from a "holiday," and Europeans clearly prefer the latter. Their normal pattern is to get as quickly as possible from home to the desired destination—no small achievement given the frequent summer traffic jams on European roads—and then spend the entire holiday there, perhaps making day excursions to other, nearby attractions. Self-contained holiday resorts offering diverse amusements have recently gained in popularity, catering to the European mode of tourist travel.

Linking the penchant for single-destination tourism to the craving of the urban European for the rural countryside led also to the widespread practice of owning vacation homes. Most of these are modest cottages of recent construction, but some are old farmhouses abandoned as the agrarian population left the land and migrated to urban areas. In some Spanish provinces, over 30% of all residences are vacation homes. The rural environs of Helsinki in southern Finland average more than 5 vacation cottages per square kilometer. In eastern Europe, where tourism remains a less important activity due to lower living standards, the *dacha*, or country cottage, has long been common. In Bulgaria, for example, 32% of all city dwellers own a dacha in the countryside.

Another distinctly European type of tourism involves "taking the waters" at one or another of a huge assortment of health resorts, a practice most common in Germany and France. The generous health care systems of such countries make it possible for citizens to receive treatment, at government expense, for real, imagined, or pretended ailments and afflictions. The road signs posted at the limits of many towns in Germany tell the traveler that the name of the place is *Heilbad* or *Kurort* Such-and-Such, treating one or more problem of the lungs, kidneys, joints, stomach, or some other part of the anatomy. Amusements receive abundant attention as part of the cure, and the stay at such a place can be most enjoyable. Visitors spend a pleasant holiday, often drawing full wages from work all the while. Needless to say, spas have prospered and proliferated in this subsidized system of health-related tourism.

The removal of most political barriers to travel in eastern Europe recently opened up that huge area to mass tourism from the affluent west.

Virtually every formerly communist country benefits from this west–east tourist flow, and some places and regions, such as Praha, Budapest, Dresden, the Harz Mountains and Thüringer Wald of eastern Germany, St. Petersburg, Moskva, Riga, and Tallinn are especially popular.

A Mixed Blessing

When mass tourism arrives in full force, residents find it a mixed blessing. Economic benefits come with tourism but so do assorted problems. The experience of the Alps is instructive. As late as 1955, most of that mountain range remained a land of traditional, anachronistic, and in places impoverished dairy farmers living in picturesque log houses. The elitist tourism of the previous century had touched few of these residents and changed little in their way of life. Many young people fled the mountains, seeking a better living in the lowland cities. Then, in a single generation between 1955 and 1975, mass tourism came to the Alps, prompting a pervasive shift from dairying to dependence upon winter and summer visitors. Certain isolated, poverty-stricken places became prosperous, highly desired tourist destinations within a span of 2 decades. Money injected into the rural Alps by tourism provided a cure for the depressed economy, prompted the construction of an excellent road network, and halted the emigration of the young. As a result, most residents of the Alps benefit from tourism and regard it as a good thing.

Even so, they paid a high price. The local mountain culture underwent disruption. A folk society based upon mutual cooperation, egalitarianism, and respect for tradition gave way to a popular culture in which neighbors competed for tourist income and the old ways were discarded. An ancient adaptive system of land use in ecological balance with the fragile Alpine environment yielded to a new one that required massive and necessarily destructive habitat modification. Ski runs cut through protective belts of communal forests on slopes above the valley floors—the *Bannwälder*—scarred the mountainsides, caused erosion, and removed the natural protection against avalanches. Also, tourism greatly increased the number of people tramping about the Alpine countryside, further damaging the local flora and fauna. Highway construction brought additional massive damage. In short, the people of the Alps lost their ancient traditional culture and the land suffered extensive ecological modification as a result of mass tourism. A proven, sustainable system of land use gave way to an unsustainable and economically vulnerable one.

The legendary Greek isle of Kriti provides another cautionary tale. Home of the ancient Minoan civilization, Kriti was long sought out mainly by culturally oriented tourists who visited its numerous archaeological sites. As recently as 1971, only 15,000 tourists visited the isle annually. True, Kriti was impoverished and suffering from emigration to the mainland, but it was home to a traditional Mediterranean way of life that possessed both charm and dignity. Then, in the 1980s, came mass tourism—fun-in-the-sun, beach-based, and wildly successful. The number of tourists rose to 2 million by 1995, and much of the island's beautiful north coast was converted into an unbroken row of hotels—a "vacationer ghetto." Almost no planning or restrictions were imposed. Today, 160,000 inhabitants find work in the hotel industry alone, in addition to many others in businesses such as car rental—Kriti now has 580 such agencies. Most of Spain's best beaches and the Algarve region of southern Portugal have similarly been overdeveloped.

Tourism of any sort has the tendency to destroy the basis of its existence. Mass tourism will certainly do that. Is there an alternative? Intelligently written land use zoning and building codes can retard the worst excesses of mass tourism. The French Riviera provides an encouraging example, though at the cost of creating an "elitist landscape" inaccessible to the average tourist.

Ecotourism offers yet another alternative. Its goal is sustainability, causing no damage to nature or local cultures. Necessarily, ecotourism involves small numbers of tourists willing to "rough it" in less than resort conditions. Europeans, by and large, do not want that sort of vacation, and in any case Europe has few natural habitats or native cultures left.

Europe, then, has evolved into a postindustrial status, in which most people find employment in a diverse array of service industries. This development leads the Europeans into uncharted waters, just as the original Industrial Revolution did 250 years ago. As always, change remains the hallmark of the European way of life. Uncertainties, even pessimism, about the postindustrial future abound among Europeans, including the wealthiest lands, but change is sibling to risk just as innovation is to its sinister twin, destruction. Europeans would have things no other way, unsustainable though they be.

Pervasive change has also come to the agricultural sector of the European economy, with results as unsettling as those in industry. The following chapter is devoted to agrarian Europe.

Sources and Suggested Readings

Amin, A., and N. Thrift, eds. 1995. *Globalization, Institutions and Regional Development in Europe.* Oxford, GB: Oxford University Press.

Ashworth, G. J., and Peter J. Larkham, eds. 1994. *Building a New Heritage: Tourism, Culture and Identity in the New Europe.* London, GB: Routledge.

Bailly, Antoine S. 1995. "Producer Services Research in Europe." *Professional Geographer* 47:70–74.

Barke, Michael. 1991. "The Growth and Changing Pattern of Second Homes in Spain." *Scottish Geographical Magazine* 107:12–21.

ter Brugge, R. 1984. "Nuclear Energy in the Netherlands." *Tijdschift voor Economi-sche en Sociale Geografie* 75:300–304.

Bryson, Bill, and Gerd Ludwig. 1992. "Main–Danube Canal: Linking Europe's Wa-terways." *National Geographic* 182 (2): 3–31.

Burghardt, Andrew F. 1979. "The Origin of the Road and City Network of Roman Pannonia." *Journal of Historical Geography* 5:1–20.

Cater, Erlet, and Gwen Lowman, eds. 1994. *Ecotourism: A Sustainable Option?* Chich-ester, GB: John Wiley and the Royal Geographical Society.

Cermakian, Jean. 1975. *The Moselle River and Canal from the Roman Empire to the European Economic Community.* Toronto, CDN: University of Toronto, Department of Geography, Research Publication No. 14.

Dawson, Andrew H. 1993. "The Service Industries." In *A Geography of European Integration.* London, GB: Belhaven, 122–131.

Dicken, Peter, and Michel Quevit, eds. 1994. *Transnational Corporations and European Regional Restructuring.* Utrecht, NL: Royal Dutch Geographical Society.

European Conference of Ministers of Transport. 1991. *Prospects for East–west Euro-pean Transport.* Paris, F: Organization for Economic Cooperation and Develop-ment Publications.

Gade, Daniel W. 1982. "The French Riviera as Elitist Space." *Journal of Cultural Geography* 3 (1): 19–28.

Gaspar, Jorge. 1995. "New Forms of Transport and Communication, New Patterns of Disadvantage." In *Europe at the Margins: New Mosaics of Inequality,* ed. Costis Hadjimichalis and David Sadler. Chichester, GB: Wiley, 123–132.

Giannopoulos, G., and A. Gillespie, eds. 1993. *Transport and Communications Innova-tion in Europe.* London, GB: Belhaven.

Gibb, Richard, ed. 1994. *The Channel Tunnel: A Geographical Perspective.* Chichester, GB: Wiley.

Gonen, Amiram. 1981. "Tourism and Coastal Settlement Processes in the Mediter-ranean Region." *Ekistics* 290:378–381.

Green, A. E., and J. R. Howells. 1988. "Information Services and Spatial Develop-ment in the UK Economy." *Tijdschrift voor Economische en Sociale Geografie* 79:266–277.

Gudkova, G. N., and B. V. Moskvin. 1974. "The Development of Motor Roads in the USSR." *Soviet Geography: Review and Translation* 15:573–581.

Hall, Derek R. 1992. "Albania's Changing Tourism Environment." *Journal of Cul-tural Geography* 12 (2): 35–44.

———. 1993a. "Impacts of Economic and Political Transition on the Transport Ge-ography of Central and Eastern Europe." *Journal of Transport Geography* 1:20–35.

———, ed. 1993b. *Transport and Economic Development in the New Central and Eastern Europe.* London, GB: Belhaven.

Helvig, Magne. 1990. "Transportation, Settlement Structure and Journey to Work in Western Norway." *Norsk Geografisk Tidsskrift* 44:61–75.

Hoffman, George W., ed. 1969. *A Geography of Europe.* 3rd ed. New York, USA: Ronald Press.

———, ed. 1989. *Europe in the 1990s: A Geographical Analysis.* New York, USA: Wiley.

Howells, J.R.L. 1984. "The Location of Research and Development: Some Observa-tions and Evidence from Britain." *Regional Studies* 18:13–29.

Hoyle, Brian S., and David A. Pinder, eds. 1992. *European Port Cities in Transition.* London, GB: Belhaven.

Illeris, Sven. 1989. *Services and Regions in Europe.* Aldershot, GB: Avebury.

International Petroleum Encyclopedia. 1999. Tulsa, Okla., USA: Penn Well.

Ivy, Russell L. 1995. "The Restructuring of Air Transport Linkages in the New Europe." *Professional Geographer* 47:280–288.

Kariel, Herbert G., and Patricia E. Kariel. 1982. "Socio-cultural Impacts of Tourism: An Example from the Austrian Alps." *Geografiska Annaler* 64B:1–16.

Kiriazidis, Theo. 1994. *European Transport: Problems and Policies*. Aldershot, GB: Avebury.

Lockhart, Douglas G., and Susan E. Ashton. 1991. "Tourism in Malta." *Scottish Geographical Magazine* 107:22–32.

Marples, David R. 1997. "The Legacy of Chernobyl in 1997: Impact on Ukraine and Belarus." *Post-Soviet Geography and Economics* 38:163–170.

Mayer, Ferdinand, ed. 1975. *Diercke Weltatlas*. Braunschweig, D: Georg Westermann.

Mellor, Roy E. H. 1992. "Railways and German Unification." *Geography* 77:261–264.

Montanari, Armando, and Allan M. Williams, eds. 1995. *European Tourism: Regions, Spaces and Restructuring*. Chichester, GB: Wiley.

Morris, Arthur, and Gordon Dickinson. 1987. "Tourism Development in Spain: Growth versus Conservation on the Costa Brava." *Geography* 72:16–26.

Nijkamp, Peter, ed. 1993. *Europe on the Move: Recent Developments in European Communications and Transport Activity Research*. Aldershot, GB: Avebury.

Nijkamp, Peter, Shalom Reichman, and Michael Wegener, eds. 1990. *Euromobile: Transport, Communications and Mobility in Europe, a Cross-national Comparative Overview*. Aldershot, GB: Avebury.

Nijkamp, Peter, Jaap Vleugel, Ricco Maggi, and Ian Masser. 1994. *Missing Transport Networks in Europe*. Aldershot, GB: Avebury.

Park, Chris. 1989. *Chernobyl: The Long Shadow*. London, GB: Routledge.

Peattie, Roderick. 1954. "The Ruts and Routes of Europe: A Study in Historical Geography." *Journal of Geography* 53:336–341.

Selstad, Tor. 1990. "The Rise of the Quaternary Sector: The Regional Dimension of Knowledge-based Services in Norway, 1970–1985." *Norsk Geografisk Tiksskrift* 44:21–37.

Shaw, Gareth, and Allan M. Williams. 1990. "Tourism and Development." In *Western Europe: Challenge and Change*, ed. David Pinder. London, GB: Belhaven, 240–257.

Stiglbauer, Karl. 1992. "Regional Development and the Service Sector in Austria." *Geographia Polonica* 59:7–19.

Svalastog, Sondre. 1988. "Tourism in Norway's Rural Mountain Districts Twenty-five Years after the Mountain Planning Team's Report." *Norsk Geografisk Tidsskrift* 42:103–120.

Turnock, David. 1986. "The Danube–Black Sea Canal and its Impact on Southern Romania." *GeoJournal* 12:65–79.

Vance, James E., Jr. 1986. *Capturing the Horizon: The Historical Geography of Transportation*. New York, USA: Harper & Row.

Westermanns Grosser Atlas zur Weltgeschichte. 1956. Braunschweig, D: Georg Westermann.

White, Paul E. 1974. *The Social Impact of Tourism on Host Communities: A Study of Language Change in Switzerland*. Oxford, GB: Oxford University School of Geography, Research Paper No. 9.

———. 1987. "Italy: Grand Tour to Package Tour." *Geographical Magazine* 59:554–559.

Whitelegg, John. 1989. *Transport Policy in the EEC*. London, GB: Routledge.

Williams, Allan M., and Gareth Shaw, eds. 1988. *Tourism and Economic Development: Western European Experiences*. London, GB: Belhaven.

CHAPTER 11

Agriculture

Europeans find numerous ways to obtain a living, but one of the oldest and most fundamental involves tilling the soil and tending herds—in short, agriculture. For most of European history, farming remained the dominant aspect of the economy. The great majority of Europeans no longer farm, but the transition away from agriculture occurred relatively recently. To comprehend the remnant agrarian nature of Europe is essential to any broader understanding of the culture area at large. Indeed, agriculture played a role in the very creation of European culture.

Origin and Diffusion

In common with Christianity, the political state, the city, and the Indo-European languages, agriculture did not originate in Europe. Instead, as suggested earlier, the domestication of plants and animals—the **Neolithic** revolution—occurred in the Near East and entered Europe later, apparently borne by the proto-Indo-Europeans. For that reason, the maps of linguistic and agricultural diffusion largely match (figs. 4.2 and 11.1). Both language and agrarian technology advanced from southeast to northwest over a period of about 4 millennia. Agriculture first came to Greece and arrived last in the lands beyond the North and Baltic Seas.

The advent of agriculture seems to have occurred in 2 ways. In southeastern and central Europe, agriculture made a sudden intrusion, producing a sharp break in the archaeological record and implying a displacement of hunters by farmers (fig. 11.1). This also forms the region of greatest Anatolian impact on blood chemistry in Europe (fig. 5.7), and no non-Indo-European linguistic remnants survived there. Elsewhere, the advent of farming occurred more gradually. Indigenous groups such as the Etruscans in Italy and Uralic speakers in the north often adopted agriculture rather than being displaced or absorbed. Transitional economies based both upon

347

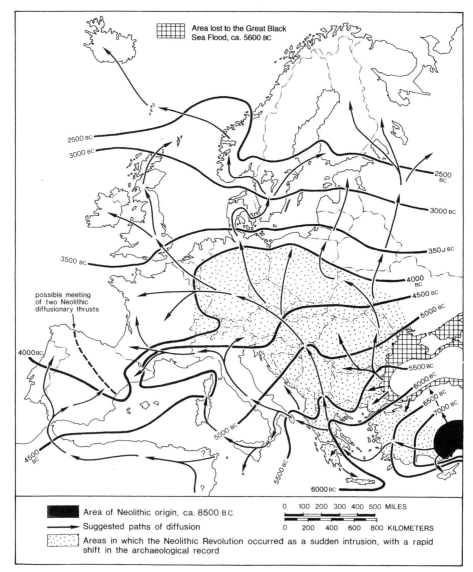

Figure 11.1. Neolithic origins and the diffusion of agriculture in Europe. Domesticated plants and animals reached Europe from the Near East. The map is based upon archaeological finds but nevertheless remains speculative and controversial in detail. (*Sources:* Chapman and Müller 1990, 128; Breunig 1987; Zilhão 1993; Renfrew 1989; Krantz 1988; Ryan and Pitman 1998; Sokal, Ogden, and Wilson 1991; Thorpe 1996.)

farming and hunting–gathering became typical, blurring the archaeological distinction between Mesolithic and Neolithic.

The earliest Neolithic crop complex included wheat, barley, lentils, peas, and flax. Other crops came later, after the Neolithic diffusion had reached Europe, but their origins almost invariably lay in the same Near

Eastern zone. Most Old World garden vegetables, orchard trees, and the grapevine belong among these later introductions from the Near East by way of Anatolia. Grapes may first have been made into wine in Georgia, an outpost of Europe in the Caucasus region.

Domestic herd animals also came from the Near East. Cattle, pigs, sheep, goats, donkeys, and horses all first entered Europe by way of Anatolia, as did poultry. So did the basic tools of agriculture, such as the hoe and plow, the technique of terracing, and irrigation technology. In the formation of early agriculture, then, Europe borrowed from higher civilizations to the east and south.

Spreading through Europe, agriculture, adjusting to different environments and cultures, fragmented into traditional regional types. The major ancient and traditional agrarian systems include: (1) *Mediterranean agriculture;* (2) *three-field farming;* (3) *hardscrabble herding–farming;* (4) *burnbeating;* and (5) *nomadic herding.*

Mediterranean Agriculture: The Ager

The rural folk of Cyprus, Greece, the eastern Adriatic coast, peninsular Italy, the Languedoc Plain, and southern Iberia traditionally practiced a distinctive agrarian system appropriately referred to as **Mediterranean agriculture** (fig. 11.2). This system came unaltered from the Neolithic hearth to the east. Agriculture had arisen in an eastern extension of the Mediterranean climate zone, and the southern European peninsulas offered a sufficiently similar setting that few adaptive changes were necessary.

By the time of classical Greco-Roman civilization, Mediterranean agriculture consisted of a trinity of distinct elements: a threefold system of *ager, hortus,* and *saltus* beautifully adapted to the unique climate and rugged terrain of southern Europe. The Mediterranean climate, described in chapter 2, has a long summer drought and mild, rainy winters. The ager, or field, involved the winter cultivation of small grains. These thrived in the cool, wet season, without irrigation. Wheat and barley, sown with the arrival of the first autumnal rain showers, grew slowly through the winter months and reached maturity in the warm, sunny days of late spring. Harvesting occurred before the annual drought tightened its grip on the land (fig. 11.3). The great harvest festivals of Mediterranean folk accordingly came in the spring rather than fall. Typically, a two-field rotational system was employed in which farmers cultivated the land only every other year to prevent soil exhaustion. In many districts, the grain ager lay in the alluvial lowlands, often at the base of slopes. Wheat was generally the more important of the two grain crops, for Mediterranean peoples prefer light bread. Barley achieved greater importance in drier areas with poor soils, for it is

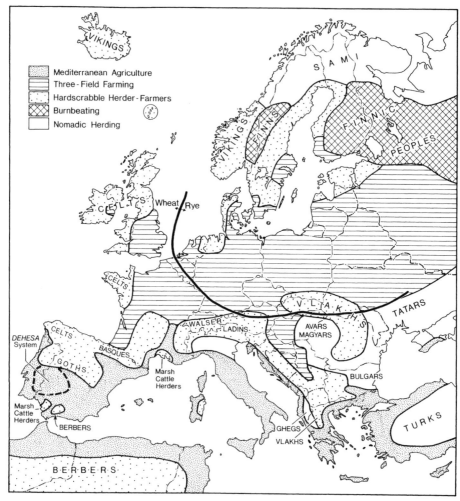

Figure 11.2.   Ancient and traditional types of agriculture. The division between wheat and rye as the dominant bread grain is as of about A.D. 1900. Ancient and traditional systems gave way at widely different periods in the various parts of Europe.

hardier than wheat. In the middle 1900s, wheat and barley still accounted for 40% of all tilled land in Italy and 50% in Greece. Many classical farmers also raised millet, a hardy grain that tolerates heat, drought, and poor soils. Millet, a warm season crop, is sown in the early spring and ripens by July, still ahead of the worst part of the dry season.

The Hortus

Horticulture provided the second element of the traditional Mediterranean agricultural trinity. This *hortus* included orchards and vineyards of drought-

Figure 11.3.   Intertillage of wheat and olives in an alluvial valley in Greece. Two typical Mediterranean crops share the same field on the island of Kriti. The wheat has only recently been reaped by hand and tied into bundles to be carried in for threshing. Intertillage is common in traditional Mediterranean agriculture. The month is May, the time of grain harvest before the drought of summer. Olives from these young trees will be ready for harvest in autumn. (Photo by T.G.J.-B. 1971.)

resistant perennials native to the Mediterranean region and able to withstand the summer dry season. The *grapevine* belongs in this category. From it Mediterranean farmers derived table grapes, raisins dried after the late summer harvest before the onset of rain, and wine. In the middle 1900s in Greece, about 40% of the harvest went to make wine, 25% for raisins, and 35% for table grapes. Southern Europeans are partial to wine, and in fact this alcoholic beverage has an ancient and enduring link to religion among them. About 1000 B.C., in the Greek lands, a cult devoted to the god Dionysus arose, in which wine and alcoholic intoxication served as aids to religious experience. The cult, not surprisingly, became very popular among the common folk and by the sixth century B.C. gained governmental approval. Dionysus and wine spread to the western Mediterranean in part with Greek colonists, and the Romans subsequently accepted the cult, renaming the wine god Bacchus. After Christianization of the Roman Empire, wine retained its ancient Dionysian sacredness by finding a place in the Eucharist as the symbolic blood of Christ. Vineyards grow both on terraced hillsides and on alluvial valley floors. The vine produces a crop of high value on a wide variety of surfaces and soils, including steep slopes, without irrigation.

The *olive* is a splendid, long-lived native tree, drought resistant but not tolerant of a hard frost, long recognized as the single best indicator of the presence of Mediterranean climate and horticulture (figs. 11.2 and 11.3). Some of these gnarled, twisted trees survive for a thousand years or more. The olive tree yields a crop only in alternate years, blossoming in the first year and bearing the next; harvesting is accomplished by hitting the branches with a pole. While Mediterranean peoples eat many olives, the principal value of the olive tree, both in ancient times and today, is as a source of fat and cooking oil. Butter has never been produced in southern Europe, and olive oil provides a needed substitute. The image of butter-eating Germanic tribesmen was repulsive to the Roman writers who left behind descriptions of their northern neighbors. Italy, Spain, and Greece alone account for 73% of the world olive oil production today. The olive tree thrives on slopes and hillsides as well as in valleys and does well in thin, rocky soils.

Other orchard trees of the classical Mediterranean included the *fig,* also drought resistant, native to the area, and suited to hillsides; the *pistacio;* the *carob;* and the *pomegranate,* a small tree that yields a tasty acidic flesh from the outer coating of its numerous seeds. While hortus and ager typically occupied different areas within the village lands of the Mediterranean, *intertillage* also occurred. In this system, wheat and barley were sown among the widely spaced orchard trees (fig. 11.3). While not actually part of the hortus, the *cork oak* also played an important role in some Mediterranean regions. Every 7 to 9 years, the outer bark of this wild tree can be stripped, using a pointed stick, producing a commercially valuable item of trade (fig. 11.4).

The Saltus

The third element of traditional Mediterranean agriculture consisted of the *saltus,* or pasture. Village herders raised mainly small livestock, particularly sheep, goats, and swine. These animals survive on the scanty forage offered by the rugged highland pastures and mountain oak forests of southern Europe. Goats and sheep moved with agility through the rocky landscape, and pigs thrived on the mast of the native live oak forests. Sheep, the most numerous livestock, provided wool, hides, and some meat, though the Mediterranean diet remained heavily vegetarian. Goats yielded mohair, milk, and hides, and to a certain extent they took the place of dairy cattle in southern Europe (fig. 11.5). The cheeses produced in Mediterranean districts come from goat's milk or, more rarely, from sheep's milk, as in Roquefort. Classical references to swine, such as the Homeric episode concerning Circe turning Ulysses' companions into pigs, suggest a widespread importance, but swine are now the least important of the three small live-

Figure 11.4. **Cork newly stripped** from the trunk of this oak tree in Extremadura, in south-western Spain, near the pilgrimage town of Guadalupe. (Photo by T.G.J.-B. 1986.)

stock, in part because the forests that provided their food steadily diminished. Today, swine remain common only in the remnant oak forests, such as those on the rainier slopes of mountains in southwestern Iberia, especially Extremadura, where air-cured pork remains a regional delicacy. Even so, pigs provide another index for determining the southern boundary of Europe. By calculating the ratio of swine to population, we can reveal a

Figure 11.5.   A herd of goats and sheep being driven to pasture near the Guadiana River in far southeastern Portugal. These two types of livestock are the most common in traditional Mediterranean agriculture. (Photo by T.G.J.-B. 1986.)

sharp line separating Europeans from the Muslim and Jewish peoples to the south, based on the fact that Christians eat pork while both Islam and Judaism forbid its consumption (fig. 11.6).

The Mediterranean saltus remained largely divorced from the ager and hortus. No crop harvests went as feed or fodder for the herds, and animal manure was not collected as fertilizer for the fields or orchards. In fact, livestock often ranged very far from villages, under the care of migrant shepherds and swineherders. In the dry, hot summer, sheep and goats moved to high pastures in the mountains, where grass grew more abundantly, and during the winter they migrated down to marshy parts of the alluvial lowlands. The herders went with them, in a system called *transhumance*, and often months passed between the herders' visits to the home village. Well-established routes of transhumance, in places lined with rock fences, crisscrossed the countryside. When ranging near the village, herds sometimes grazed on the stubble of the harvested, fallow ager, but in general the raising of crops and livestock remained divorced.

The beast of burden of the traditional Mediterranean agriculture was the donkey, though some farmers did not own one, making do instead entirely with human labor. Even today, donkeys pulling the typical Mediterranean two-wheeled farm cart or being ridden to the fields can occasionally be seen on rural roads.

In traditional Mediterranean agriculture, the land belonged to the nobility in the form of large estates, or *latifundia*. Three thousand years ago, Homer described peasant reapers who "drive their swaths through a rich

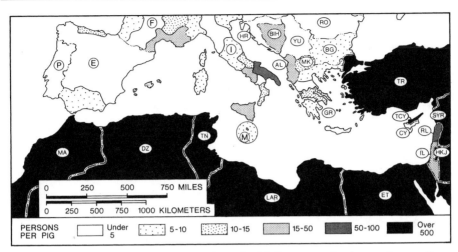

Figure 11.6.   The population-to-swine ratio in the Mediterranean lands reveals a southern border for Europe. Pigs and pork are typical of almost all traditional European farming systems and regional diets, but Islamic and Judaic law forbids the consumption of pork. Some European Mediterranean lands became too deforested to permit large droves of pigs, but they never disappeared altogether.

man's field of wheat or barley." On these estates, some of which survive to the present day, tenants scratched out a living from tiny farms. A crude hand plow, called an *aratro*, broke the soil so that the seeds would germinate and the winter rains would not run off and erode the grain fields. The aratro merely scratched the surface and did not turn a furrow. A hoe, perhaps the main farming tool, was employed to weed the fields and vineyards to retard loss of moisture.

This, then, was the agriculture of classical times. All 3 of the basic enterprises were practiced on each farm, though one or another might have been emphasized. From the diverse unspecialized trinity of small grains, vine and tree crops, and small livestock, nearly all of life's necessities could be obtained, including woolen and leather clothing, bread, beverages, fruit, cheese, cooking oil, and even a cork for the leather wine container. Homer described this diverse system in the *Iliad*, mentioning a district with "wheat-bearing fields and many orchards of trees apart, and many sheep."

In certain Mediterranean regions, truly ancient farming techniques survived even into the twentieth century. An example is the *dehesa* (or *montado*) system of southwestern Iberia (fig. 11.2), under which the ager was placed in the saltus. Dehesa farmers selected an area of open oak woods, the typical native vegetation of the ancient Mediterranean. They thinned out the foliage by removing some tree limbs to allow more sunlight to reach the ground, then plowed and sowed grain beneath the pruned forest. A crop could be obtained only about once in every 5 years in the dehesa system, and the fields had to be relocated every year, but the system proved sustainable and did not destroy the forest. Perhaps as a result, the greatest survival of native oak woodland in all the Mediterranean occurs in the dehesa region. Dehesa represents an archaic form of orchard intertillage. In fact, it may fairly accurately preserve the most ancient technique of grain farming, the type practiced at the dawn of agriculture in the Near East, 9,000 years before Christ. It could also reflect an Afro-Asiatic, as opposed to an Indo-European, method, anciently diffused by way of North Africa. Rural Europe, even today, abounds in hints concerning ancient ways and diffusions.

Mediterranean Rural Landscapes

This traditional Mediterranean agrarian system produced an equally distinctive landscape. Most farmers in the region resided in large, tightly clustered villages of irregular plan, often situated on high points for defensive advantage (figs. 11.7 and 11.8). These villages grew, without planning, over many centuries, and their irregular layout mirrors that of the earliest Neolithic villages in the Anatolian agricultural hearth. They are ancient, older than memory, and in every Mediterranean farm village one truly walks the streets of antiquity.

Figure 11.7. A large irregular clustered farm village of the type found in southern Iberia and much of the Mediterranean area. This village, or "agrotown," lies in the hills of southern Portugal. (Photo by T.G.J.-B. 1986.)

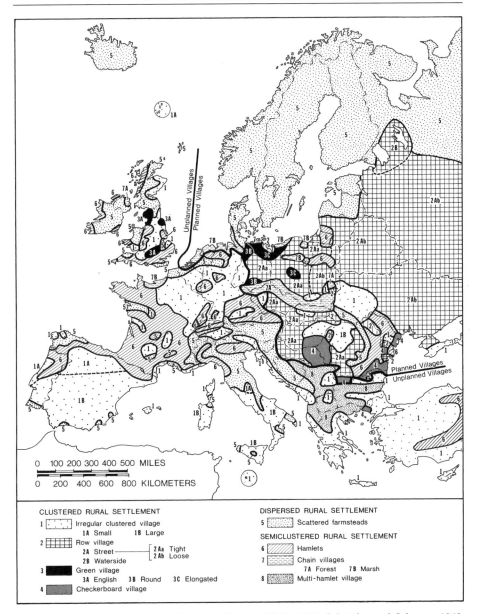

Figure 11.8. Forms of rural settlement. (*Sources:* Uhlig 1961; Schröder and Schwarz 1969; Roberts 1979; Thorpe 1961; Demangeon 1939; Otremba 1961; Wagstaff 1969; Wilhelmy 1936.)

The typical Mediterranean farmstead is built of stone or, less commonly, mud brick and covered with a heavy tile roof. Because of deforestation, wood for construction had largely disappeared, leaving only earth and rock as building materials (fig. 11.9). The Mediterranean farmstead is multistoried, with the ground level and cellar devoted to food storage and cheese and wine making. The upper stories contain the living quarters (see

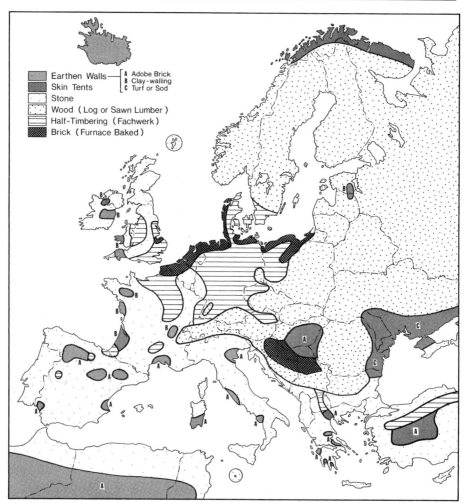

Figure 11.9.   Traditional rural building materials. (*Sources:* Vidal de la Blache 1926; Meirion-Jones 1982; Smith 1988.)

fig. 11.14). Many such farmsteads survive to the present day, as do the venerable villages, lending a traditional charm to the southern European countryside.

The ager and hortus were divided into countless block-shaped parcels, forming a complicated patchwork of fragmented holdings. In districts colonized during Roman times, a more rigid checkerboard pattern survives in places, a legacy of the imperial land survey system (fig. 11.10). Again, antiquity is rarely out of sight, even in modern Europe.

Three-Field Farming

North of the Mediterranean, in fertile lands beyond the mountains and centered in the Great and East European Plains and the Hungarian Basin, a

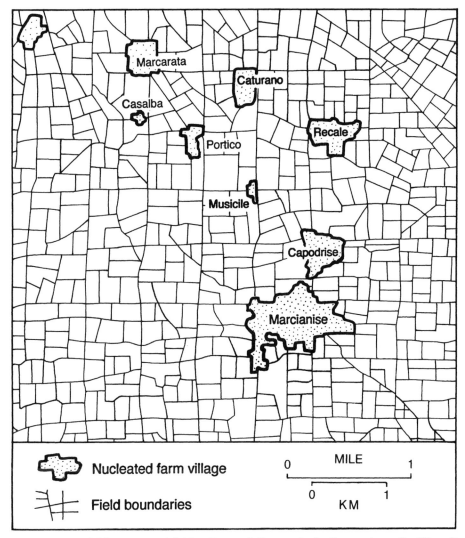

Figure 11.10.   Field patterns exhibiting Roman influence, in the Campania north of Napoli, Italy. Fields in the Mediterranean areas, dominated by use of the small plow, take on rectangular shape. In this instance, the rectangularity has been made even more pronounced by the survival of the Roman rectangular survey system.

second traditional agricultural system once prevailed—**three-field farming** (fig. 11.2). In this system, found mainly among Germanic and Slavic peoples, grains were raised on a three-field rotation, in which the land was cropped 2 out of every 3 years. In this succession, any particular field was planted first to a summer crop, next to a winter grain, and then allowed to lie fallow for a year. At any given time, one-third of the land was at each stage in the cycle (fig. 11.11).

The grains differed somewhat within the area of three-field farming. In southern and western areas, including England, France, and northwestern

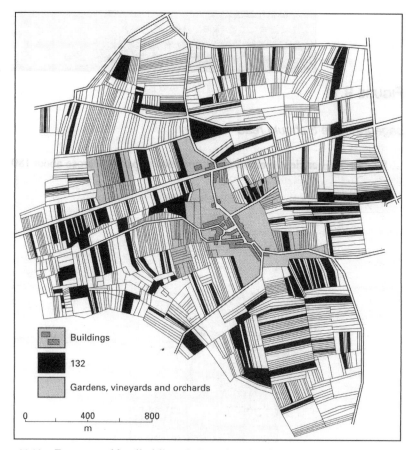

Figure 11.11.   Fragmented landholdings in Lorraine. Small strip fields typical of three-field farming survived in the irregular clustered village of Seichamp, near Nancy in northeastern France, into the twentieth century. The 132 separate strips belonging to one sample farm are shown. (*Source:* Demangeon 1946, with modifications.)

Iberia, *wheat* was the principal and preferred bread grain. *Rye*, the second great bread grain, dominated the north, in Germany, Scandinavia, Poland, and Russia, where dark bread was preferred. Poland and Russia together produce nearly half of the world's rye today. Rye has greater resistance to cold and more tolerance for acidic, sandy soils than does wheat, allowing it to succeed better in northern and eastern regions. *Oats* share the hardiness of rye and grow, usually as a summer grain, throughout the three-field area, providing oatcakes, gruel, and—most important—the major livestock feed grain of the system. The fourth major grain, *barley*, provided beer, the northern substitute for wine, but was also raised primarily as a feed grain.

Oats and rye apparently joined the ancient Indo-European agrarian system as it spread north, into colder lands beyond the Vardar–Morava rift valley and Danube River (figs. 4.2 and 11.1). Earlier, these 2 grains had apparently grown only as weeds in the wheat and barley fields of early agriculturists in the south and east. Rye and oats may be the only crops domesticated within Europe.

Flax, one of the original Near Eastern crops, made the transition northward to find an important place in three-field farming as the major fiber crop. Linen garments are made from flax. Still today, the old three-field countries, led by Russia, produce much of the world's flax.

Horticulture also survived the northward diffusion into colder lands, though a different array of fruit trees from those of the Mediterranean prevailed. In place of the olive, almond, fig, and pomegranate came the apple, pear, peach, cherry, and plum, all of Asian origin but also able to grow in the north. The grapevine eventually struggled northward, but reached its climatic limits roughly along the line of the Seine, Rhine, and Danube Rivers. Even there, it thrived best on south-facing, sunny slopes, and the German word for vineyard, *weinberg*, literally means "vine hill."

Another basic part of three-field farming, the cutting of hay from meadowland, provided additional sustenance for livestock during the winter season. In our modern urban society, the meanings of "meadow" and "pasture" have become blurred, trending toward synonymity. Traditionally, livestock grazed pastures but not meadows, from which hay was to be cut. As the famous nursery rhyme admonishes, "sheep's in the meadow" was a state of affairs to be corrected. During much of the winter season, the livestock remained in stalls to consume hay and feed grains. At the opposite season, they grazed fallow fields, pastures, and remnant forests, which usually lay toward the periphery of village lands.

Livestock played a much greater role in three-field farming than in Mediterranean agriculture, supplying a larger part of the rural diet. *Cattle*, the dominant animals, provided meat, dairy products, manure for the fields, and, as oxen, power to pull the bulky plow characteristic of the Germanic and Slavic lands. In much of central Europe, including Germany and Poland, *swine* were a more important source of meat than cattle, and pork is still a mainstay of the diet there. The unique value of swine is their ability to convert even the least savory garbage and waste into high-quality meat, and the mast of remnant oak and beech forests added to their diet. Few areas lacked flocks of *sheep*, but only in areas of poor quality, such as the Lüneburger Heath of northern Germany, did they serve as the most important livestock.

Perhaps the key difference between three-field farming and Mediterranean agriculture was the close relationship in the former between crops and livestock. The Mediterranean farmer raised both plants and animals, but there was little or no tie between the two, and animal husbandry remained separate from tillage. In the three-field system, crops and livestock were inseparable, for the animals provided the manure used to maintain soil fertility and the power for plowing the fields. In turn, much of the produce of the cropland, particularly the barley and oats, went to feed the livestock, and meadows and pastures occupied extensive acreage.

In other respects, the traditional agricultural systems of northern and southern Europe were similar. A landed aristocracy dominated a tenant peasantry in both, and the individual farms were small. Both three-field farming and Mediterranean agriculture were unspecialized, subsistence types of farming, designed to produce all of life's necessities.

Villages and Fields

The rural landscape of the three-field farming area also bore some resemblance to that of southern Europe. Here, too, farmers lived in a myriad of clustered villages. In western areas, especially among the Germanic peoples, these were irregular in plan, similar to those of the Mediterranean. To the east, the Slavic farmers generally lived in villages of more regular layout, most typically *street villages,* in which the farmsteads lay on either side of a single road. Less common were villages grouped around a central green or commons (fig. 11.12). The ancient cultural divide between German and Slav can still today be seen in the border between planned and irregular farm villages (fig. 11.8).

In place of the stone farmsteads of the south, Slavic wooden buildings and Germanic half-timbering dominated the three-field region. Half-timbering consists of a heavy framework of oaken beams, morticed and tenoned together and left exposed as the skeleton of the structure (fig. 11.13). The spaces between the beams are filled in with brick or, more commonly, with *wattle and daub,* a wickerwork of sticks daubed with clay and plastered. The folk architecture of these farmsteads was also distinctive. Typically, the stead consisted of multiple buildings, grouped tightly around a central courtyard, a type closely associated with the Franks, a German tribe influential in spreading both the farmstead and three-field farming itself (fig. 11.14).

Even more closely linked to three-field farming was a highly distinctive field pattern, in which each land parcel consisted of a long, narrow strip (fig. 11.11). These presented a marked contrast to the block-shaped fields of the Mediterranean. The strip field accommodated the massive moldboard plow of the three-field farmers, a device that cut deeply into the earth and turned the soil over, creating a furrow. Invented by the Slavs and later adopted among the Germanic peoples, the moldboard plow was pulled by teams of oxen. It was difficult to turn around. By laying the fields out in long, narrow strips, the number of times the plow and team needed to be turned was minimized.

The modern rural landscape retains many reminders of these villages, fields, and farmsteads even though the three-field system that created them

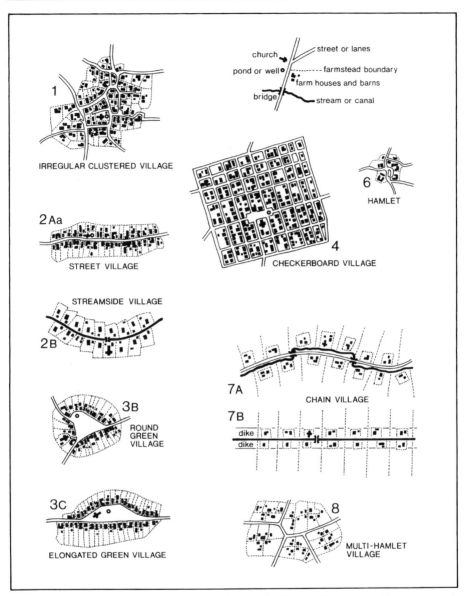

Figure 11.12.   Different types of rural settlement in Europe. For the distribution of each type, see figure 11.8. (*Sources:* Wilhelmy 1936; Demangeon 1939; Mayhew 1973; Schröder and Schwarz 1969; Thorpe 1961.)

Figure 11.13. Hessian half-timbering, or *Fachwerk,* adds a distinctive appearance to the cultural landscape in this farm village on the Lahn River in Germany. (Photo by T.G.J.-B. 1991.)

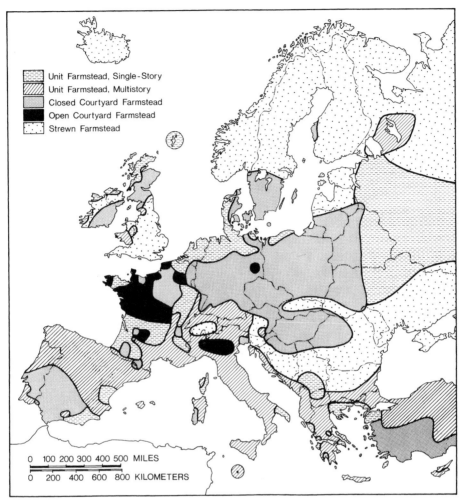

Figure 11.14.   Traditional rural house and farmstead types. (*Sources:* Buschan 1926, following p. 176; Demangeon 1920; Hance 1951; Meirion-Jones 1982; Müller-Wille 1936; Smith 1988.)

has vanished. Particularly in the East European Plain, Russian street villages retain the appearance of times long past.

Hardscrabble Herder–Farmers

Separating and surrounding the favored "fat lands" of the three-field farming and Mediterranean agriculture lay hardscrabble belts, afflicted with broken terrain, excessive cloudiness, and/or sterile soils (fig. 11.2). In these regions, open-range livestock herding constituted the dominant traditional activity, with crop farming minor and secondary in importance. From ancient times, stable village-dwelling farmers of the Mediterranean and Germano-Slavic lands both vilified and romanticized the herders of the peripheries—Celts, Vikings, Basques, Berbers, Vlakhs, and others.

In common with Mediterranean shepherds, the herder–farmer hard-scrabble folk relied heavily upon transhumance, shifting their herds seasonally. While these shifts usually occurred between highlands in the summer and lowlands in the winter, other patterns also developed. For example, in Las Marismas, the great marsh at the mouth of the Guadalquivir River in Spain, Iberian longhorn cattle entered the core of the wetlands in the dry summer and then retreated to the peripheries of the marsh as the floods of winter turned the area into a huge lake. In Somersetshire, England, an expanse of low wetlands also provided the summer pastures, and in fact the word *Somerset* means "summer pastures."

Cattle were the favored animals of the herder–farmers, as in Las Marismas, the Rhône Delta, Celtic fringes, Alps, Massif Central, and Kjølen Range. A milking culture complex characterized most of these areas, and bovine dairying provided an important component of the diet. Alpine areas, even before the beginning of the Christian Era, exported cheese, and by about A.D. 1100 a distinctive high-mountain system of dairy cattle herding developed among the Walser people there, involving transhumance, hay cutting, winter stall feeding, milk products, and sheep raising. Sheep dominated most of the other hill and mountain areas and were the favored animal of the Vlakhs, Basques, and Dinaric folk. In response to the demands of late medieval and Renaissance woolen textile industries, as well as the mechanized woolen mills of the Industrial Revolution, many highland herding areas shifted from cattle to sheep.

The role of crops in this traditional system, while secondary, was still significant. In most areas, an *infield–outfield* system was practiced, involving a small, continuously cropped area close to the farmstead, the "infield," surrounded by a much more extensive "outfield." Only a small part of the outfield was planted at any given time, and a lengthy fallow period of a decade or more was needed to restore fertility after several crops. During the fallow period, the outfield served as pasture. Rye, oats, and barley grew as the principal grains, and the hardscrabble farmers regularly consumed oats—a livestock feed elsewhere in Europe—either as gruel or oatcakes. Wheat did not thrive in these hard lands.

In the British Isles, the infield lay enclosed by a rock fence called the *inner dyke,* allowing the most prized livestock to be penned there after the harvest and fed through the winter. Their manure fertilized the infield, permitting it to be planted every year. The outfield, too, was ringed by a fence, the *acrewall,* and the less-valuable animals foraged there in the cold season. Beyond and above the acrewall lay the permanent cattle pasture, used during the crop season when all livestock were banished from both infield and outfield. Still higher stood the *moor wall,* separating the good-quality cattle pastures from the poorer sheep-grazing lands of the heath and moor.

The dominant rural settlement form of the hardscrabble districts, the *hamlet* (figs. 11.8 and 11.12), consists of a small number of farmsteads, loosely clustered. These might best be regarded as embryonic villages, whose growth was stunted by the want of good soil.

Burnbeaters of the North

In the subarctic expanse of taiga and sterile podsols, Finnic peoples of the forests practiced another traditional farming system called **burnbeating** or **shifting cultivation** (fig. 11.2). They cut down trees in small clearings, allowed the dead vegetation to dry, burned it, and then sowed rye and barley in the fertile ashes among the stumps (fig. 11.15). After a year or two, burnbeaters abandoned the clearing and made another. One important variant of this system, called *huuhta*, possessed the unique advantage of rendering the infertile, acidic soils of the virgin *taiga* highly productive for one crop year. Farmers practicing huuhta cut or girdled trees in the early spring of the first year and allowed the wood to dry until midsummer of the third year and then set fire to the clearing. They then planted rye, which came to harvest in the fourth summer, after which the field was abandoned. A sec-

Figure 11.15. Finnish farmers in the interior of their country practicing a traditional form of shifting cultivation that required the repeated clearing and burning of woodland. The fields were used only for 1 or 2 years before being abandoned. (Photo by T.G.J.-B. 1985, at the Kuopion Museo in Kuopio, SF.)

ond method of shifting cultivation, called *kaski,* occurred in areas covered with birch and other deciduous trees, a second-growth forest that appeared after 20 or 30 years in the old huuhta fields. In kaski, the woodland was felled in summer at maximum leaf and burned early in the following summer, followed by rye and barley planting. Either system offered the spectacular sight of flaming tree trunks being rolled over the ground by soot-blackened men and women to ignite the leaf mold. Finnish burnbeaters also kept cattle herds in the woods, and they relied as much on hunting and fishing as upon agriculture for livelihood. So successful was their system that the Swedish crown introduced Finnish burnbeaters into interior Scandinavia as colonists after about 1575. In the long run, however, population pressures made shifting cultivation untenable in northern Europe, and it has not been practiced since about 1920.

The Finnic burnbeating system represented a partial acceptance of agriculture by non-Indo-Europeans. Before the coming of agriculture, the Uralic peoples lived solely by hunting, fishing, and gathering in the forests. All of these traditional activities survived in burnbeating to the extent that a total crop failure did not bring starvation or even severe deprivation.

Nomadic Herding

In the outermost peripheries of Europe, crops failed to gain acceptance, in part due to climatic extremes of cold, infertility, or aridity and also as a result of Asian invasions. Only the herd animals, not the crops of the ancient Near East agricultural hearth, reached the Asiatic nomadic peoples. They wandered from place to place, seeking fresh pastures for their animals, and had no fixed residence. The steppe corridor of the southeast and the Hungarian Puszta received wave after wave of such nomadic herders, who raised horses, sheep, goats, and cattle. Among them were the Magyars, Avars, Bulgars, Tatars, and many others, driving their flocks and herds westward in a competition for land, pitting Europe against Asia. Europe eventually won this contest but only with difficulty and amid cultural compromise.

A unique group of nomadic herders, the Sami, inhabited Sapmi (Lapland) in the far north. None of the Near Eastern herd animals could survive in the arctic tundra, but the Sami observed their linguistic cousins, the Finns, herding cattle. Following that example, they or some neighboring tundra people domesticated the reindeer, which became the sole basis of their herding system (fig. 11.16). The Sami had no other animals and no crops at all. Like the Finns, they also engaged in hunting and fishing, but Sami herders acquired many of the necessities of life from the reindeer: meat for food, skins for housing and clothing, and bone for tools and instruments. They spent the summer herding stock on the tundras of the hilly interior and northern Scandinavian coastal fringe, including some islands

Figure 11.16.   Reindeer herds belonging to the Sami in northern Scandinavia. The formerly nomadic system has evolved into ranching today. (Photo by T.G.J.-B. 1985.)

off the coast of Norway. In wintertime, the reindeer migrated into the protective coniferous forests adjacent to the tundra, which afforded shelter from the bitterly cold winds of the open tundra. Autumn and spring were spent en route to and from the summer pastures on the tundra. The Sami had no awareness of international boundaries and moved freely through what is today Norwegian, Swedish, Finnish, and Russian territory.

Little survives today of traditional agricultural systems. Here and there, in remote hill areas of rural Europe one can occasionally glimpse archaic elements of the older, largely vanished ways, but for the most part pervasive change meets the eye. These changes occurred in the types of crops raised, land tenure, field systems, levels of commercialization and specialization, intensity of land use, and the proportion of the population working in agriculture.

New Crop Introductions

Two enormously significant diffusions brought exotic crops to Europe during the past two millennia, radically altering agriculture. The first wave came from the Arabic Muslim lands across the Mediterranean, bearing the *citrus fruits*, which had apparently been unknown to the classical Greeks, though the mythological eleventh labor of the mythical Hercules had been to obtain the "golden apple" from the Garden of the Hesperides, a probable reference to the orange. Hercules' quest took him into the warm lands to the south, where the orange in fact grew in the irrigated gardens of Arabia. He failed to get the job done properly, but the Arabs brought citrus into Europe when they conquered Iberia and parts of Italy in the Middle Ages. The Arab word *naranj*, accepted into Spanish as *naranja*, later entered English corrupted as *orange*. Citrus quickly became a basic part of Mediterranean horticulture, though these fruits lacked drought resistance and required extensive development of irrigation. The Arabs also added apricots and sugar cane to the Mediterranean hortus, as well as sorghum, cotton, and rice to the ager.

The second revolutionary introduction of crops came from the American Indian as a result of the Age of Discovery. Two distinct diffusions occurred. The first involved the intertilled Mesoamerican food complex of *maize* (corn), *chili peppers, squash, beans*, and *pumpkins*, to which was appended the *turkey* and perhaps the *tomato*. Improbably, this food complex did not reach Europe directly, by way of the Spaniards in Mexico. Indeed, Iberians largely rejected these foods and still do. Instead, the complex of Mexican domesticates accompanied the Portuguese around Africa to India and from there to Turkey, gaining acceptance at every stop. All spread into Balkan Europe with the Turkish conquests, and adoption of the Mesoamerican complex remains greatest there, even to the present day. Taste the paprika in Hungarian food, observe the expansive tomato fields of Bulgaria, watch stick-wielding Peloponnesian women drive flocks of turkeys through the streets, see the festival corn decorations of the South Slavs, consider that *mamaliga* (cornmeal mush) serves as a main Romanian food staple, and you will grasp the extent to which Balkan agriculture has been reshaped in a Mesoamerican image.

Andean Indians of highland South America provided the other major New World crop, the so-called Irish *potato*. It spread to Europe by an altogether different route. Arriving in Spain from Peru in 1565, the potato quickly reached Spanish-ruled Belgium. Within 2 centuries, it gained acceptance throughout most of the three-field farming region and the herder–farmer hardscrabble periphery, completely revolutionizing both. The potato provided 4 times as much carbohydrate per hectare as wheat and became the principal food crop of most peoples living north of the Alps and Pyrenees. It yielded large amounts of food from small fields, even in a cloudy, cool climate. Temporarily, at least, the potato ended famines wherever it gained acceptance. Hunger returned again only when the potato itself became blighted in the 1840s.

Specialization and Commercialization

Even more radical changes in European agriculture occurred after about 1850 as a result of the urbanization and industrialization of the culture area.

Farmers stopped producing at a subsistence level, no longer content merely to provide their own needs and have a small surplus left over to sell. Instead, the large urban markets prompted them to focus on production of commodities for sale.

Subsistence breeds diversity, while market orientation usually leads to **specialization.** No longer would the Mediterranean farmer pursue a threefold system; no longer would three-field agriculture retain its multiplicity of crops and livestock. Small aspects of the traditional diversified systems would become the only agricultural pursuit. Specialization remains an ongoing process in Europe, increasing decade by decade. As a result, the map of agricultural types in Europe has been almost totally redrawn, with focus on individual cash products replacing the older, many-faceted systems (fig. 11.17). In Mediterranean Europe, specialization was usually achieved by elevating the hortus to the only agricultural pursuit. Ager and saltus shrank and disappeared, crowded out by the expansion of orchards, vineyards, and vegetable fields or else abandoned. The result was a modern, specialized type of agriculture called **market gardening** or truck farming.

Market Gardening

Mediterranean specialization centered not merely upon the hortus, but upon specific elements within it. A farmer might choose to produce olives or oranges, wine grapes, or garden vegetables. Entire districts focused upon a single orchard or vineyard product. The Languedoc Plain, for example, became one huge "sea of vines"; the irrigated *huertas* of eastern coastal Spain developed specialized citrus cultivation and gave the name to the Valencia orange; while Andalucía, the Adriatic coast of Italy, and the Riviera achieved fame for their olives. Northern Sicilia and the area around Napoli also became noted for citrus, and the valley of the Douro River in Portugal expanded production of the famous *port* wines. One of the most remarkable agricultural sights in the Mediterranean lands is the view from adjacent mountain heights of the olive-clad expanse of the once-sacred Plain of Krissa, near Delfi in Greece. This plain, now one solid olive orchard to the almost complete exclusion of other trees or crops, gives the appearance from above of a gray-green embayment of the adjacent Gulf of Kórinthos. Nearby, Homer's "wheat-bearing Argos" became one immense citrus orchard.

The older, diversified Mediterranean system has not completely disappeared. Rougher, interior districts, poorly endowed with irrigation water or sufficient flat land, retain relics of the older system. Fine examples of traditional Mediterranean agriculture can be seen in such districts as the southern flank of the Pyrenees in Spain, and in the mountains of Kriti in insular Greece. In effect, two quite different agricultural types developed in southern Europe, one preserving the traditional system and the other evolving into market gardening. Alongside methods dating to the time of

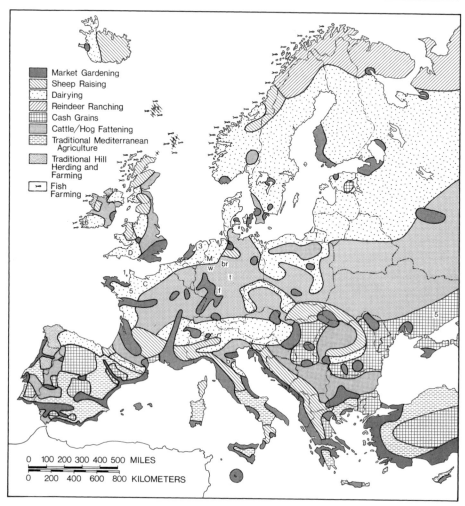

Figure 11.17.   Specialized types of agriculture in modern Europe. Numbers refer to source regions of selected dairy breeds: 1. Guernsey and Jersey; 2. Ayrshire; 3. Friesian; 4. Holstein; 5. Maine–Anjou; and 6. Kerry. Capital letters refer to the place of origin of selected generic cheeses: C = Camembert, D = Cheddar, G = Gruyère, M = Muenster, and T = Tilsit. Lowercase letters refer to the origin of selected generic meat products: b = bologna, br = braunschweiger, f = frankfurter, and w = westphalian ham. (*Sources:* Kostrowicki 1984; Fry 1971.)

Homer, we find modern scientific agriculture. Here we can view two worlds—one reminiscent of the Neolithic and classical past, which survives in small holdings where people live their lives traditionally, and one inhabited by the specialized, cash-crop farmers serving the world markets. In places, the juxtaposition of traditional Mediterranean farming and modern agribusiness is quite startling. For example, the district called Las Alpujarras, south of Granada in the Spanish Bética Range, displays an almost unaltered ancient agrarian system. Tiny fields and orchards, laboriously won from mountainside and flood plain, yield a variety of Mediterranean crops, while sheep and goats graze high above. Machines are few, with the necessary labor provided by people and donkeys. Little in the way of agricultural produce reaches the market from Las Alpujarras. Homer would find the district a familiar place. Journey a very short distance southward toward the Mediterranean shore, over the Sierra de Gádor, and you enter the altogether different agricultural world of the flat Campo de Dalías. Most of these plains are covered with huge sheets of white plastic, beneath which grow irrigated winter vegetables in one of the most impressive market-gardening enterprises anywhere in the world. The boomtowns of the Campo de Dalías offer agribusiness sales and service outlets for plastic sheeting, pipe, insecticides, and pump systems. Perhaps nowhere else in the world do such contrasting types of agriculture coexist in such a small area.

Market gardening also emerged north of the Alps, mainly in small pockets of the old three-field region. Each sizable city there acquired a surrounding "halo" of truck farms producing fruit and vegetables for the nearby urban market (fig. 11.17). Other local districts of northern market gardening appeared in climatically favored places, where one or another crop thrived particularly well. For example, Bretagne in France today specializes in apples and cider; nearby Picardie produces potatoes; Holland is a center for flowers and bulbs; Bulgaria is known for tomatoes; and cherries thrive on the shores of the Bodensee in southern Germany.

The most impressive and lucrative northern example of market gardening is found in the wine-producing vineyards of the Bordeaux region, Champagne, Bourgogne, the middle Rhine Valley, Austria's Weinviertel (wine region) north of Wien (itself named for wine in Roman times), and certain other favored districts (fig. 11.18). Traceable to monastic settlements of the fourth century founded to produce sacramental wine, northern viticulture expanded rapidly to supply growing urban and export markets.

Dairying

Milk cows enjoyed importance in several traditional agricultural systems, especially in the three-field system and highland herding–farming of Scandinavia, the Alps, Celtic fringe, Massif Central, and Pyrenees. When specialization and commercialization came, many such districts elevated bovine **dairying** to their only major activity. Cropland was converted to pasture and meadow, herd size increased on each farm, and an elaborate network of milk processing plants, creameries, cheese factories, and milk transport systems developed. As a result, the great European *dairy belt* took shape around the shores of the North and Baltic Seas, including much of northern Russia, the British Isles, coastal France, the Low Country, northern

Figure 11.18.   Wine grape monoculture in the Bordeaux area of southwestern France. The specialization and commercialization of European agriculture produced such landscapes. (Photo by T.G.J.-B. 1999.)

Germany, and the Scandinavian lands. An outlier lies to the south, in the Alps of Switzerland and Austria (fig. 11.17). The dairy belt occupies the cloudiest, coolest part of northwestern Europe, a land better suited to pasture and the raising of hay than to field crops such as wheat. Similarly, the rugged mountain terrain of the Alps is more easily adapted to the raising of grasses, and hay can be mown on the steep slopes where crop tillage would be difficult. Extensive areas of mountain pasture, the *almen*, lie too high to be farmed but serve well a livestock-based economy.

The trend toward specialized dairying can be traced to the Middle Ages in some parts of northern Europe. In England, the counties of Essex and adjacent East Suffolk, on the North Sea coast northeast of London, became known for dairying in the late Middle Ages. In the 1600s, the shires of Hertford and Buckingham north of the British capital adopted the same agricultural specialty, as did certain districts in the English Midlands. Generally, the more peripheral dairy areas produced cheese, which was less perishable. Also in the 1600s, the French provinces of Normandie on the English Channel and Brie near Paris became famous as dairy areas, as did parts of the Low Country. In the nineteenth century, commercial dairying spread to its present limits, displacing grain farming in countries such as Denmark. Dairying now enjoys overwhelming importance in the belt devoted to it. In Finland, for example, milk production accounts for 38% of the total agricultural income of the country, while meadow, pasture, and silage crops cover a third of the arable land.

Every major breed of dairy cattle in the world today derives from the European dairy belt, and the breeds bear names indicative of their origin. The Jersey and Guernsey commemorate the names of two of the Channel Islands, which lie between France and England; the Ayrshire breed reminds us of a Scottish county; the Holstein–Friesian comes from Friesland in the Netherlands and the north German province of Holstein; the Brown Swiss was originally bred in the canton of Schwyz in central Switzerland; the Maine–Anjou breed honors two old provinces of western France; and the Kerry breed reveals its Irish county of origin. The famous cheeses and butters of the world often have the names of towns, cities, or provinces in the European dairy belt, including Edam (Netherlands), Münster (Germany), Camembert (Normandie), Gruyères (Switzerland), Cheddar (English Somerset), and many others. In Russia, "Vologda" butter, bearing the name of a province north of Moskva, is synonymous with the highest quality product.

Pronounced regional contrasts exist within the European dairy belt, both in type of produce and intensity of farming. Denmark, which specializes in butter production and contributes a substantial percentage of all butter entering international trade, exemplifies highly developed dairying. The Danish farmers banded into local cooperatives, mainly for purposes of marketing but also for the construction of creameries. Land and livestock remain privately owned. Each package of butter bears a stamp with the code number of the cooperative and the individual farmer so that customer complaints concerning quality can be directed to the farmer responsible and fines levied. This system produces the highest-quality butter found anywhere, supplemented by fine pork and bacon from swine fattened on skim milk, a by-product of the butter-making process. In the Netherlands, attention is focused on milk and high-quality cheeses. Another advanced dairy country, the United Kingdom, has farmers specializing in fluid milk.

The rise of specialized dairying brought a profound change to the rural landscape. Villages and hamlets disappeared, replaced by scattered farmsteads, standing apart from each other in the American manner (figs. 11.8 and 11.19). The field patterns of the older land use systems were completely obliterated, replaced by pasture expanses.

Cattle and Hog Fattening

Another element of traditional three-field farming that survived into the modern age of commercialization and specialization is the breeding and fattening of cattle and hogs. Germanic and Slavic Europeans retain their preference for beef and pork. Most of the protein in their diet comes from these sources. As a result, an elongated belt of commercial cattle and hog

Figure 11.19. A modern, isolated dairy farmstead on the coastal plain of southwestern Iceland. Dairying tended to disperse the rural population from villages and hamlets, in the American manner. The farmstead retains no traditional architectural elements. (Photo by T.G.J.-B. 1994.)

fattening farms now stretches from the Paris Basin through Germany, Poland, and Ukraine into Russia (fig. 11.17). Feeder specialization began at least as early as the 1600s in parts of England, particularly in East Anglia northeast of London and Leicestershire in the Midlands. Similar developments occurred about the same time in parts of Germany and the Netherlands, but most such developments awaited the growth of urban markets in the 1800s.

Raising of livestock feed replaced production for human consumption, and a pronounced regional contrast developed in the choice of crops. South of a rather sharp line across the neck of the Balkan Peninsula, the Alps, and on through central France, maize is the principal feed crop used to fatten livestock, as in the American corn belt, but north of the line small grains and root crops dominate, including barley, oats, potatoes, and sugar beets. In Germany, 70% or more of the potato harvest goes for livestock feed.

Just as the European dairy belt gave names to many important breeds and dairy products, so the livestock feeder area influenced the names of meats and sausages. For example, thüringer, braunschweiger, and westphalian ham (actually beef) all derive from the names of provinces in the cattle and hog fattening areas, while frankfurter, wiener, and bologna bear the names of cities there.

Sheep Raising

A great portion of the hardscrabble regions originally devoted to herding with secondary crop farming is now engaged in specialized **sheep raising.** The Celtic fringes of the British Isles, Massif Central, Dinaric Range, Carpathians, and Iceland all contain important sheep raising districts today (fig. 11.17).

The market that prompted this specialization lay in the woolen textile districts, especially in Great Britain. In the 1700s and 1800s, landlords in the British highlands converted the far greater part of their estates to sheep pasture. Raising sheep required only a small resident population of herders. Most of the tenant farmers pursuing the traditional agricultural system became superfluous and found themselves cruelly evicted from the land in a long series of "clearances," their houses pulled down stone by stone and their stored food destroyed to make sure they could not return. Many perished. Others fled to Australia or North America, leaving behind hilly homelands devoted almost solely to sheep raising. Cattle largely disappeared from these areas, as did crops. The visitor to the British sheep raising districts today should be aware of the enormous human suffering and death caused by the advent of specialized agriculture.

Sheep are raised for both wool and meat, and most European pastures support very large flocks by world standards. In the Shetland Islands of Scotland, for example, 1.6 sheep can be kept on each hectare. Europeans consume far more mutton and lamb than do Americans, giving an added market impetus to raising sheep.

Cash Grain Farming

In some regions, the grain ager prevailed in the age of specialization and commercialization (fig. 11.17). *Wheat* became the most common cash grain and today dominates the former nomadic herding region in the steppes of Ukraine and Russia, forming Europe's greatest wheat belt. Large wheat farms also appear in parts of the Castilian Plateau and in the Paris Basin, served by migratory harvesting crews using giant American-made combines. Tall grain elevators now compete visually with Castilian church spires in local market towns, and much of the landscape has taken on the appearance of Kansas or Saskatchewan. The Seine River port of Rouen exports huge amounts of wheat.

Reindeer Ranching

Not even Sapmi, in the remotest northern fringes of Europe, has been immune to the far-reaching changes in the agricultural economy. Traditional nomadic herding by the Sami has been destroyed. Beginning in 1852, certain borders closed to their international migration, forcing the Sami to accept citizenship in one or another country and disrupting many routes of seasonal movement. An agreement allowed some Swedish Sami to use summer tundra pastures in Norway in exchange for the use of Swedish forests for winter refuge by Norwegian Sami, but border crossings are generally rare. Another significant change involved range fencing, separating the herds of adjacent groups and ending the traditional open-range system. One such fence parallels most of the Norwegian–Finnish border, and others have been built within the various nations. Sweden designated a Sapmi (*Lappmark*) border within its territory, north of which the Sami have precedence in rural land use. Even so, the Sami lost large areas that once belonged to them, particularly in Finland, where dairy farmers pushed far to the north. Commercial lumbering, utilizing large machines and clear-cutting techniques, damaged woodlands that once supported large herds.

Those who remain herders have adopted new, different methods. Snowmobiles replaced skis in reindeer herding, and the stock receives less frequent attention nowadays, owing to the fencing of ranges and the reduction of predators. Herders now belong to cooperatives, which operate much like collective farms. Norway established a Reindeer Office within its Ministry of Agriculture, and the Sami herders of that country belong to the National Association of Reindeer Herders. The Reindeer Office requires reports of the number of livestock each year, supervises migrations, and demands that each owner mark his or her deer and register the mark. Sanitary slaughter sheds and meat-freezing plants have been built, and commercial marketing of reindeer meat advanced. Most Sami abandoned herding altogether, accepting employment in fishing, mining, and other industries. Only about 7,000 still engage in reindeer raising, with cumulative herds totaling about 700,000. In the Swedish province of Västerbotten, for example, about 100 herder families remain in business, owning an average of 500 reindeer each.

Fish Farming

Some modern types of agriculture do not derive from traditional types. One example is hothouse market gardening near Reykjavik in Iceland, where all sorts of warmth-loving crops such as bananas grow beneath glass. **Fish farming** provides another example. In the past 3 decades or so, northern Scotland, parts of Ireland, western Norway, and the Faeroe Islands have become fish farming centers, an enterprise that grew out of the traditional importance of fishing (figs. 11.17 and 11.20). Fish farming focuses mainly upon salmon, raised in anchored cages moored in the saltwater inlets, bays, and channels of peripheral northwestern Europe. In the same region, trout grow to maturity in freshwater ponds, often providing

Figure 11.20.   A salmon fish farm in Sundini, the saltwater sound between the two main Faeroe Islands, Eysturoy and Streymoy. The fish are confined to the circular enclosures, and food for them is being strewn from the boat. (Photo by T.G.J.-B. 1994.)

a second income on sheep farms. These valued fish find a ready market in the urban areas of western Europe and now offer significant competition for the fishing industry.

Agricultural change in Europe extended far beyond new crop introductions and the rise of specialized, market-oriented types. Radical changes occurred and are still happening in land consolidation and land tenure.

Land Consolidation

All traditional crop farming systems in Europe involved fragmented holdings. Farmers had many different fields, at varying distances and directions from the village or hamlet (fig. 11.11). For example, in a village near Zamora, in Spain, one particular farmer owned 394 separate parcels, each averaging only 0.07 hectare. Such a field system put European farmers at a distinct disadvantage in producing cash crops. As a result, all governments took steps to bring about **land consolidation,** redrawing property lines to reduce or eliminate the fragmentation of holdings.

Land consolidation began as the *enclosure* movement in the United Kingdom, where the process was completed in the late 1700s. Scandinavian countries followed the British example, and in the twentieth century most other western European countries followed suit. The process was slow. In western Germany, only half of all agricultural land had undergone consolidation by the middle 1970s.

Eastern Europe experienced an altogether different process in the elimination of fragmented holdings. Under communism, large fields suited to collective agriculture abruptly replaced private farms, radically and suddenly altering the rural landscape. To the present day, the border between west and east remains vividly etched on the countryside, visible even from outer space (fig. 11.21).

Land-Tenure Changes

Traditionally, almost all of rural Europe belonged to a landed aristocracy. The peasantry, laboring as tenants, were required to pay a share of their produce as rent. Only the Finnish burnbeaters and nomadic herders escaped this pervasive bondage. In a few regions, large landed estates survive to the present day, as in southern Iberia, parts of southern Italy, and some British Highland areas.

Elsewhere, agrarian *land reform* took place. In most of western Europe, a steady move toward peasant landownership occurred between about 1650 and 1850 with a gradual elimination of the landed aristocracy. This

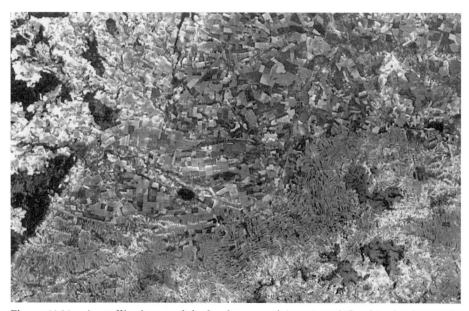

Figure 11.21.   A satellite image of the border area of Austria and Czechia clearly reveals the contrast between Austria's small, fragmented farms and the large collective enterprises of the formerly communist east. You should be able to spot the border easily. (Source: U.S. Landsat imagery.)

transition occurred in various ways, but the sequence of events in the Po Valley of northern Italy is illustrative. Landlords there by law had to pay outgoing peasant tenants for any improvements made during their terms as renters, and failure to do so forced the owner to renew the lease at no increase in rent. These improvements included clearing of woodland, marsh drainage, or even irrigation development, for which the landlords were hard pressed to pay, and typically they allowed the lease to be renewed. The rent thus remained constant while inflation lowered its relative cost, until eventually the peasant could buy the land. In Greece, the successful rebellion against Turkish rule had the side effect of destroying the landed aristocracy, composed primarily of Turks. Typical of present conditions is the Greek island of Kriti, where 96% of the farmers owned their land by 1960.

In eastern Europe the landed aristocracy persisted, and few farmers gained possession of the fields they worked. Many aspects of medieval bondage survived into the 1900s in Slavic Europe and eastern Germany. A more drastic and violent solution came there—liquidation of the landed aristocracy under communist dictatorships. Typically, the communists won early peasant support by promising the farmers landownership. In 1946, for example, such a campaign occurred in Soviet-occupied East Germany under the slogan "aristocrats' lands in farmers' hands." After a brief period of peasant ownership, the state confiscated the land and established *collective* and *state farms*. Collectives involved farmers operating as a unit, more or less in business for themselves as a group, paying rent to the state and splitting profits. In the less-common state farm system, the farmers labored as salaried state employees for a fixed wage on huge superfarms, turning all produce over to the government. Collective and state farms became dominant in most communist countries.

Since the collapse of communism, land tenure has once again undergone fundamental changes in eastern Europe. Every formerly communist country is presently experiencing privatization of the agricultural sector, with differing results and rates of progress. Some commonalties exist. In the majority of countries, most state and collective farms have been replaced with cooperative farms, owned and operated by the workers, who no longer answer to state planners. The ancient peasant collectivism of eastern Europe replaced the state-owned enterprises. In the process, almost everywhere, production levels fell sharply and many farm workers left the land.

In Russia, some collectives made the transition directly to agribusiness, when farm directors from the Soviet era seized ownership and became capitalistic entrepreneurs. Even so, some 270,000 private farms had been established in Russia by January 1994, though actual individual landownership did not exist. The greatest strides toward privatization occurred in the fertile black-earth belt of southern Eurorussia. Farm production declined in the 1990s, and today nearly half of all food grown in Russia comes from garden lands, especially in the urban peripheries, where many city dwellers own or rent plots of land. Russia has still not approved private land ownership, in the western sense of the term.

Nor has Ukraine, which possesses the richest farmlands of Europe. Only 2% of the land is tilled by private farmers, who are not allowed to control more than 100 hectares each, too little to be commercially viable. Private collectives now prevail in Ukraine, but they remain notoriously inefficient. Estonia, a Baltic republic, made the transition to private farm ownership, but in the process agricultural production fell by 56% between 1990 and 1997, and 30% of all arable land now lies fallow. In all of Estonia, only a few farms are operating at a competitive level. Neighboring Latvia seems to have made the transition to private, family-operated farms more smoothly, and agricultural production began to increase again in the middle 1990s, following an abrupt decline. In Latvia, 95% of all farms are now privately owned.

In Romania, nearly half of all parcels had passed into private hands as early as 1991, but the average size of such farms today is only 2.25 hectares. Most are seriously undercapitalized and unable to achieve more than a subsistence production. By law, they cannot exceed 10 hectares in area. The state-owned cooperative farm, a compromise between socialistic and capitalistic enterprise but retaining far more of the old system, remains important in Romania. Neighboring Bulgaria allowed each state collective to oversee its own dissolution, dividing land and fixed assets as fairly as possible.

By contrast, in Czechia, Slovakia, and Hungary, most land reverted to private ownership but was then promptly pooled into cooperatives or rented to agribusiness enterprises. Many people own land while the number of renters is small. Hungary reached a similar solution, allowing the old collectives to survive as cooperatives. About a third of Hungarian farmland in cooperatives is privately owned and 61% collectively owned. For example, the area of the former Noble Grape Collective near Lake Balaton in western Hungary is now in the hands of about 2,000 private landowners, most of whom rent their property to one of several successor wine-producing companies. Slovakia has favored cooperatives over agribusiness enterprises.

In the former East Germany, yet another solution was found. The 4,500 state-owned farms in 1990, at the close of the communist period, gave way to 20,000 corporate and private enterprises by 1993. Corporate agribusiness now owns 80% of all east German livestock. In the process, the farm population plummeted from 850,000 in 1989 to 160,000 by 1995! The restoration of rural property to private owners is complete, but most east German landowners are absentee and lease their property to corporate agribusinesses.

Development of Core and Periphery

The commercialization of European agriculture led to another fundamental change—the emergence of a pronounced core–periphery pattern. Land use intensified throughout Europe in the modern age but most profoundly in the central regions closest to the industrial complexes and growing cities. Any number of statistical measures reveal the agrarian core–periphery pattern of Europe, including grain productivity per hectare, percentage of land cultivated, livestock density, amount of fertilizer applied per hectare, value of agricultural produce per capita, and the distribution of economically distressed rural regions (fig. 11.22).

Increased intensity of land use in the European core began in England in the 1700s and is sometimes referred to as the Agricultural Revolution. One of its first victims was the traditional three-field system. Fallowing 1 year in 3 disappeared from the three-field rotation, greatly increasing the acreage and production of feed crops. Fallowing had always been something of a problem, because the field quickly became choked with grass and weeds in the idle year unless the farmers continually cultivated it. In many areas, turnip crops replaced the fallow, with repeated hoeing employed to keep the weeds out. Improved, more complicated crop rotations were developed, such as the *Norfolk four-course rotation*, which included turnips. Improved pastures and meadows resulted from the spread of new varieties of clover, and the increased planting of turnips and sugar beets added significantly to the amount of livestock feed. The amount of pastureland declined, and many old grazing areas became cropland. The net result of the changes was a marked increase in the amount of feed available for livestock, and the numbers of animals rose accordingly. Stall feeding became all-important, for many stock were kept penned rather than roaming about in pastures and forests. Increased confinement of animals also allowed a more complete collection of manure, which in turn aided the elimination of fallowing. The changes occurred in a spiral: the elimination of fallowing, an increase in yield of feed crops, more livestock per farm, more manure per farm, increased fertility of fields, increased yields of feed crops, and so on. Chemical fertilizers, invented by the Germans, assisted the upward spiral, as did agricultural machinery of various kinds. Later, in the twentieth century, pesticides further enhanced productivity. Increased attention to selective breeding produced better-quality livestock and hybrid seeds.

In all of these changes, peripheral parts of Europe lagged behind the core. The reason lay largely in the geographical principle of *land rent*, originally revealed in the work of J. H. von Thünen. Land rent, the return for the use of land in excess of the minimum expenditure required to operate

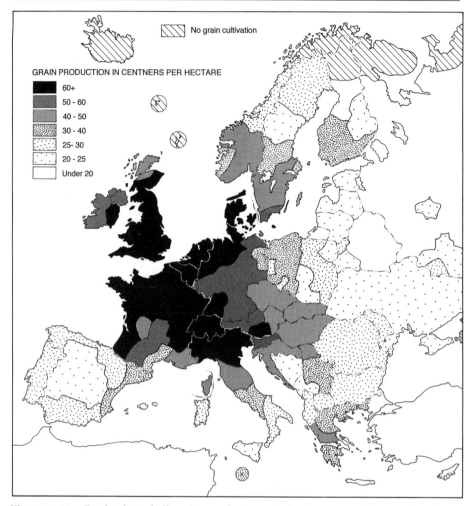

Figure 11.22.   Production of all grains per hectare. A classic core–periphery pattern is revealed, a recurring geographical configuration in Europe. Anomalies include the cultivation of irrigated rice in some small Mediterranean districts and maize in the Balkans, which yields far more per unit of land than the European small grains. The principle of land rent is evident in this pattern.

a farm, is directly proportional to land value, and both of these decrease with increasing distance from market, all other factors being equal. Assuming that all farmers will maximize land rent and possess the knowledge to do so, then an orderly set of concentric zones of land use ought to surround a market. For any particular crop, the intensity of production decreases with increasing distance from market since more and more capital and time must be expended on transportation rather than on production. The most intensive forms of agriculture, then, will lie closest to the market, thereby producing a core–periphery pattern. Figure 11.22 reveals the geographical impact of the land-rent principle in commercialized agricultural Europe. As early as the 1920s, the Swedish geographer Olaf Jonasson demonstrated that the industrial belt of northwestern Europe constituted one huge urban area or supercity, flanked by an inner zone of market gardening and dairying.

Rural Depopulation

Another profound agricultural change in Europe during the past 2 centuries has been the flight of people from the land. Today, only a small minority of Europeans still work in agriculture, constituting in some districts less than 3% of the labor force (fig. 11.23). The decline of farm population has been absolute as well as proportional, and flight to the cities continues today.

In large part, economic causes explain the emigration of rural people. Europe's small farms simply could not effectively compete on the world market when the commercialization of agriculture occurred. At the same time, the growing cities offered abundant jobs at salaries allowing a higher standard of living. One of the criteria defining economically depressed regions in Europe today is a higher-than-average proportion of the workforce in agriculture. Those who remain in farming often take second jobs to augment their income. Increasingly, people left in the countryside are elderly. Aging of the agricultural population guarantees that the numbers engaged in farming will continue to dwindle.

The map showing the proportion of the labor force working in agriculture reveals several basic geographical patterns that should by now be familiar to you. A core–periphery configuration appears, in which the lands bordering the North Sea rank lowest in percentage employed in farming (fig. 11.23). The eye also detects north–south and east–west contrasts.

Emigration from the countryside caused both a decline in the number of farms and an increase in their size. In western Germany, for example, the number of farms declined by 57% between 1949 and 1986, and in Finland by half between 1960 and 1990. A third of all French vineyards disappeared since 1960. In every country, the agricultural contribution to the national economy declined sharply. Some countries, most notably Norway, provide subsidies designed to keep people working the land, with results readily visible when one crosses the Norwegian–Swedish border, but the trend nevertheless continues.

Rural depopulation produced not merely larger farms, but also large-scale land abandonment. In particular, farmland of marginal quality has gone out of production. In eastern Germany's sandy Brandenburg Province, for example, almost one-fifth of the farmland was abandoned at the

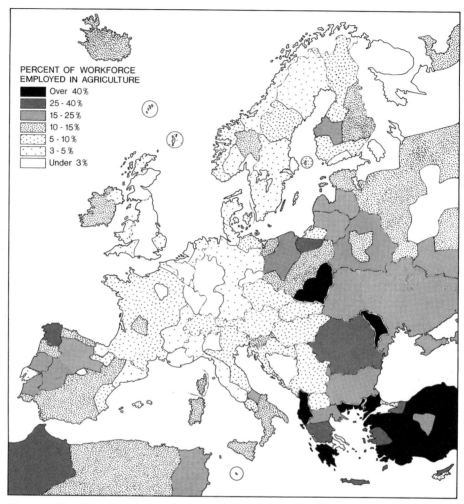

Figure 11.23. Percentage of workforce employed in agriculture. The pattern is complicated, revealing north–south, east–west, and core–periphery elements.

collapse of the communist collectives in 1991–1992. One Brandenburg collective, in a conversion loaded with irony and symbolism, became a golf
course for affluent former West Berliners.

Indeed, recreational land use of one type or another, including tourism,
has taken over much of Europe's abandoned farmland, a trend likely to
continue (fig. 11.24). Many Europeans own second homes in the countryside, often converted farmhouses purchased cheaply from departing agriculturists. Also helping to fill the rural void are large-scale afforestation
projects, especially in the Mediterranean and Celtic fringe, as mentioned in
chapter 2.

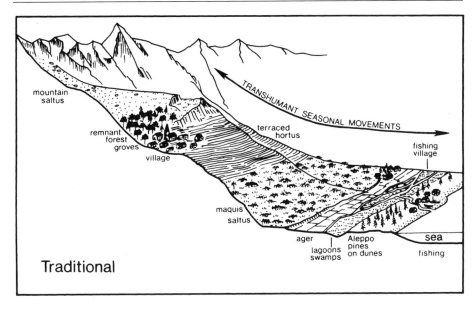

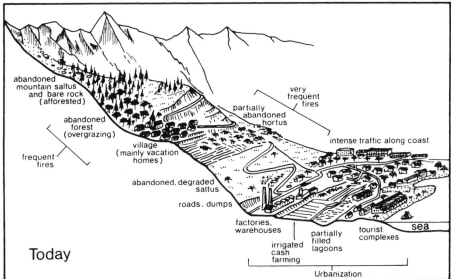

Figure 11.24.   Change comes to a rural Mediterranean slope. Many of the modern changes in European agriculture discussed in the text are summarized in this sketch. (*Source:* Modified from Grenon and Batisse 1989, figure 1.3.)

Preserving Rural Landscapes

As European agriculture changes, the venerable villages, hamlets, and farmsteads that provide beauty and charm to the countryside stand at risk. The traditional landscape, often so ancient as to confound those who seek its origins, proves ill-suited to the demands of the modern age. Europe could quickly lose much of its aesthetic appeal. Europeans in many countries responded to the endangerment of their rural landscapes with effective, subsidized preservation programs. In the Netherlands, for example, some 43,000 features of the cultural landscape were listed and protected by the middle 1980s, including 5,300 farm buildings, 1,000 mills, and an array of other objects such as wayside shrines. In various countries, rigorously enforced building codes restrict the demolition of traditional structures and regulate their renovation. Beneath the façade of a seventeenth-century farmhouse may lie a modern suburban home equipped with central heating, modern appliances, and a Jacuzzi. New buildings often must be architecturally compatible with traditional ones. In short, many countries have inventoried their rural landscapes, passed protective legislation, implemented preservation, aggressively resorted to rural land use zoning, and subsidized these enterprises with tax monies.

The core countries in Europe have been most active in such undertakings, while those of the peripheries have been more lax. Much of the rural charm of countries such as Spain, Romania, and Russia has been squandered and cannot be retrieved. Hopefully, enough will survive to perpetuate the rich mosaic of rural landscapes.

The time has come now for a summing up of the geography of Europe, a daunting task at best. In the final chapter, we will seek to join and mingle the findings of the first 11 chapters by proposing an overarching framework of regions within Europe.

Sources and Suggested Readings

Agnew, Swanzie. 1946. "The Vine in Bas Languedoc." *Geographical Review* 36:67–79.

Aitken, Robert. 1945. "Routes of Transhumance on the Spanish Meseta." *Geographical Journal* 106:59–69.

Andrews, Jean. 1993. "Diffusion of Mesoamerican Food Complex to Southeastern Europe." *Geographical Review* 83:194–204.

Black, Richard. 1992. *Crisis and Change in Rural Europe: Agricultural Development in the Portuguese Mountains.* Aldershot, GB: Avebury.

Boyazoglu, Jean, and Jean-Claude Flamant. 1990. "Mediterranean Systems of Animal Production." In *The World of Pastoralism,* ed. John G. Galaty and Douglas L. Johnson. London, GB: Belhaven, 353–393.

Breunig, Peter. 1987. ^{14}C-*Chronologie des vorderasiatischen, südost- und mitteleuropäischen Neolithikums*. Köln, D: Böhlau.

Buschan, Georg, ed. 1926. *Illustrierte Völkerkunde*. Vol. 2. Pt. 2. Stuttgart, D: Strecker & Schröder.

Chapman, John, and Johannes Müller. 1990. "Early Farmers in the Mediterranean Basin." *Antiquity* 64:128.

Cleary, M. C. 1987. "Contemporary Transhumance in Languedoc." *Geografiska Annaler* 69B:107–114.

Clout, Hugh. 1991. "The Recomposition of Rural Europe." *Annales de Géographie* 100:714–729.

Coull, James R. 1988. "Fish Farming in the Highlands and Islands: Boom Industry of the 1980s." *Scottish Geographical Magazine* 104:4–13.

Crowley, William K. 1993. "Changes in the French Winescape." *Geographical Review* 83:252–268.

Demangeon, Albert. 1920. "L'habitation rurale en France: essai de clasification des principaux types." *Annales de Géographie* 29:352–375.

———. 1939. "Types de villages en France." *Annales de Géographie* 48:1–21.

———. 1946. *La France*. Paris, F: Armand Colin.

Epstein, D. M., and A. Valmari. 1984. "Reindeer Herding and Ecology in Finnish Lapland." *GeoJournal* 8:159–169.

Evans, E. Estyn. 1956. "The Ecology of Peasant Life in Western Europe." In *Man's Role in Changing the Face of the Earth*, ed. William L. Thomas Jr. Chicago, USA: University of Chicago Press, 217–239.

Fry, Virginia K. 1971. "Reindeer Ranching in Northern Russia." *Professional Geographer* 23:146–151.

Gardner, Brian. 1996. *European Agriculture: Policies, Production, and Trade*. London, GB: Routledge.

Grenon, Michel, and Michel Batisse, eds. 1989. *Futures for the Mediterranean Basin: The Blue Plan*. Oxford, GB: Oxford University Press.

Häkkilä, Matti. 1991. "Some Regional Trends in Finnish Farming with Special Reference to Agricultural Policy." *Fennia* 169:39–56.

Hance, William A. 1951. "Crofting Settlements and Housing in the Outer Hebrides." *Annals of the Association of American Geographers* 41:75–87.

Helle, Reijo K. 1979. "Reindeer Husbandry in Finland." *Geographical Journal* 145:254–264.

Hofmeister, Burkhard. 1971. "Four Types of Agriculture with Predominant Olive Growing in Southern Spain: A Case Study." *Geoforum* 8:15–30.

Hoggart, Keith, Henry Buller, and Richard Black. 1995. *Rural Europe: Identity and Change*. London, GB: Arnold.

Hoskins, W. G. 1957. *The Making of the English Landscape*. London, GB: Hodder & Stoughton.

Ioffe, Grigory, and Tatyana Nefedova. 1997. *Continuity and Change in Rural Russia: A Geographical Perspective*. Boulder, Colo., USA: Westview.

———. 2000. *The Environs of Russian Cities*. Lampeter, Wales, GB: Edwin Mellen.

Johnston, W. B., and I. Crkvencic. 1957. "Examples of Changing Peasant Agriculture in Croatia." *Economic Geography* 33:50–71.

Jonasson, Olaf. 1925–1926. "The Agricultural Regions of Europe." *Economic Geography* 1:277–314; 2:19–48.

King, Russell L., and Alan Strachan. 1978. "Sicilian Agro-towns." *Erdkunde* 32:110–123.

King, Russell L., and Laurence Took. 1983. "Land Tenure and Rural Social Change: The Italian Case." *Erdkunde* 37:186–198.

Kostrowicki, Jerzy. 1984. "The Types of Agriculture Map of Europe." Nine sheets, scale 1:2,500,000. Warszawa, PL: Institute of Geography and Spatial Organization, Polish Academy of Sciences.

Krantz, Grover S. 1988. *Geographical Development of European Languages.* New York, USA: Peter Lang.

Lovell, W. George. 1996. "The Solitude of Solanell." *Geographical Review* 86:259–269.

Lydolph, Paul E. 1964. "The Russian Sukhovey." *Annals of the Association of American Geographers* 54:291–309.

Marañón, Teodoro. 1988. "Agro-Sylvo-Pastoral Systems in the Iberian Peninsula: Dehesas and Montados." *Rangelands* 10 (6): 255–258.

Matley, Ian M. 1968. "Transhumance in Bosnia and Herzegovina." *Geographical Review* 58:231–261.

Mayhew, Alan. 1973. *Rural Settlement and Farming in Germany.* New York, USA: Barnes & Noble.

Meirion-Jones, Gwyn I. 1982. *The Vernacular Architecture of Brittany: An Essay in Historical Geography.* Edinburgh, GB: Donald.

Millman, R. N. 1975. *The Making of the Scottish Landscape.* London, GB: Batsford.

Montelius, Sigvard. 1953. "The Burning of Forest Land for the Cultivation of Crops: Svedjebruk in Central Sweden." *Geografiska Annaler* 35:41–54.

Müller-Wille, Wilhelm. 1936. "Haus- und Gehöftformen in Mitteleuropa." *Geographische Zeitschrift* 42:121–138.

Netting, Robert M. 1981. *Balancing on an Alp: Ecological Change and Continuity in a Swiss Mountain Community.* Cambridge, GB: Cambridge University Press.

Otremba, Erich. 1961. "Die deutsche Agrarlandschaft." *Geographische Zeitschrift Beiheft* 3.

Overton, Mark. 1985. "Diffusion of Agricultural Innovations in Early Modern England, 1580–1740." *Transactions of the Institute of British Geographers* 10:205–221.

Pallot, J. 1984. "Open Fields and Individual Farms: Land Reform in Pre-revolutionary Russia." *Tijdschrift voor Economische en Sociale Geografie* 75:46–60.

Palomäki, Mauri J., and Allen G. Noble. 1995. "Greenhouse Horticulture and Economic Transition." *Geographical Review* 85:173–184.

Parsons, James J. 1962. "The Acorn-hog Economy of the Oak Woodlands of Southwestern Spain." *Geographical Review* 52:211–235.

Pfeifer, Gottfried. 1956. "The Quality of Peasant Living in Central Europe." In *Man's Role in Changing the Face of the Earth,* ed. William L. Thomas Jr. Chicago, USA: University of Chicago Press, 240–277.

Renfrew, Colin. 1989. "The Origins of Indo-European Languages." *Scientific American* 261 (4): 106–114.

Roberts, Brian K. 1979. *Rural Settlement in Britain.* London, GB: Hutchinson.

Rose, Richard, and Yevgeniy Tikhomirov. 1993. "Who Grows Food in Russia and Eastern Europe?" *Post-Soviet Geography* 34:111–126.

Rother, Klaus. 1986. "Agrarian Development and Conflicts of Land Utilization in the Coastal Plain of Calabria (South Italy)." *GeoJournal* 13:27–35.

Ryan, William, and Walter Pitman. 1998. *Noah's Flood.* New York, USA: Simon & Schuster.

Schacht, Siegfried. 1988. "Portuguese Agrarian Reform and Its Effects on Rural Property and Agricultural Enterprise Conditions." *Erdkunde* 42:203–213.

Schröder, Karl H., and Gabriele Schwarz. 1969. *Die ländlichen Siedlungsformen in*

Mitteleuropa. Bad Godesberg, D: Bundesforschungsanstalt für Landeskunde und Raumordnung.

Semple, Ellen Churchill. 1928. "Ancient Mediterranean Agriculture." *Agricultural History* 2:61–98, 129–156.

Smith, Peter. 1988. *Houses of the Welsh Countryside: A Study in Historical Geography.* 2nd ed. London, GB: Her Majesty's Stationery Office.

Sokal, Robert R., Neal L. Ogden, and Chester Wilson. 1991. "Genetic Evidence for the Spread of Agriculture in Europe by Demic Diffusion." *Nature* 351:143–145.

Stanislawski, Dan. 1970. *Landscapes of Bacchus: The Vine in Portugal.* Austin, USA: University of Texas Press.

———. 1975. "Dionysius Westward: Early Religion and the Economic Geography of Wine." *Geographical Review* 65:427–444.

Stroyev, K. F. 1975. "Agriculture in the Non-chernozem Zone of the RSFSR." *Soviet Geography: Review and Translation* 16:186–196.

Sylvester, Dorothy. 1969. *The Rural Landscape of the Welsh Borderland: A Study in Historical Geography.* London, GB: Macmillan.

Thorpe, Harry. 1961. "The Green Village as a Distinctive Form of Settlement on the North European Plain." *Bulletin de la Société Belge d'Ètudes Géographiques* 30:93–134.

Thorpe, I. J. 1996. *The Origins of Agriculture in Europe.* London, GB: Routledge.

Troll, Karl. 1925. "Die Landbauzonen Europas in ihrer Beziehung zur natürlichen Vegetation." *Geographische Zeitschrift* 31:265–280.

Uhlig, Harald. 1961. "Old Hamlets with Infield and Outfield Systems in Western and Central Europe." *Geografiska Annaler* 43:285–312.

Valdes, Alberto, Casaba Csaki, and Achim Fock. 1998. "Estonian Agriculture in Efforts to Accede to the European Union." *Post-Soviet Geography and Economics* 39:518–548.

van Valkenburg, Samuel. 1960. "An Evaluation of the Standard of Land Use in Western Europe." *Economic Geography* 36:283–295.

Vidal de la Blache, Paul. 1926. *Principles of Human Geography.* New York, USA: Henry Holt.

Vogeler, Ingolf. 1996. "State Hegemony in Transforming the Rural Landscapes of Eastern Germany." *Annals of the Association of American Geographers* 86:432–458.

Wagstaff, John M. 1969. "The Study of Greek Rural Settlements." *Erdkunde* 23:306–317.

Wilhelmy, Herbert. 1936. "Völkische und koloniale Siedlungsformen der Slawen." *Geographische Zeitschrift* 42:81–97.

Woodruffe, Brian J. 1990. "Conservation and the Rural Landscape." In *Western Europe: Challenge and Change,* ed. David Pinder. London, GB: Belhaven, 258–276.

Zilhão, João. 1993. "The Spread of Agro-pastoral Economies across Mediterranean Europe." *Journal of Mediterranean Archaeology* 6:5–63.

CHAPTER 12

Regions

Europe emerges from our geographical study, paradoxically, as both *one* and *many*. Beneath the overarching unity that prompted our use of the phrase "European culture area," beneath the façade of a "common European home," we have uncovered major, often ancient cultural fault lines and divides. So far, our overview of this internal division has remained fragmented. We proceeded through 10 topical chapters, each devoted to a different aspect of geography and each presenting Europe as both one and many. Confusingly, each chapter revealed a different internal division of Europe. Now, in the final chapter, we must try to make sense of all this.

The Europe of the Regions

The temptation is to surrender to the seemingly overwhelming internal diversity of the culture area and accept the increasingly popular notion of a multiple "Europe of the Regions" or "Europe of the Homelands." To do so is to shatter Europe into well over a hundred separate pieces (fig. 12.1). Actually, the 117 regions shown in figure 12.1 represent a coarse grouping. We could justifiably split many of the 117 further, recognizing 200, 300, or even 500 regions. Such a map would attain a Medusa-like capacity to turn the viewer into stone. And to what purpose? Such geographical complexity, even at the level of 117 regions, simply boggles the mind.

Let us, instead, reject "splitting" for "lumping." A simpler regional classification of Europe is both feasible and potentially instructive. We find recurrent regional patterns presented in the preceding topical chapters, including east versus west, north versus south, and core versus periphery. These can be combined to yield a more rational regional classification.

West versus East

Repeatedly in our study, contrasts between *eastern* and *western* Europe appeared (fig. 12.2). This sectional difference often enjoys fundamental

393

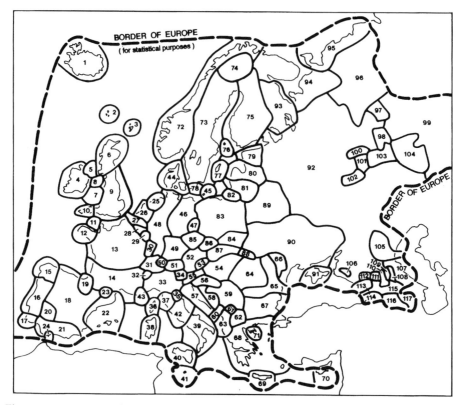

Figure 12.1.   Europe of the 117 regions. *Key:* 1. Iceland; 2. Faeroes; 3. Shetlands; 4. Ireland; 5. Ulster; 6. Scotland; 7. Wales; 8. Man; 9. England; 10. Cornwall; 11. Channel Islands; 12. Bretagne/Brittany; 13. Paris Basin; 14. Occitania; 15. Galiza; 16. Portugal; 17. The Algarve; 18. Castilla and León; 19. Pais Vasco/Euskera; 20. Extremadura; 21. Andalucía; 22. Catalunya; 23. Andorra; 24. Gibraltar; 25. Friesen; 26. Holland; 27. Vlaanderen; 28. Wallonia; 29. Luxembourg; 30. Alsace; 31. Helvetia; 32. Val d'Aosta; 33. Padania; 34. Friulia; 35. San Marino; 36. Corsica; 37. Toscana; 38. Sardegna; 39. Mezzogiorno; 40. Sicilia; 41. Malta; 42. Central Italy/Roma; 43. Monaco; 44. Denmark; 45. Bornholm; 46. East Germany; 47. Lusatia/Lausitz; 48. West Germany; 49. Bayern; 50. Liechtenstein; 51. Tirol; 52. Austria; 53. Burgenland; 54. Hungary; 55. Slovenia; 56. Croatia/Slavonia; 57. Dalmacija; 58. Bosnia; 59. Serbia; 60. Crna Gora; 61. Kosovo; 62. Macedonia; 63. Albania; 64. Transylvania; 65. Romania proper/Old Kingdom; 66. Moldova; 67. Bulgaria; 68. Greece; 69. Kriti; 70. Cyprus; 71. Athos; 72. Norway; 73. Sweden; 74. Sapmi; 75. Finland; 76. Åland; 77. Gotland; 78. Skåne; 79. Estonia; 80. Latvia; 81. Lithuania; 82. Kaliningrad/Königsberg; 83. Poland; 84. Galicia; 85. Bohemia; 86. Moravia; 87. Slovakia; 88. Transcarpathia/Ruthenia; 89. Belarus; 90. Ukraine; 91. Crimea/Krym; 92. Eurorussia; 93. Karelia; 94. Kola/Murmansk; 95. Nenetsia; 96. Komi; 97. Permyakia; 98. Udmurtia; 99. Russo-Siberia; 100. Mari El; 101. Chuvashia; 102. Mordvinia; 103. Tatarstan; 104. Bashkortostan; 105. Kalmykia; 106. Adygeya; 107. Dagestan; 108. Ichkería/Chechnya; 109. Ingushetia; 110. Ossetia; 111. Kabardino–Balkaria; 112. Karachay–Cherkessia; 113. Abkhazia; 114. Ajaria; 115. Georgia; 116. Armenia; and 117. Nagorno–Karabakh.

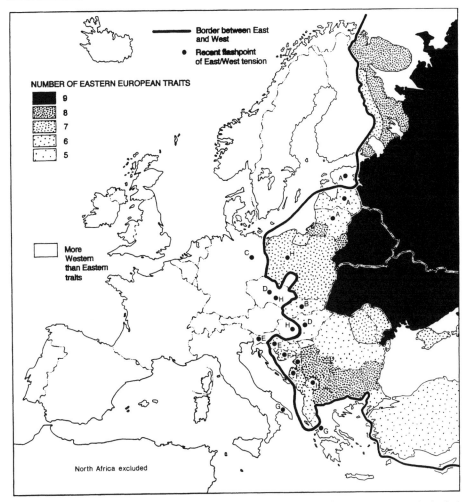

Figure 12.2.   West versus east in Europe. Nine representative characteristics are included (western trait listed first in each case): 1. Latin/Greek Christianity; 2. Latin/Greek–Cyrillic alphabet; 3. Western/Eastern Indo-European languages; 4. less than 8/greater than 8 per thousand infant mortality rate; 5. marine/continental climate; 6. less than 4/greater than 4 persons per automobile; 7. small, compartmentalized terrain units/expansive plains; 8. per capita GDP more/less than 50% of EU-15 average; and 9. more/less than 100 Internet connections per 10,000 people. Uniate Christians are counted as Greek. Uralic and Altaic languages are counted as "eastern," Basque as "western." Unshaded areas have fewer than 5 western or eastern traits. Flash points of tension include: A. Baltic republic secessions; B. Slovakia secession; C. collapse of the German Democratic Republic; D. restoration of democracy to the Czechia and Hungary; E. Croatia and Slovenia secessions from Yugoslavia; F. Bosnian Serb desire to link with Serbia; G. Italian–Greek rejection of Albanian refugees; H. Poland, Hungary, and Czechia join NATO; and I. Kosovo dispute.

importance, as for example the east–west partition between Greek and Roman Christianity and between the two main divisions of Indo-European languages. Roman, or Western, Christianity eventually provided the path to the Renaissance and the Enlightenment, to democracy, individualism, capitalism, prosperity, materialism, and creativity, while Eastern Orthodoxy, by contrast, fostered enduring paternalism, mysticism, spiritualism, collectivism, conformity, and ultimately Marxist dictatorship. The Protestant Reformation served to widen the gap.

Because eastern Europe rejected the eighteenth-century Enlightenment—the notion that if we discard the superstition of religion and use our 5 senses in a disciplined manner, we can acquire ultimate truth and knowledge—the west came to stigmatize and denigrate the east. The ancient schism between Roma and Constantinople, between Roman and Greek, opened wider. Eastern Europe's rejection of the Reformation made the east–west split a chasm. Thus, the British writer Jan Morris, visiting Trieste near the east–west divide, stood at "the cusp," looking "one way toward Rome and Paris and London, the other toward Belgrade and Bucharest and Athens" (and Moskva).

Eastern Europe, forever tainted in the minds of westerners by Asianization, by Mongol, Tatar, Hun, and Turk, must remain partly alien. Western Europe, in the minds of easterners forever tainted by secularization, materialism, and liberty-taken-to-license, must remain an entity apart. Gennadi Zuganov, leader of Russia's Communist Party at the dawn of the twenty-first century, saw Russia—his "dreamer idealist nation"—still engaged in the ancient struggle between Western and Eastern Civilization. So, it seems, does Vladimir Putin.

As a result, east versus west continues to describe the most basic internal contrast within Europe. Living standards differ strikingly between the 2 halves of the culture area, whether measured by infant mortality, employment in the service industries, automobile ownership, or more comprehensive indices of material prosperity and well being. Books bearing titles such as *East–West Life Expectancy Gap in Europe* do not startle the prospective, informed reader. Less convinced than westerners that the individual person controls his or her destiny, the fatalistic easterner is more likely to smoke, eat, and drink to excess. In Russia, 67% of all males smoke, while only 37% of German and 38% of Italian men do so. Eastern European tradition "involves badgering the guest to eat and drink more than he likes," and the east is a realm "where public lavatories are revolting" (*Economist*, 16 November, 1996, 50).

East and West further involve 2 Christian faiths, 2 major divisions of the Indo-European languages, 2 alphabets—2 separate peoples and lands. The chapter on physical environment revealed a western rimland with mild marine climate, deciduous woodlands, and small, compartmentalized terrain units, contrasted to an eastern heartland with harsh continental climate, coniferous forests, and expansive, unbroken plains. Politically, the west lies fragmented into myriad independent states, while most of the east, even after the collapse of the Soviet Union, forms part of the largest country in the world. Even seemingly trivial differences contribute to the dichotomy of east versus west. For example, the farm villages of the east obey a rigid, planned geometry, while those of the west sprawl chaotically.

Peruse the titles of books and articles at the end of this chapter. Note that 25 different ones employ the term *Western Europe* or *Eastern Europe* in their titles, a revealing measure of the importance geographers place upon this particular pattern of internal European division.

Not surprisingly, flash points of tension and disagreement continue to flare along the east–west divide in Europe. The Cold War—the most vivid and profound reflection of east–west conflict—passed into history, but harmony has hardly returned to this great cultural fault zone. Politically, the east–west divide helped prompt Slovaks to secede from Czechoslovakia, Croats and Slovenes to withdraw from Yugoslavia, Italians to repulse Albanian refugees, and the Baltic states—after 50 years of subjugation—to leave the Soviet Union. It partially explains both the demise of the German Democratic Republic and the disdain with which many west and east Germans still regard each other. It underlies the 1999 NATO bombing of Serbia and invasion of Kosovo, as well as the earlier intervention in Bosnia.

Expanding by spurts over the decades, the European Union has come to provide the most compelling statement of western Europe, representing democracy, progress, prosperity, and capitalism. Fortified by the NATO, the European Union is a formidable bastion of western Europe. Politically and economically shattered eastern Europe, loosely and ineffectually regrouped as the Commonwealth of Independent States, belongs to another world. Europe, then, continues to acknowledge an ancient cultural divide, one as old as the culture area itself. Truly, as Rudyard Kipling said, "east is east and west is west," even within Europe.

North versus South

While less profound today than the east–west divide, the contrast between *northern* and *southern* Europe remains substantial (fig. 12.3). This, too, is an ancient cleavage, along which the Greco-Roman civilization long ago battled barbarian Germans, Celts, and Slavs. The border of the Roman Empire at its apex, about A.D. 110, still possesses cultural consequence in present-day Europe. It helps explain the south–north contrast of Catholicism versus Protestantism and Romance speech versus Germanic languages. For reasons that remain unclear, women more easily obtain high elected positions in government in the European north than in the south.

Chapter 2, on the physical environment, revealed the south as a land of young folded and faulted mountains, earthquakes, warmth, and summer drought, while the north features plains, hills, and year-round damp. To

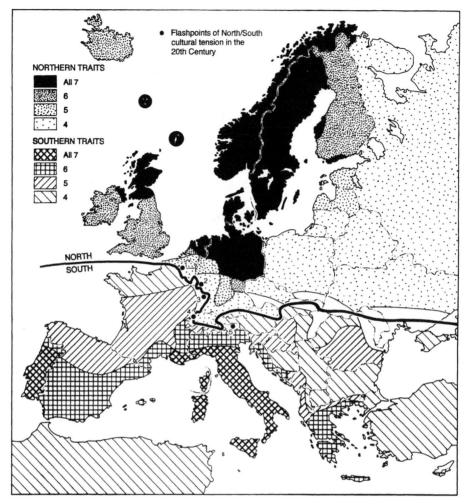

Figure 12.3. North versus south in Europe. Seven selected characteristics are included (southern trait listed first in each case): 1. Romance (and Greek)/Germanic languages; 2. Catholicism/Protestantism; 3. part/not part of Roman Empire, A.D. 100; 4. wine making present/absent; 5. summer drought/year-round precipitation; 6. young folded and faulted mountain ranges present/absent; and 7. women hold less/more than 15% of parliamentary seats. Flash points of south–north conflict in the past century include: 1. French–Dutch tension in Belgium; 2. France's attempts to seize Saarland; 3. French–German dispute over Alsace–Lorraine; 4. Jura cantonal secession in Switzerland; and 5. Italian–Austrian dispute in the South Tirol. Unshaded areas have 4 or fewer northern *or* southern traits.

the south, too, belong viticulture, religious pilgrimage, multistory stone farmsteads, and the Mediterranean city, while the northerners drink beer, live in different types of cities, and more often exhibit religious secularization. North and south look toward different seas, separated by the European continental divide.

Cultural conflict along the north–south line, while presently muted, has flared regularly since classical times. The horrible Thirty Years' War, pitting Catholic against Protestant, ravaged the central section of the divide in the 1600s. Perhaps that great and destructive conflict released all the pressure along this cultural fault line, for only minor conflicts, generally of an ethno-linguistic nature, have occurred since (fig. 12.3). The Dutch–French tension in Belgium, the Alsace–Lorraine border dispute between France and Germany, secession of French-speaking Jura canton from German-speaking Bern in Switzerland, and the restiveness of German-speaking South Tirolers in Italy offer reminders of the north–south split within the last century. All of these disputes are either dormant or resolved today, but the north–south cultural division remains viable, if peaceful.

Core versus Periphery

The contrasts among east, west, south, and north would alone, as the bases for a regional scheme, produce a simple division of Europe into quarters. The resultant spatial classification would be sectorial, with 4 regions shaped like pieces of a pie. Europe, however, is not that simply described geographically. Repeatedly in our study, another pattern has been revealed: *core* versus *periphery*. Indeed, the very essence of European culture was presented as weakening from core toward peripheries, where Europe meets non-Europe (fig. 1.12).

The idea of core versus periphery is deeply embedded in the European self-image (fig. 12.4). For centuries, residents of Europe's core have looked down upon the peoples of the periphery, disparaging their quasi-European character. The snobbery of the core and inferiority complex of the periphery find expression in some of the quotations cited earlier, in chapter 1. Figure 12.4 lists many of these, and others as well. In countries such as Italy, whose borders overlap core and periphery, separatist movements often exist and sectional biases are strong. In one 1950s Italian movie comedy, a policeman from northern Italy—part of the European core—is stationed in Sicilia, the epitome of the Mezzogiorno and south. Frustrated by the local lawless ways, an affront to his orderly world, the policeman, in one wordless but revealing scene, approaches a large map of Italy on the wall. With one hand he conceals Sicilia, to see how his country would look without that troublesome, peripheral island!

An equally revealing example of the core–periphery mindset can be found in the linkages of "sister cities," a system in which urban areas in different countries are "twinned" for the purposes of increasing international contacts and understanding. Student exchanges and other regular contacts are established between the sister cities. Such ties disproportionately link cities *within* the European core, rather than linking a core city to one in a periphery. In France, for example, 1,500 towns and cities are twinned with places in Germany and 664 with the United Kingdom, but

Figure 12.4. European core and periphery in stereotype and myth, a subjective and big-oted delimitation. Cultural residues of African and Asian rule persist, and Europeans them-selves recognize and stigmatize these spatial patterns. These quotations generally emanate from the inhabitants of the European core, reflecting their biases and prejudices. (*Sources:* Spenser 1970, 1; Kazantzakis 1966, 410; Peltzer 1957, 11; Dumas 1928, 34; Huisman 1965, 5; Nickels et al. 1973, 302; Barzini 1971, 68, 259; Evans 1968, 602; Yapp 1983, 6, 54, 158, 185, 428, 693; Michener 1968.)

only 134 French sister cities lie across the Pyrenees, in peripheral, "African-ized" Iberia. Truly, in the French mind, "Africa begins at the Pyrenees," and the French turn their backs on Spain to embrace Germany and En-gland.

So profound is the core–periphery contrast that Francis Delaisi gave the title *Two Europes* to an early book on the subject (fig. 12.5). Traditionally, geographers often recognized the core region through their use of the term *central Europe,* or the German word *Mitteleuropa.* They argued about the

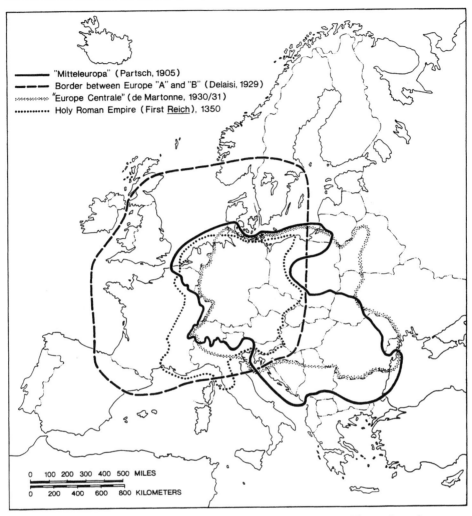

Figure 12.5.   Some additional expressions of the European core. The notion of a core, whether expressed by geographers as Mitteleuropa (central Europe), as "Europe A" (industrial core), or as the German Reich, is quite venerable. (*Sources:* Delaisi 1929, 24–25; Partsch 1905, frontispiece; Mutton 1961, 3.)

boundaries of central Europe but never questioned its existence. Most acknowledged that the concept of core or central Europe must somehow be linked to Germany and the other German-speaking lands. The unification of the German empire in 1871 gave a political expression to central Europe, as had its medieval predecessor, the Holy Roman Empire (or First *Reich*) (fig. 12.5). The total defeat and disintegration of Germany in 1945, coupled with the east–west Cold War that ensued, caused the notion of central Europe to lose favor temporarily, but today we see the core vigorously reascendant. The German task, performed with varying degrees of success,

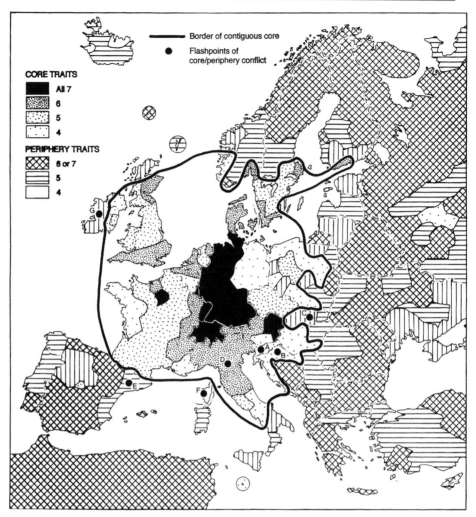

Figure 12.6.   Core and periphery in Europe, measured statistically. The 7 defining traits used for the core are: 1. unemployment rate under 12% (see fig. 9.5); 2. grain yields 30 centners per hectare or more (see fig. 11.22); 3. population 50% or more urban (see fig. 8.1); 4. "Green" vote substantial to modest (see fig. 9.7); 5. 500 or more kilometers of highways per 1,000 square kilometers (see fig. 10.2); 6. 50 or more kilometers of railroad per 1,000 square kilometers (see fig. 10.9); and 7. GDP per capita is 100%+ of the EU-15 average (see fig. 6.11). The selected flash points of core–periphery conflict extend back as much as one century and include: A. Slovenia secedes from Yugoslavia; B. Croatia does likewise; C. Slovakia secedes from Czechoslovakia; D. Padania separatism; E. Catalonian separatism; F. Corsican separatism; and G. Ireland secedes from United Kingdom.

through the centuries, has always been to join together east and west as well as north and south into a viable European core.

Other scholars view the European core in nonpolitical, less German ways. Delaisi in 1929 distinguished "Europe A" (core, industrial) from "Europe B" (peripheral, agrarian), and he included all of France, England, and Benelux in the core (fig. 12.5). His classification corresponded well to the designation we made earlier of a "manufacturing core" (fig. 9.2).

We need to seek a more objective way to delimit the European core, one devoid of German chauvinism and snobbish denigrations. This is easily attained simply by combining the various features from the preceding chapters that reveal a core–periphery configuration (fig. 12.6). The European core, by this measure, becomes the region with the densest, most urbanized population, most prosperous economy, lowest unemployment, most productive agriculture (as far back as the medieval advent of the three-field system), most conservative politics, the greatest concentration of highways and railroads, and highest levels of crowding, congestion, and pollution.

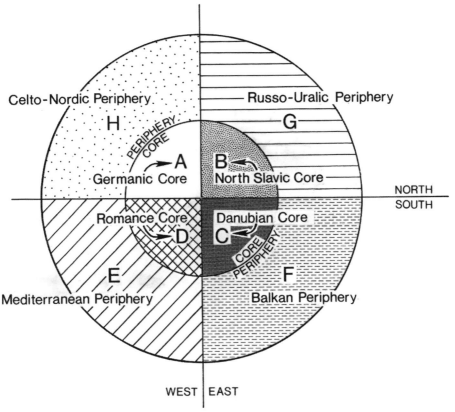

Figure 12.7.   Europe: a regional model. The bases of the model are north–south, east–west, and core–periphery divisions. Compare the model to figure 12.8.

The core–periphery contact zone, too, contains flash points of cultural tension. Many northern Italians, citizens of the European core, seek to secede, separating themselves from southern, peripheral Italy. Catalan, Corsican, Scottish, Breton, Welsh, Slovak, Croat, Slovene, and, earlier, Irish separatism can all partly be understood in core–periphery terms.

Eight Regions

Superimposing the core–periphery division upon a Europe already quartered by east–west and north–south partitions produces a more compli-

Figure 12.8.   A regional classification of Europe, based on the model shown in figure 12.7 and taking into consideration east versus west, north versus south, and core versus periphery. The real world produces great distortions in the neatly geometric model, but all 8 of the regional components survive. Why are the Danubian and north Slavic cores so small? This map draws upon figures 12.2, 12.3, and 12.6.

cated, eightfold regional scheme. Such a classification can be presented as an abstract model that resembles a bull's-eye target placed over a crosshairs sight as in figure 12.7.

The industrial–urban European core thus becomes divided into 4 regions: Germanic, north Slavic, Danubian, and Romance. Likewise, peripheral Europe becomes fourfold by being divided into the Mediterranean, the Balkans, the Russo-Uralic periphery, and the Celto-Nordic fringe. Some regions appear larger than the neatly geometric model would predict and others smaller (fig. 12.8). Reality is always complicated. The atrophied character of the eastern half of the European core, including the north Slavic and Danubian regions, perhaps suggests the lower level of prosperity there.

As a general rule, cores tend to dominate peripheries. Marxist doctrine holds, in fact, that such a relationship is inherent in capitalistic systems. If so, the future of Russia and most of eastern Europe can hardly be happy, nor can the Mediterranean crescent or Celto-Nordic fringe aspire to greatness.

We end where we began with the seemingly paradoxical proposition that Europe, geographically, is both many and one. Perhaps to the European mind, trained for 2 millennia to accept the notion of one God as a Trinity, that proposition makes perfect sense.

Sources and Suggested Readings

Barzini, L. G. 1971. *From Caesar to the Mafia.* New York, USA: Library Press.

Bater, James H. 1996. *Russia and the Post-Soviet Scene.* New York, USA: Wiley.

Breathnach, Proinnsias. 1988. "Uneven Development and Capitalist Peripheralisation: The Case of Ireland." *Antipode* 20:122–141.

Brunt, Barry M. 1991. *Western Europe: A Social and Economic Geography.* Dublin, IRL: Gill & Macmillan.

———. 1995. "Regions and Western Europe." *Journal of Geography* 94:306–316.

Burtenshaw, David, M. Bateman, and G. J. Ashworth. 1981. *The City in West Europe.* New York, USA: Wiley.

Cahnman, Werner J. 1949. "Frontiers between East and West in Europe." *Geographical Review* 39:605–624.

Chisholm, Michael. 1995. *Britain on the Edge of Europe.* London, GB: Routledge.

Clout, Hugh. 1986. *Regional Variations in the European Community.* Cambridge, GB: Cambridge University Press.

Clout, Hugh, Mark Blacksell, Russel King, and David Pinder. 1993. *Western Europe: Geographical Perspectives.* 3rd ed. London, GB: Longman.

Coleman, David A. 1993. "Contrasting Age Structures of Western Europe and of Eastern Europe." *Population and Development Review* 19:523–555.

Conrad, Victor, 1943. "The Climate of the Mediterranean Region." *Bulletin of the American Meteorological Society* 24:127–145.

Cvijic, Jovan. 1918. "The Zones of Civilization of the Balkan Peninsula." *Geographical Review* 5:470–481.

Delaisi, Francis. 1929. *Les deux Europes.* Paris, F: Payot.

Delamaide, Darrell. 1994. *The New Superregions of Europe*. New York, USA: Plume/ Penguin.

Dickinson, Robert E. 1951. *The West European City: A Geographical Interpretation*. London, GB: Routledge & Kegan Paul.

Dumas, Alexandre. 1928. *The Corsican Brothers*. London, GB: Readers Library.

Dyson, K.H.F. 1980. *The State Tradition in Western Europe*. Oxford, GB: Martin Robertson.

Ehlers, Eckart. 1997. "Zentren und Peripherien—Strukturen einer Geographie der europäischen Integration." *Colloquium Geographicum* 24:149–171.

Evans, B. 1968. *Dictionary of Quotations*. New York, USA: Delacorte.

George, Pierre, and Jean Tricart. 1954. *L'Europe centrale*. 2 vols. Paris, F.: Presses Universitaires de France.

Graubard, Stephen R. 1990. "Eastern Europe/Central Europe/Europe." *Daedalus* 119:1–344.

Hadjimichalis, Costis, and David Sadler, eds. 1995. *Europe at the Margins: New Mosaics of Inequality*. New York, USA: Wiley.

Hamilton, F. E. Ian. 1978. "The East European and Soviet City." *Geographical Magazine* 50:511–515.

Hertzman, Clyde, Shona Kelly, and Martin Bobak. 1996. *East–west Life Expectancy Gap in Europe*. Hingham, Mass., USA: Kluwer Academic.

Hudson, Ray, and Allan M. Williams. 1999. *Divided Europe: Society and Territory*. London, GB: Sage.

Huisman, P. 1965. *René Jacques' Brittany*. Garden City, USA: Doubleday.

Ilbery, Brian W. 1984. "Core–periphery Contrasts in European Social Well-Being." *Geography* 69:289–302.

———. 1986. *Western Europe: A Systematic Human Geography*. 2nd ed. Oxford, GB: Oxford University Press.

Kazantzakis, N. 1966. *Report to Greco*. New York, USA: Bantam.

Keeble, D. 1989. "Core–periphery Disparities, Recession and New Regional Dynamism in the E.C." *Geography* 74 (1): 1–11.

King, Russell L., Lindsay Proudfoot, and Bernard Smith, eds. 1997. *The Mediterranean: Environment and Society*. London, GB: Arnold.

Knox, P. L. 1984. *The Geography of Western Europe: A Socio-economic Survey*. London, GB: Croom Helm.

Kretschmer, Konrad. 1904. *Historische Geographie von Mitteleuropa*. München, D: R. Oldenbourg.

Lewis, J. R., and Allan M. Williams. 1981. "Regional Uneven Development on the European Periphery: The Case of Portugal, 1950–1978." *Tijdschrift voor Economische en Sociale Geografie* 72:81–98.

Lewis, Jim, and Alan Townsend, eds. 1988. *The North–south Divide: Regional Change in Britain in the 1980s*. London, GB: Paul Chapman.

Machatschek, Fritz. 1931. *Länderkunde von Mitteleuropa*. 2 vols. Breslau, D: F. Hirt.

Malmström, Vincent H. 1971. *Geography of Europe: A Regional Analysis*. Englewood Cliffs, N.J., USA: Prentice Hall.

de Martonne, Emmanuel. 1930–1931. *Europe centrale*. 2 vols. Paris, F: Armand Colin.

Matvejevic, Predrag. 1999. *Mediterranean: A Cultural Landscape*. Berkeley, USA: University of California Press.

Mellor, Roy E. H. 1975. *Eastern Europe: Geography of COMECON Countries*. London, GB: Macmillan.

Michener, James A. 1968. *Iberia*. New York, USA: Random House.

Monkhouse, Francis J. 1974. *A Regional Geography of Western Europe*. 4th ed. London, GB: Longman.

Morris, Jan. 1997. *Fifty Years of Europe*. New York, USA: Villard.

Mountjoy, Alan B. 1973. *The Mezzogiorno*. Oxford, GB: Oxford University Press.

Mutton, Alice F. A. 1961. *Central Europe: A Regional and Human Geography*. London, GB: Longmans, Green.

Myklebost, Hallstein. 1993. "Regionalism in Western Europe." *Norsk Geografisk Tidsskrift* 47:79–91.

Newbigin, Marion I. 1924. *The Mediterranean Lands: An Introductory Study in Human and Historical Geography*. London, GB: Christophers.

Nickels, S., et al. 1973. *Finland: An Introduction*. New York, USA: Praeger.

O'Loughlin, John, and Herman van der Wusten, eds. 1993. *The New Political Geography of Eastern Europe*. London, GB: Belhaven.

Ormsby, Hilda. 1935. "The Definition of Mitteleuropa and its Relation to the Conception of Deutschland in the Writings of Modern German Geographers." *Scottish Geographical Magazine* 51:337–347.

Partsch, Josef F. M. 1905. *Central Europe*. Trans. Clementina Black. London, GB: H. Frowde.

Pedersen, Roy N. 1992. *One Europe/100 Nations*. Clevedon, GB: Channel View.

Peltzer, K. 1957. *Das Treffende Zitat*. Thun, CH: Ott.

Pinder, David, ed. 1990. *Western Europe: Challenge and Change*. London, GB: Belhaven.

Rhodes, Martin, ed. 1995. *The Regions and the New Europe: Patterns in Core and Periphery Development*. Manchester, GB: Manchester University Press.

Rodwin, Lloyd, and Hidehiko Sazanami, eds. 1991. *Industrial Change and Regional Economic Transformation: The Experience of Western Europe*. London, GB: HarperCollins Academic.

Rugg, Dean S. 1986. *Eastern Europe*. London, GB: Longman Scientific & Technical.

Schöpflin, George, and Nancy Wood, eds. 1989. *In Search of Central Europe*. Cambridge, GB: Polity Press.

Schultz, Hans-Dietrich. 1989. "Fantasies of *Mitte: Mittellage* and *Mitteleuropa* in German Geographical Discussion in the 19th and 20th Centuries." *Political Geography Quarterly* 8:315–339.

Seers, Dudley B., Bernard Schaeffer, and Marja-Liisa Kiljunen, eds. 1979. *Underdeveloped Europe: Studies in Core–periphery Relations*. Hassock, GB: Harvester.

Semple, Ellen C. 1931. *The Geography of the Mediterranean Region*. New York, USA: Henry Holt.

Shmueli, Avshalom. 1981. "Countries of the Mediterranean Basin as a Geographic Region." *Ekistics* 48:359–369.

Siegfried, André. 1948. *The Mediterranean*. Trans. Doris Hemming. London, GB: Jonathan Cape.

Smith, Clifford T. 1978. *An Historical Geography of Western Europe before 1800*. 2nd ed. London, GB: Longman.

Sömme, Axel, ed. 1960. *A Geography of Norden*. Oslo, N: J. W. Cappelen.

Spenser, E. 1970. *A View of the Present State of Ireland*. Oxford, GB: Clarendon.

Stiglbauer, Karl. 1992. "Die Kulturregionen Europas." *Mitteilungen der österreichischen Geographischen Gesellschaft* 134:93–114.

Turnock. David. 1988a. *Eastern Europe: An Economic and Political Geography*. London, GB: Routledge.

———. 1988b. *Eastern Europe: A Historical Geography, 1815–1945*. London, GB: Routledge.

————. 1989. *The Human Geography of Eastern Europe*. London, GB: Routledge.

William-Olsson, William. 1975. "A Prelude to Regional Geography: Two Maps of Europe." *Geografiska Annaler* 57B:1–19.

Williams, Allan M., ed. 1984. *Southern Europe Transformed*. London, GB: Harper & Row.

————. 1987. *The Western European Economy: A Geography of Post-war Development*. London, GB: Hutchinson.

Wolff, Larry. 1994. *Inventing Eastern Europe: The Map of Civilization on the Mind of the Enlightenment*. Stanford, Calif., USA: Stanford University Press.

Yapp, P. 1983. *The Traveler's Dictionary of Quotations*. Boston, USA: Routledge & Kegan Paul.

Zelinsky, Wilbur. 1991. "The Twinning of the World: Sister Cities in Geographic and Historical Perspective." *Annals of the Association of American Geographers* 81:1–31.

Index

Abkhazia, 187, *187*, 189
Abkhazis, 20, 107, 108
abortions, 172, *173*
acid rain, 52–53, *53*, 65
Acquired Immune Deficiency Syndrome (AIDS), 178, *179*
acrewall, 366
Adriatic Sea, 41, 78, 212, 243, 297
Adzharia, 187
Aegean Sea, 1, 3, 20, 68, 118
aeolic power, 334
afforestation, 56, *56*, 58
Africa, 1, 3, 11; agriculture in, 13; geopolitics in, 13, 14; health in, 177–78; Islam in, 25–26; migration from, 143–44, 161, 166, *167*, 168, 173; modern Europeans from, 151–52, 156; per capita income in, 13; population change and, 170; population size and, 12; Spain and, 207, 208; transportation in, 13
Afro-Asiatic languages, 10, 134
Afro-Asiatics, 118, 120, 121, *235*
Afro-Caribbeans, 142–43, *143*, 144, 166
Afsluitdijk, 74
age of countries, *191*, 191–93, *192*, *194*
ager, 354, 355
agglutinogens, 147–48, *149*, *150*, *151*, *152*
aging of population, 174, 241–42
agribusiness, 371–73, *372*
agriculture, 13, 25, 347–92; burnbeating and, *350*, *367*, 367–68, 380; cash grain farming and, *372*, 377; cattle and hog fattening and, 348, *372*, 375–76; cities and, 233, *235*; commercialization and, 370–71; core versus periphery and,

383–85, *384*; cottage industry and, 286; dairying and, 352, 366, *372*, 373–75, *376*; depopulation and, 385–86, *386*, *387*; Europe defined with, *22*; fish farming and, *372*, 378–79, *379*; forests cleared for, 54, 55, *59*, 59–60, *60*; Germanic people and, 124–25; Group 4 immigration and, 154; hardscrabble herder-farmers and, *350*, *357*, *363*, 365–67, 370, *372*, 377; huertas and, 31; Indo-Europeans and, 149; land consolidation and, 379–80, *380*; language and, 118; market gardening and, 371–73, *372*, *374*, 378; marshes converted to, 70; new crop introductions and, 368–70; nomadic herding and, *350*, 368–69, *369*; origin and diffusion of, 347–49, *348*; pollution and, 336; regional differences in, 397, *398*, *403*; reindeer ranching and, *369*, *372*, 377–78; sheep raising and, 349, *350*, *372*, 377; specialization and, *369*, 371–85, *372*, *374*, *376*, *384*. *See also* land holding; Mediterranean agriculture; rural settlement; soils; three-field farming
Agriculture Revolution, 383
agrotown, 356
air masses, 44, 49
air transport, 330–32
Albania: automobile ownership in, 318; cities in, 270; core area absent from, 193; education in, 175, 176; European Union and, 220, *222*; fertility decline in, 172; health in, 177; language in, 115, *116*, 117, 132; migration from, 169;